The Cinema and the Origins of Literary Modernism

Routledge Interdisciplinary Perspectives on Literature

The Cinema and the Origins of Literary Modernism

Andrew Shail

 Routledge
Taylor & Francis Group

NEW YORK   LONDON

First published 2012
by Routledge
711 Third Avenue, New York, NY 10017

Simultaneously published in the UK
by Routledge
2 Park Square, Milton Park, Abingdon, Oxon OX14 4RN

*Routledge is an imprint of the Taylor & Francis Group,
an informa business*

Library of Congress Cataloging-in-Publication Data
Shail, Andrew, 1978–
    The cinema and the origins of literary modernism / Andrew Shail.
      p. cm. — (Routledge interdisciplinary perspectives on literature ; 7)
    Includes bibliographical references and index.
    1. Motion pictures and literature.   2. English literature—20th
century—History and criticism.   3. Modernism (Literature)—Great
Britain.   I. Title.
    PN1995.3.S53 2012
    820.9'112—dc23
    2011036724

ISBN13: 978-0-415-80699-2 (hbk)
ISBN13: 978-0-203-12628-8 (ebk)

Typeset in Sabon by IBT Global.

To Bean and Plum (both of whom first encountered *Ulysses in utero*) and to Stacy (who didn't mind).

Contents

Note on Presentation

This book makes extensive use of regular features in popular film magazines, most of which were published anonymously. To reference such works, the referencing system used here therefore adapts the current MLA system: references are given in full in endnotes for these articles, but for ease of reference full endnoting is not used. Instead, short-form references to the list of works cited, which would ordinarily be given parenthetically, are also given in endnotes. In addition, many of the articles in the magazines cited in this book are only one page long, so the page given in reference refers both to the page range of the article *and* to the page of the quotation. As numbers 3.68 to 4.81 of the weekly magazine *The Pictures* magazine give no date, and as it is not possible to work out the dates of these issues from the dates of those before (3.67, 22 Jan 1913) and after (4.82, 29 April 1913), I have given a rough estimate of the date within this window in the text, although the entry states that the date is unspecified. Lastly, emphases are always in the original unless otherwise stated.

Figures

Acknowledgments

Thanks to all who have made it possible to employ the range of materials at the Bill Douglas Centre for the History of Cinema and Popular Culture at the University of Exeter, in particular Jessica Gardner, Michelle Allen and Mike Rickard. This book has had an Exeter-Northumbria-Oxford-Newcastle trajectory, so colleagues near and far to whom I'm indebted include David Trotter, Duncan Petrie, Steve Neale, Joe Kember, Ian Christie, Stacy Gillis, Colin MacCabe, Dan North, Susan Hayward, Karen Edwards, Min Wild, Becky Munford, Peter Hutchings, Michael Hammond, Laura Salisbury, Jon Burrows, Simon Brown and Gerry Turvey.

COPYRIGHT ACKNOWLEDGMENTS

Figures 0.2, 0.3, 0.4, 0.11, 1.1, 1.3, 1.4, 2.2, 3.1, 3.2 and 3.3: Courtesy of the Bill Douglas Centre for the History of Cinema and Popular Culture, University of Exeter.

Figure 1.5: By kind permission of the Syndics of Cambridge University Library.

Figure 1.6: Courtesy of the Bodleian Library, University of Oxford.

Brief elements of Chapter 2 appeared in *The Oxford History of the Novel: 1880–1940*, ed. Patrick Parrinder and Andrzej Gasiorek (Oxford University Press, 2010) as part of my and David Trotter's piece on 'Cinema and the Novel'.

Introduction
From 'The Cinematograph' to 'The Pictures'

This book approaches the appearance of cinema and its attendant institutions as a major cause for the emergence of modernism in literature in the United Kingdom. In each of the three chapters, I detail a major area of the literary terrain for which the new institution 'the cinema' was the architect, areas that together comprised some major characteristics of the modernist 'mode'. Each of the three chapters outlines a major, and historically specific, characteristic of the common experience of cinema in the UK, and relates this characteristic to contemporary changes in literary form.

In understanding literature's various influences, there are (at least) two ways of defining 'influence'. In the first definition, 'influence' alludes to a process wherein a literary practitioner chooses to draw on certain ideas: s/he chooses, or is motivated in some way, to take up a certain cultural object (such as a philosophical work), digest its contents, engage with the ideas proposed therein, adopt some, adapt others and refuse still others, and, through such contemplation, develop, or develop further, their own aesthetic precepts.

The second version of influence concerns changes in the everyday mental landscape of whole populations, changes in such basic conceptions as the substance of thought, the functions of the senses, the nature of time, the dividing line between consciousness and matter and the purpose of language, and the pressure these changes exert on the underlying and shared machinery that produces literary works, pressure that re-tunes existing protocols on such dimensions as the nature of the relation between narrator and quoted speech, dominant use of verb tenses, the degree of agency assumed in description, governing modes of narratorial discourse and the prescribed destination of the literary utterance.

Cinema exerted influence on writing via both of these mechanisms. Yet the overwhelming majority of investigations into cinema as an influence on literary modernism have fallen into the first category.[1] Most recently, in *The Tenth Muse* (2008), Laura Marcus has deftly analysed the changing influence of cinema on Virginia Woolf's fiction from *Jacob's Room* (1922) to *Between the Acts* (1941), and done so by scrutinising Woolf's own stated attitudes towards film; for Marcus the impact of cinema on Woolf's fiction would have been the impact of Woolf's *regard* for cinema, impact wrought under her supervision, as with many others similarly "incorporating the cinematic into their fictional or poetic texts."[2] The first definition of influence has proven attractive, in part, because cinema has an established place in art history as the motive for the emergence of modernist painting: cinema exacerbated an aesthetic retreat from representation which had first been triggered by the popular dissemination of photography during the 1840s and 1850s. Applying this model to writing suggests in turn that there is nothing more to be said about cinema regarding this second definition of influence. A link in art history between the emergence of the cinematograph in 1895 and a perceived second-wave 'retreat' by painters over representational ground in the move from impressionism to post-impressionism was in place as early as Clive Bell's 1922 essay 'Art and the Cinema',[3] and has been bolstered by perceptions that literary modernism was itself motivated by aspirations to the condition of painting.[4] It is not merely the case that this model fails to translate to the different mechanisms behind the process of literature, however. Emerging out of modernists' own commentaries, this model was a product of modernist gestures of art's contemporaneity rather than an account of modernism's generative causes. Moreover, recent re-examinations of the impact of optical technologies on the visual arts have pointed out that the model of cinema as super-representational ignores the capacity of photo-chemical processes to produce *non*-representational images, and to do so solely via their technological bases (e.g. instantaneous photography makes bodily attitudes available to everyday perception that normally occur too briefly to be perceived) or to contrast all the more strongly with visual perception *because* they replicate aspects of optics without an attendant consciousness (e.g. film renders the visual field of a seer who does not have the selective and unconscious attenuation mechanisms built into human perception).[5]

The first category of influence, as applied to cinema and modernism, has also, more recently, come to attract disdain because of its fruitlessness, in part because accounts of modernism's 'cinematic' frissons have become restrictively orthodox. Most recently, David Trotter has expounded the shortcomings of common assumptions about modernist 'cinematicity' and proposed instead "to substitute for the model of an exchange of transferable techniques the model of parallelism", in which both filmic and literary practice of the modernist period drew on "a fund of shared preoccupation".[6] For Trotter, each therefore comprised one field of a more widespread fixation about, amongst other concepts, sensory automatism. For him, "[t]he relation between cinema and literature can best be understood as a shared preoccupation with the capacities and incapacities of . . . the instrumentality of a nonliving agent."[7] He admirably moves the debate on from the well-worn argument that cinema's intrinsic properties and modernist techniques seem analogous with each other because of the causal effects of the former. But although he leaves off conceiving of the relationship between cinema and modernism as one of influence, Trotter only provides a reason to abandon the first definition of influence, not both. I would certainly agree that reasons other than influence must be sought for why literary modernism looks 'cinematic', but this is only a reason to abandon influence as a part of our history of cinema and modernism *if* the limit of our perception of the influence of cinema is in noticing bits of literary modernism that look 'like' cinema. The emulation seen to result from the first type of influence—the 'cinematicity' repeatedly diagnosed as a typical feature of literary modernism—is very different from those changes in literary form that arise from new arrivals in the cultural landscape according to the second category of influence. The latter are symptoms rather than analogues, products of unconscious developments rather than conscious engagement and general rather than writer-specific. And only in the absence of accounts that examine cinema and literature according to the second definition of influence has it been possible to summarise influence as producing analogy.

This book investigates the part played by cinema if it is construed as exerting influence on literature along this second channel. It approaches the emergence of cinema—both image type *and* institution—as substantial enough a historical event for the shifts it occasioned in literary production to rank alongside those occasioned by the rise of eugenics, the development of the interventionist nation state, the birth of relativity in physics, the growth of historical linguistics, the relativising of world views in modern anthropology, the invention of the notion of the psychodynamic unconscious/preconscious/conscious psyche, the ideological restructurings of the First World War and the political ascendancy of notions of collective consciousness: the other major, first-order, historical causes of the emergence of literary modernism given by recent literary historians.[8] It tackles cinema as a popular experience rather than as a stylistic toolkit to be sampled and emulated, and it charts an influence exerted on the machinery of literary production that occurred in ways too complex to have caused literature to become merely like (or unlike) the filmic image. It details a history in which modernism was not an aesthetic reformation in response to cinema, but a consequence in literary practice of its appearance.

In this book I use 'modernism' in its narrower sense. Rather than the neophilic literature of the literary period 1890–1939, or even the more technically innovative literature of that period, my subject is the formally identifiable line of stylistic development in literature—which emerged in 1914 and continued until the late 1920s—that is more commonly known as 'high' literary modernism. As with many contemporary literary historians, however, I view definitions that pivot 'high' modernism on poesis, opposed to realist mimesis, and difficulty, opposed to realist cuddliness, as too heavily saturated with the inherited influence of modernists' own efforts as self-delineation (as Stan Smith has noted, even though 'modernism' was a retrospective epithet, it was "also a real element in their discourse of themselves").[9] Modernism does, nonetheless, hold together as a formal movement, on the basis of such characteristics as hypermimesis, a pervasive relativising of metalanguage, a particular relation of narrative time to story time and a mixture of interior monologue given in free indirect discourse with impersonal third-person narration (although I will show in Chapter 2 that 'spatial form', usually placed on this list of formal attributes, does not fit the bill). The tenacity of modernism as a category in the history of aesthetics derives from the intensity of the exchange between the various art forms at the time, making any distinction between modernist aesthetics in literature and in other forms provisional, but this book will examine literature alone, on the basis of the supposition that the mechanisms which underpin linguistic meaning-making would have been influenced differently than those underpinning music or the plastic arts.

READING CINEMA

The relative dearth of studies of cinema as a historical cause for the whole aesthetic refrain of literary modernism is not a result of neglect. In addition to the influence exerted by the authority adhering to the model of cinema's purported influence on painting, other factors have thrown up definitions and tenets that have worked to refer scholars away from examining generative causality.

The first of these is the 'cinematicity' tradition, as long-established as the idea that modernism in literature was a retreat from the representational ground annexed by cinema in the guise of the second assault of photochemical reproduction. From as early as 1932, when Joseph Warren Beach commented that "[i]t is very probable that the moving picture has had a very strong influence on the stream-of-consciousness technique",[10] the orthodoxy that certain moments in modernism were instances of borrowings of film form has gradually cohered.[11] In 2004, Rachel Connor remarked that "[t]he often 'cinematic' style of writers like Joseph Conrad, Beckett, Woolf and Joyce, as well as lesser known writers like Rhys or Richardson, attests to the huge impact of film in the early years of the twentieth century."[12] The property defined as 'cinematic' (usually 'montage'),[13] however, almost always serves to de-historicise one historically specific theory of the essence of cinema as a description of the medium in general. Montage, for example, was both a minority idea—even during the time that modernists were writing—and a product of the application, to film, of the formalist aesthetics associated with fully-formed modernism during the late 1920s. This model has also functioned to prevent an analysis of cinema as a generative influence on modernism by assigning cinema the status of an influence on writers who were *already* modernist, *and* only on *some* of these writers, *and* only when they chose to emulate it, rather than an influence on the aesthetic parameters of modernism that distinguished it as a literary mode:

a dusting of formal cinematicity does not constitute a distinct segment and phase of literary practice.

The idea that modernism and cinema were sibling consequences of an earlier cause has also recently come to the fore.[14] Drawing on André Bazin's c. 1958 insistence that "the American [modernist] novel belongs not so much to the age of cinema as to a certain vision of the world",[15] it has been proposed that a 'cinematic' protocol for relating to the world came about, before the emergence of cinema, as a consequence of such new forces as behaviourist psychology (which reduced the psyche to a product of the interaction with the outside world), criminological discoveries that identity is carried by the body, ergonomic understandings of the body's neurological habits and increasingly sophisticated analyses of the mediating mechanics of sensory perception. While this approach is not flawed, it has implied, by apprehending cinema as a sibling product of modernism's socio-historical causes, that cinema was not itself a socio-historical phenomenon.

Recently, new notions of modernist affinity with popular culture[16] have encouraged analyses of the explicit flirtations that comprised the European and North American 'intellectual film culture' that began to emerge in the early 1920s, as evidence of modernism's relationship with cinema.[17] These instances of contact include the body of abstract short films made by modernist painters in 1924,[18] the special cinema items in the Autumn–Winter 1924–1925 and Winter 1926 issues of the *Little Review*, the involvement of several Bloomsbury group members in the London-based Film Society, founded by Ivor Montagu and actor Hugh Miller in October 1925 (Roger Fry and John Maynard Keynes were amongst the founding members), the involvement of *Nation and Athenaeum* in announcing and reviewing Film Society events while under the literary editorship of Leonard Woolf, the publication by the Hogarth Press of Eric Walter White's early work of film theory, *Parnassus to Let: An Essay About Rhythm in Films* (1928), and the preponderance of female modernists editing and contributing to the little/film magazine *Close Up* during its short life between July 1927 and December 1933, with H.D. contributing and co-editing (alongside Kenneth Macpherson, later replaced by Oswell Blakeston), 'Bryher' (Winnifred Ellerman) and Dorothy Richardson both contributing regularly, and Gertrude Stein and Marianne Moore writing occasional pieces also.

This line of inquiry nevertheless leads away from unearthing historical conceptions of cinema. Like Fernand Léger, who argued in 1926 that his "new point of view [the 'cinematographic value' of the object] is the exact opposite of everything that has been done in the cinema up to the present",[19] like Etienne de Beaumont, who asserted in the same issue of the *Little Review* that the language of film had not yet been spoken,[20] like Walter Hanks Shaw, who announced, in the January 1926 *New Criterion*, that de Beaumont's *A Quoi Rêvent les Jeunes Films? [Of What Are the Young Films Dreaming?]* (1924), Léger and Marcel L'Herbier's *L'Inhumain* (1924) and René Clair and Francis Picabia's *Entr'acte* (1924) were all good for "those who believe in the future of the cinema",[21] like Ralph Block, who argued in his October 1922 'When the Movies Come of Age' that anything more than the tiny suggestion of cinema's powers apparent in Chaplin's films was "still to be accomplished",[22] and like Woolf, whose article 'The Cinema', forthcoming in the June 1926 issue, was boosted to Americans in the May 1926 *The Arts* as 'The Future of Cinema',[23] the writers in *Close Up* were mainly concerned only with the aesthetic outlay they saw as *made possible* by cinema, the "new beginning" forecast in the manifesto of the POOL group in April 1927.[24] These envisioned futures for cinema provide an account of cinema as modernists refashioned it to their own ends, a refashioning that occurred *after* the emergence of modernism, and taking this modernist-authored film culture as indicative of the profile of cinema during the earlier emergence of modernist aesthetics risks confusing evidence of a conscious decision to go *against* the grain of popular thought on the institution cinema with evidence of precisely that popular thought. This approach has also led to such extreme avoidances of cinema history as Maggie Humm's persistent description of the films influencing modernists, in her 2002 work, as "experimental independent art films": i.e. only those recent and minority products that were *already* modernist.[25] This tendency continues to influence thought on film. Though expertly nuanced, the chapters of Marcus's *The Tenth Muse* specifically on overt commentaries on cinema typify the now ubiquitous scholarly pre-conception that the important writing on cinema during "the Modernist Period" of her book's subtitle was *modernist* writing on film (she makes a few exceptions), hence the focus on the attempt to erect cinema as an aesthetic category in, for example, the allusions to cinema's own muse that she unearths from the period 1921 to 1942.[26] For literary historians, minority definitions of film have widely taken the place of the medium's popular profile.[27]

In his 2003 work on modernism, David Bradshaw included "cinematography" on a lengthy list of modernism's second-tier generative influences.[28] In the same year, Colin MacCabe claimed that "it is impossible to imagine the form of either *Ulysses* or *The Waste Land* without the developments of film editing".[29] These two literary historians' shared assumption that the influence of cinema was that of film *technique* reflects an ongoing tendency to discover cinema's singularity in its incarnation as an art form rather than in its historical aspect. As a consequence, in part, of the influence of modernism's own film theory, cinema appears as a new aesthetic toolkit to be consciously deployed by its own *auteur* practitioners, and equally consciously emulated by writers, rather than as a set of institutional and social practice. Bradshaw thus inherently bars cinema from his own list of modernism's first-tier causes. Modernism, already formed, went on to superintend at the birth of esoteric theories that militated for cinema's aesthetic purity, insisting that it was no longer possible to regard it as a mere mechanism, but this does not mean that, prior to the early 1920s, in the years when it *was* commonly conceived as a mere mechanism, cinema meant nothing to modernists. Although some attention has been paid to cinema before 1920 (in particular to cinema before 1908) as a particular influence on literary modernism, this is again denoted as a cinema exercising influence because it unwittingly exhibited sparks of aesthetic novelty in its infancy.[30]

Amongst the reasons proffered for modernists' shared affinity for cinema has been the idea that cinema was an innately modernist medium. Even modernism's contemporaries witnessed an affinity on this basis. For example, Ralph Block argued in October 1922 that, when cinema 'came of age',

> a modern and somewhat neurasthenic world will find in [cinema's] flow of action, this instrument of becoming, a fitting carriage for what is imperfectly poured into James Joyce's *Ulysses*, *A La Recherche du Temps Perdu* of Marcel Proust, and the works of Dorothy Richardson, and to some extent the works of May Sinclair . . . Here will be reality, tragic-comedic, humourless, flat—with and without the inspired human attitude—heads, shoulders, torsos of a mad accidental world, moving with that absence of reason which is completely rhythmic.[31]

Cinema, for Block, would one day bring its powers to bear on the established primary task of literary modernism, which, it is implied, did not derive any of its preoccupations from cinema in the first place.[32] Block's 'longing for a coming of age' model, reiterated most influentially by Woolf in 'The Cinema', has been passed down through the historiography of modernism, surviving other now disputed modernist-authored pictures of literary history to imply both that modernists only registered cinema as an empty capacity to be modernist, and that cinema before modernists found anything of worth in it was an empty space in the history of modernism. Cinema has thus appeared as so small a dose that it can only have influenced modernism by eking out the influences of modernism's more substantial generative forces. For Susan McCabe, for example, cinema comprised an influence on her chosen American modernists because its account of the body was 'like' the model of embodiment of both psychodynamics and behaviourism, 'like' the bodily dislocation of the hysteric body and the male hysteria of shell shock, 'like' the bodily distortion and exaggeration resulting from repressed psychic processes, 'like' the piecing of disparate temporal and spatial elements undertaken in psychoanalytic processes, 'like' the gap-ridden phallic economy of bodies, 'like' sexed identity crisis, 'like' the dismembered body of the war and 'like' the increasing availability of an account of cultural identities as malleable.[33] While influences on literature, as Chapter 3 in particular will stress, do not exist in isolation, cinema appears in McCabe's study only as banned from the category of influence altogether.

A strand of cinema studies has also worked to curb studies of cinema as a causal force for modernism, in spite of ostensibly seeking to achieve the opposite. Ben Singer, drawing on David Bordwell, has called this strand the 'modernity thesis'.[34] Invoking Stephen Kern's definition of modernity, to which a scopic technicity is fundamental,[35] the 'modernity thesis' treats cinema as 1) an aspect of the sensory environment of urban modernity, 2) one of many late nineteenth-century technologies designed for sensory notation, 3) a member of the corps of visual forms allied to consumer capitalism, and 4) a method for reproducing the phenomenal experience of modern life. In 1999, for example, Miriam Bratu Hansen insisted that cinema was "not only part and symptom of modernity's experience and perception of crisis and upheaval; it was also . . . the single most inclusive cultural horizon in which the traumatic effects of modernity were reflected, rejected or disavowed, transmuted or negotiated."[36] Singer pointed out in 2001 that silent cinema had come to be seen as a fulcrum of modern experience because it was *like*, a *part of*, a *consequence of* and a *reflexive aspect of* modernity: characterised by rapidly changing visual attractions, part of a range of new scopic technologies (like sideshow illusions), entertainments (like the myriorama), visual displays (like billboards) and social spaces (like department stores), an outgrowth of inventions designed to supplant the human perceptual apparatus in the task of making recordings of the sensory world and an unintended apparatus for becoming active participants in urban existence during the twentieth century.[37] In her 1997 introduction to Siegfried Kracauer's 1960 *Theory of Film*, Hansen described cinema as: the expression of accelerating technological expansion, standardisation, the disembedding of social relations, the industrialization of culture, a form of address to an emerging heterogeneous urban mass public, a force restructuring sense perception and practical critique of the sovereign subject, all of which make it difficult not to read cinema as exemplar of modernity, and to see cinema impacting on modernism as the foremost representative of the experiences involved in modernity.[38] When modernism is interpreted as primarily neophilia, it is easy to perceive cinema as one of the recent facets of technological modernity about which modernists were characteristically enthusiastic and paranoid by turns.[39] But this approach has inhibited studies of cinema as a modernist cause in three ways, first by inserting cinema into another larger cause, second by interpreting modernism in terms of shared content rather than as a formal mode and third by defining cinema as a part of the texture of modern life just as literary historians began to produce explanations for the emergence of modernism that depart from the idea that it was the simple cultural refrain of the period of modernity. Indeed, the very idea that modernity was a definable historical period is a consequence, in part, of modernism's auto-critical insistence on its contemporaneity.

Supplementing the diverting channels that these otherwise productive approaches—and models of relationships between cinema and modernism other than causal influence—have inadvertently dug across inquiries into the second type of influence is the seeming outright foolhardiness of proposing that cinema ought to rank alongside modernism's other chief generative causes. With material histories of modernism appearing in strength during the past two decades, an attempt to place another art form in the position of the historical cause for changes in writing may well seem to express an unstated desire to revert to the New Critics' description of modernism as intensified aesthetic autonomy, an account that, with its roots in the 1920s, dominated literary scholarship in the 1940s and 1950s. Rather than contributing to the current displacement of modernism's own rationale of aesthetic purity by detailing its embeddedness in subtle developments in material history, arguing that modernism as a product of cinema would seem to seek to return the discussion of modernism's root causes to the aesthetic realm. But the aesthetic is just one of cinema's faces (and not *even* one—at least in popular, widespread conceptions—during the period when literary modernism was forming), as is the identity of 'cultural form'. Cinema was and is 'the cinema' of this book's title: an aspect of everyday life, an item on a citizen's menu of pastimes, a social interaction and a form of knowledge. As Gilles Deleuze has argued, 'cinema' is not 'moving projected photographic images' but a "regime of the image",[40] a widespread and historically specific set of perceived properties and operational categories which constitutes a historical entity in itself, and without which a 'first-hand' experience of the 'core' text—projected motion photographs—is incapable of achieving meaning. Cinema may have been a 'mere' medium, but as Jay Bolter and Richard Grusin remark, media are very real in that they "make reality over in the same way that all Western technologies have sought to reform reality", not by *mediating* a reality but by insisting that a certain set of interactions between human and artefact is "the locus and presence of meaning for us".[41] 'The cinema' of this book's title was a mounting wave of everyday discourse, a change in the social behaviour of populations, which, although it did not occur the length and breadth of the UK, was a widespread aspect of urban experience, even for those who did not regularly attend films. It incorporates cinema culture, defined by Michael Hammond as "a realm of discursive exchange in which film industry producers . . ., distributors, exhibitors and subsidiary media such as the fan and trade press as well as the national and local press participate."[42] Where beliefs that 'cinema' consists merely in films have, for example, led Michael North to perceive that Eugene Jolas's "synesthetic portmanteau" words, like "lightshriek", were the product of "attempts to produce a verbal montage that would mimic the juxtapositional syntax of modern film editing",[43] I will here uncover literary modernism's origins not in films but in an image-regime comprised of explorations, assumptions, assertions, borrowings and guesses that established how the product, experience and public comprising the institution cinema was to be regarded. While cinema in its guise as an art form *did* offer stylistic possibilities to literature,[44] this guise was one of the *last* it assumed, some years after the emergence of the parameters of literary modernism.

An analysis of cinema as one of modernism's major causes might also seem inadvisable because cinema was far from a novelty at the time of its 'birth' in 1895. In the UK alone, well before the Lumières' Cinématographe debuted to a paying public on 21 February 1896, the British public had been able to sample animated photographs for almost 17 months, since the arrival of the first 'parlour' of single-viewer Edison kinetoscopes on 18 October 1894. Ottomar Anschütz's 'Electrotachyscope', which debuted in Berlin in 1887 (consisting of a large glass disc with 24 images ranged around the circumference, which rotated while being illuminated intermittently from behind) and could be viewed by small groups of people through a hole in a wall, was first exhibited in London no later than 1893 as the 'Electrical Wonder'. Attempts at converting the praxinoscope (an optical toy invented in 1877) for projection had proliferated after Eadweard Muybridge's zoopraxiscope first brought projected moving images comprised of silhouettes based on photographs to lecture halls around Britain in 1881. Even between the mid-1850s and the early 1870s—before the introduction of forms of gelatine to emulsions in photographic plates greatly increased sensitivity and permitted the brevity of exposure that together were necessary for taking enough photographs of objects in motion to permit reconstitution as a single 'moving' image—attempts had been made, with varying success, to produce the illusion of movement by combing optical toys with sequences of posed photographs.[45] Contemporaries in Britain in 1896 recalled a range of patents and designs for devices that could project still photographs in series to suggest movement between 1856 and 1870.[46] Another contemporary of the arrival of cinema recalled that "the projection of rapidly consecutive [presumably hand-drawn] pictures on a lantern screen, giving the illusion of motion, . . . was done more than thirty years ago at the old Polytechnic Institution in Regent Street."[47] Projected still photographs, using positives printed on glass slides, had first appeared at the Great Exhibition in 1851. Technologies and techniques for producing movement on, or with, magic lantern slides had been the major developments in lantern exhibition during the nineteenth century, and by the 1890s slides incorporating intricate hinged figures had reached a level of sophistication sufficient to warrant the introduction of the separate category of 'shadowgraph'. In addition, when cinema emerged at the end of the Victorian era, it was as a new component to an already packed array of visual media, information technologies and public amusements, which included variety theatre, public lecturing, dioramas, travelling fairs, stage illusionism and urban 'freak' show. Several questions arise. If cinema did have an identifiable impact on literary practice, what aspect of cinema distinguished it from its various forebears? And if cinema was a historical product, in what sense did it distinguish itself from such neighbouring technologies and media such as x-rays and wireless telegraphy (both also 'born' in 1895), given that these manifested the same historical directives? And if cinema can be taken as a product of modernism's own socio-historical causes, how can it also have influenced modernism?

In this book I take the view that although cinema was both an outgrowth of existing technologies and a historically determined invention, 1) this does not meant that its image type or exhibition modes were without novelty (indeed, if there was nothing novel about the cinematograph, there would have been no reason to invent it), and 2) it displayed properties, led to institutional structures and functioned in ways that were not anticipated by its developers. Does this mean, however, that a study of the impact of cinema on modernism in the UK ought to begin shortly after February 1896? One strand of cinema research suggests that it should. In defining the 'cinema of attractions'—the chief characteristic of cinema from its invention in 1895 until roughly 1908 being the exhibitionism of the direct address to the spectator—Tom Gunning notes that Futurist, Dadaists and Surrealist enthusiasm for this early incarnation of cinema "was at least partly an enthusiasm for a mass culture that was emerging at the beginning of the century, offering a new sort of stimulus for an audience not acculturated to the traditional arts."[48] Modernist fascination with the shock format of the cinema of attractions explains, for Gunning, a pattern of disappointment found in later modernist comments on cinema across Europe. He argues that "it was precisely the exhibitionist quality of turn-of-the-century popular art that made it attractive to the avant-garde—its freedom from the creation of a diegesis [a story-space], its accent on direct stimulation".[49] With the gradual turn away from attractionist cinema to what Gunning calls a 'cinema of narrative integration'[50] around 1908, modernist fascination with the transformative possibilities of cinema appeared to fade away.[51] Gunning is evidently disinclined to claim that 'kine-attractography' (as André Gaudreault has recently proposed it be known)[52] was a catalyst of modernist aesthetics, restricting his analysis to a fascination about cinema on the part of modernists that provides evidence about the cultural texture of early cinema, but his analysis betrays (and has encouraged) a picture of early cinema as only novel enough to effect changes in trends in literary form up until c. 1908, and has led to conclusions that it was only in its early shock aspect that cinema provoked modernist aesthetics.

Of course, kine-attractography *did* have an identifiable generative impact on modernist aesthetics. In his 1917 essay 'Inferior Religions' (probably written in 1914), Wyndham Lewis elaborated the aesthetic rationale of the short stories he wrote about his time in Brittany in 1908, and which were published between May 1909 and February 1911, at the end of the kine-attractography period. "To introduce my puppets, and the Wild Body, the generic puppet of all," he wrote, "I must look back to a time when the antics and solemn gambols of those wild children filled me with triumph . . . These studies of rather primitive people are studies in a savage worship and attraction."⁵³ As this essay suggests, Lewis's visual rendering of the comic in these stories had value to him other than merely according with his painterly consciousness. They approximated the comic bodies of the attractionist cinema that Lewis had seen in Paris and London just before his trip to Brittany, particularly as cinema's attractionist violence was often distinguished by occurring outside performance frameworks. The cinema of the years 1905–1910 was dominated by the entry of a generation of music hall entrepreneurs, who replaced the film performance style of an industry previously influenced by magicians. *Rinking World and Picture Theatre News* (albeit dismissively) called music hall performance style, borrowing the playwright Henry Arthur Jones's phrase, "legs and tom-foolery", in 1910.⁵⁴ As late as September 1911 a journalist wrote in the *Evening Times* that violence was still the fundamental of many of the comic films on the 'picture theatre' programme: "The best of the comic productions come from America. Those from the Continent—sometimes good—usually convey the impression that the essential of humour is violence, such as smashing everything within reach."⁵⁵ *Punch* noted the same as late as the end of 1913 (see Figure 0.1).

OCTOBER 15, 1913.]   PUNCH, OR THE LONDON CHARIVARI.   323

Bailiff. "OH NO, YOUR LADYSHIP, I DON'T MIND THE BATTLE PICTURES—THEY DON'T DO MUCH DAMAGE, BUT IT'S THESE *COMIC* ONES THAT MESS THE PLACE UP THE WAY YOU SEE IT."

["Several owners of large estates are allowing the use of their grounds for the production of cinema pictures."]

Figure 0.1 Punch cites comic violence as a major characteristic of cinema.⁵⁶

In addition to such originating forces for Lewis's 'Wild Body' stories as the Primitivist impulse to journey into the authentic and uncorrupted rural, a critique of these aims, an explication of Henri Bergson's idea that comedy exists when bodies act mechanically,[57] or an agreement with anarcho-syndicalist thought on the transformative potential of violence (see Chapter 3), Lewis's admiration, in 'Inferior Religions', for his own stories' circus and comedy, as well as his 12 points on the importance of laughter, suggests that the attractionist aesthetics of comedy provided fond models for characters who, Lewis explained, "are only shadows of energy, and not living beings".[58] In the earliest of the stories, the May 1909 'The "Pole"', the narrator describes a dance organised to celebrate the completion of a violent quarrel between hostess and guest, "their two gaunt and violent forms whirling round the narrow room, quite indifferent to the other dancers, giving them terrible blows with their driving elbows."[59] His description of a crowd encapsulates the impression of 'kine-attractography':

> Crowded in the narrow and twilight pavilion of the Saltimbanques at the Breton "pardons," the audience will remain motionless for minutes together. Their imagination is awoken by the sight of the flags, the tent, the drums, and the bedizened people. Thenceforth it rules them, controlling the senses. They enter the tent with a feeling almost of awe. They are "suggestionné," [influenced by suggestion] and in a dream the whole time. All they see they change, add to, and colour. When a joke is made that requires a burst of merriment, or when a turn is finished, they all begin moving themselves as though they had just woken up, changing their attitude, shaking off a magnetic sleep.[60]

The August 1909 'Les Saltimbanques' describes a circus proprietor slapping a clown as "[a]woken to the sudden violence of an automatic figure set in motion",[61] again suggesting the de-familiarising effects of movement and the predominance of violence in kine-attractography. In the June 1909 'Some Innkeepers and Bestre', the protagonist has always "in his moments of most violent action something of his dumb-passivity—he never seems quite entering into reality."[62]

Despite the likelihood of a wider influence of the first 15 years of cinema on literary protocols, however, a study of the relationship between cinema and modernism in the attractionist period could not properly be called a study of cinema, as it was only in the period after roughly 1910 that the technology acquired an identity that fully distinguished it, for the first time, from those performance and amusement practices that had employed it as a labour-saving technology immediately on its emergence. As André Gaudreault and Philippe Marion have recently asserted, cinema is best described as having experienced two births: the first birth at the 'moment' of its appearance in 1895 as a technological process, "as an extension of earlier practices, to which it was at first subservient",[63] and the second birth "when it set out on a path that enabled the resources it had developed to acquire an institutional legitimacy that acknowledged their specificity", this second birth leading to "the *constitution* of an established medium that transcends and in some way sublimates the apparatus."[64] They stress that for even its most informed contemporaries, who knew only of a procedure called 'animated photography', before cinema attained its 'identity card'—its 'mediativity'[65]—during this second birth, "early cinema was not, in fact, early cinema."[66] Rather, it was a continuation of earlier cultural practices by other means. The cinematograph did have a 'culture' between the first and second births, but Gaudreault and Marion stress that this "was of necessity intermedial and was characterised ... by a hodgepodge of neighbouring institutions which by definition were not 'cinematic'."[67] While a medium can be intermedial in that it can establish an alliance with another medium or operate under its aegis, during this initial period, before a technology acquires the status of a medium, merely being employed by existing media, it operates 'spontaneous intermedaility':[68] it is 'intermedial' in the sense that the technology is spread across several medialities. Thus while Trotter is right to point out that cinema first confronted modernists as a medium rather than an art form,[69] for over a decade after its arrival it was not *even* a medium.

From its debut in the UK in February 1896 until c. 1908, the practices of the cinematograph were continuous with both the performance and amusement institutions out of which the cinematograph had grown *and* the neighbouring performance and amusement institutions of the late-Victorian and Edwardian era. The magic lantern provided practice and business bases for films and technological preoccupations for inventions until well into the 1900s.[70] In what he designates as a history of 'screen practice' rather than 'pre-cinema', Charles Musser observes that "cinema appears as a continuation and transformation of magic-lantern traditions in which showmen displayed images on a screen, accompanying them with voice, music, and sound effects", a sense of continuity frequently articulated in the US between 1895 and 1908.[71] Sax Rohmer (at the time writing under his real name, Arthur Henry Sarsfield Ward) called the technology "a magic-lantern ... with cinematograph attachment" in his October 1904 short story 'The Green Spider', and H.G. Wells likened the cinematograph to "people going to and fro in front of the circle of a rather defective lantern" in his novel *A Modern Utopia*, which began serialisation in the *Fortnightly Review* in the same month, suggesting the tenacity of initial perceptions that cinema was a mere addendum to the lantern.[72] Valentia Steer would write in 1913 that the technology had only recently shed its image as "an adjunct to the 'Fat Lady' and the 'Two-headed Calf!'",[73] an allusion to a lengthy and only recently curtailed incorporation of the cinematograph into the entertainment context of fairground attractions and urban shop shows. Fairground entrepreneurs and itinerant town hall showmen appropriating a new technology constituted a significant slew of the UK's first film showmen, and, as recent histories of early cinema have shown, at the turn of the century the idea that films produced their own meaning was alien to a mode of presentation in which showmen 'sold' their exhibited items through their own overarching narratives: films were components of a much larger meaning system.[74]

KETTNER'S RESTAURANT.

THE PALACE THEATRE of VARIETIES

Managing Director	-	-	Mr. ALFRED BUTT.

9/3/1909

Programme - - **6d.**

The Management politely request that where necessary Ladies will remove their hats in order not to obstruct the view of those sitting behind.

1.	March ... ... "The Little Drummer" ... *Hugo Felix*.	8.0
2.	MISS HETTIE LEE Comedienne and Dancer	8.5
3.	MISS ANITA BARTLING in a Juggling Scena	8.15
4.	LA CONTADINA Italian Violinist.	8.25
5.	J. P. LING in a Mimetic Monologue	8.35
6.	THE PALACE GIRLS	8.50
7.	CARLTON Comic Card Manipulator	9.0
8.	First appearance in England LAS FLORIDOS—MARIE AND PEPE From Seville	9.15
9.	The First Presentation of **"KINEMACOLOR"** URBAN-SMITH PATENTS (Animated Scenes and Moving Objects Bioscoped in the Actual Tints of Nature.)	9.25

"Sweet Flowers." This picture will first be shown as an ordinary Black and White Bioscope view. After an interval of two seconds for adjusting Colour Filters to the Urban Bioscope Machine, this same picture will be shown in its natural hues and tints.

Farmyard Visit: The Rabbits—Sheep—A Carrot for the Donkey—Swans.

Reaping.

Sailing at Southwick. (Note effect of sunshine on varnish of Boat rounding the Buoy.)

View of Brighton Front from West Pier.

Band of Queen's Highlanders on West Pier.

Carnival at Cannes. (Taken Sunday, Feb. 21st, '09.)

"Waves and Spray." (Examples of Rocky Coast and Beach Scenery.)

Incidental Music by HERMAN FINCK.

MATINEE OF THE FULL EVENING PROGRAMME SATURDAY NEXT AT 2.

10.	"Collection" by the Orchestra— "Now and Then" ... *Arranged by Herman Finck*	9.40
11.	First Appearance in Vaudeville MR. LOUIS CALVERT Supported by Mr. WILLIAM HAVILAND AND COMPANY, in a New One-Act Play, **"EZRA SOLOMON"** By ARTHUR LAYARD and LEOPOLD PAM.	9.55

PRINCE SARATOFF ... ... (High Chancellor) ... ... MR. WILLIAM HAVILAND.
IVAN ... ... (Servant) ... ... MR. SEBASTIEN SMITH.
ANNA ... ... (Daughter of the Prince's Lodgekeeper) ... MISS LUCIE CAINE.
EZRA SOLOMON ... ... (A Rich Jew) ... ... Mr. LOUIS CALVERT.
SCENE—The Courtyard of Prince Saratoff's Palace at Moscow. TIME—The Present.

12.	MISS MAUD ALLAN In Selections from her famous Classical Dances. For full particulars of programme to be presented each performance, see separate slip.	10.15
13.	ARTHUR PRINCE and his Sailor Boy "JIM"	10.40
14.	**"URBANORA" BIOSCOPE.**	10.55

Alpine Winter Sports.

Invasion—Its Possibilities. Showing Naval and Military Activity—
(a) As it is. (b) As it might be.

Incidental Music by HERMAN FINCK.

Pictures by THE CHARLES URBAN TRADING CO., Ltd., London, Paris, Berlin and New York

Treasurer—Mr. THOMAS MILLER. Stage Manager—Mr. FRANK DAMER.

NOTICE.—The Public can leave the Theatre at the end of the performance by all exit and entrance doors which open outwards. All gangways, passages and staircases must be kept free from chairs or any other obstructions. Persons must not be permitted to stand or sit in any of the intersecting gangways, and if standing be permitted in the gangways at the sides and rear of the seating, sufficient space must be left for persons to pass easily to and fro. The safety curtain must be lowered about the middle of the performance so as to ensure its being in proper working order.

The order and composition of this Programme may be varied as circumstances require.

BOX OFFICE open from 10 a.m. to 11 p.m. TELEPHONE No. 6834 GERRARD (2 lines)

Figure 0.2 Programme for the Palace Theatre of Varieties, week commencing 9 March 1909.

In the UK, early film production and exhibition was also continuous with the dominant entertainment institution of the late-Victorian and Edwardian era, the music hall or variety theatre, which began to feature animated photography 'turns' in the spring of 1896.[75] From March 1896, when the Lumiéres' Cinématographe began its 18-month engagement at the Empire and R.W. Paul's Theatrograph/Animatograph began its 13-month engagement at the Alhambra (both in Leicester Square), starting a movement that would, by the end of the year, put 'animated pictures' on the programme of most major variety theatres in the UK, such outfits did not even significantly alter music hall programmes. In many cases they merely took the place of the popular *tableaux vivants* (still live scenes, often from classical paintings and often in series) or the 'moving panorama' (a strip painting that would be scrolled horizontally across the stage). Music halls advertised not films but 'the Bioscope' or 'the Biograph', the technology's ability to animate figures, in line with the spectatorial amazement also generated by acrobats in the music hall, defining its appeal. These 'turns' featured in a dense entertainments field. Even the prestigious touring of the new Kinemacolor process featured on the 9 March 1909 programme at the Palace Theatre of Varieties (the Shaftesbury Avenue venue that opened as a music hall in 1892) comprised just 20 minutes of a three-hour evening made up of 14 acts, including a comedienne, juggler, violinist, card trickster, dance act, a sketch and orchestral pieces (see Figure 0.2). The fairground film show, which went by such names as Wadbrook's Royal Electrograph of 1900, emerged in 1897 within the architectural and presentational mode of, for example, the ghost show (see Figure 0.3). Both had, behind the wide show front covered in carved and gilded figures, rows of upholstered seats and a stage equipped with elaborate scenic effects.[76] The cinematograph even co-existed in the same mobile auditoria as other optical forms, in such outfits as 'Colonel' Clark's 1905 Ghost Show and Cinematograph.[77] The touring showpeople who have recently been championed as comprising the most significant exhibition channel for films during the Edwardian period, though they were the first to create film-only shows, also exhibited films in line with a tradition of town hall showmanship figured around such large-scale optical installations as dioramas (scenes comprised of painted canvases and models) and the more elaborate magic lantern shows.[78]

As the cinematograph, from its emergence in the UK in 1896 until well into the Edwardian period, was used as a component of these multiple existing cultural series—'polysystems' to which "various forms of signification (literature, painting, art, popular tradition, etc.) . . . are subordinated as sub-systems"[79]—a study of the impact of 'kine-attractography' on modernism could only be a study of the impact on modernism of, for example, public amusements, or magic theatre, or touring spectacles. The impact of kine-attractography on Lewis, for example, was *also* the impact of the performance mode endemic, at the time, to music hall comedy. Indeed, during the first roughly 15 years, cinematograph 'views'

Figure 0.3 James Brighton's travelling Bioscope at Boston, Lincolnshire, 1904.

were produced and exhibited in a schema far *more* continuous with, for example, nineteenth-century practices of optical spectacle than with the media mode of later cinema. As Gaudreault writes,

> everything is to be gained, I believe, by looking at so-called early cinema not from the point of view of what it would become, the new "cultural series" called the cinema, but from the point of view of the other cultural series which annexed, in a sense, the kinematograph, in order to do differently what was already being done within these cultural series even before the introduction of the new device.[80]

The cinematograph during its first roughly 15 years was a labour-saving device both in the sense that it enhanced the technological array of various travelling and static shows *and* in the sense that it provided new ways of "presenting already well-established entertainment 'genres'" such as magic and travelogue.[81] Indeed, as Gaudreault insists, instead of separating early cinema out as a distinct historical phase in a still unified larger entity 'the cinema', "it would be better to connect films from the early days to a non-cinematic cultural series than to cinema itself".[82] Indeed, in the Edwardian period futures were envisioned for cinema in which it would be a tele-communicative utterance, a stage magic trick, a four-dimensional panoramic photograph, a press illustration, a simulation of neurological input, a record of the perceptually invisible, a spirit medium's 'apparition', a fictional utterance, a news-maker, a deletion of bourgeois privacy or an ethnographic archival imprint.[83]

Given that the constitution of cinema as a medium was, for Gaudreault and Marion, developed out of the unstable culture of the proto-medium of 'animated photography', they have been reticent about assigning cinema's second birth a single date, giving both 1908 and 1910 as candidate years, and linking the second birth to the rise of, firstly, the job category and then the institutional power of the film director.[84] Rick Altman has also dated this second birth to 1910.[85] When, then, did a discrete medium 'the cinema' come about in the UK, if we define a medium, to follow Gaudreault and Marion, as "a relatively specific semiotic configuration supported by a technology of communication, in relation to social and institutional practices of producing and appropriating public messages"?[86] When, for the purposes of this study, to start? Although a clutch of historical changes was involved, one year stands out: 1911.

1911: "THE PICTURE THEATRE AND THE NEWSAGENTS"[87]

R.D. Blumenfeld, editor of the Pearson publishing empire's *Daily Express* from 1904 to 1932, wrote a diary entry for 17 February 1908 about a meeting with the legitimate stage actor Jimmy Welch:

> Welch was contemptuous about kinematograph shows, which appear to be frightening other theatrical folk. He does not think they can ever compete with the legitimate stage, and that in any case the music-hall has nothing to fear from moving pictures as a means of full-programme entertainment. The music-hall, he says, will absorb the moving picture, and in the meantime the variety stage will be improved by the absorption of legitimate actors. In confirmation, he pointed to the fact that Constance Collier, so well known in connection with Beerbohm Tree's productions, is to go to the Empire next week.[88]

Published in 1930, and the object of both 'revisions' and a process of selection from a mass of longer material (the effect of which was to make Blumenfeld appear prescient in contrast to unprophetic counterparts), this diary is no simple historical document, but the mention of the small number of lendings of legitimate stage personnel to the recently-established high-class 'variety theatres' that occurred in the late 1900s suggests that Welch's attitude as Blumenfeld reported it was not just a foil to Blumenfeld's retrospective prescience. In early 1908 the cinematograph was still so closely linked with such music hall turns as comic whistlers and dancing dogs that it was common for contemporaries to expect it to be permanently absorbed by the music hall. This reflected the perception of "kinematograph shows" held by a public that had seen just a smattering of film-only venues so far (the trade press having only announced the emergence of the static, film-only show in late 1907).[89] As Nicholas Hiley points out, in 1908, although audiences were known to exist for urban amusements and for travelling shows and fairs, there was no such confidence about the possibility of constituting a habitual film-watching audience, as reflected

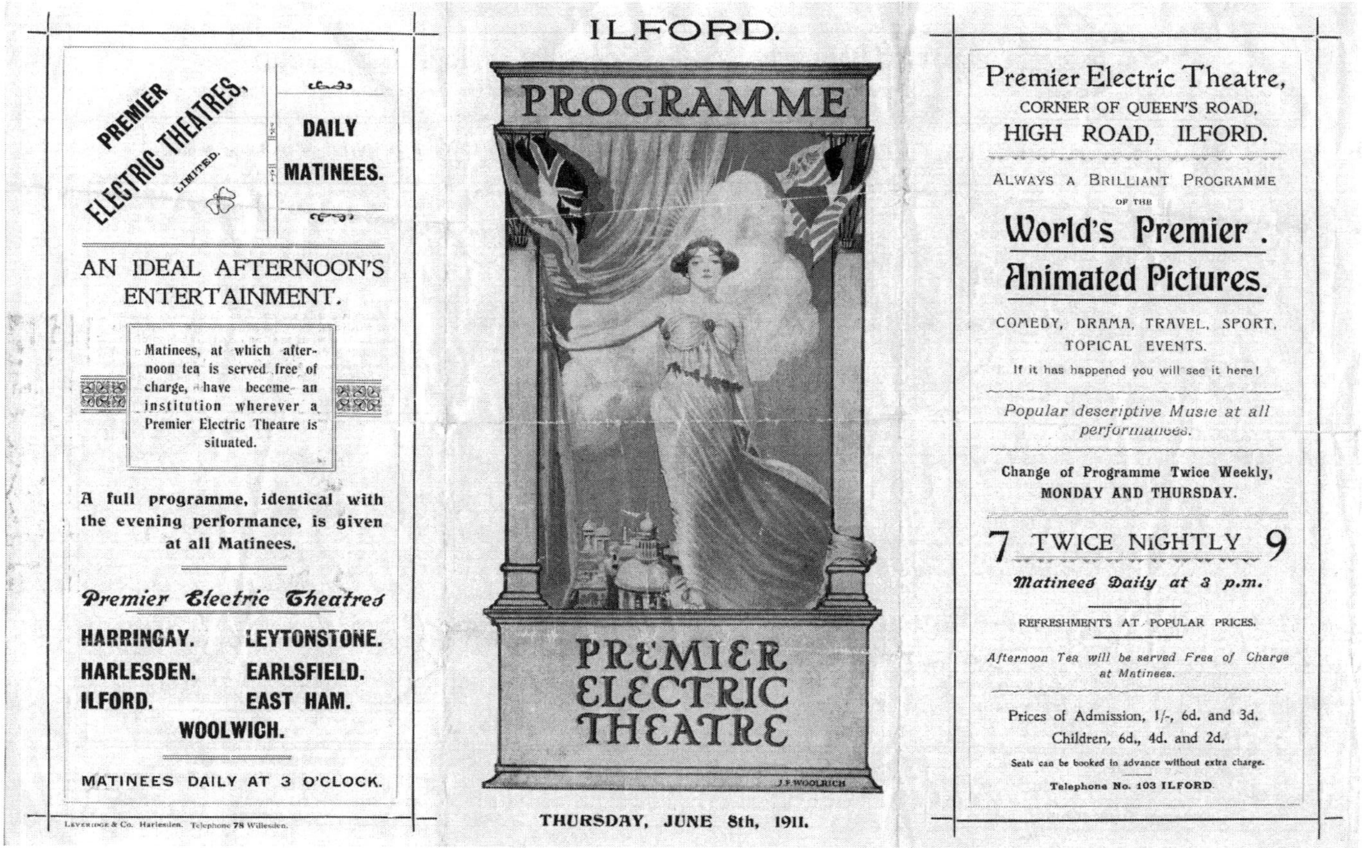

Figure 0.4 Cover of programme for the Premier Electric Theatre, Ilford, 8 June 1911.

in the extreme difficulty of motivating private investment in companies seeking to construct 'picture theatres'.[90]

Blumenfeld's encounter highlights how dramatic the transformation in cinema discourse in the UK would be during the following decade. The rest of 1908 would see the beginning of an avalanche of film-only venues. In January 1917, F.R. Goodwin, Chairman of the London branch of the Cinematograph Exhibitors Association, explained that "the beginning of 1908 . . . may roughly be taken as the beginning of the moving picture boom".[91] Between 1908 and 1916, with a widespread investments boom in building and converting 'picture theatres' that produced between 4,500 and 5,000 such venues nation-wide, a revolution in film exhibition occurred (see Figure 0.5). Indeed, the number of venues that accommodated peak sales of almost 21 million tickets per week in the year up to January 1917 (numbers only ever exceeded during and after the Second World War, between 1941 and 1956) was, by and large, in place before the war started.[92] Although this new entertainments investment boom established venues that were by no means the first static or regular motion picture-only venues in the UK (Jon Burrows has recently identified 154 shop-front venues showing films operating in London between 1906 and 1911),[93] these earlier venues had not altered perceptions of the cinematograph as a constituent of the urban shop show experience, particularly given that the 'nickelodeon' showpeople presented cinema in the vein of the titillations of the urban penny shop show, with, for example, its fat lady, strongman, waxwork chamber of horrors and mutoscopes, until their demise around 1914.[94] In *The History of Mr Polly* (begun in May 1909 and published in April 1910), H.G. Wells typified contemporary opinions that the cinematograph was both temporary *and* remained embedded within existing urban amusements when he had Mr Polly, at the time a shop-keeper in Fishbourne High Street in c. 1905, notice that the failed businessmen using a neighbouring building included "the exploiter of a cinematograph peep-show": film-viewing was still subsumed by definitions provided by such existing encounters as the peep show.[95] These British 'nickelodeons' were also in the a minority, outnumbered in a summer 1907 survey, as Burrows notes, eight to one by those Salvation Army halls, chapels and mission halls regularly hosting film shows.[96] The construction of purpose-built/converted 'picture theatres' on the basis of the new private investment in cinema companies (in contrast to the 'nickelodeons', which were funded by the individual showmen) generated a semantic clout which served to amputate the practice from those sibling forms with which it had, so far, shared space in fairgrounds, music halls, public halls and shop shows. By May 1908 Gaumont executive A.C. Bromhead claimed that the opinion held by Jimmy Welch in February had just been relinquished in popular opinion.[97] A very common industry opinion, during the 1910s, that the cinematograph's first 15 years represented a kind of stasis, reflects just how much of a reinvention was involved in the period beginning in 1908 (see Figure 0.4).

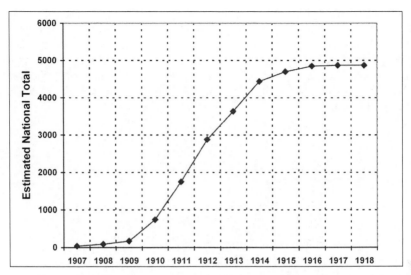

Figure 0.5 The construction/conversion of purpose-built cinemas in the UK, 1907–1916.[98]

1911 saw the fastest yearly increase in the number of picture theatres in the UK of this pre-war boom, the total nearing 3,000 venues at the end of the year. While, by the end of 1909, the 90 cinema companies established in the last two years had a nominal capital of only £875,000, by the end of 1911, 575 cinema companies had been floated on a nominal capital of £4,300,000.[99] 1911 was also the year when the number of cinemas licensed to show films first exceeded the number of other venues holding cinematograph licenses. The new picture theatres and the diverting of money to invest in them were also responsible for the demise in these other venues, from roughly 1,900 in 1910 to just 200 by 1913.[100] When the government responded to the flood of new venues with the safety and licensing requirements of the 1909 Cinematograph Act (which became law in January 1910), they illustrated the speedy expansions of the exhibition industry. By 1911 the rapid emergence of the new venues had reached a point sufficient to trigger *Kinematograph and Lantern Weekly* to produce handbooks for static cinema technical know-how and management, published in early 1911 and 1912 respectively.[101] By August 1912 the new venue was such a part of urban life that *The Era* placed picture theatres and music halls on the same par, as equal as Adam and Eve, in one of its allegorical cartoons,[102] and by 1914 most of the fairground cinematograph showpeople had adopted other shows. On the basis of extensive research into early London film exhibition, Luke McKernan describes the 1906–1909 period as defined by shop shows, with the purpose-built cinema first dominating the shape of film exhibition in 1910.[103] 1911 also emerges as a key date in McKernan's findings, with daily London cinema seating capacity, for example, reaching roughly half a million by 1911.[104] In this virtually nation-wide business venture, a range of names for filming and projection technologies became 'the pictures', 'cinema' now referred to a type of building as well as the entertainment form it delivered (see Figure 0.6) and by late 1911 the terms 'cinematograph audience' and 'cinematograph show' attached to very different referents from those to which they had attached in 1907.

IF YOU SHOULD SEE ANY LITTLE THING YOU WANT IN THAT PET OLD CURIOSITY SHOP OF YOURS, BUY IT NOW.

TO-MORROW MAY BE TOO LATE.   NEIGHBOURHOODS CHANGE SO QUICKLY NOWADAYS.

Figure 0.6 The rapidly erected cinema venue as exemplar of urban modernity.[105]

The new venue type was accompanied by a further catalogue of intersecting developments. For instance, the audience for this new form of urban entertainment was increasing very fast in 1911 (see Figure 0.7). A September 1911 estimate put average weekly UK picture theatre attendance at four million,[106] a figure which has not been exceeded in the period from 1970 to the present.[107] Hiley's own research into ticket sales indicates that 1911 was the first year that these figures could reasonably be counted in cinema tickets per household per week, even though a quarter of these households—i.e. the middle-classes and above—were by and large not visiting these 'electric palaces' at all.[108] 1911 also saw the founding, in August, by William Jeapes and Herbert Wrench, of the first British-produced regular 'animated newssheet' company, the Topical Film Company. The first issue of their twice-weekly *Topical Budget*, what we would now call a 'newsreel' (the term was not used in the UK until the 1920s), was released on 1 September 1911. While this 'animated newssheet' was preceded in the UK by *Pathé's Animated Gazette* and *Gaumont Graphic* (launched in June and October 1910 respectively), the Topical Film Company, as McKernan points out, was unlike Pathé and Gaumont in that it produced no other films, had no sidelines in equipment manufacturing or exhibition, and had no diversified parent company to carry its losses. Given that the 'animated newssheet' automatically becomes rapidly obsolete, it requires a regular audience, and the successful launch of a company producing nothing else indicates that by late 1911 the picture theatre boom had generated a nation-wide film audience that was visiting with some frequency.[109]

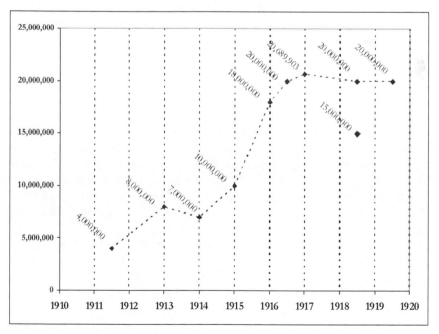

Figure 0.7   Estimated total cinema audience per week in the UK, 1911–1919.[110]

1911 was also the year in which, as a result of the demand for films created by the new method of changing the film programme twice a week (itinerant showmen had made films last much longer), the number of 'entertainment films' produced by UK producers (known as 'manufacturers' at the time) rose at the fastest rate in the 1895–1914 period, increasing from under 400 releases in 1910 to almost 600 in 1912, the highest it had ever been.[111] Film distribution in the UK was also growing fast. The total number of films released in the UK rose from 1,842 in 1909 to 7,554 in 1913.[112] The numbers of companies selling films to distributors in the UK (or acting as selling agents for other minor producers) rose from seven on 16 May 1907, to 16 on 14 May 1908, to 23 on 1 April 1909, to 29 on 15 December 1910, and to 37 on 21 September 1911, and the total length of footage of the titles on recent release rose from 59,719 feet on 1 April 1909 to 78,870 feet on 21 September 1911.[113] The *Evening Standard and St James's Gazette* announced in January 1912 that producers had only recently taken up fiction films as a reaction to an expanding audience that could not be served by topicals and factuals alone.[114] In addition, while an average weekly attendance of four million at the end of 1911 does not mean that four million UK citizens were visiting a picture theatre each week (repeat attendance was estimated at half of all weekly ticket sales in 1917),[115] as 1911 approached it was becoming *apparent* that a certain number of these were repeat attendances, the writer of the anonymous 1910 *Historical Review of the Cinematograph* referring to audience behaviour in terms of the "Cinema Habit".[116] Frequent attendance by the same people was also one of the factors motivating the uptake, at this time, of a blanket twice-weekly programme change in UK picture theatres, the intermittent display of films by itinerant showmen touring the same films around different locations giving way to the exhibition of a steady stream of films in one place. Any mediativity depends on the existence of a self-identifying consumption community, a corresponding public, and this public of 'picturegoers' seems to have come into being in 1911: the writer of the first regular newspaper column devoted to film, begun in June 1911, cited the needs of the new "picture theatre habitué" as the reason for its inception.[117] 1912 saw the first uses of the term 'fan' (imported from American English) in British English to describe this new kind of habitual media consumer.[118] Ian McDonald also identifies 1911 as the year when the earliest screenwriting manual—E.J. Muddle's *Picture Plays and How to Write Them*—was published in the UK, which also signals the assumed existence of a substantial 'picture theatre public'.[119]

In 1911 the new picture theatres also amounted to a significant enough proportion of the market for films to elicit a new distribution system. In open market rental, which had been the dominant film distribution system in the UK since the end of 1907, production companies sold prints of their films to as many hirers as they could, their ownership of the prints ending at this point, and the hirers then leased films to as many exhibitors as they could and for as long as the prints remained usable. In the exclusive rental system, which was first used in the UK in February 1911, a production company would retain ownership of a film and lease a small number of prints to a limited number of hirers (with the highest bidder in each locality securing the sole rights for a particular film), and the hirers in turn leased these few prints to cinemas in a system of run zones. This new system, which involved the substantial risk of refusing to sell films to all-comers, could only work if the dominant mode of film exhibition was static, and where, instead of various showmen exhausting and renewing their *audience* supply by regularly moving on, film exhibition was now committed to the exhaustion and renewal of *film* supply.[120] Moreover, exclusive rentals, and the associated structure of run zones, led to a higher uniformity of exhibition: unlike 'open market' rental, where films had no set return date, the exclusive rental system required hirers to sign contracts with the production companies which set a film's release and withdrawal dates. As the number of production companies using the new system grew rapidly in the years immediately before the First World War, films thus began to commence and end their runs in a hierarchy of dates that was roughly uniform across the UK, meaning that the individual film product gradually came to be defined as consumed with nation-wide uniformity. This transition also hastened the shift in definitions of the product 'regarded' in the act of film-watching from the 'animated photographs' of the pre-'picture theatre' period to specific film titles. In addition, because hirers would often refuse altogether to take bookings from music halls, exclusive rental also served to push the picture theatre as the home of film.

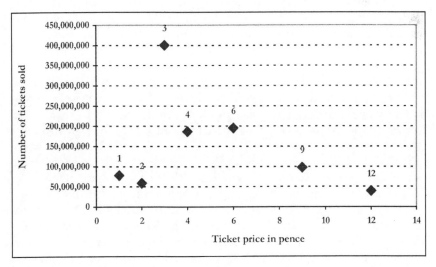

Figure 0.8 Nicholas Hiley's analysis of seats occupied in UK picture theatres on weekdays in the year up to January 1917.[121]

Hiley also gives 1911 as the date when the new picture theatres came to be popularly regarded as shifting the recreational habits of the average working-class person, as this was the first year in which rivalry with the pub was perceived to be within the capacity of the rituals of picture-going.[122] Pricing scales appealed directly to working-class pockets. It was commented in July 1914 that "people who never went to theatres or music halls, today go into picture theatres, simply because a nominal price is charged",[123] and, as Rachael Low recorded, no exhibition company manager or picture theatre manager could do without "a businesslike acceptance of the humble foundations of his rapidly growing fortunes".[124] At the end of 1911 and beginning of 1912 a mode ticket price of just 2d was commonly reported.[125] Even with the price increase occasioned by the mid-1916 Entertainments Tax, evidence given to the National Council of Public Morals Cinema Commission of Inquiry in January 1917 put the mode ticket price at 3d (see Figure 0.8), and by 1918 this had risen to no more than 4½d.[126] As Burrows has pointed out, this was much closer to the pricing scale of music halls and variety theatres than that of legitimate theatres.[127] Amongst the 30 picture theatres opening in Newcastle upon Tyne between June 1908 and May 1914, the most common price stratification was a 2d pit, 4d stalls and 6d circle.[128] In March 1911, tickets at Newcastle's Grey St. Theatre Royal started at 1s for a pit or amphitheatre seat, rising to 2s for an upper circle seat, 3s for unreserved stalls and 4s for reserved stalls, with only the distant 'gods' or 'gallery' seating available for under 1s at 6d. At the Palace Theatre of Varieties in nearby Sunderland, however (albeit in August 1907), the gallery was 2d, a pit seat was 4d, a balcony seat 6d and stalls and grand circle seats were both 1s.[129] The new institution's reliance on the industrial working-class was evidenced by the fact that, in 1914, "heavily industrialised cities had by far the highest proportion of picture theatres per head".[130] A 1912 guide to running a picture theatre was clear that 'disinfectant' sprays were actually deodorants for Edmund Burke's "great unwashed".[131]

1911 also saw the dissemination, in the UK, of the first national publicity campaigns aimed at the general public for celebrities whose fame was based solely on their appearances in films. From June 1911 a handful of American 'picture players' (from the American Biograph, Kalem, Lubin, IMP, Edison and Essanay companies) were advertised in national newspapers in the UK, in some cases under pseudonyms. This range of American producers expanded, Hepworth began the first systematic publicity of UK players in November 1911 and public appearances of the new 'picture personalities' began to be seen as a viable form of publicity towards the end of the year. Not only is a celebrity system another major aspect of a distinct mediativity, it permitted cinema to encompass a range of attributes which it was not previously seen to possess. The often strongly gendered but extremely productive discursive mechanism of gossip was attached to film by the reinvention of bodies in films (already understood as undertaking a task akin to acting), as entities whose lives were relevant to their being

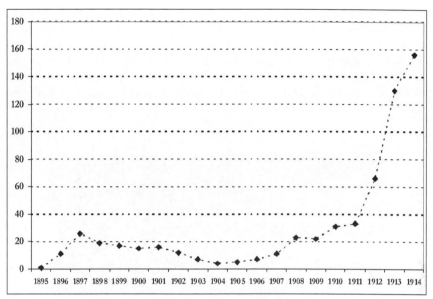

Figure 0.9 Date breakdown of 639 cartoons about film world-wide, 1895–1914.[132]

screened. While descriptions of a player's personality and private life aimed primarily to ensure interest amongst picturegoers in her/his future films, they also enlarged film as a realm of knowledge.

1911 also saw a significant expansion of avenues of film discourse. The *Evening Standard and St James's Gazette* began a 'Cinematography' column in June 1911, in September 1911 the *Evening Times* began a 'Motion Picture and Photo-Play' column and the *Pall Mall Gazette* began a 'Cinematography' column and the *Daily Express* was producing a daily 'Cinematograph News and Notes' section by October 1911. The *Evening Standard* stated in June 1911 that "[t]he rapid growth of the motion picture business, and the increasing interest and appreciation accorded it by the public, both from a scientific and social standpoint, clearly indicate that cinematography now takes an established and important place amongst the industries of this country."[133] In 1911 *Punch* featured its first cartoons concerning the 'picture theatre' (see Figure 0.10), suggesting that this was the first year that the new institution constituted a significant enough aspect of its readers' diverse experiences for the editorial team to be confident that jokes about it would evoke humour in the general public, and cinema's place in this avenue of discourse expanded: it featured in three *Punch* cartoons for 1911, rising to 10 for 1913. Stephen Bottomore's survey of cartoons about films in newspapers and magazines world-wide between 1895 and 1914 also provides evidence that this form of discourse on cinema attained a new scale from the end of 1911. Plotting the number of cartoons on film found year by year, it becomes clear that after an initial flurry of cartoons on the new form rising to no higher than 26 per year in 1897, the intensity of discourse on film dipped until 1904, then began to gradually grow until the number drastically doubled from 33 in 1911 to 66 in 1912, then to 130 in 1913, beginning to level out at 156 in 1914 (see Figure 0.9). His survey of the appearance of cinema in short stories during the same period also shows 1911 to be a year of drastic increase in the volume of discourse.[134]

THE STAY-AS-YOU-PLEASE CINEMA PALACE.

Boy (to Lady just arrived). "Please, will you tell me the time, Lady?"
Lady. "Half-past eleven."
Boy. "Will you please tell me when it's six o'clock, Lady, cos I've got to go out and sell papers!"

Figure 0.10   *Punch*'s first reference to the 'picture theatre', February 1911.[135]

1911 also saw the launch of the UK's first popular film magazine when, in October, Benito Nichols of Markt & Co. (the UK sales agent for the US production companies American Biograph, Lubin and Kalem) supplemented the film still postcards, picture player postcards, picture player photographs and picture player brooches that their subsidiary the Picture Publishing Company had been selling to cinema managers since c. July 1911 with *The Pictures: An Illustrated Weekly Magazine of Fiction for Lovers of Moving Pictures*. Modelled on the American *Motion Picture Story Magazine*, itself launched in February 1911 by the Motion Picture Patents Company (hereafter MPPC), of which American Biograph, Lubin and Kalem were members, *The Pictures* advertised their films, initially with motion picture stories of forthcoming films but also with an increasing proportion of 'fan' matter. As with *Topical Budget*, *The Pictures* suggests the recent appearance of a nation-wide habitual audience for film-only shows. The number of production companies placing motion picture stories steadily increased, the UK firm British & Colonial Kinematograph investing in both motion picture stories and picture personality publicity from February 1912. When Markt & Co. disposed of the magazine to the Queenhithe Press in December 1912 and it became open to all who wished to advertise, most major North American and European production companies with a publicity budget used motion picture stories to advertise their films. *The Pictures* was joined in 1913 by *Illustrated Films Monthly and Picture Stories Magazine* (in September) and *Picturegoer: The Picture Theatre Magazine* (on 11 October). All steadily increased their proportions of 'fan' matter for the duration of the 1910s. This new arena of film discourse, described by one columnist in late 1912 as "a moving picture magazine for the Public",[136] now incorporated such knowledges into popular film discourse as transfers of personnel between production companies, company projects and screen conventions, and it focused information that had previously been scattered across trade showings, distributors' and producers' publicity, daily papers and trade papers. In contrast to such trade papers as *Optical Lantern and Kinematograph Journal/Kinematograph and Lantern Weekly/Kinematograph Weekly* (November 1904–April 1907/May 1907–Nov 1919/Dec 1919–Dec 1959) and *Bioscope* (Oct 1908–May 1932), which were already presiding over definitions of the apparatus and practice, and which circulated in the thousands, the new popular film magazines circulated in the hundreds of thousands.[137] With the emergence of such magazines, newsstands became mechanisms for nationally disseminating a nationally standard discourse on cinema.[138] In October 1911 the *Evening Times* remarked that the launch of *The Pictures* was

> a very interesting departure, which is sure to be popular with some people who would often like some souvenir of a particularly good picture, and this penny weekly puts one in the same position as the person who sees a spoken play written round a well-known book, and afterwards

reads the book, which is recognised to be a more satisfactory proceed-
ing than reading the book first, and afterwards seeing the play.[139]

For this journalist, even when the film was perceived as an adaptation of
the motion picture story rather than vice versa, the fact of the film's literari-
ness awarded it significant prestige.

Like any knowledge, popular film discourse is constituted *as* a knowledge only by the statements used to refer to it. In January 1912 *The Pictures*
magazine explained its role:

> The remarkable interest evoked by a vast community of picture play-
> goers in matters cinematographic has not only rendered necessary
> the existence of a weekly magazine of fiction . . . but has created
> a need for a *newspaper*, publishing items of topical interest in the
> picture theatre world and incidentally affording 'a peep behind the
> scenes' of the silent stage.[140]

This sense of a discrete sphere of activity beyond and influencing the picture theatre auditorium—that there was *something* "behind the scenes"—
evidences the proliferation by 1912 of cinema as a discrete realm of, and
in, popular discourse. The emergence of such terms as "pictureland"[141] and
"filmland"[142] in the pre-war period reflected popular convictions of the new
existence of this discrete knowledge. *The Pictures* alone enmeshed a series of
ideas about education, entertainment, representation, moral hygiene, celebrity,
reportage, nationality, quality, business, cultural reception, class and artistic
ambition in popular discourse, rendering a much higher degree of uniformity
in popular thought about 'the pictures' than had existed for 'the cinematograph'. That the basic unit of cinema was a narrative rather than a reel of film,
that the image was the result of a creative effort (in its first version seen as a
partnership between a production company director and the company's stock
company of players), that directing filming was as relevant a component as
directing acting, that a film had parameters measurable as duration of narrative rather than the length in feet of the film strip, that it was an arena of activity for a particular kind of endeavour on the part of the participating actants,
and that it had an existence beyond the duration of projection: all were now
being packed into cinema's new image-regime from 1911.

Such specifications of the kind of knowledge included under the term
'cinema' determined the ritualised meaning of cinemagoing as a cultural
event, and these new, national, forms of cinema culture were fundamental tools in making available what James Donald and Stephanie Hemelryk
Donald call "structures of visibility, modes of conduct, and practices of
judgement, which together constitute a culture of public participation."[143]
Given that nothing of the institution cinema that originated at the end of
the Edwardian period was implicit in the cinematic apparatus itself, the
production of the parameters of 'cinema' was related to the efforts of
film discourse to relinquish previous pedigrees and establish new ones.[144]

Change of Programme every Monday and Thursday.

Acknowledged by all to be THE COOLEST THEATRE IN THE SUMMER, THE WARMEST IN WINTER, and the THE BEST VENTILATED IN OXFORD.

Watch this Space *for Special Announcements.*

MONDAY NEXT, MARCH 16th and following 5 days,

FROM

THE QUEEN'S HALL, LONDON,

THE

"CLARENDON SPEAKING PICTURES"

The Latest Artistic Development of Cinematography.

The HUMAN VOICE with the marvels of photography. NOT a Gramophone.

SPECIAL NOTICE.—Showing at 3, 7 and 9 p.m. only.

MUSICAL SELECTIONS.

During the showing of the Programme the following will be played by Miss GWENYDD MANNERS, and Miss MARGERY QUAINTON on two Pianos.

"DOLLAR PRINCESS" ... *Leo Fall*
"AISHA" ... *John Lindsay*
"DANSE DU PARAGUAY" ... *Valverde*
"THE MOUSME" ... *Howeton & Talbot*
"POLKA-CAPRICE" ... *E. Meyer-Helmund*
"PUPPCHEN" ... *Jean Gilbert*

On request others will be played if suitable for the Picture.

NOTE.—Patrons are respectfully informed that Pictures of an objectionable nature will never be shown at THE ELECTRA PALACE. The Management exercise the strictest censorship in the selection of every picture exhibited.

PROGRAMME.

(Subject to alteration at the discretion of the Management.)

Monday, Tuesday, Wednesday, Mar. 9th, 10th and 11th.

1. The Schemers ... Comedy—Vitagraph.
2. The Tiger Cat ... Interest—Premier.
3. Lieut. Daring and the Aerial Scout
    Drama—B. & C.
4. Is it not wonderful! Trick—Anderson.
5. Eclair Weekly Journal.
    (The latest news from North, South, East and West.)
    (Exclusive to this Theatre.)
6. "THE GREAT GOLD ROBBERY" or A STORY OF OLD FATHER THAMES.
7. Love Sickness at Sea ... Comic—Keystone.
8. Some Garden Flowers ... Coloured Nature Series.
9. Proving a Lover ... Comic—Pathe.

Thursday, Friday, Saturday, March 12th, 13th and 14th.

1. Broncho Billy's Squareness ... Drama—Essanay.
2. Through the Canadian Rockies ... Scenic—Kineto.
3. Tangled Treads ... Comedy—Vitagraph.
4. Eclair Weekly Journal.
    (The latest news from North, South, East and West.)
5. A Pill-Box Cupid ... Comic—Lubin.
6. The Fruits of Vengeance ... Drama—Vitagraph.
    (Exclusive to this Theatre.)
7. "THE GIRL FROM SCHOOL" A Charming Study of a "TOMBOY" replete with laughter-provoking situations.
    (Exclusive to this Theatre.)
8. "DOWN THE CRATER OF VESUVIUS"
    (The most wonderful film ever taken.)
    THE HEART OF VESUVIUS PHOTOGRAPHED IN A TEMPERATURE OF 1,112 DEGREES FAHR. BY MR. FREDERICK BURLINGHAM.
    SPECIAL NOTICE—This Film will be shown at 3, 7 and 9 p.m. only.

Figure 0.11 Programme for the Electra Palace, Oxford, week commencing 9 March 1914.

Popular film magazines even contributed to the creation of a viable habitual national picturegoing public, notably by disseminating the identity of 'picturegoer' through such techniques as conditioning the new term 'fan' away from synonymy with 'loon' and towards synonymy with 'enthusiast' during 1912 and 1913.

While 1911 was neither the only eventful year nor saw the radical beginning of a new film product, it did see 'the pictures' emerge as a largely new dimension of the common cultural landscape of the UK; cinema was now popularly framed by its own venues, specialist personnel, a popularly identifiable place of emanation, common conventions, bug-bears, an interplay of popular conceptions and misconceptions, economic institutions with a degree of permanence in public consciousness and, perhaps most crucial to the naissance of 'the cinema' as a national entity, a self-identifying and habitual national audience relating to a practice that had until very recently been foreign to the idea of patronage. This is not to claim that schemas of the methods and personnel of the cinematograph did not exist before 1911, but that before this point, as an influence on writing, these cannot be accurately called schemas specifically and solely of cinema.[145] While, therefore, Stephen Donovan has made a coherent case that Conrad's 'Preface to *The Nigger of the "Narcissus"*' (written in the summer of 1897, after the novel was finished in January, and first published in the December 1897 *New Review*) represents "a literary counter-manifesto, as it were, to the New Year One of the New Photography",[146] then *if* the "scenes of spectatorship"[147] that began to appear in Conrad's work thereafter were the product of the cinematograph, they were *also*, as Donovan makes clear, the product of x-ray photography (like cinema, known as 'the new photography'), spectacular theatre, ghost shows and moving panoramas, i.e. a range of visual forms that, together, comprised one of the 'cultural series' of Britain's complex visual culture at the end of the 1890s. (These "scenes of spectatorship" are also, notably, the habitual content of some proto-modernist novels rather than any aspect of their form.) In neighbouring work, a small tradition of work on the impact of cinema on painting which perceives Cubist and Futurist painting as emulating cinema has been unable to pare the impact of cinema away from the impact of chronophotography.[148]

This study therefore takes up the story at cinema's 'second birth' at the beginning of the 1910s not out of a belief in the immaturity or irrelevance of earlier cinema, but because it was only in 1911 that the cinematograph was disembedded from its earlier continuity with the information, entertainment and instructional practices which had encompassed it on its emergence, a continuity that would make any study of the influence of the cinematograph pre-c. 1910 on literary practice the study of the impact, for example, of advanced stage illusionism, Edwardian fairground, or amateur photography in the wake of the democratisation of the Kodak, on literary practice, and therefore distinct from the study undertaken here.

Even *after* 1911, the ongoing relationships between, for instance, cinema and music hall (including the use of the variety programme format in picture theatres (see Figure 0.11)) and between cinema and the legitimate theatre (the use of legitimate stage stars being a major prestige factor for the UK film industry during the 1910s)[149] were just the most explicit of the ongoing contacts established between cinema and other media during the period covered by this study. Cinema was not now 'clean' of its relatives, and continued to be produced and experienced according to various implicit influences and explicit alliances. As Gaudreault and Burrows have both argued, it is incumbent on cinema historians to excavate a history of the practice that observes its fundamental dependence on other media and cultural spheres,[150] a dependence that, as Burrows has argued, does not necessarily disappear with the establishment of a discursively distinct media institution 'the cinema'.[151] This second form of intermediality, however, was not constitutive but subjugated, no longer spontaneous but negotiated: a matter of alliances formed to fulfil conscious aspirations to cultural status. For Gaudreault and Marion, this second intermediality is "the intermediality found in any process of cultural production".[152]

Cinema's second birth was also clear to contemporaries. Even those commentators who were intent on disseminating a history of cinema's unbroken teleological growth from the moment of its appearance in 1895 could not avoid having to describe the point around 1911 as a disjunction of some kind. "Not until motion-photography made a genuine intellectual appeal was it anything more than an amusing novelty", wrote Fred Dangerfield, editor of the newly amalgamated *Pictures and the Picturegoer*, in 1914: "now it is rapidly developing into the finest of the fine arts."[153] Although an industry-friendly assertion of aesthetic status rather than a representative slice of film discourse, Dangerfield's remark is telling for its tendency to periodise. Iris Barry would much later date the point at which cinema's intellectual evolution had begun by citing the emergence of cinema as a mode of public participation in c. 1910, explaining in 1927 that "[t]he cinema . . . is still only at the mental age of seventeen".[154]

The following three chapters will therefore consider literary works written immediately after the emergence of a distinct institution cinema in 1911 as the very first to be able to bear the impact of a force that can plausibly be isolated as solely that exerted by cinema. Indeed, given that nineteenth-century poetry, for example, bears the imprint of a range of mid-Victorian scene-changing, stereo-optic, movement-based, telescopic, microscopic and photographic forms of visual culture,[155] the emergence of the technology of the cinematograph out of its initial embedding in such technologies and its metamorphosis from a technology to a distinct medium with its own characteristic image-regime, its second birth as 'the cinema', suggests a basis for the change in currents amongst the literary imaginary that gave rise to the modes and methods of literary modernism.

EXCAVATIONS: "CLIVE HAD BEEN UP LATE. SO HAD I—AT THE PICTURES"[156]

In the 1910s, cinema's 'regime of the image' arose from the efforts that popular channels of film culture made to generate terms for understanding cinema's distinctiveness as a practice, institution and medium. Such popular publications on film have a double usefulness for this study. First, although not always produced at the hands of film industry bodies, they exemplify efforts being made at the time to describe cinema in ways more amenable to its longevity. As Christian Metz writes, even writers on cinema with no industrial role are motivated by the urge "to maintain a good object relation with as many films as possible, and at any rate with the cinema as such."[157] Popular publications on film represent one–half of a conversation with the institution's real and imagined critics, which can be used to extrapolate the rest of this conversation. Second, they comprise a detailed, albeit sometimes heavily encoded, record of the observations of typical picturegoers, their descriptions of their mediated experience of films and the social practices cohering around them. These popular publications did include fan-authored matter, but even the specialists (editors, regular columnists, interviewers and interviewees) were also just witnesses to a new institution. Jennifer Bean comments that, "[i]neluctably linked to the crisis of the archives and to the paucity of film remnants from the period [the 1910s], with surviving prints in often precarious condition, elisions of all sorts haunt the historical register of early cinema".[158] The print version of this historical register is significantly less impoverished.

While Anne Friedberg is certainly right to point out that writing on cinema is a record of "discursive documents that impart their own form of historical knowledge",[159] the predominant form of this writing and richest "archaeological site for the aesthetic, economic, ideological and technological questions posed to a cinema [always] struggling to form itself"[160] was not the minority film culture that began in the late 1920s in such periodicals as *Close Up* but the majority film culture that had emerged at the beginning of the previous decade. To praise such 1920s film journalists as Iris Barry or Dorothy Richardson as spirited advocates writing against the grain is to risk dismissing as inane chatter the film journalism of the 1910s which they opposed, journalism which contains vital clues to the shape of cinema's image-regime at the time of the emergence of literary modernism.[161] This book therefore excavates the historical 'cinema' impacting on literary practice not by looking solely to films, but by surveying examples of popular cinema discourse in given historical moments, using selected films as examples of much wider trends. It treats these remarks and commentaries on the many aspects of the institution cinema as archaeological remains of the image regime for cinema that pertained during the period of literary modernism's emergence, handling cinema's singular formal tendencies only via their particular historical manifestations and the categories applied to these manifestations in popular thought.

There are further reasons to avoid construing modernist form as a product solely of certain films. In 1911 a picturegoer with access to just one 'picture theatre' with a twice-weekly change of programme and five films on each programme (see Figure 1.1) would have had the opportunity to see over 500 films a year. In April 1914 one avid picturegoer recorded that in the previous 12 months s/he had seen 1,375 films.[162] Therefore, even with the few records of modernist picturegoing that have survived, it is most likely that the films that we *know* that modernists saw are vastly outnumbered by the films that they saw but left no record of seeing. Although the number of films available each year was reduced as the variety format began to diminish with the gradual rise of the feature film in the years immediately before the First World War, meaning that the lack of evidence about whether certain modernists saw any given film becomes a slightly smaller problem for anyone researching the impact of certain films, to look at any of the common traits of literary modernism as the result of watching certain films would be to assume that all modernists would have seen those films, whereas cinema's image-regime influenced anyone who was an occasional patron of the new institution, making the latter more likely to have comprised a historical basis for all of 'high' literary modernism. Even in cases where the influence that I identify is primarily that of watching films rather than inhaling cinema's profile as constituted in popular discourse (Chapter 2 in particular), this was an influence generated by the experience of film-watching in general rather than the experience of watching certain films and not others, and this experience was not available without accompanying accounts of such categories as the film's origins, genre, virtues and purpose. Lastly, while certain films *would* undoubtedly have had identifiable impacts on literary practice *as well*, I see this as the subject of a different study, in particular because this was more likely to have been an impact on literary content rather than literary form, and I concentrate here on literary form in trying to explain cinema's place in the emergence of modernism as a literary mode.[163]

Given that the cinema was experienced as an image-regime, the question of whether individual modernists were picturegoers becomes less important. In Ford's *Mr. Fleight* (commenced c. April 1912, finished very early in 1913, and published in April 1913), Mrs Leroy disagrees with Fleight that the very rich could never see all of their wealth: "Sir Pompey Munro, where I was in service, he had a strong room in Lowndes Square. Two foot thick the walls was, and it had a circular door that worked like the back end of the big cannons you sometimes see in the picture theatres."[164] Even if Ford had not yet encountered any films when he wrote this text in the second half of 1912, these kinds of discussions of the typical characteristics of the cinematic image would still have been available to him through popular discourse. Nonetheless, many of the writers we now call modernist *were* distinguished as regular picturegoers. In spite of making only a handful of mentions of cinemagoing in her diaries and letters, Woolf, in writing her 1926 article 'The Cinema', clearly drew on more than a mixture of Film Society visits and second-hand enthusiasm. Lewis's frequent references to film, although usually derogatory and concentrated during the sound period, were replete with specifics of film discourse, including production companies, actors, films and perceived film movements, and William Wees has discovered that he was an enthusiastic picturegoer in the period immediately before the First World War.[165] Joyce first made mention of occasional-to-regular experience of film shows when in Rome in 1907,[166] saw films during his third stint in Trieste from March 1907 to June 1915 (the city had 21 cinemas by 1909),[167] initiated the opening in Dublin, in December 1909, of one of its first cinemas (a branch of the International Cinematograph Society Volta), even briefly programming the venue's films,[168] and made mention of regularly attending cinemas during the evening when he was living in Paris (from July 1920) because his poor sight prevented him from writing in artificial light, which suggests that he may have done the same during his lengthy period in Zurich (June 1915 to October 1919).[169] The film-watching in America on which Eliot based his mock film scenario *Effie the Waif* (composed in letters to Eleanor Hinkley shortly after he arrived at Merton College, Oxford, in late 1914 and early 1915)[170] continued on his arrival in the UK.[171] Pound's mentions of cinema in his 'Art Notes' columns for *New Age* in 1918–1919 resemble the complaints voiced by the average picturegoer.[172] All suggest that even those other modernists who made no note of an experience of this major new aspect of their social landscape were members of a public unable to completely avoid it, in spite of common tendencies to associate it with an exclusively working-class public.

Many of the overt commentaries on cinema produced by modernists tended to subject the institution to ridicule.[173] Writing of the state of the legitimate stage in 1921, Eliot remarked that "[a]n optimist might even affirm that when everything is bad and expensive is removed, its place may be supplied by something good and cheap; on the other hand it is more likely to be supplied by what is called, in the language of the day, the 'super-cinema.'"[174] "The film he thought milk for very young children", Conrad's long-term friend Grace Willard recalled shortly after Conrad's death on 3 August 1924,[175] while the following year Walter Tittle recalled much the same of conversations with Conrad during January 1924:

> 'They are absolutely the lowest form of amusement. I hate them!' he said, with quite a considerable show of heat. 'They are stupid, and can never be of real value. The cinema is not a great medium. It merely affords entertainment for people who enjoy sitting with thought utterly suspended and watching a changing pattern flickering before their eyes.'[176]

These attitudes have also diverted attention away from cinema as a causal force for modernism by suggesting that modernists' limited affinity for cinema would have limited its impact on them. But I will show that, in spite of conscious approaches ranging from the enthusiasm mentioned above to the disdain shown by Eliot and Conrad, cinema exercised an extensive unconscious influence on modernist writing.

The generative force that I identify in this book is 'the cinema' in Britain rather than British films. The film fare consumed by the average picturegoer was at no point, during the period under scrutiny, exclusively or even predominantly British. Indeed, the point at which cinema emerged as a distinct institution in the UK was also the point at which American films first achieved a substantial hold in the UK exhibition market. The Vitagraph Company had established regular exports to the UK at the end of 1906, but even on 4 March 1909 just two American producers were exporting to the UK, comprising just 8.7% of the 23 producers with films on release at the time.[177] An influx of American exports to the UK began in April 1909, however, and, by 21 September 1911, 16 (43.2%) of 37 companies with films being distributed in the UK were American. American films leapt from comprising 12.9% of the total negative footage on recent release on 1 April 1909 to 30% on 15 December 1910, and then to 46.2% on 21 September 1911. While the total available negative footage represents only those films on *recent* release during a specific week and does not reflect total film production or the number of prints of each title produced (a more accurate indicator of market share), it is nonetheless notable that the total length of negative footage on recent release from native producers fell from 25,900 on 1 April 1909 to 6,940 on 21 September 1911 (a drop of 73.2%, while the amount of negative footage available from Italy, France and Denmark remained stable).[178] Of the 18 films 'trailed' by motion picture stories in an August 1913 issue of *The Pictures* (which at the time was open to all producers), 13 were American, three were British, one was Italian and one was Danish.[179] In one May 1913 article in *The Pictures*, readers with an interest in writing scenarios were given the addresses of 14 American, nine British and one Danish production company.[180] Picturegoers reported similar proportions of films watched. The regular who reported, in April 1914, that s/he had seen 1,375 films in the preceding 12 months reported that of the 836 whose production company s/he had noted, 64.7% were American, 29.5% French, 3.9% Italian, 1% British and 0.8% Danish.[181] In a May 1915 article, a Brighton picturegoer did the same with the films he had seen in the first three months of 1915: 112 were American, 14 English, six Italian, five French, and three Danish.[182] Thus while films produced in the UK by British production companies did comprise a segment of the films being exhibited and watched around the country during the period chosen for this study, the experience of cinema in the UK was the experience of much more than British films. Even British cinema culture incorporated a number of discursive imports, although the configuration given to these imports was particularly British, which provides a reason other than borders to limit this study geographically.

In picking out avenues of influence, cinema and modernism are both in need of clarification, modernism for cinema scholars and cinema for modernism's scholars. This study is therefore both an analysis of the media institution 'the cinema' in the UK during the 1910s and early 1920s and a re-reading of certain avenues of literary modernism. The ordering of the chapters also reflects the need to distinguish stages in this new, but by no means unchanging, institution. That 30 years of modernist practice and theory are often taken as a single utterance and compared with 30 years of film practice has only hampered work in this area. It is only by isolating phases in film form and film discourse that the impact of cinema's evolving image-regime can be reckoned in terms of changes in central literary principles. By describing both the image-regime of cinema and the texture of literary modernism with precision, it is possible to excavate at least parts of several imprints made by cinema on a section of literary practice that contributed to the parameters of modernism. It is also possible to isolate areas where cinema had *no* impact. In addition, when synchronised sound was adopted in the UK film industry at the close of the 1920s, the institution cinema was generally reinvented, meaning that while cinema continued to condition literary form after the 'coming of sound', a study of this influence would comprise a conceptually distinct work. 1928 is therefore taken as a cut-off point.

As this work considers literary modernism *produced* in the UK (before 1922 also including the whole of Ireland), it incorporates works by a number of ex-patriot Americans written while they were living in the UK, but also excludes those works they wrote when they were not in Britain (hence the exclusion, for example, of T.S. Eliot's 'The Love Song of J. Alfred Prufrock', written in 1910–1911, before Eliot's 1914 move to the UK). It does however incorporate one text *not* written in the UK. Although Joyce had left the UK permanently before he started *Ulysses*, and although praise for *Ulysses* as "the most important expression which the present age has found"[183] was, as Chapter 3 will indicate, tied into an attempt to increase the market value of the book's first edition, it is precisely because of its internationalism that I see it as appropriate to include it in the remit of this otherwise exclusive study of UK literary modernism. The influence of *Ulysses* on perceptions amongst literary practitioners across Europe—including the UK—that they were part of a movement means that it would be reductive to leave *Ulysses* out of this study. *Ulysses* features in Chapter 3 as the subject of a marketing project in which other modernists participated, and in Chapter 2 as one of the literary 'results' of the emergence of a filmic rendition of temporality that was, of the major dimensions examined in these three chapters, the most trans-national.

In addition, while the works examined are only taken as samples, meaning that most of the works not discussed here are not deliberately excluded, the rapid changes that the institution cinema underwent during its formative years mean that it is only appropriate to examine those literary works whose dates of composition can be stated with some precision. Because of this, I will exclude Lewis's *Tarr* (1918), as it was in progress for a six-year period (c. July 1909 to c. July 1915) that straddles several of the major historical landmarks in the development of the institution cinema (including its appearance), and therefore, because none of the manuscripts have survived, cannot be dated, even in part, to either before or after these changes. Lastly, while including some discussions of modernist poetry, critical writing and marketing institutions, I will concentrate on modernist prose.

What, then, of cinema's impact on realism? If cinema occasioned a widespread revolution in literary protocols rather than a small-scale flirtation with cinematic techniques amongst a minority of writers who were *already* committed to engaging formally with the modern world, why did the majority of literary practice continue in a realist mode? Is not the common perception that cinema's impact on modernism was not matched in realist writing simply a consequence of imagining modernism to be either a flight from the 'verisimilitude' of cinema or a reflexive corner of literature drawing on 'cinematic' alternatives to realist form? If the second birth of cinema was a major force determining the appearance and parameters of literary modernism, modernists alone were uniformly influenced by it because they experienced cinema as part of, for example, their existing political commitments to connecting with the proletariat, which means that they must be understood as *already* constituting a group before cinema impacted on their practice. How then can cinema be one of modernism's causes? If cinema was a common historical context for all literary practitioners, both realist and modernist, meaning therefore that realist writing will also be found to bear the signs of the impact of cinema, then how can cinema be one of the specific distinguishing contexts of literary modernism? Assuming that modernism was just one of several types of product created by the impact of cinema on the institution literature as a whole, this book will distinguish between modernism as a *formal* product of the impact of cinema, in contrast to the changes wrought by cinema in the *content* of ongoing realist literary production, changes not sufficient to create a new literary mode.

In addition, while cinema's own modernist activities are worthy of study, this book does not tackle the question of whether cinema was capable of modernist activity itself, because 1) this risks limiting the study of influence to the realm of modernists' conscious regard for cinema as intrinsically either anti-modernist or modernist (i.e. cinema only in relation to their own consciously held categories), and 2) if cinema is found to have been one of the historical forces giving rise to modernist literary form—if cinema was already 'in' modernism in at least one of the established arts before modernist form was applied to cinema by those such as Lêger—complications follow for the use of the term 'modernist cinema' to describe film at any point in film history.[184] This is not to argue that cinema cannot be modernist, but that it is necessary to bracket the discussion of cinema's capacity to be modernist for the purposes of this study.

The gesture of unprecedentedness is a sign of a paranoid scholar. This book is impelled, in part, by the impetus to find a version of the aesthetic, economic and technological relationship between cinema and modernism that is *not* based on a view of cinema formed either by modernists' own writing on film or by thinking on film that has descended, via academic film studies, from modernist priorities. In doing this any scholar would be desperately outmatched by the complexity of the historical picture were it not for the current renaissance in studies of early cinema in Britain. To my advantage, in such works as Andrew Higson's collection *Young and Innocent?* (2002), Simon Popple and Vanessa Toulmin's collections *Visual Delights 1&2* (1999 & 2005), Burrows's *Legitimate Cinema* (2003), Michael Hammond's *The Big Show* (2006), Joe Kember's *Marketing Modernity* (2009) and Gaudreault's *Cinema delle origini. O della 'cinematografia-attrazione'* (2004) (translated into English as *Film and Attraction: From Kinematography to Cinema* in 2011); and in a vast body of articles, a community of scholars have recently committed to producing the most accurate possible map of the cultural topography of cinema before and during the period when literary modernism emerged in the UK. In seeking to add to our picture of the societal developments of the period, I also draw heavily on both the histories and the methodologies of recent works on modernism's major cause, in particular Michael Tratner's *Modernism and Mass Politics* (1995), Lawrence Rainey's *Institutions of Modernism* (1998), Sara Danius's *The Senses of Modernism* (2002) and Vincent Sherry's *The Great War and the Language of Modernism* (2003), and several of the contributions to Michael Levenson's (1999) and David Bradshaw's (2003) collections.

The following three chapters will match three aspects of the institution cinema during the 1910s with three historically specific formal and institutional characteristics of modernism. These pairings are: 1) the emergence of a structural narrativity in cinema and the beginnings of a radical revision of the narrational status of language with the demise of 'literary impressionism' immediately before the First World War, 2) the time-sense of an increasingly narrational cinema and the turn to interior monologue and 3) cinema's wartime articulations of collective consciousness (and its influence on the parallel causal force of collectivist philosophy) and the marketing practices adopted by modernism immediately after the War. To these can be added a fourth aspect, the film discourse figure of the 'picture personality' as the basis of the fictio-biography imagined by Woolf in *Orlando*, as outlined in my 2006 article 'She looks just like one of we-all!'.

What, then, was the experience of cinema's form of public participation at the time when literary modernism emerged in the UK? What purposes and properties was the process of film-making believed to entail? What ventures defined the sphere of activity of the media institution cinema? What practice, habit, visual mode, originating space, viewing space, implied spectator, effect, structure of observation, political representational mode and guiding principle were involved in picturegoing during the 1910s and early 1920s? And in what ways would the development of this complex new cultural architecture have impacted on literary practice so as to generate the formal literary refrain we now call modernism? I begin to answer these questions by looking at the first major phenomenon to signal the emergence of 'high' literary modernism: the dissolution of the pre-modernist mode known in the UK as 'literary impressionism' as it was championed by the group of poets associated with Imagism, and as it was practised in the writing of Joseph Conrad and Ford Madox Ford.

1 The Cinema of Narrative Integration, the Demise of Impressionism and the Rise of Modernism

> There has been a systematic failure, in discussions of early cinema and literary modernism, to take proper account either of films made before the First World War, or of films made after it for a mass audience.
>
> —David Trotter, *Cinema and Modernism*, 8.

In charting how the turn to a "cinema of narrative integration" at cinema's 'second birth' expunged the attractionist aesthetics that, he argues, fascinated several early modernists,[1] Tom Gunning's seminal 1986 article suggested *not* that disappointed fascination constituted the totality of the cinema/modernism relationship, but that it is crucial to notice in retrospect that attractionist cinema confronted aesthetic thought with a presence very different from later formal delineations of the photo-chemically-based moving image. His work is nonetheless often used to imply that cinema *after* 1908 was subsumed by pre-existing and familiar bourgeois narrative protocols. Mary Ann Doane's 2002 book, for example (to which I will return in Chapter 2), summarises pre-1908 cinema as liberatory, using such terms as "contingency", "chance", "reversibility" and "interactivity" to describe the alternative possibilities offered by 1895–1908 cinema. By contrast, for her, "inevitability", "irreversibility", "dominance" and "control" describe the behaviour of film after 1908. "Unabashedly exhibitionistic," Doane comments of the films of the cinema of attractions, "they differ from the classical cinema".[2] She issues the common warning against understanding early cinema as merely an immature version of later cinema, but in doing so is *as* reductive of the post-1908 cinema as she hopes to avoid being about pre-1908 cinema, defining it solely as a later norm from which early cinema differed, as a closing down of possibilities. Under the influence of Gunning's otherwise very useful paradigm, studies linking modernism with cinema have focused almost exclusively on cinema before 1908 and the underground persistence of its modes of operation in later cinema.[3] While the new institution cinema between 1908 and 1920 did depart from attractionist aesthetics, it was just as novel a cultural arrival as the cinema of attractions had been (not because of any subterranean persistence of the attractionist dynamic of early cinema). The 'transitional'[4] decade of the 1910s by no means merely anticipated the ensuing 'classical' cinema, nor did it merely (as Bazin and Wood have both argued) appear to its contemporaries as a new constituent of the range of bourgeois cultural forms with which they were familiar, even though it newly sought to emulate such forms.[5] This chapter will examine the four-year period from 1911 to 1915, relating the changes in modernist prose during this period to the particularities of the two major new features of cinema's image-regime during this period: narrativity and a discourse of realism.

"[N]EW RULES FOR DEVELOPING THE PLOT AND REVEALING CHARACTER WITHOUT THE AID OF WORDS"[6]: NARRATIVE INTEGRATION

In 1908, the system of meaning behind films released in the UK was still based on the idea that a cut from one shot the next was the same as a set change. For example, Hepworth's *That Fatal Sneeze* (1907) and Edison's *Jack the Kisser* (1907), both examples of the common 'chase' sub-genre of the comic genre that, at the time, was the primary fictional genre, were comprised of a series of episodes where the culprit (the sneezer and the kisser) causes mischief to bystanders and passers-by and so attracts a growing group of pursuers. In each mischief scene, the shot begins before the culprit appears, then the culprit enters and the mischief occurs, causing people nearby to become pursuers, then the culprit flees into off-screen space, the pursuers follow, and then the shot ends. Interspersed are further scenes of simple pursuit: the shot begins on an empty scene, the culprit enters from off-screen space and crosses the shot, and either before or after he leaves the shot the pursuers enter from off-screen space, then both leave the shot in turn, and then the shot ends. Each film is rounded off by a concluding scene: the sneezer explodes and the kisser is caught. The story was based on the principle of allowing all action occurring in one location to play out before permitting the shot to end.

The major development in narrative cinema in the period from 1908 was the development of new ways of connecting shots and so moving beyond this linked-episode principle. Cutting as the transition from one scene to the next gradually came to be replaced by the editing *together* of shots of the same action taken from different positions, either in multiple simultaneous scenes (cross-cutting) or in the same scene (scene dissection). As these methods came into common use in North America and Europe, editing shifted away from following action and towards articulating the dramatic links involved in complex narrative. Even in February 1909 a writer in the US trade magazine *Moving Picture World* described the linked-episode films still being made in the vein of *That Fatal Sneeze* as afflicted with an "obvious disconnectedness in action"[7].

This transition was particularly acute in the American films beginning to flood into the US in 1911 (though European producers were by no means excluded from these developments). With its pool of patents, exclusive contract with Eastman Kodak for use of film stock, its exchange licences, release and pricing schedules, distribution agreements and control of projection equipment, the MPPC created, from its inception on 1 January 1909, a centralised, permanent and stable US film industry out of previously artisanal and ad-hoc film production methods. The industry-wide drive to generate a product type that was amenable to industrial mass production prompted producers further towards narrative cinema, which could be produced on a production-line basis as the raw material was hypothetically infinite and did not involve depending for product on intermittent and unpredictable real-world events, and also concentrated their attention on a search for ways of disposing of the need for external narration (and so eliminate variations at the site of exhibition and limit exhibitors' abilities to manipulate the product). Constructing editing structures around plot structures offered one method of achieving this enhanced control over the product, a method that seemed particularly attractive in the US given that, as the major producers knew, the immigrant populations of America's major cities constituted a significant part of their audience (almost a majority in Chicago), meaning that they could not expect film spectators to comprehend films on the basis of recognising the narrative events of adapted pre-texts. American cinema in particular thus began to explore editing structures that could explain any sequence of events (and to make use of images and narratives that did not draw on culturally specific structures).

The films released in Britain in the 1911–1914 period under consideration here began to draw UK filmgoers away from a conception of cinema in which edits were markers of the beginning and end of scenes. Such films were not solely American. Pathé Frèrés's *Le Médecin du château* (1908) employed the technique of cross-cutting between a distress scene and those contacted for help as they raced to the rescue, the point of view transferring freely between the two spheres of action while action is ongoing to generate suspense and dramatise the nearing of a deadline. As with most race-to-the-rescue films, *Le Médecin du château* used a physical connection between the two spheres of action—the telephone line—to initiate and rationalise what was widely seen at the time as the viewpoint 'jumping' from place to place.[8] Cross-cutting had appeared in race-against-time situations as early as Vitagraph's *The Hundred-to-One Shot* (1906) and Pathé's *The Runaway Horse* (1907), but 1908 was the year of its wide-scale inception in the films issued in the UK. Gunning points out that the race-to-the-rescue film would come to entirely displace the linked-episode chase film from American cinema by 1909. Based on a story-space event linking two locales (usually a telegram or a telephone call, but also emotional or economic connections between individuals), the technique of cross-cutting between these locales began to establish cinema as a "specification of temporal and spatial relations between shots."[9] Charles Musser argues that it was from D.W. Griffith's *The Fatal Hour* (1908), the first film in which he used extensive cross-cutting between multiple parallel actions, that action began to exist *across* shots in a larger story-space, not just *within* shots (shots that could, consequently, be conscribed as 'scenes').[10] Gunning refers to a sequence in Griffith's 1908 *A Salvation Army Lass* where a tough, having just scorned his girlfriend to take part in a burglary, stops and looks off screen. Two edits, first a cut to a shot of his girlfriend and then a cut back to him as he hands a gun back to his companions, insist that the tough's actions are to be understood in terms of his motives, thereby dramatising the shown action in relation to changes in a larger story-space.[11] Although the dramatising of action across a larger story-space was by no means a Griffithian, American or late-Edwardian invention, notably featuring in several British films of the early Edwardian period, Griffith's films can be regarded as a useful example of the narrative, and narrational, status of cinema at the point in 1911 when 'the cinema' presented as a distinct medium, because his innovatory status derives from his collecting and collating multiple techniques in general (though less frequent) use. His films will feature in the following analysis not because they were exceptional but because they were a concentration of a more general landscape of narrativity in film. Griffith was one of the many film production personnel who were moving away from identifying shots with scenes during the turn to dramatic narrative cinema after 1907, and one of the many American directors concentrating his efforts on techniques for lengthening narrative after the loosening of film length standardisation in the US in 1910;[12] the "cinema of narrative integration" of the post-1908 period derived as much from George Loane Tucker's use of point-of-view structure as it did from Griffith's 'innovation' of cross-cutting.

As several film historians have recently pointed out, even the earliest 50-second single-shot films made by the Lumière brothers in the first five months of 1895 for their cinématographe projector were constructed along narrative lines. It is difficult, Gunning indicates, "to find moments even in early [i.e. pre-1908] cinema that are totally bereft of narrative development".[13] The Lumières' *Demolition of a Wall* (1896) incorporates pick-axing of the wall to weaken it before the jacks are brought into use to generate gradual suspense over whether the wall will be successfully demolished and, when it is demolished (at roughly the mid-point of the film), enacts a transition from equilibrium, via percussive disequilibrium, to a new equilibrium. But even in work where he highlights narrative conventions in even the earliest Lumière films that have gone unobserved by Barry Salt,[14] Gaudreault nevertheless comments that "[i]n my view, the narrative of, for example, [*The*]*Birth of a Nation* [1915] is of a quite different order from that of *L'Arroseur Arrosé* (*The Waterer Watered*) [1896] and the relationship between these two orders of narrative is far from being merely quantitative."[15] Gunning, Gaudreault, Richard deCordova, Noël Burch, Charles Musser and Stephen Bottomore have all emphasised that the transition to the cinema of narrative integration was based not on cinema 'discovering' narrative but on the promotion of narrative from a secondary to a primary function via the unification of two levels of narrativity: narrativity within shots and narrativity *across* shots,[16] what Christian Metz calls "a second complex of codified instructions".[17] For Gaudreault, the editing structure of cross-cutting, originating as a narrational technique around 1908, represents "[t]he genesis of filmic expression" because it occasioned "the convergence of narrativity and cinema."[18]

At the beginning of the second decade of the twentieth century, existing editing conventions with previously disparate and often exhibitionist functions were being integrated into a primarily narrative system: hence Gunning's term 'narrative integration' to distinguish cinema after 1908 from pre-1908 fictional narrative films. By 1912, for example, facial close-ups were being revived, reinventing a 'technique' that, in G.A. Smith's *Grandma's Reading Glass* (1900) and James Williamson's *The Big Swallow* (1901) had served to render the everyday risible and, at the beginning/end of Edwin S. Porter's *The Great Train Robbery* (1903), absented a character from a narrative context, turning it into a method of uttering emotional depth or, when used to match with the eyeline of a previous shot, iterating emotional intimacy between characters. Close-ups were re-purposed, altered from a necessity in situations where details could not be seen in long shot—as in G.A. Smith's *Sick Kitten* (1903) and *Mary Jane's Mishap* (1903)—to a way of concentrating attention on pertinent story events. The shot/countershot pattern, which arose before 1900 from the demands of filming actualities that could not be orchestrated in front of a single camera position, was also reinvented as a narrative device. Narrative film techniques in use by 1909 included cross-cutting, eye-line matches, shot/countershot, point-of-view structure, the emotional use of lighting and a shorter average shooting distance for characterisation.[19] Cross-cutting was increasingly used from this point to iterate motivation, generate dramatic irony, specific moral status and even to illustrate mental images. By 1912, with the increasing use of cross-cutting and scene-dissection in the US and Europe, the cut was detached from the convention of ending a scene and attached instead to an 'articulating' agency.[20] Even by 1910 cinema musicians were being advised by *Moving Picture World* not to change music for each scene, because, as the word 'scene' referred to what we would now call a 'shot', a 'scene' was just one of many functional components of the scene as laid out in a script.[21]

Notably, the rise of the imports to the UK from the US discussed above was the rise of a more exclusively narrational product. 70.2% of the titles released in America by American producers between 5 June and 1 July 1911 were classified as 'dramatic', as compared to just 50% of the films released in America by non-American companies during the same time period.[22] 69.8% of the identifiably American titles on release in the UK on the 21 September 1911 were dramatic, as compared to 31.2% of French titles, 35.7% of British films and 25% of Italian titles. Only the Danish company Nordisk, with just one exceptional three-reel, dramatic 'feature film' on recent release on that date, had a higher percentage.[23] Even with dramatic fiction as the dominant film product in the UK, the first picture theatre programmes maintained a variety format which included scenic, educational, industrial, topical and travel films (see Figure 1.1). But by January 1913,

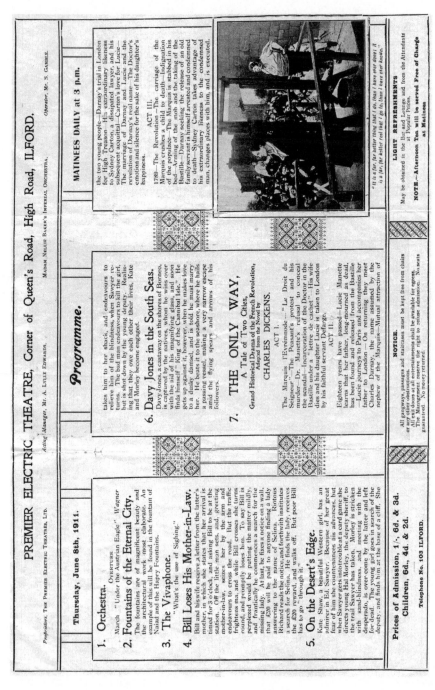

Figure 1.1   Programme for the Premier Electric Theatre, Ilford, 8 June 1911.

as one industry spokesperson wrote, while "scenic or industrial" films still comprised a part of the programme, they were now merely "a splendid stop-gap between comedy and tragedy [i.e. dramatic] films".[24] French, Danish, Italian and British films released in the UK continued to innovate formally as much as did the new American product (and even more so in terms of introducing the 'feature' film), but the latter nonetheless illustrates the formal status of film in the UK by 1914.

Griffith's *The Girl and Her Trust* (American Biograph, released in the US in March 1912 and in the UK c. June 1912) typifies the range of narrational techniques available to film-makers shortly before the First World War. A narrativity operating through editing structures manifests in a range of ways in this film. The first was the cut on action, here used both to change angle *and* to progressively alter camera distance, and which, as distinct from previous uses of the close-up to show detail, was shot and edited to maintain the unity of the story-space: instead of showing the heroine fit the bullet into the keyhole and then showing her do it *again* from a closer distance, the film is structured so that the edit to a closer distance occurs as she walks intently towards to the door with the bullet in her hand. The denotation of the ensuing action is also completed in two stages. First an edit takes the viewpoint from a medium shot of her moving towards the door to a medium close-up of her as she crouches by the door, then a further edit takes the viewer to a close-up of her hand inserting the bullet into the keyhole. An edit from a close-up of her fitting the scissors to the bullet to a medium close-up of her drawing back the hammer to strike also articulates this action across multiple shots (Figure 1.2a). After the tramps steal the strong-box, the heroine realises, as she leaves the station building in pursuit of them, that they are about to make their getaway on a handcar. She then enters a shot of the handcar (taken from 45 degrees to the track) and clambers on board the handcar to grapple with them, and this grappling is denoted by an edit to a closer shot, now directly in front of the handcar on the tracks (Figure 1.2b). Again several changes of camera position render a privileged point of view on action.

The second structure was scene dissection, here used to specify characters' knowledge: a shot of the tramps emerging from between train cars (taken along a line at 90 degrees to the train) cuts to a shot taken parallel with the train (a 90 degree angle change) to show that the hero is oblivious of their presence (Figure 1.2c). The third structure was the eye-line match, here based on the engine drivers: a shot of the engine moving in a curve from deep space centre towards front frame right, cuts to a reverse angle shot of the engine taken from the coal car, and the environment just denoted in the previous shot from the opposite angle, visible over the engine's roof (Figure 1.2d). Such edits articulate the action of 'the pursuit' through the potential disjunctions of editing: narrative unity is achieved through a higher synthesis which nonetheless presents as a simple articulation of the story-space. The last scene includes an instance of scene dissection for the purpose of connoting intimacy: a cut from a long shot of the hero and heroine sitting on the fender of the engine, taken from a position slightly off to the right of the track, to a medium shot of them, taken from a point on the track, and they playfully squabble over his packed lunch as the engine reverses away from this camera position (Figure 1.2e).

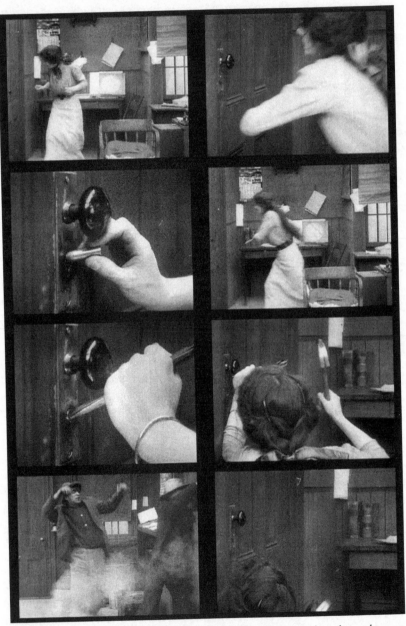

Figure 1.2a Frames from each of the eight shots showing the telegraph operator using a hammer and scissors to fire at the tramps. *The Girl and Her Trust* (Dir. D.W. Griffith, American Biograph, 1912).

Figure 1.2b   Frames from each of the three shots (with two from the second) showing the telegraph operator chasing the tramps.

Figure 1.2c   Frames from each of the three shots showing the tramps getting off the train.

Figure 1.2d   Frames from three shots in a part of the sequence showing the pursuit by the engine.

Figure 1.2e   Frames from each of the two shots showing the reunited couple on the engine returning to the station.

Narrativity in the form of all of these structures, based on what had up until recently been treated as disjunction, constituted the cinema of narrative integration as a distinct experience of space. Scene dissection through editing became even more elaborate in Griffith's ensuing films. Instances of narrative conveyed solely within shots did persist. For example, Griffith ordered shots in his *The Painted Lady* (October 1912) so that an intertitle reading 'Unpopular' is followed by a shot composed to show the isolation of Blanche Sweet's character. But in such 1912 films as *The Female of the Species* (April 1912), through *One is Business, The Other Crime* (April 1912), *An Unseen Enemy* (Sept 1912) and *The Painted Lady* (Oct 1912), Griffith made increasing use of edits to transfer the viewpoint on action around space in line with the motivations and actions of characters. This method, as it became an aspect of narrative construction, rendered a particular experience of action via a unique experience of space. Eileen Bowser remarks that audiences must have at least been accustomed to the editing practice of alternation between multiple locations by February 1912.[25] By 1914, scene dissection was common practice at all American film companies, with the exception of Vitagraph, the latter instead leading the way in adopting point-of-view shots in the latter part of 1912 and 1913.[26] As Gunning explains, "[c]oherence of story and storytelling allows the classical mode to fashion a unity from a proliferation of viewpoints and shots, through *identification of the camera with an act of narration*. The classical film can absorb sudden ubiquitous switches in viewpoint into an act of storytelling".[27] Unlike such attractionist early films as Hepworth's *How it Feels to be Run Over* (1900), in which the spectator is approached and then 'hit' by a car, spectatorial identification with the camera in the cinema of narrative integration was mediated through her/his engagement with the unfolding of the story.

In 1907 some American producers were still providing intertitles for every shot, a consequence of a still widespread perception that the images were illustrations for a pre-existing textual 'track'. In the turn to narrative integration, two growing ideas—that intertitles contravened an illusion of reality and that cinema's events should be able to self-narrate—led to the emergence in 1911 of a new ambition to abandon the expository intertitle. Eileen Bowser remarks that while a group of *post*-War film-makers wanted to get rid of *dialogue* intertitles (and thus expunge films of text altogether), between 1911 and 1914 the industry saw a widespread attempt to eject expository intertitles for their implication that action was textual, as a direct consequence of the new ideal that action should instead be described by editing.[28] An April 1913 article in *The Pictures* described the founding of Famous Players: "Mr. [Adolph] Zukor said that one of the objects sought by the director of the Famous Players is the elimination of sub-titles or at least the reduction of the number. 'We are trying to let the story tell itself so far as possible,' said he; 'to do this we are introducing more scenes and connecting links.'"[29] This was a 'story' that told itself through editing structures. The glut of mockery, at this time, for those cinema managers who employed sound-effects men also suggests a growing notion of cinema as capable of nar-rational self-sufficiency. One October 1912 editorial argued that "[i]t is time that the showman . . . awakened to the fact that, generally speaking, his effects are not true, and nine times out of ten, give dissatisfaction, . . . distracting the audiences' attention, and making one feel that you want to shout . . . 'Shut up, while I look at the pictures.'"[30] The temporarily renewed usefulness of film lecturers during 1908–1909 with the turn to dramatic fictional productions as the industry staple (see Figure 1.3) had abated by 1912.

Cueing viewers to diminish their awareness of themselves as addressees positioned before a series of images on display, Miriam Bratu Hansen comments, "the systematic improvement of cinematic techniques that guarantee the complete absorption of the spectator into the fictional world of the film and the imaginary flow of linear narrative"[31] involved disposing of external narrators and internalising that narrator into film style. Gunning opines that in the US by 1913 such fissures in continuity of action as the interruption of the tough's change of heart in *A Salvation Army Lass* were being commonly understood in terms of the new synthesis denoted by edit-ing techniques.[32] Evidence survives that this second level of narrativity was being noticed in the UK also. In popular scenario-writing advice published in November 1913, although the columnist still used the word 'scene' to refer to a single shot and 'illustration' to refer to a scene, s/he described the multiple shots necessary to narrate one scene, endorsing the process of com-posing a scene out of several shots as intensifying rather than disrupting the coherence of an action.[33] One August 1914 article clearly demonstrates the

Figure 1.3 The 'Bioscope' lecturer, c. 1908. Postcard.

endorsement of narrative integration as the standard method for conceiving of filmic narrativity. The 'office hack', holidaying at an unnamed seaside town, quotes a picture theatre manager:

> Another amusing patron I once had was an old countryman who had, obviously, never been to 'the pictures' before. As he came out his face was beaming and he looked altogether very pleased with himself. He walked up to me and said: 'Be you tha' manager?' I acknowledged that

I was. 'Well, then' he said, 'Oie jest want to tell 'ee that's the foinest play Oive ever seed!' I told him that I was very pleased to hear that our programme had delighted him so much.

'Yes,' he continued, 'but Oi must say I found it a trifle 'ard to follow!' Then it was that I learnt that the old chap had been under the impression that each separate film was a different scene in the same play![34]

This anecdote concerns a failure to distinguish between linked-episode narrative (the basis of the chase film) and the articulation of a story-space (the basis of the race-to-the-rescue film), the bumpkin figure interpreting the fact that one *film* followed another as signifying as much of a link as that now involved in one *shot* following another. As the ridiculed audience member in such anecdotes fails to perceive the 'self-evident' fact perceived by the majority, this in turn suggests that the distinct quality of a spatio-temporal coherence constructed between shots by continuity editing was being apprehended, at least unconsciously, as an aspect of the profile of the new media institution by 1914.[35]

One July 1914 article in *The Pictures* explained recent mentions of the previously obscure figure of the 'producer' (also beginning to be known as the director) with reference to the act of transforming a film "from a collection of isolated happenings into a series of logically interwoven events".[36] Bannister Merwin was quoted in *The Pictures* in January 1914: "The photo-play has a technique of its own. As yet it is not fully developed. We are learning every day that things which we had thought could not be indicated in dumb show can be 'got to the screen' effectively."[37] Given that Merwin excluded acting, he seems to have been referring to the narrative capacities of editing structures as the basis of this act—percolating into popular understandings by 1914—of 'getting to the screen'. When both Ernest Dunlop Swinton in December 1912 and Harry Furniss, in his *Our Lady Cinema* (1914), gave accounts of a linked-episode comic chase film and a cross-cut race-to-the-rescue film which ridiculed the former, they did not just express their regard for the medium as more properly intimate with suspense than slapstick, they independently warmed to the spatio-temporal articulation achieved in the latter by editing, a result of the widespread re-definition and re-purposing of cinema as narrational.[38]

The rise of the cinema of narrative integration was also popularly avowed in that the industry made efforts to instigate an education in cine-literacy, to shift popular perceptions away from a tendency to experience a close-up, for example, as the subject doubling in size and recommending instead that uncertainties about film meaning be referred to the idea of a required change of perception in the agent articulating the narrative. The anonymous writer of the opening editorial of *The Pictures* in October 1911 explained that each motion picture story "correspond[ed] to a set of films about to be shown in the picture theatres."[39] As virtually all stories in the magazine corresponded to entire film narratives rather than serial episodes, this usage suggests that even in late 1911 the term 'film' still meant what we now call 'shot'. The cinema of narrative integration was still not spontaneously generating the sense that those pieces of positive film corresponding to the negatives were integrated into a singular whole, so 'film' still referred to the positive print of one uncut piece of negative footage, rather than to a film title. The magazine itself, with its motion picture stories, was a significant part of the transition, in the UK, from this conception of the ordering of shots as merely sequential and non-associative to a perception of a suturing narrative matter linking many shots.[40] For "the devotees of this form of popular entertainment", the opening editorial insisted, a mere description "might be deemed unsatisfactory and inconclusive evidence of the value of the forthcoming pictures." "[T]he usefulness of such a publication" lay in the fact that the motion picture stories "will make the picture actors real and living personages, invest them with human interest, and lay bare their characters, motives, passions, and mutual relations". This rationale implied that character, rather than, for example, the gag, ought to comprise the core and operating unit of film. Having read a motion picture story, the picturegoer would, it was promised, "enter into the drama enacted before his eyes with a thoroughness of sympathy and appreciation which he could not feel were he witnessing it without having read the story." 'Entering' into the real of the story is here contrasted to the 'witnessing' to which a person not cognisant of fictional reality on the level of character would be limited. A cinema based on character was also contrasted to an earlier cinema described as a lack. The reader was informed that "[i]f, like the lady of Shalott, bewildered by the multitude of sights afforded by her magic mirror, he is beginning to long for human company, in addition to that of shadows, beings who talk and feel as well as move and act, his desire will be gratified by this Magazine."[41] The term 'shadow' had featured previously in allusions to the disquieting and bewildering aspects of films. Maxim Gorky had used the term when writing on watching the first Lumière programme in July 1896,[42] and in 1908 Leo Tolstoy had referred to "the shadowy screen and the cold machine".[43] Here in late 1911 the supernatural connotations of the cinematic image were disavowed as an aspect of the medium's immaturity.

The motion picture story also implied that external narration via such methods as the synopsis posted in the foyer was now inappropriate. While the stories may have been *read* to 'enable' the film, by iterating film's equivalence with literary fiction they cited film as formally, rather than superficially, narrational. Articles on film quality in *The Pictures* also consistently favoured literary adaptations, with one article describing the category of 'living pictures' (i.e. the best pictures) as those that "reproduce chiefly works of great authors successfully".[44] The description of cinema as narrative entered even the most prosaic discussions of cinematic etiquette, as in one article from October 1912:

A man comes in whilst a picture is showing and, instead of waiting, he causes half a row of people to rise, brushes carelessly against them, and seldom takes the trouble to apologise . . . Then once seated, he must discuss the picture, its subject, and the players with his companion, regardless of the fact that other people around him are trying to gather up the thread of the plot which they have lost while he has been taking up his seat.[45]

For this commentator, the core act involved in film spectatorship was construing a cause-and-effect thread rather than merely understanding on-screen events. This likening of film to psychological fiction was also driven, for example, by the attempt to underwrite the assertion that "the modern cinematograph theatre has become entirely dissociated with, and is a thing apart from, the 'gaff' or penny peep-show", as *The Pictures* argued in February 1912.[46] The turn to cinema as an intrinsically narrative form was of course gradual. The first mention of a fan taking pride in the number of times s/he had seen a certain film rather than the number of films seen in a year was at the end of 1917,[47] but narrativity in cinema directed picturegoers' inquiries about what cinema was like to a new common reference point.

One July 1913 article stated the desirability of a wholly self-narrating cinema:

It is so easy to explain the action by means of wordy sub-titles and long letters—but often so crude. . . . In a film we once saw the hero proposed by letter and the heroine answered by the same medium, but the correspondence was not shown on the screen. There was no need for it. The young man put an engagement ring inside his letter, and the girl put the ring on her finger and danced round the room before she wrote her reply.[48]

In February 1912 one contributor opined that "[t]he cinematograph is developing two new arts, one for the actors who have to put the essentials of a three hours' dialogue into perhaps eighteen minutes of action, and one for the writers who must discover new rules for developing the plot and revealing character without the aid of words."[49] An account of a new school of acting corresponding to the former 'art' did indeed emerge. One April 1914 account of a manager of an acting school who had recently set up a new cinema acting department quoted his understanding of cinematic acting: "We teach people to exercise their hands, to 'loosen' them, to have an action for every thought. . . . The actor or actress who has mastered the art of pantomime . . . is the one required by cinema firms."[50] Another contributor argued that pantomime was so endemic to film acting that, where stage acting norms had not contravened the British tendency towards reservation, "[i]t is not so far-fetched to suppose that a much greater freedom of gesticulation than English people have practised for two or three generations may come into vogue".[51] Columnists in *The Pictures* referred to "the pantomime of the actors"[52] and often preferred the term "pantomimes"[53] instead of 'photoplays'. Coming *after* the demise of pantomimic acting in UK films in 1912, this discourse lauding pantomimic acting in popular film culture did not just provide a template for an anti-stage account of film acting, it also indicated how widely cinema's meaning-making function was being seen to inhere solely in the images (disavowing such extra-filmic channels as intertitles, lecturers, actors talking behind the screen, early sound-on-disc technologies or such ramshackle techniques as posting the synopses provided by distributors in the foyer).

NARRATION/NARRATOR

Cinema's adoption of this narrative-by-structure does not, however, equate to the achievement of a narrator. In the three years immediately before the First World War, cinema attained the formal status of a narrative composed of spatio-temporal articulations. Point-of-view structure, "[w]ith its specification of temporal/spatial relations [and] its effect of an omniscient point of view on action,"[54] its ability to portray, create, specify, underscore, reveal and predict, specified the filmic entity as narrational. Bowser observes that "[t]he added implications of a change of angle is that it is no longer necessarily the point of view of one of the characters: it may be a privileged point of view, that of the 'narrator'".[55] However, whereas the enunciator of cinema before 1908 had been either a live showman or an implicit 'monstrator', in the cinema of narrative integration cinema's utterances were produced structurally, by cinema itself. David Bordwell has pointed out that although character narrators and non-character narrators are used in some films, there is no way in which they can be said to *produce* the narrational process of the film. Instead, narrative is achieved by "an implicit, nonpersonified narrator".[56] Film theorists commonly refer to the creations of this structural, non-personified narrator as 'diegesis'. Coined by Étienne Souriau in 1953, the term refers to "all that belongs, 'by inference', to the narrated story, to the world supposed or proposed by the film's fiction".[57] Narrational editing structures motivate the viewer to suppose that the film's 'views' are part of a larger story-space. Defining 'diegesis' in February 1964, Christian Metz explained that film, denoting 'house', does not do so in the same way as a photograph:

> In film a house would be a shot of a staircase, a shot of one of the walls taken from the outside, a close-up of a window, a brief establishing shot of the [outside of the] building etc. etc. Thus a kind of filmic *articulation* appears, which has no equivalent in photography: It is the denotation itself that is being constructed, organized, and to a certain extent codified.[58]

The 'wholeness' conveyed by this articulation, the structuring together of a series of cones of space, each with its tip at the lens of the camera, is qualitatively different from the 'wholeness' of a photograph of the house, or of an establishing shot of the whole house. As a codification existed in denotation that was and is usually seen to originate in merely showing, film was experienced both as an articulation—the space is experienced as qualitatively different from simply 'space seen'—*and* as devoid of the connotative articulating figure usually implied by a written text.'

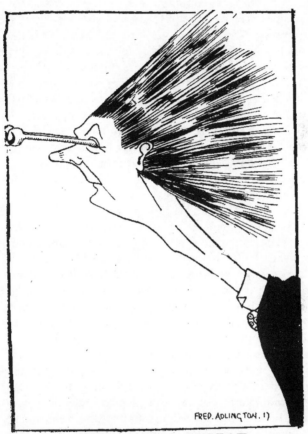

CAUSE AND EFFECT

Complaints frequently reach us that owing to the rapidity with which the scenes succeed one another on the screen, it has been impossible to follow the action without making an intolerable mental effort—
EDITOR.

Figure 1.4 A reference to the 'sights of a different order' of narrational editing from October 1917.[59]

A number of film theorists have argued that in the impersonal narration deployed by film since the rise of the cinema of narrative integration, the fictional world appears "not as the discourse of a narrator situated outside the story but rather directly as the autonomous facts of the fictional universe".[60] It appears to its viewers as the simultaneous spokenness *and* givenness of a space. The impersonal narrator, for Robert Burgoyne, "produces a type of discourse that is read directly as the facts of the 'real world' of the fictional universe",[61] and not—as in the case of writing—as the process by which that universe is created and communicated. The edit from shot to shot in a dissected scene is perceived as a revelation of space (albeit space of a distinct quality), rather than a narratorial process. Metz holds that although film functions on the basis of certain systems, its defining quality is that it "abolishes all traces of the subject of the enunciation".[62] Diegesis, in his description, is *both* "the narration itself [and] . . . the fictional space and time dimensions implied in and by the narrative".[63] It is both act of narration and the place narrated, both the result of certain editing structures and a space, it is implied, existing regardless of process. Although—as both Souriau and Metz stressed—this place vaguely suggests its articulation (see Figure 1.4), it is simultaneously incompatible with the status of 'being spoken'.

Cinema also troubles narratorial status because of what Metz calls its "dearth of linguisticity".[64] For him the dominant misconception held by film theory since the 1920s, and still held by his contemporaries, was that while film *is* a kind of language (*langage*), it was considered by extension to also be a specific language system (*langue*): an organised code for producing statements.[65] But, he writes, while some film techniques "which, through long previous use in [filmic] speech, have been solidified so that they acquire stable and conventional meanings, become kinds of signs", these techniques are not the basis of any language system.[66] In part because the range of other paradigmatic possibilities against which every unit in a film 'sentence' would get its meaning is, "if not limitless, at least more "open" than the "most open' linguistic inventory", "[t]he clarification of present by absent units occurs much less than in verbal language".[67] Cinema is thus paradigmatically impoverished, lacking the necessary limits to the range of paradigmatic alternatives which generate meaning in true language systems. In addition, cinema also has no direct equivalent of words, in that "the cinema begins where ordinary language ends: at the level of the 'sentence'—the film-maker's minimum unit and the highest properly linguistic unit of language."[68] As Metz explains, "[a] close-up of a revolver does not mean 'revolver' (a purely virtual lexical unit), but at the very least, and without speaking of the connotations, it signifies 'Here is a revolver!' It carries with it a kind of *here*. . . . Even when the shot is a 'word', it remains a kind of sentence-word".[69] Cinema's 'structural narrator' is the undertaker of this diectic act, a shifting of attention *away* from narration. Instead of a code, cinema possesses merely a "certain number of dominant habits"[70] for producing meaning. In the immediate pre-First World War period, the first period when it functioned as "a language without a system",[71] cinema would have impressed itself on its viewers as lacking any narratorial figure in spite of its newly narrational profile.

Metz himself suggested that because of the impossibility of identifying cinema as a system for producing statements, narrators are not 'spotted' in film; for him "the film-maker can express himself by showing us directly the diversity of the world, and in this he differs from the reciter of tales."[72] Canted framings, re-framings that reveal or dismiss visual information, edits between static and swiftly moving cameras and the 'following' of certain characters while others appear from and disappear into off-screen space: these all, by differing from standards, constitute modelled stimuli which *may* lead viewers to attribute them to an entity with the human capacity of making choices. But, as Bordwell wrote in 1985, "[f]ilm's lack of . . . person, tense, mode, etc. . . . . makes it difficult to account systematically for the speaker, situation, and means of enunciation."[73] In film, he writes, "no trail we could assign to an implied author of a film could not more simply be ascribed to the narration itself: it sometimes suppresses information, it often restricts our knowledge, it generates curiosity, it creates a tone, and so on." Thus film's organization of cues for constructing a story "presupposes a receiver, but not any sender, of a message."[74] In terms of Emile Benveniste's distinctions between *énoncé* (the utterance) and *énonciation* (the general process of enunciating) and *discours* (an enunciation assuming a speaker and a hearer and in the speaker the intention of influencing the hearer) and *histoire* (the presentation of facts outside a concrete communicative situation),[75] that cinema is enunciative does not mean that it is *discours*, since cinema assumes no speaker or hearer, describing a space which ostensibly exists regardless of utterances.

Alongside the inception of Bordwell's formalist mode of film studies in the mid-1980s, Deleuze's break with the semiotic bent of film theory occurred, he explained, because it was a fundamental mistake to perceive film as even 'like' a language: "if the frame has an analogue, it is to be found in an information system rather than a linguistic one."[76] As *any* utterance is "construed with respect to a putative source",[77] it would seem that film viewers are led to an 'implied author',[78] a principle within the text to which the enunciative quality of the film is attributed rather than any narrating voice. Jerrold Levinson speaks of a "perceptual enabler" to 'whom' is attributed the giving of access to a diegesis.[79] Gunning also describes the structural narrator developing after 1908 as an "invisible but *sensed* hand".[80] But as Jakob Lothe has pointed out, this sender is composed of *links*.[81] While perceptions of film in the 1911–1914 period did resonate under the influence of a *potential* narratorial figure, and while film was firmly reinvented at this time as narrational, the structural narrator in place by the beginning of 1914 did not approximate the narrativity of written fiction. Film's new status as narratorial and yet lacking in linguisticity continued to render the medium strange.

"[A]ND YOU NEVER NOTICED THE CAMERA, DID YOU?": 'REEL LIFE'

The second most significant and persistent element of cinema's image-regime in the 1911–1914 period was what I will call the 'cinema-real.' In popular film discourse in the UK throughout the 1910s, the term 'realism' was ubiquitous. Rather than denoting a historically specific mode of literary discourse, it was chiefly used to mean 'realisticness'. It covered:

1. dangerous action sequences
2. instances when exciting events occurred spontaneously and yet were caught on camera
3. the favourable comparison between outdoor shooting and the sets seen as endemic to various forms of stage performance
4. company directors' capacity to license virtually unlimited expenditure
5. the effects of films on naive members of a cinemagoing public
6. real-world incidents caught on camera by chance
7. skilled make-up and costume
8. commitments on the part of producers to finely-honed historical verisimilitude
9. travel to authentic locations, such as the exact spots where recreated historical events occurred or where fictional events were set

Widely used in popular film discourse in the UK, the term 'reel life' fondly described gripping cinematic stunts happening off-screen, stunts-gone-wrong while filming (but proving more exciting nonetheless), the tendency of picture players to voluntarily do all their own stunts (indeed, the absence for most of this period of a distinction between acting and action), heroic acts performed either to get the best footage or to save the film once exposed and the mistaking of filmed events for real ones by passers-by.

As the new dramatic narratives were based on editing techniques that were often drawn from the earliest actualities like *Henley Regatta* (Hepworth, 1899; an early use of the shot/countershot), filmic narrative in 1911 was not so exclusive of 'reality' (and reality so exclusive of a narrative format) as we tend to see it today.[82] But the perceived importance of 'realism' in narrative film was also the product of a widespread effort to re-purpose cinema after 1910. While the many developments that led to cinema's new industrial incarnation around 1911—the move to a statistically dominant output of dramatic fiction, the establishment of a celebrity system, the emergence of nationally uniform publicity formats, the emergence of virtually uniform nationwide release dates, the new numerical dominance of the exhibition venue of the 'picture theatre'—comprised more of a "crescendo of change", as Cecil Hepworth called

it,[83] than a single cataclysmic event, the discursive counterpart of the
new institution cinema generated by this accumulation of lengthy processes was a widespread drive in film discourse in the UK to re-describe
cinema as foreign to the type of film practice fostered by the various low-
prestige parent media and entertainments forms that had made use of
the cinematograph during the kine-attractography era. These forms had
widely emphasised the capacity of the technology and its practitioners to
manipulate the film strip during and after filming. Magic films, which
comprised the chief 'arranged' genre during the kine-attractography
period, generated images of appearance/disappearance, transformation,
levitation, reversing and acceleration/deceleration by means of multiple
exposures, forced perspective and temporarily stopping or over-cranking
or under-cranking the camera during filming, and by means of splices
and inverting the film during editing, and so strongly implied a transfor-
mational agent, usually also emphasised by an on-screen conjuror figure.
These techniques were also widespread in less fantastical films; violent
events were commonly rendered through the use of dummies, the transition between performer and dummy and back again being achieved by
the 'stop trick': stopping the camera, exchanging one object/person for
another, and re-starting the camera.

If the technology was intrinsically non-transformative, then the contemporary institution cinema could not be regarded as the continuation
of the often disreputable and macabre practice that the cinematograph
had been allied with previously, because these were mostly artisanal,
small-scale, amusement-based, and low-expenditure.[84] Indeed, the UK-
specific attempt to dignify the new institution cinema by reinventing it
as intimately allied with the legitimate stage, although ostensibly a push
to simply encourage a popular association between cinema and a form
possessing much higher established cultural respectability, was also
part of the more general drive to inscribe an understanding of cinema
as non-transformative, displacing ideas of cinematic artifice from the
camera or editing to the artifice of contriving the scene being recorded.
This image of similarity between cinema and the legitimate stage was
broadcast by such dominant terms as 'shadow stage' and the ever-pop-
ular 'photoplay', and the new conviction—increasing in currency in the
immediate pre-war period—that as films of famous legitimate stage
actors and current theatrical productions would communicate with a
larger constituency rather than compete for established theatre patrons,
one of cinema's defining powers was its ability to bring theatre to
new audiences.[85]

In America, as the MPPC companies and the 'independent' producers
associated with the MPDSC could not increase the prices of the fixed
contracts that their distribution arms had with exhibitors by increasing
the length of their films, production values (such as colouring, acting, set
costs and dramatic tension) were referenced by the producers as extras.

This was the case with the introduction of distinct pricing scales for the new 'feature films' (productions of three reels or more), that began to emerge in America in 1910. When the MPPC's hiring exchange, General Film, set up their feature film service in May 1912, their publicity stressed the quality of acting to justify its higher costs.[86] But even those American producers not dabbling in feature films (and one-reel and two-reel dramas and comedies remained the staple of American film production well into 1915) were using their own publicity to elicit audience demands that would encourage exhibitors to demand specific products so that they could manipulate prices with the distributors. In the UK, by 1911 intense open-market competition had been keeping down the prices for which producers sold copies of their films at an almost unworkable 4d per foot (regardless of subject) since mid-1907, and because producers were now (since late 1907) selling these prints to hiring companies rather than directly to exhibitors, sales volumes were dangerously low. Revenue could therefore only be enhanced through such means as generating an audience demand for their films alone that would maximise both the number of hirers willing to buy copies of the films and the number of copies they would buy. On both sides of the Atlantic, the solution to these problems was to seek for fiction films a market status equivalent to exclusive films of one-off (and inherently unrepeatable) real-world events by inventing an equal unrepeatability for fiction films, an unrepeatability occasioned by set costs, remote locations, expenditures on one-shot events like train crashes and the potential in the pro-filmic event for spontaneity and unpredictability. For example, one July 1914 columnist remarked that James Youngdeer, a producer working at British & Colonial's outdoor studio in Finchley, "is never so happy as when he is burning down or blowing up something or somebody for the benefit of the picture public."[87]

When it was controlled exclusively by MPPC companies, *The Pictures* consistently ascribed cinema's freedom to become a modern industry to Lubin company manager Siegmund Lubin and his quest to import the principle of 'realism'. One November 1912 article described this 'originary' moment:

> One day he saw a crude reproduction of 'Uncle Tom's Cabin.' The fugitive slave girl was shown walking on sheets of white paper. The lecturer had to explain that the paper was supposed to represent ice.
> "If we are going to have motion pictures, let's have the real thing!" said Lubin; and realism became his special study.[88]

One major aspect of the cinema/stage distinction was the expenditure which only needing to produce the performance *once* made possible for that performance. Cinema was widely identified by vast expenditures in the immediate pre-war period, accounts of high-cost film-making endorsing a move in public perceptions of cinema to abandon definitions of the technology which likened it to a toy or amusement. This was even the case with a filmed play, *Vanity Fair* reporting in September 1913 that in Hepworth's *Hamlet* (starring Johnston Forbes-Robertson), the building of the castle of Elsinore "called for an expenditure of £2,000", meaning that just one two-minute scene "cost over £15 a second".[89] An article on *The Golden God* (1914) explained that with costs of $45,000–$50,000, it was expected to be the most expensive film ever made in America, with much of the money having been spent on large battle scenes.[90] Headlines in the form of 'Warren Kerrigan in "Samson": The Costliest Set Ever Erected for a Moving Picture Spectacle is Wrecked in One Minute' were common.[91] One March 1914 article gave an account of how, in the US, "entire companies of trained and practised actors are carried to every interesting spot on the Continent, and carefully drilled to enact pantomimes which will concentrate within the space of a few minutes the world's most entertaining and instructive incidents".[92] These players were not fictionalising, they were 'delivering incidents'. That many cowboy film actors had formerly been cowboys in real life, one October 1912 article argued, followed from the requirements of film performance: "Only men accustomed to the reckless life of the prairie could give such splendid displays of horsemanship as are sometime seen on the screen."[93]

The cinema-real presented the new institution as capable of communicating vast and novel realities in which the technologies of cinema—even when recording a synthesised reality—were used solely in their documentary capacity. The degree to which *every* corporeal state is the result of labour was exploited by descriptions of cinema's 'fictionalised' realities:

> Wilbert Melville, one of Lubin's directors, recently required a small, isolated railway station, with an old-fashioned chimney built against the outside. Miles and miles of adjacent country were searched but no such structure could be found. Realism in both acting and atmosphere is Director Melville's hobby, and as he could not find the railway station he required he determined to erect one . . . The station was complete with signal-box, telegraph wires and all detail. It cost over £250 to erect, and was only used in one scene.[94]

The travels of Sidney Olcott's itinerant Kalem stock company across Ireland, Palestine and Egypt between 1911 and 1913 provided a prototype for popular accounts of the work involved in film-making. In reports on the filming of *From the Manger to the Cross* in early 1912, Kalem actor J.P. McGowan was quoted equating quality with verisimilitude:

"Each and every scene in the films is being localised, the traditional and historic spots used whenever possible, and, as the authentic spot for the calling of the Fishermen was the Lake of Galilee, we travelled 224 miles, by wagon and horse, to obtain a few small scenes, and established a record in moving picture circles."[95] McGowan later reported that since Olcott had taken the Kalem travelling company off around the world,

> the Company has travelled: By steamer, 18,230 miles; by motor, 600; by donkeys, 830; by horses, 900; by rail 7,121; by jaunting car, 1,430; by camels, 270; by rowing boats, etc., 297; total, 29,647 miles; a collective total of 355,764 miles. The cost for transportation alone has exceeded £2,500, and yet the movement is practically in its infancy. It has marked a new epoch in the history of the moving picture industry.

That the endeavour of cinema was one of logistics and that the resulting image was "a view of the Holy Land that has never yet appeared on canvas"[96] cited cinema as peripatetic rather than pictorialist, and the idea that the endeavours of production around the world—breaking travel records, having unplanned adventures—constituted news also unsettled a simple definition of cinema as fictional narrative in the same sense as prose. Through this discourse of 'realism', narrative cinema was re-described as the conceptual *opposite* of a code. One January 1912 journalist explained that the 'photoplay' "speaks all languages, and even he who can speak no language may see and understand."[97] The pervasiveness of this new orthodoxy expunged references to any kind of mediation. The verisimilitude and historical actuality of *From the Manger to the Cross* were stressed with reference to "the unchanging East", this reviewer remarking that "in all the long succession of scenes to the terrible end there was never one failure to produce such an effect as if one stood oneself in the midst of the scene and watched things as they happened."[98] Here the facticity of the representation was willingly conflated with the historical reality of the events recreated.

Logistical endeavour was also discovered in historical and sociological accuracy. *Pictures and the Picturegoer* editor Fred Dangerfield informed readers that Hepworth actor/producer Hay Plumb

> has recognised the necessity for accuracy in the manners, customs, clothing, architecture, and other details of the period. If this recognition were more generally adopted, it would, I am certain, tend to raise the standard of all cinematography, and lift it into the region of serious art, worthy of criticism far more valuable than lengthy statements as to the number of feet taken and the amount of money expended.[99]

The idea that cinema's artistic quality was dependent upon the representative fidelity of both the device and the events filmed was fully developed by the beginning of 1914. A May 1914 article reported that the X.L. Film Company's producer had "carefully studied mines and their working 'on the spot' to ensure details as well as main incidents being correct"[100] for their picture *Trapped in a Mine* (1914). "The Selig 'Jungle' affords one of the first instances on record of a permanent menagerie being maintained for the purpose of moving picture production", another stated. "Lions, tigers, elephants, and many other wild animals are there in profusion— some in a state of native ferocity".[101] Stories of wild animal scenes, in which sharp-shooters were often required to shoot the animals just before they could savage the actors, were plentiful.

Just as the travelling capacity of the various studios' stock companies was frequently cited to reflect the rapid growth of the industry in both the UK and the US, by 1910 the movement of the American film industry towards the West Coast was cited as evidence of its exceptional logistical capacities. Because the long winters of New York and Chicago began to present problems for the steady film production demanded by the conditions of an organised distribution system, Essanay, Selig, Bison, Biograph, Lubin, Kalem and Nestor all began filming in sites around southern California between 1910 and 1914, not all permanently but as the start of a general movement west, and by 1915 the Los Angeles Chamber of Commerce claimed that 80% of US film production occurred in California.[102] This move to the rugged landscapes and wide-open spaces of southern California (which added extra impetus to development of the Western genre) was just the most tenacious of a series of outdoor excursions in American fiction film production, all of which sought to assert the increased scale and expenditure and new cleanliness of the film production industry. The New York studios, with their simple rooftop sets, did not constitute blatant expenditures for a business claiming both economic capacities unmatched by French rivals and an absolute lack of resemblance to such forms of urban visual culture as peep shows. Up until 1913 the area around Jacksonville in Florida promised to become a permanent film-production venue, with much the same potential as southern California. In early 1912 the figure of the 'producer' (what we now know as the director) began to appear in discussions of the creative labour involved in cinema, a direct consequence of the new public recognition that labour pertinent to the final product occurred in orchestrating large-scale outdoor scenes.

This turn to outdoor filming gave UK film discourse a way of defining the new institution. In one October 1912 article, the superiority of moving pictures over the stage was explained with reference to the realism of scenery and weather, the unlimited potential for scene changes, the opportunity for vast variations in distance from shot to shot and the almost infinite capacity for the enlargement of detail.[103]

Pictures and the Picturegoer amplified this line from its launch in February 1914, asserting that "in countless instances the 'pictures' are acted amid natural scenery and surroundings" and are "often twenty times bigger than anything ever seen on our largest stages."[104] Popular film discourse also cited real film settings as the cause of the demise of stage melodrama. "[T]he old order of palpably absurd and wholly impossible barn-storming melodrama", one writer claimed in May 1912, "had no chance against the perfect vraisemblance of the photographic film."[105] In the 1910–1914 period, the conventions of 'stage distance' that still, despite a general reduction in shooting distance from the 'stage distance' of 12 feet to nine feet in 1909, characterised shooting, were further relaxed by this outdoor turn. Central and balanced composition began to fade in the face of deeper staging, extreme long shots and high-angle shots, further absenting cinema from the codes of self-evident artifice that had tended to distinguish film fiction so far. The pan—a technique previously associated with and restricted to actualities—was gradually reintegrated as directors found it harder to keep subjects in the centre of the frame by pre-arrangement. Outdoor shooting—in films and in popular discourse—thus invigorated the cinema-real. Popular film magazines reported film events with little distinction from news: "A train travelling at fifty miles an hour rolled down an embankment. The engine exploded and the coaches burst into flame. Don't be alarmed. It was only a film scene."[106]

By 1912 the idea that cinematic endeavour might involve interposing a creative force between obtaining images and creating the finished product was all but outlawed. One June 1912 article on special effects stated that "[u]pon the production of 'fake' pictures we do not wish to dwell. The *impossible and ridiculous* trips to the moon; the collapse of buildings and manifold eccentricities with which the picture patron will be familiar, are more frequently than not enacted within the four walls of the studio."[107] So compelling was the new sense of cinema as a logistical achievement placed before a camera that this 'how it is done' article disregarded accounts of trick cinematography. "The moving-picture dummy has had its day,"[108] one August 1914 writer remarked. De-emphasising the *transformatively* spectacular while still employing the spectacular as a production value, popular film culture celebrated spectacle, in the new discourse of realism, as the grand pro-filmic contrivance. As Lucille Love explained to one interviewee: "Oh yes, please don't imagine that the exciting scenes you will see on the screen were 'faked' in a studio or in a back garden! Dear, no! When, on the screen, you see me in a jungle please remember that I was really in a jungle. All the scenes you see are real."[109] Verifiability became a major scale of quality. In just one May 1914 article, for example, variations on the 'telegraph wires in the background' complaint were stated several times.[110]

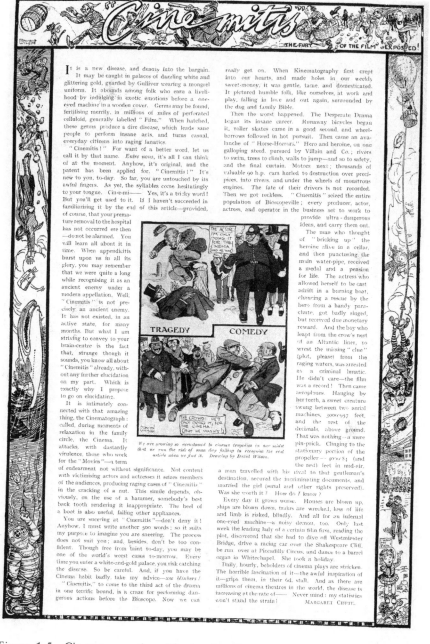

Figure 1.5 Cinema as action. The border illustrations in particular pinpoint the perceived defining factor of cinema for this November 1913 writer in the *Graphic*.[111]

In addition, existing popular accounts of film history were also disavowed, as they derived from film practice of the 1896–1908 period, which included the high degree of 'post-production' manipulation employed in magic films.[112] An early form of film history emerged in which cinema before c. 1910 was a wasted youth. Another attempt to disavow ideas of cinemas as transformative came in the shape of a series of potted pre-histories of cinema in *The Pictures* in early 1912, for which chronophotography was established as the originating point for cinema, in part because it lacked connotations of transformativeness.[113]

In the popular film discourse of the immediate pre-war years, the sheer frequency of stories in which locals mistook staged events for real events (usually because they could not see the camera) provides evidence less of how little technology was used in the outdoor film set at this time than it does of a willing ignorance in accounts of film-making, for the sake of the discourse of realism, of what technology *was* present (see Figures 1.6 & 1.7). The following was typical of both factual anecdotes and jokes during the 1911–1914 period:

> "Help! Help! Help!"
> The frantic man stood on the pier end tearing his hair.

PEOPLE WE ADMIRE.
The cinematograph actor, to whom this sort of thing is an ordinary day's work.

Figure 1.6   Cinema labour envisioned in a London paper, February 1914.[114] Courtesy of the Bodleian Libraries, University of Oxford. Shelfmark: N. 2289 d. 10 p. 340.

"My wife is drowning!" he screamed. "Five pounds to the man who saves her!"

A grizzled boatman plunged into the water and speedily brought the imperilled woman to safety.

"My five pounds, sir," he gently reminded.

"When I made that offer," the man said, "I thought it was my wife who was drowning. I was mistaken. It was my wife's mother."

"Just my luck!" exclaimed the boatman, lengthening his face. "How much do I owe you sir?"

"Take this half-sovereign and call it quits," was the reply, "I forgot to mention it was for our film, and you never noticed the camera, did you?"[115]

One October 1912 item described how a local farmer mistook a highway robbery scene for the real thing, attacked the actor 'holding up' Daphne Wayne, and had to be instructed on the event's fictionality,[116] while one March 1914 'Reel Life in Real Life' article told of such open-air dupings as police taken in by a car chase, a Parisian woman taken in by a kidnapping and children taken in by a bag of 'cash' dropped by a bus driver. The crowning confusion had occurred in central London:

Londoners had several views of thrilling occurrences on the Thames a few months ago when scenes in 'The Great Gold Robbery' were being 'filmed'. . . . the crowd passing over Westminster Bride at a certain hour one day were astounded to see below them a fierce hand-to-hand fight, in which revolvers were freely used, taking place on a barge. The Londoners stopped and gasped. Where were the police?[117]

As it was insisted repeatedly that "[i]t all happened exactly as recorded by the camera",[118] accounts of high-expenditure film-making ensured that the defining quality of 'cinema' in popular consciousness was that it occasioned a unique event that was then recorded, rather than inhering in the transformations possible in recording and post-production manipulation. In Figure 1.7, for example, not only is the contrivance behind cinema now located in arranging the pro-filmic event, even this contrivance is minimised: while the action is known to be performed, it is only *stated* to be in three of nine images.

It would be a mistake to see the cinema-real as the symptom of a vacuum in film theory which authorial accounts would later fill. It was an industry discourse derived from a particular economic situation in which it was seen to be necessary to eradicate older accounts of the technology. It was also an interpretation of the nature of the image. As Doane points out,

[f]rom Rudolf Arnheim, for whom the deviation from the real assured the status of film as art, to *Screen* film theory of the 1970s and its

Figure 1.7   Cinema as danger in *Punch*'s medley of found film footage, July 1914.[119]

critique of realism as ideological, the cinema's alleged adherence to the referent was something to be denied, rejected, transcended. But indexicality can and must be dissociated from is sole connection to the concept of realism, the reflection of a coherent, familiar, and recognizable world. Indexicality is a function that is essentially without content—in language, it is allied with the pure denotation of "this" or "here it is".[120]

The cinema-real alluded to the impression that, as Metz writes, in cinema "the signifier is coextensive with the whole of the significate, the spectacle is its own signification, thus short-circuiting the sign itself".[121] Because the event narrated and the act of narration are simultaneous in film, the event narrated is much less likely, compared to other narrative forms, to be seen as a mere function of the act of narration. The spatio-temporal continuity fabricated by structural narration, while linked to a narrative act, already adhered more closely to the event narrated than a narration of that event.

The cinema-real also sought to compensate for those transformative aspects of film that *did* persist. Jennifer Bean explains, in reference to US film discourse, that "the emphasis on realism in industrial publications coincides with the emergence of textual systems—incorporations of point of view and combinations of shot-matching and continuity-editing—increasingly capable of supporting a film's referentiality in space and time".[122] In the UK too, just at the point when the coherence of the story-space began to inhere more in the structure of the text, the term 'realism' was used to insist to picturegoers that it actually inhered in the material filmed. The ubiquity of the cinema-real evidences a 'realism anxiety' in the 1911–1914 period. As Elsaesser explains of the principle of alternation between images involved in the turn to narrative cinema,

> [a]nalytical editing, or scene dissection . . . breaks with the possibility of cinematic images being seen as records of (actual) objects or events. Instead they become motivated views (implying an act of showing) and semiotic acts (elements of a discourse): evidence that the cinema's representational space is not given but constructed, existing in an imaginary as well as a perceptual dimension.[123]

As its 'reality' increasingly inhered in the codification of editing structures, film was now potentially even *more* of a transformative medium, and so was potentially increasing its affinities with those amusements predecessors from which the industry wished to distance it. Production companies themselves attempted to address this. Between 1911 and 1912 in the US, for example, conspicuously displaying company trademarks on sets was finally phased out as part of an effort to purge cinema of its associations with monstration and establish it as a conveyer of the illusion of reality. In popular UK film discourse, the term 'realism', when used to describe the unrehearsed, likewise insisted on the absence from film of any gap between the pre-filmic and the filmic. The cinema-real described cinema as distinct from even prestigious cultural forms by virtue of a purportedly innate tendency to show events as they really were, often unrehearsed and always without codification. While Elsaesser implies that it is possible that cinema would have been sensed as 'narrated' at this historical juncture, the popular discourse of the 1910s regarded public perceptions that cinema's images were 'spoken' as a threat, and so used the cinema-real to distance cinema from these earlier permutations in which authorship was deceit. The discourse of realism was also compensatory precisely because of cinema's narrativity-by-story-space: because it was so easy to regard cinema outside the bounds of a constructive or authorial act, film journalists tended to generate definitions of cinema which avoided an account of film-making as purely descriptive, looking to the *pro*-filmic as intensely constructive. The authorial labour went into building, for example, the bridge to be destroyed in the climactic scene.

The term 'realism' also achieved dominance in films discourse because of developments in cinema's intermediality. The popular profile of pre-1908 cinema was conglomerated from a range of definitions borrowed from the existing media genealogies informing its practice: local film shows, travel films and topicals drew on the principles of panoramas and the illustrated press, early narrative films drew on the principles of *tableaux vivants*, trick films drew on stage magic and children's theatre, science films drew on public lecturing, comedy films drew on comic strips, exhibitionistic 'scenes' drew on titillatory 'freak' shows and peep shows and film practice in general drew on fairground showmanship, lantern lecturing and variety and penny theatre. At cinema's second birth, these spontaneous intermedial relationships were exchanged for more consciously negotiated intermediality. In this process of exchange, this wide range of contacts was reduced to the three major identities of 1) fictional narrative, 2) news reportage and 3) travel narrative, particularly after the launch of the first three 'animated newssheets' in the UK in 1910 and 1911.[124] With news reporting and travelogue preserved in the popular account of cinema's propensities, cinema was subject to a new force of description that defined it as "capable of trapping events in all their unpredictability and pure factualness",[125] but, unlike in the earlier period, to the exclusion of most other potential definitions.

The cinema-real was not an onanistic dialogue. It had significant effects. Nicholas Reeves explains that the UK government's decisions to create film propaganda during the First World War could easily have produced a variation of the fictional atrocity propaganda that was so popular with the press and the unofficial propaganda organisations, but, because of a widespread commitment to factual film, this was never considered: "if those who argued the case for official film propaganda had been willing to conceive of it in terms of fiction, then it could have been initiated without delay. As it was, they were committed to the factual film, and therefore they had to win the active support of the service departments."[126] The year-long delay between the start of the war and the eventual granting of official permission for cameraman to travel to the front derived, in spite of a history of co-operation between the cinema trade and the service departments before the war, from fears about what the cinema-real would reveal of the battle front. By 1914, cinema was now very different from the various projected motion picture apparatuses of attractions-era cinema, which were defined by their unreality, not because the kine-attractography era was saturated by fantastic films, but because it was not produced within the same cultural understanding of the purpose and action of the process. By 1914, these two major components of the cinema's image-regime—that it narrated itself and that it interposed no presence between filmed material and screened material—presented to the UK public a radical new definition of narrativity.

MODERNIST PRE-HISTORY: LITERARY IMPRESSIONISM

Colin MacCabe's 1974 model of realism can suggest *how* this radical new definition of narrativity impacted on literary practice. Realism, for Mac-Cabe, is a historically contingent literary mode based on, amongst other factors, a hierarchy made up of two distinct levels of discourse: 1) quoted speech or thought and 2) the narrative 'metalanguage' that takes the quoted language as its object. "In the classical realist novel", he writes, "the narrative prose functions as a metalanguage that can state all the truths in the object language—those words held in inverted commas—and can also explain the relation of this object language to the real."[127] Difficulties produced in any instance of object language tend to be resolved by the metalanguage which accompanies it. The metalanguage explains "the strange methods by which the object languages [i.e. the utterances and thoughts of the characters] attempt to express truths which are straightforwardly conveyed in the metalanguage."[128] Treating object languages "as certain material expressions which express certain meanings", narratorial metalanguage, in realist texts, "regards those same meanings as finding transparent expression within the metalanguage itself. Transparent in the sense that the metalanguage is not regarded as material; it is dematerialised to achieve perfect representation."[129] This relationship between metalanguage and object language, where the metalanguage opposes itself to the object language, allows the former to pervasively dematerialise itself *as* speech, designating itself the 'revealer' of that which the object language avoids, regarding "its object discourses as material but itself as transparent".[130]

While certain aspects of MacCabe's case have been disputed, a persistently dematerialised metalanguage (relative to an object language) remains a key component of critical definitions of literary realism, and is borne out far beyond MacCabe's attention solely to the novels of George Eliot (specifically *Romola* (serialised July 1862 to August 1863), *Daniel Deronda* (serialised February to September 1876) and *Middlemarch* (serialised December 1871 to December 1872)). In Arnold Bennett's *The Old Wives' Tale* (1908), for example, the eloping couple Sophia and Gerald meet up in a hotel in Paris:

> "I've got no one but you now," she murmured in a melting voice.
>
> She fancied in her ignorance that the expression of this sentiment would please him. She was not aware that a man is usually rather chilled by it, because it proves to him that the other is thinking about his responsibilities and not about his privileges. Certainly it calmed Gerald, though without imparting to him her sense of his responsibilities. He smiled vaguely. To Sophia his smile was a miracle continually renewed; it mingled dashing gaiety with a hint of wistful appeal in a manner that never failed to bewitch her. A less innocent girl than Sophia might have divined from that adorable half-feminine smile that she could do anything with Gerald except rely on him. But Sophia had to learn.[131]

The metalinguistic commentary on this one utterance from Sophia serves to specify the various levels of miscomprehension held by both Sophia and Gerald, miscomprehensions that denote their own utterances as subjectively implicated. In strict contrast to this hierarchical two-tier relationship endemic to realism, MacCabe argues, literary modernism emerged as a departure from this realist relation between the two levels of language. Modernism refused to offer, via metalanguage, a stable position from which the true meaning of the instances of object language was explained and the meaning of the story's real iterated. In MacCabe's post-First World War examples, modernism either replaced realist metalanguage with unmediated character consciousness or employed multiple and incompatible competing metalanguages.[132]

Although Bordwell refutes MacCabe's ensuing attempt to apply the same two-tier model to film narrative, arguing that cinema's viewers derive no sense of a self 'speaking' the fictional world from the majority of films,[133] this notion of a language about a language can nonetheless describe the *historical status* of literary language. The metalanguage of the realist novel, MacCabe points out, de-emphasises its own linguisticity by emphasising the linguisticity of the object language. However, at the time of the establishment of cinema's own implicit, structural—and discursively disavowed—metalanguage, even the most self-effacing *literary* metalanguage would have appeared to viewers, by contrast, *as* linguistic. Given that, as demonstrated above, cinema's transition to a practice defined by narrativity was not, as is frequently claimed, a transition from an early flaunting of textuality to "the transparent realism that modernism in the other arts contested",[134] cinema's narratorial mode, even if cinema by 1914 could now be called 'realist', was tangibly very different from that of *literary* realism. Even though literary realist metalanguage dematerialised itself in relation to instances of object language, it could not be *as* dematerialised as the narrator-less narrational process which the public were encountering in cinema. Even as cinema came to acquire several of the trappings of narrative in the popular imagination,[135] the popular discourse of the cinema-real asserted a dearth of metalanguage. Compared to a metalanguage functioning not just self-effacingly but *invisibly* in cinema, a metalanguage with a dearth of linguisticty *in spite of* its new use of narrational codes, any *literary* metalanguage would have appeared not as the opposite of an object language but merely as another form of object language. The narrative dynamic of a form that narrated itself yet which was also merely 'happenings'—'cinema-as-narrator' *and* 'cinema-as-events'—rendered literary metalanguage highly tangible.

What changes, then, did this increased relative tangibility of literary metalanguage occasion in literary practice? I will examine one of the premodernist literary groupings in the UK—those associated with what was known at the time as 'literary impressionism'—to ask why, at the time of the maturation of cinema's new image-regime at the beginning of 1914, the characteristics we associate with 'high' modernism began to emerge.

Ford Madox Hueffer (who changed his name to Ford Madox Ford in June 1919) in particular, both as editor of the *English Review* 1908–1909 and in critical articles written between 1909 and 1914, became both "the acknowledged representative" and the most outspoken proponent of 'literary impressionism' in the years leading up to the war.[136] Ezra Pound, for example, would later credit Ford with turning his head to impressionism in writing in around 1911.[137] In the work of Henry James and Joseph Conrad in particular, this mode concretised in the UK in the first decade of the twentieth century, and, as several have been careful to point out in recent years, it was *not* the mere literary corollary of impressionism in painting.[138] It can be defined as the result of an elaborate dialectic between, 1) the positivist belief that all knowledge could be obtained through falsifiable investigation, and 2) the assertion, by late nineteenth-century positivistic disciplines of the mind, that all bodies of knowledge are products of neurological operations. "The fundamental presuppositions and artistic techniques of realism and naturalism are essentially scientific", John Peters argues, while *impressionism* perceived that the possibility of knowing everything actually revealed that there was nothing to know except the productions of the mind; a 'fact' was therefore only the experience of an idea *as* verifiable by a consciousness.[139] Literary impressionism's rendering of events and objects 'as they really are' followed from the abandonment of previous conventions of omniscient access to all internal spaces by the narrator, but the school of thought also saw events as mute if not subject to the illumination of a consciousness, 'sense' now being the requirement of intelligibility for all things previously metaphysical. Consequently, literary impressionists employed limited, mostly first-person, narratorial consciousnesses to undertake the meaning-generating process of 'recording' their sense of the world. The impression, a product of the meeting of sensation and intellection, an objective sensory input that might be shared by others *and* an idiosyncratic experience of that input, was seen as completing otherwise inert objects and events by adding meaning and value.[140] As literary impressionism regarded objectivity as no more than a function of subjectivity, a subjective view did not prevent accurate perception of the world. Rather, an objective view of a sensory experience was seen as *only* possible if the intersection of sensory data with the subject's intellection was witnessed. Germinal in criticism in Walter Pater's *The Renaissance* (1873), his essay 'Style' (1888), and Henry James's preface to *The Princess Casamassima* (1886), this literary school of thought understood aesthetic production as the transcribing of a consciousness's sense of the world, "[s]o that the artist drawing life," as Ford wrote in 1911, "sombre more or less according to its latitude, is the true, is the only moralist. All the rest are only moralizers: they say what they like, not what is."[141]

The omniscient narrator was virtually incompatible with literary impressionism because it did not comprise a subject. Instead impressionism replaced the metalanguage of the omniscient commentator with another, subject-derived metalanguage, in both first-person narrators and limited third-person narrators focalising in just one character so as to imitate an experiencer of impressions. For these writers, narrative should also include only short dialogue that was credible as having been remembered by the narrator, and the narrator should record their impressions of other characters' internal states as they occurred on visible exteriors, recount impressions without poetic diction and never become surrogate commentators for authors (as Ford deplored of William Makepeace Thackeray).[142] Ford wrote in 1911 that "the general effect of a novel must be the general effect that life makes on mankind."[143] For him,

> any piece of Impressionism whether it be prose, or verse, or painting, or sculpture, is the record of the impression of a moment; it is not a sort of rounded, annotated record of a set of circumstances—it is the record of the recollection in your mind of a set of circumstances that happened ten years ago—or ten minutes. It might even be the impression of the moment—but it is the impression, not the corrected chronicle.[144]

This is why literary impressionism, Michael Levenson argues, "has been characterized as both a precise rendering of objects and an unrepentant subjectivizing",[145] because it takes the former as meaningful only in the context of the latter. 'Mere' sensory apprehension and psychological depth were no longer opposed: moral, religious and aesthetic preoccupations were now merely functions of consciousness, and consciousness was neurologically very real. Pound wrote in 1913 that "the arts give us our best data for determining what sort of creature man is. As our treatment of man must be determined by our knowledge or conception of what man is, the arts provide data for ethics."[146] "The Impressionist author", Ford wrote in early 1914 (in an article published in December 1914), "is sedulous to avoid letting his personality appear in the course of his book. On the other hand, his whole book, his whole poem is merely an expression of his personality."[147] Ford argued in 1911 that although what the artist "has to avoid is an intrusion of his own personality into the current of his work," events must be presented only as a subject would perceive them.[148] To achieve poetic sincerity, Ford wrote in 1909, "[i]t does not much matter where the poet goes or what he does, so long as he turns inquiring, sincere, and properly humble eyes upon the life that is around him."[149] He was still saying much the same in September 1913: "It is the duty of the poet to reflect his own day as it appears to him, as it has impressed itself upon him".[150] "The main thing is the genuine love and the faithful rendering of the received impression",[151] he argued. His 1911 command "*Never comment: state*"[152] was echoed in Pound's March 1913 'Don'ts' on Imagism, which cited Shakespeare's evasion of description for simple presentation as an ideal.[153]

These principles comprised the stated underpinning of Imagism for several of its proponents. T.E. Hulme wrote in 1909 of just such a primacy of verifiable visual impressions as an antidote to the redundancy of epic metaphysical anxieties. Ideal modern poetry, he argued, "always endeavours to arrest you, and to make you continuously see a physical thing, to prevent you gliding through an abstract process".[154] He defended free verse in his 1911 'Lecture on Modern Poetry' as servicing the drive towards "the maximum of individual and personal expression" because the psyche being expressed was the only place where an idea had any kind of truth.[155] He advocated poetry that emulated impressionism in painting: "where the old [painter] endeavoured to tell a story, the modern attempts to fix an impression",[156] admitting that "the first time I ever felt the necessity or inevitableness of verse, was in the desire to reproduce the peculiar quality of feeling which is induced by the flat spaces and wide horizons of the virgin prairie of western Canada."[157] The tendency for language to age away from impressions into abstractions, Hulme argued in 1911, meant that only poetry, by providing new linguistic conjunctions, could create original visual effects, whereas prose is 'creative', dealing in figures of speech rather than poetry's pictures. Free verse, "this method of recording impressions by visual images", Hulme wrote, "resembles sculpture rather than music; it appeals to the eye rather than to the ear."[158] Commenting on Yeats's rhetorical glamour in early 1913, Pound would praise Ford as believing "in an exact rendering of things. He would strip words of all 'association' for the sake of getting a precise meaning . . . He is objective."[159] In the same article, Pound went on to associate Imagism with the same priorities, asserting that the watchword of the 'Imagistes' was "Precision".[160] "Bad art is inaccurate art", Pound wrote in 1913: "It is art that makes false reports."[161] Good artists, he wrote, must "have discovered something—either of life itself or of the means of expression" through a "strength of perception."[162]

Even in the works that he wrote immediately before early 1914, Conrad maintained these principles. In *Under Western Eyes*, in progress from December 1907 to May 1910 and published in October 1911, the first-person narrator, a language professor, has access only to his own impressions and to those of one other character, Razumov, who has left a memoir. That it is not, ostensibly, written for anyone's consumption makes it, in the narrator's opinion, acceptable as an uncorrupted record of impressions.[163] Parts One and Three and sections of Part Four are given in the third-person by the character-narrator as a summing-up of Razumov's memoirs, and Part Two and the remaining sections of Part Four, the parts of the narrative at which the narrator *was* present, are given in the first person. The novel hinges on the discrepancy between the impressions experienced by the 'western eyes' (those of the language professor) and those experienced by the Russians he meets in Geneva, particularly Razumov, whose diary is itself a rendering of impressions. Everything known about Razumov is either taken from the language professor's brief meetings with him or derived from the impressions recorded in Razumov's memoir. The language professor merely records Razumov's sense impressions, even though he is able to interpret what those sense impressions mean. For example, when called to his attorney's office, Razumov is introduced to

> a tall, aristocratic-looking personage with silky, grey side-whiskers . . . To his intense surprise Razumov saw a white shapely hand extended to him. He took it in great confusion (it was soft and passive) and heard at the same time a condescending murmur in which he caught only the words 'Satisfactory' and 'Persevere'. But the most amazing thing of all was to feel suddenly a distinct pressure of the white shapely hand just before it was withdrawn: a light pressure like a secret sign. The emotion of it was terrible. Razumov's heart seemed to leap in his throat. When he raised his eyes the aristocratic personage, motioning the little lawyer aside, had opened the door and was going out.[164]

The narrator's possession of knowledge of Razumov's later discoveries that could be—but has not been—used to modify this record of impressions is stressed by the fact that, as he remarks, he has read the whole memoir before beginning his account of Razumov's life. As is later found out, the narrator has chosen not to remark that this was Razumov's unknowing first contact with his own father: instead he gives an uncorrected record of impressions.

Likewise, when the narrator recounts his first encounter with Razumov in Geneva, his wonder at the supposed 'hero' Razumov's avoidance of Miss

Haldin is 'faithfully' recounted even though the narrator, at the time of writing this, knows that Razumov is not a revolutionary hero but a counter-revolutionary agent responsible for the death of Miss Haldin's brother's.[165] Indeed, the two sets of impressions that comprise the book—the language professor who accompanies the revolutionary Haldin's mother and sister, and Razumov (who betrays Haldin to the government, causes his death and becomes a counter-revolutionary agent simply as a consequence of the threat to his university career posed by government suspicions of him for ever having known Haldin) are given even though they demand opposing sympathies. The language professor's memories are likewise given as the memories of impressions. Towards the end of the narrated action, Razumov comes to Miss Haldin to confess:

> The next moment he gave me a very special impression beyond the range of commonplace definitions. It was as though he had stabbed himself outside and had come in there to show it; and more than that—as though he were turning the knife in the wound and watching the effect. That was the impression rendered in physical terms. One could not defend oneself from a certain amount of pity.[166]

Even though he is writing from a viewpoint that allows him to explain *why* Razumov is behaving so strangely (i.e. out of a double guilt at having caused Haldin's execution *and* having been received by Haldin's family as Haldin's closest friend), the narrator records only the strangeness, at the time, of the impressions he experienced. It is important to note, however, that *even* in this novel in which, out of all his works, Conrad *most* explicitly set out to contrast world views, he achieved one of the abilities of an omniscient third-person narrator: to access multiple consciousnesses and arbitrate between multiple object languages, merely doing so via impressionist first-person rules.

Conrad also achieved a first-person equivalent to the multiple psychological intimacy of omniscient third-person narration in his next novel, *Chance*, started in the summer of 1905 but mostly written between May 1911 and 25 March 1912 (serialised 21 January—30 June 1912 and published in book form in January 1914). The character-narrator, the two 'recounters' (Marlow and Powell) who, combined, give the character-narrator the complete story, and each of the secondary 'recounters' who have in turn given Marlow and Powell *their* parts of the story, all record only the experience of their own impressions, and no knowledge is recounted that does not have a chain of confidantes by which it has (or might have) been acquired by Marlow or Powell. One impression, which explains much of Flora's behaviour in later marrying Captain Anthony, is related by her to Mrs Fyne, to Marlow and then to the narrator (and given in Marlow's words). When Flora is berated by her governess, who is abandoning her, and Charley,

There was something like an emanation of evil from her eyes and from the face of the other, who, exactly behind her and overtopping her by half a head, kept his eyelids lowered in a sinister fashion—which in the poor girl, reached, stirred, set free that faculty of unreasoning explosive terror lying locked up at the bottom of all human hearts and of the hearts of animals as well.[167]

Impressions are also recounted in spite of their relevance. When Marlow is talking to Fyne after Anthony and Flora's elopement, Marlow betrays by his speech that he has forgotten that Flora's father will soon be discharged from prison:

Fyne made an extraordinary simiesque grimace. I believe it was quite involuntary, but you know that a grave, much-lined, shaven countenance when distorted in an unusual way is extremely apelike. It was a surprising sight, and rendered me not only speechless but stopped the progress of my thought completely. I must have presented a remarkably imbecile appearance.[168]

This impression is as important as the immensely consequential impression that, as Powell later recounts to Marlow, made Powell pause just as he was about to dispose of Captain Anthony's glass because he has just seen Flora's father poison it:

He held the glass in his hand; all he had to do was to vanish back beyond the curtains, flee with it noiselessly into the night on deck, fling it unseen overboard. A minute or less. And then all that would have happened would have been the wonder at the utter disappearance of a glass tumbler, a ridiculous riddle in pantry-affairs beyond the wit of anyone on board to solve. The grain of sand against which Powell stumbled in his headlong career was a moment of incredulity as to the truth of his own conviction because it had failed to affect the safe aspect of familiar things. He doubted his eyes too. He must have dreamt it all! 'I am dreaming now,' he said to himself. And very likely for a few seconds he must have looked like a man in a trance or profoundly asleep on his feet, and with a glass of brandy-and-water in his hand.[169]

This impression causes Powell to pause just long enough for Captain Anthony to return to his drink and demand why his second mate is in his rooms, which in turn causes the discovery and consequent suicide of Flora's father.

Chance also, in its extreme complexity of indirect storytelling, reflects the centrality, to any event, of the act of experiencing impressions. In addition to the frequent variation between levels of recounters, an even more frequent variation of whose words the narration is stated *in* emphasises this too. Even in the case of the handful of psychological moments in the story recounted by Marlow and Powell that (in spite of the large number of accounts which contribute to the overall story of Flora de Barral) seem unlikely to have been related to either of them, each of these is stated by the recounting character to be conjecture. Many more moments, particularly at the end of the story, which seem to be impossible for either of the two 'recounters' to know about, are found just 1.3% from the end to be have been told, by Flora ("a most unexpected source of information"),[170] who is currently living nearby, to Powell and then to Marlow. Impressionist equivalents of a de-materialising metalanguage are still possible.

Conrad's short stories likewise adhered to the impressionist principle well into the early 1910s. In 'The Partner', written between October 1910 and March 1911 (and published in November 1911), a first-person narrator is told the story by a stranger, who in turn has parts of the story second-hand, the narrative encompassing the impressions experienced by the narrator, by the 'recounter' and by the protagonists whose stories have been told to the 'recounter'. The narrator remarks on his impression of the stranger's immobility, which, when the stranger gets to the story of George and Harry Dunbar, changes: "He drew a breath, and I noticed his hand, lying loosely on the table, close slowly into a fist. In that immovable man it was startling, ominous, like the framed nod of the Commander."[171] As with *Under Western Eyes* and *Chance*, each of the accounts relayed by the 'recounter' to the narrator revises his understanding of the protagonist, in this case both Harry Dunbar and the stranger's own attitude to the local boatmen who, it is now clear, falsely inform tourists that Dunbar committed suicide. In 'The Inn of the Two Witches', written in late 1912 (published in March 1913), the narrator conveys 'found' writing, as in *Under Western Eyes* and, as distinct from the framed stories that were popular in Edwardian short fiction, relays Edgar Byrne's story as the impressions experienced by Byrne. For example, the fact that Cuba Tom was Byrne's boyhood mentor when Byrne joined the navy is not stated by the narrator of the story. It is implied only at the end of the description of Tom through a reference to Byrne's joy, when he comes aboard, at meeting him *again*.[172] The series of impressions experienced by Byrne is more important than an account of the history which has led to them, so as their past together when Byrne was a boy exists for this record *only* as the reason for Byrne's joy at meeting Tom again, the narrator does not subsume impressions into a chronology of the circumstances which led to them.

After the completion of 'The Inn of the Two Witches', however, and shortly after the emergence of cinema's radical new definition of narrativity, a major change occurred in Conrad's work. In 'The Planter of Malata', written during November and December 1913 (and published in January 1914), while the story of Renouard is similar to that of *Under Western Eyes* in that it concentrates on the impressions of a man who has told a lie and found it to have had major consequences, and while, describing Miss

Moorsom's shallowness, the narrator states that "[i]t could not be said that she had received from the contacts of the external world impressions of a personal kind, different from other women",[173] the formal partial narrator of literary impressionism (achieved by third-person focalisation in Renouard) disappears, albeit temporarily, seven times in the second half of the story. Short focalisations in other characters are used to highlight the invasiveness that Renouard feels in the presence of those who might guess his secret. The partiality of the third-person impressionist narrator is exposed here as little different from that of a typical realist narrator. In addition, whereas Conrad's previous works withheld information from the reader that the first-person narrator or focalised character did not yet know at that time, in 'The Planter of Malata' a piece of knowledge that the story's main consciousness *does* have but has not yet shared with others is withheld. In spite of the fact that Renouard's psychological processes, which the narrative concerns through focalisation, would have included, at some point, the recollection of a memory of having buried his assistant before he left his island for the mainland, the omniscient narrator of this story is shown to have *chosen* not to narrate Renouard's thoughts on his assistant until Renouard finds that the assistant is the man that the Moorsoms are looking for and so discovers the magnitude of his earlier lie to the newspaper editor that his assistant is still alive. An impressionist tenet is here expressed not, as in 'The Inn of the Two Witches', as a record of the experience of impressions, but as a narratorial act of concealing and revealing.

In 'Because of the Dollars', written in early 1914 (first published in September 1914 as 'Laughing Anne'), written in the first-person and a record of a story told to the narrator by Hollis, *some* impressionist tenets are likewise still in evidence. There is no 'scene-setting'. As with Cuba Tom and Byrne in 'The Inn of the Two Witches', Laughing Anne and Davidson's previous acquaintance is not narrated until Hollis gets to the point in the story when they meet *again*—i.e. it does not exist until it becomes relevant to their impressions. The unnamed mutual friend of Hollis and Davidson, whom Davidson informs of his plans to go 'dollar-collecting', is not mentioned by Hollis when he narrates Davidson first entering the tiffin-room where this conversation happens: his existence is mentioned only when Davidson states his plans and is overheard by Fector. But, unlike the narrator and the two 'recounters' in *Chance*, Hollis narrates actions and thoughts that he has no means of having learned about. Neither Davidson nor the mutual friend can have known that they were being overheard while Davidson stated his plans as this would have led Davidson to be prepared for the attack, and the attack on him leads to a train of events in which the overhearer, Fector, and the other three characters involved either die or disappear at its culmination. As the reader might think that Davidson has later *guessed* that he was overheard by Fector, and told Hollis of this, Conrad also clearly demonstrates that Hollis knows even the thoughts of the four who, alone and unheard, plan the attack on Davidson: "The couple [Niclaus and the

Frenchman] were alone together loafing in the common-room of that infamous hotel when Fector turned up. After some beating about the bush, for he was doubtful how far he could trust these two, he repeated what he had overheard in the tiffin-rooms."[174] The Frenchman "saw all that lot of dollars melted into bars and disposed of somewhere on the China coast. Of the escape after the *coup* he never doubted."[175] Not merely, as in *Chance*, rendering a character who disdains to mention how he came to know this, Conrad deliberately and explicitly *prevents* a character from being able to have come to know what he knows in the first place. An impressionist conceit is paraded merely as a linguistic rule.

Victory, the novel that occupied Conrad at the time of the maturation of cinema's radical new definition of narrativity, also evidences a shift away from impressionism. Started in May 1912 but mostly written throughout 1913 and in the first half of 1914 up to the end of June (first published in March 1915), *Victory* initially employs a first-person narrator, but discards this after the first of the four sections (the first 16% of the text). Unlike preceding novels which used first-person and third-person narrative in discrete chapters or sections, *Victory*'s first-person narrator merely stops referring to himself or the method by which he has learned the narrative after the first two paragraphs of section two. Even in this first section, while this narrator has gaps in his knowledge that disclose his existence in the narrated world through his limited abilities to know, the care that the narrator and 'recounters' of *Chance* take to signal the route via which the story has come to them does not reappear in *Victory*. This narrator, an unnamed peripheral character, only twice mentions himself speaking.[176] Otherwise his presence in the story is as one of a group of bystanders. He reports popular opinion of Axel Heyst, and recalls that "[a] few of us who were sufficiently interested went to Davidson [Heyst's friend] for details".[177] Shortly after the beginning of section two, the narrator who, with the last reference to himself, describes Heyst as "[h]e whom we used to refer to as the Enchanted Heyst",[178] soon graduates to omniscience. This occurs in a single paragraph. Telling of Heyst's morose mood one night at Schomberg's hotel in Sourabaya in Java, he comments,

> Perhaps this [the spell of the Malay Archipelago] was the very spell which had enchanted Heyst in the early days. For him, however, that was broken. He was no longer enchanted, though he was still a captive of the islands. He had no intention to leave them ever. Where could he have gone to, after all these years? Not a single soul belonging to him lived anywhere on earth. Of this fact—not such a remote one, after all—he had only lately become aware; for it is failure [the failure of the Tropical Belt Company] that makes a man enter into himself and reckon up his resources. And though he had made up his mind to retire from the world in hermit fashion, yet he was irrationally moved by this sense of loneliness which had come to him in the hour of renunciation.

> It hurt him. Nothing is more painful than the shock of sharp contradic-
> tions that lacerate our intelligence and our feelings.[179]

The book's last instance of conjecture—the "perhaps" which begins this
paragraph—is for this work shown to be exactly the same as the metalinguistic commentary which extrapolates from Heyst's experience of impressions
that "[nothing] is more painful than the shock of sharp contradictions".

The last 84% of the book continues via this 'promoted' narrator. This
narrator continues to extrapolate, remarking, for example, in discussing
Heyst's upbringing by a father committed to "absolute moral and intellectual liberty", that "[t]he young man learned to reflect, which is a destruc-
tive process, a reckoning of the cost. It is not the clear-sighted who lead
the world. Great achievements are accomplished in a blessed, warm mental
fog".[180] The consciousnesses in whom the narrator temporarily focalises
do continue to experience the world around them as impressions, but the
narrator adds his own commentaries. For example, when the narrative is
focalised in Schomberg, the narrator records that Schomberg tells Mr Jones
and his secretary Ricardo about his hotel, and "the new guest made answer
that he liked a hotel where one could find some local people in the evening.
It was infernally dull otherwise. The secretary, in sign of approval, emitted
a grunt of astonishing ferocity, as if proposing to himself to eat the local
people."[181] The narrator later tells how Schomberg expresses his fury to his
wife that Jones and Ricardo are using his hotel for gambling:

> He was beside himself in his lurid, heavy, Teutonic manner, so unlike
> the picturesque, lively rage of the Latin races; and though his eyes
> strayed about irresolutely, yet his swollen, angry features awakened
> in the miserable woman over whom he had been tyrannising for years
> a fear for his precious carcass, since the poor creature had nothing
> else but that to hold on to in the world. She knew him well; but she
> did not know him altogether. The last thing a woman will consent to
> discover in a man whom she loves, or on whom she simply depends,
> is want of courage. [182]

Not only is the narration no longer first-person—able to narrate the perspectives of Schomberg and his wife without needing to rely on accounts later
given by each independently to someone else and then to the narrator—it
is not even partial, able to move between Schomberg and Mrs Schomberg,
following a principle of universal access to consciousness.

Partial narration *is* used later in the story, taking up roughly the last half
of the book, but this partiality is highly portable, anticipating the method
of Joyce's *Ulysses* and Woolf's *Mrs Dalloway*. Parts Three and Four are
comprised of a series of switches of focalisation, initially between Heyst,
Lena and Wang, and then between Heyst, Lena, Wang, Ricardo and Jones.
For example, Heyst and Lena are talking:

He was moved by the vibrating quality of the last words. She seemed to be talking low of some wonderful enchantment, in mysterious terms of special significance. He thought that if she only could talk to him in some unknown tongue, she would enslave him altogether by the sheer beauty of the sound, suggesting infinite depths of wisdom and feeling.

"But," she went on, "the name stuck in my head, it seems; and when you mentioned it-"

"It broke the spell," muttered Heyst in angry disappointment, as if he had been deceived in some hope.

The girl, from her position a little above him, surveyed with still eyes the abstracted silence of the man on whom she now depended with a completeness of which she had not been vividly conscious before, because, till then, she had never felt herself swinging between the abysses of earth and heaven in the hollow of his arm. What if he should grow weary of the burden.[183]

While this frequent switching between focalisations sometimes coincides with chapter beginnings, it much more often disregards these 'natural' boundaries. In addition, rather than simply being non-exclusive in its knowledge of characters' thoughts, the narrator of the second half of *Victory* limits itself to exclusive focalisations for lengthy blocks of text, not availing itself of the ability to know the thoughts of another character, even when the focalised character (and thus also the reader) wants to know what others are thinking. Brief moments of omniscience are not taboo, the narrator commenting at one point that Ricardo "did not know that he was striking terror into her [Lena's] breast now."[184] But largely the narration refuses to switch focalisation between characters when knowledge of others' thoughts would qualify the situation. Distinct from impressionism's partial views, this localisation also differs from the realist omniscience that usually underpins the dramatic iteration of what characters do and do not know of each other, restricting the reader to character consciousness in turn. When Ricardo leaves Heyst at the door to Jones's cabin, the strictness of this new injunction to focalise temporarily means that at the end of the chapter focalised in Heyst, the next chapter's focalisation in Ricardo only lets the reader know by implication that this is occurring at the same time as the discussion between Heyst and Jones narrated in the previous chapter.

In *Victory*, omniscient narrative is no longer simulated via impressionist rules, as it was in *Under Western Eyes* and *Chance*, by having narrators or characters 'research' the thoughts of others. In addition, combined with Conrad's continued commitment to registering visual information rather than objects, this mode in which not only no narrator but no *character* is the exclusive seer of the sight makes for moments when a sight is seen even when no subject exists to see it. For example, while the narrative is focalised with Lena, she leaves Heyst and goes alone into her room: "When the curtain had fallen behind her, she turned her head back with an expression of infinite and tender concern for him—for him whom she could never hope to understand".[185] The turning of her head and the expression on her face are reported as sights in spite of there being no character able to see them and the narrator also being unable to see them because the narrative is focalised in Lena. The narration still 'sees', but it relinquishes the association between the describing of that sight and the description being that of a specific character or narrator. Lastly, also prefiguring a characteristic of later modernist works, at the point when Jones and Ricardo arrive in Heyst's island (the narrative at the time being focalised in Heyst), the narrator names them before Heyst discovers their names.[186] As he wrote *Victory*, then, Conrad, it appears, had chosen to expose his previous impressionist works as metalinguistic. While the epistemological priorities underpinning the content of Conrad's novels may not have been altered,[187] his formal priorities radically changed.[188]

Ford's writing also underwent a major alteration at the same time. His impressionist collaborations with Conrad (*The Inheritors* (written in late 1899 and published in June 1901) and *Romance* (written between mid-1900 and September 1903 and published in October 1903)) were both first-person narratives which employed Conrad's "primitive perception" and "delayed decoding", where sense impressions are first images and are developed only after a time lag into perceptions of recognisable entities.[189] While Ford's novels in the years immediately before 1914 included strains of social satire and historical romance that generically absented them from the injunctions of impressionism, he is also generally seen to have been already developing, in the remaining "novels of small circles", *The Benefactor* (1905) and *A Call* (1910), a template for his *ostensibly* most 'impressionist' work, *The Good Soldier* (1915).[190] In 1962 John Meixner was already referring to *A Call* as "a first experiment" in anticipation of *The Good Soldier*.[191] Written between late 1908 and early 1909, *A Call* was serialised in the *English Review* from August to November 1909 and then revised for its early 1910 publication in book form. The novel shows the state of Ford's literary consciousness before his exposure to the new image-regime of cinema. In the work's epistolary epilogue, added during his revisions, Ford, describing himself as "your poor Impressionist", wrote of his ambition, in writing the book, "to render a little episode—a small 'affair' affecting a little circle of people—exactly as it would have happened. He desired neither to comment nor explain."[192] *A Call*'s third-person narrator is impressionistically partial, seeming, in chapter 1.1, to describe Robert Grimshaw but only relaying a series of exchanges which exclude explanations of 1) the terms imposed by Katya Lascarides that Robert Grimshaw refused to agree to, 2) why she imposed them, 3) why Robert, Ellida and Katya grew up together, 4) how Robert influenced Dudley Leicester away from Etta Stackpole or 5) why Robert wants Pauline married. These major pieces of information, which determine the rest of the action, are revealed only as chapters 're-introduce' characters, inviting revisions of their interests and motivations, and are only completely revealed as characters cite them in explaining the actions initiating and resulting from the titular phone call of chapter 2.1. Dramatic facts are secondary to an account of the intersection of sensory data with intellection in the protagonists.

The Good Soldier, however (written between c. December 1913 and September 1914 and published in March 1915), rather than constituting an *intensification* of this literary impressionism, has a number of characteristics that strongly distinguish it from the impressionist credo. First, Dowell, the first-person narrator, consistently rather than sporadically addresses the reader/hearer in the second-person, remarking "you must expect", "you understand", "[y]ou don't tell me anything", "I am, at any rate, trying to get you to see", "now you understand", "I . . . beg you to think of that poor wretch", "I have never told you anything about my marriage", "I suppose I have not conveyed it to you", "[y]ou will remember I said", "you see", "I hope I have not given you the idea", "you understand", "you are to remember", "it may strike you", and beginning to draw his commentary to a close by stating, twice, "I leave it to you".[193] Spread throughout the text, these lay stress on the production of the text, its status as a speech act in the present.

Indeed, Ford so intensely styled *The Good Soldier* as an utterance in the present that not only is much of the story to be reassembled from the many versions of it that Dowell recounts, Dowell often leaves the meaning of many of his utterances unexplained. For example, in the opening chapter, he states that

> I don't, you understand, blame Florence. But how can she have known what she knew? How could she have got to know it? To know it so fully. Heavens! There doesn't seem to have been the actual time. It must have been when I was taking my baths, and my Swedish exercises, being manicured. Leading the life I did, of the sedulous, strained nurse, I had to do something to keep myself fit. It must have been then![194]

"It" is later retrospectively implied to have been Florence's knowledge of and participation in Edward Ashburnham's affairs, her attempts to try to end Edward's affairs while also openly, to Leonora Ashburnham, being his mistress. "Is the whole thing a folly and a mockery?", Dowell asks: "Am I no better than a eunuch or is the proper man—the man with the right to existence—a raging stallion forever neighing after his neighbour's womankind?"[195] Not yet stating that Edward Ashburnham routinely cheated on his wife, and so not yet making clear what "the whole thing" is, the text is an occurrence in the narrator's present, a materialised linguistic product, rather than an account of plot events.

In the earlier *Romance*, in a seemingly similar opening half-chapter, the narrator Castro recounts an event that happens in the middle of the story that he then goes on to narrate from the beginning. In part of this he recalls that "[t]he spirit of the age has changed; everything has changed so utterly that one can hardly believe in the existence of one's earlier self. But I can still remember how, at that moment, I made the acquaintance of my heart—a thing that bounded and leapt within my chest, a little sickeningly."[196] This is a memory taken out of the chronological order followed by the rest of the first-person novel. In *The Good Soldier*, however, the opening chapter is a present-day reflection on what the events mean, not a recounting of *any* kind:

> what do I know of the smoking-room? Fellows come in and tell the most extraordinary gross stories—stories so gross that they will positively give you a pain. And yet they'd be offended if you suggested that they weren't the sort of person you could trust your wife alone with. And very likely they'd be quite properly offended—that is if you can trust anybody alone with anybody. But that sort of fellow obviously takes more delight in listening to or in telling gross stories—more delight than in anything else in the world. They'll hunt languidly and dress languidly and dine languidly and work without enthusiasm and find it a bore to carry on three minutes' conversation about anything whatever and yet, when the other sort of conversation begins, they'll laugh and wake up and throw themselves about in their chairs.[197]

Also unlike *Romance*, this is not a 'pre-amble' to a narrative. While the later chapters do involve some sequential narration by Dowell, he continues to ask himself these questions.

In *The Good Soldier*, events in the narrator's past are also to be gleaned *only* from the aspects of it that come to the narrator's mind in the present because they are relevant at a certain moment in the present of the linguistic act that is the novel. Dowell recalls Florence's reasons for concealing her affair with Jimmy before he mentions that the affair is with Jimmy, and Nancy Rufford is alluded to as 'the girl' or 'the poor girl' five times before her name is given or her relationship with anyone stated. This is, of course, a vital step towards the literary mode in which the plot time of *Ulysses*, *Asphodel* and *Mrs Dalloway* acquires a past through the recollection, by characters, of certain aspects of that past only because they are relevant to the thought process of that certain characters in the present. (I will discuss the important distinction between this occurring in the consciousness of the *narrator* in *The Good Soldier* and in the consciousness of *characters* in *Ulysses*, *Asphodel* and *Mrs Dalloway* in Chapter 2.) Dowell's past self is also not the impressionist 'experiencer' of the moment. In contrast to the first-person narrators of Conrad's and Ford's earlier impressionism, in spite of several points where Dowell recalls the experience of impressions at a certain time and place, the knowledge that Dowell has in the present constantly leaks into his narration. Introducing Edward Ashburnham, he also introduces Leonora's hatred of him in spite of having yet not yet given the reason for this.[198] Starting his account of Edward's affairs, he also mentions that Florence was one of Edward's lovers even though his discovery of this occurred, as is later stated, after both Edward and Florence died.[199]

In 1924 Ford recalled his conversations with Conrad about technique, stating that they had together reached the awareness

> that what was the matter with the Novel, and the British novel in particular, was that it went straight forward, whereas in your gradual making acquaintance with your fellows you never do go straight forward. You meet an English gentleman at your golf club. He is beefy, full of health, the moral of the boy from an English Public School of the finest type. You discover, gradually, that he is hopelessly neurasthenic, dishonest in matters of small change, but unexpectedly self-sacrificing, a dreadful liar but a most painfully careful student of Lepidoptera and, finally, from the public prints, a bigamist who was once, under another name, hammered on the Stock Exchange. . . . Still, there he is, the beefy, full-fed fellow, moral of an English Public School product. To get such a man in fiction you could not begin at his beginning and work his life chronologically back to the end. You must . . . work backwards and forwards over his past. That theory at least we gradually evolved.[200]

For Max Saunders this is a summary of Ford's method in *The Good Soldier*: the novel is an attempt to synthesise the receiving of impressions.[201] But while this aspect of 'impressionist' writing remained intact in *The Good Soldier*, the novel is not the work prescribed by the model of impressionism that Ford had produced before 1914. The repetitious revising of an initial narrative in *The Good Soldier* may somewhat resemble Conrad's technique, at its most intense in *Chance*, of presenting multiple accounts of a single event in the order in which they are recounted to a listener rather than synthesising them into the order in which they happened, and the radical nature of the novel's revisions, which include an explanation that Ashburnham's seemingly cruel affairs are a product of his own tendency to feel indebted to women, *seem* to stress an adherence to the impressionist credo.[202] But the 'account' of Edward Ashburnham in *The Good Soldier* is made available out of order because it is a record of the changing of Dowell's consciousness in the 'narrator-NOW'.[203] This ordering is not determined by the ordering of the revelation of it to Dowell, as stressed by Ford placing Dowell's learning of Florence and Edward's affair, one of Dowell's *last* discoveries, *first* in his series of recollections. Neither are the multiple revisions of each event in Dowell's narrative revisions of defined time periods. Instead they are thought processes experienced by the narrator that almost always bring what plot time exists up to the narrator's own present, the present of the linguistic act. For example, when Dowell explains that Nancy Rufford was different from Edward's previous lovers in that she was the one with whom he found himself ceasing to constantly expand his horizons, he tells that "over her he wore himself to rags and tatters and death—in the effort to leave her alone."[204] As Edward's death has occurred so soon before the 'narrator-NOW' that he does not yet have a tombstone, this version of an account of Edward's life brings the 'story-NOW' to the 'narrator-NOW' in just 755 words. Likewise, Dowell's account of the end of Ashburnham's affair with Mrs Basil is followed by an account of her life until just three days before the 'narrator-NOW'.

Impressionism had entailed organising the experience of impressions for the reader in the same order that they would have been experienced by the protagonist, eliciting in the reader the same temporary misunderstandings and delays in cognition experienced by the protagonist. In Conrad's 'The Partner', the narrator mentions that he told the stranger that he had heard the name Harry Dunbar as that of the Captain of the *Sagamore*, the reader therefore being left (like the narrator at the time of hearing the story from the stranger) with the assumption that Harry is alive and that the ship still exists. The reader then finds that Dunbar is dead and that the ship has been wrecked only at the point in the hearing of the stranger's story that the narrator also discovers this. Nonetheless, as it was practised by Conrad (and as Ford, Pound and Hulme all advocated it) impressionism had been a narrative *transcribing* of impressions, not an attempt to *synthesise* them. Undertaking this rather different project in *The Good Soldier*, Ford shifted emphasis onto the literary act, citing this act as itself capable of originating impressions. Describing 'impressionist' tenets at a time when literary impressionism had been radically modified and even, arguably, abandoned, Ford's 1924 recollection describes an intention to materialise metalanguage as a language. Notably, Ford, by placing the *reader* in the place of the experiencer of impressions in *The Good Soldier*, also departed from impressionism by locating its reader inside a hypothetical story-space of meeting and learning about Edward Ashburnham—the narrator Dowell's own part in the story is something of a cipher for a process of 'getting to know' the "English gentleman at your golf club", hence the apparent absurdity of his nine years of obliviousness to his own wife's affair with Ashburnham. Dowell is an explicit narrational process.

Literary impressionism may seem to have already attempted to dissolve the metalanguage intrinsic to the realist novels of the nineteenth century, but in spite of being set by its proponents against realist narratorial commentary, impressionism nonetheless comprised a metalanguage. As Trotter has remarked, "literary impressionism was less self-effacing than one might suppose".[205] In *Under Western Eyes*, even though Conrad obeys the dictate that, for example, the ridiculousness of Peter Ivanovitch's simultaneous intellectual deification of women and real-world cruelty to them *cannot* be remarked by a narrator (being remarked instead by a character, the language professor), impressionism's narrators achieved their own metalinguistic discussions of object language. The meaning of the spoken language is still qualified by a single subject above the meanings extracted by others. In *Chance*, for example, Marlow unifies all of the stories told to him under his discussion of the part that chance plays in life, remarking, for example, that "[i]t's certainly unwise to admit any sort of responsibility for our actions, whose consequences we are never able to foresee".[206] Such chapter headings as 'Young Powell and his Chance' do the same. Even first-person narration, one way of ensuring adherence to the impressionist credo, does not distinguish impressionist writing from its predecessors: both the language professor and Marlow, having obtained multiple accounts of the major experiences of *Under Western Eyes* and *Chance* respectively, frequently achieve the ability to access multiple consciousness—a characteristic of realism's frequently omniscient narrator—that impressionist writing only *seemed* to relinquish. The conceit that no character-narrator may back-date knowledge about another character to a point in the narrative before they discovered it—in such cases as Powell's own name at the beginning of *Chance*—was also as strict a metalinguistic rule as the omniscient injunction to comment.

What, then, was cinema's part in the abandonment of impressionism? It was certainly not to produce analogues in literary practice. When Conrad toured America in 1923 reading from *Victory* and likening his literary technique to that of a film camera he also argued, as he stated in a letter to Eric Pinker, that "the artist is a much more subtle and complicated machine than a camera",[207] and that, as he recorded in his lecture notes, novelists had been working "to present humanity in action on the background of the changing aspects of nature" since well before the advent of even still photography.[208] Even in 1918 Pound wrote that cinema, though it "asks for 'criticism'", "is not art": in "pantomime and in nothing else has the cinema any technique that a serious critic can consider."[209] In March 1912 he had made clear that cinema posed no threat to impressionist aesthetic practice, writing that care should be taken in defining impressionism as recording because

> [t]he cinematograph records, for instance, the 'impression' of any given action or place, far more exactly than the finest writing, it transmits the impression to its 'audiences' with less work on their part. A ball of gold and a gilded ball give the same 'impression' to the painter. Poetry is in some odd way concerned with the specific gravity of things, with their nature.[210]

The changes in the novels of Conrad and Ford suggest that instead of constituting an assault on the terrain of representation, cinema took a very different place in precipitating the rise of literary modernism. Cinema's newly institutionalised narrativity, in proposing a form of narrative that was popularly defined as entirely lacking a metalanguage, forced aesthetic practitioners to regard all literary metalanguage, *even* that of literary impressionism, as highly material. A literary mode that sought to erase the stable commentating metalanguage of realism in favour of the sensory experience of a human subject, impressionism was thrown into relief as a mere *alternative* metalanguage by comparison with cinema's own ostensibly non-linguistic form of narrativity. This was the basis of the two paths of disintegration taken by impressionism in *Victory* and *The Good Soldier*. With the disintegration of impressionism as a valid alternative to realism, the move to full-blown modernism was initiated. What becomes visible in these works written in 1913 and 1914 is the beginning of a materialising of metalanguage *as a language* that spread to all of the works we now call modernist. Admittedly Conrad and Ford reacted in two very different ways to this highlighting, by cinema's image-regime, of the materiality of even impressionism's metalanguage, but *Victory* and *The Good Soldier*, taken together, comprise the twin attitudes to literature—1) the deliberately inflated enacting of realist metalanguage *as a linguistic act* and 2) the replacement of stable metalanguage with the utterances of a consciousness—that were soon taken by Joyce, Woolf, H.D. and Richardson.

2   Cinema's Continuous Present and Modernist Temporality

> What the new technologies of vision allow one to see is a record of time.
> —Mary Ann Doane, *The Emergence of Cinematic Time*, 3.

> I see a cinematograph going on an on
> —James Joyce to Harriet Shaw Weaver,
> 27 June 1924, *Letters*, Gilbert, 216.

> Nothing happens. It is just life going on and on. It is Miriam Hender-
> son's stream of consciousness going on and on.
> —May Sinclair, 'The Novels of Dorothy Richardson', 444.

This chapter examines the formative influence that cinema's singular account of time exercised on the mechanics of 'high' modernist writing. It will also show that this modernist configuration of literary temporality led, in turn, to another major aspect of modernist form: the shift towards a combination of impersonal narration and interior monologue.

In her *The Emergence of Cinematic Time* (2002), Mary Ann Doane gives every reason to consider filmic temporality as just one small facet of the emergence, towards the end of the nineteenth century, of a heightened tangibility of time. The dense cluster of late nineteenth-century social developments amongst which cinema cohered, she points out, included the emergence, in popular thought, of time as a fourth dimension. Time came to be posited "as a particular object of knowledge within diverse disciplines and practices"[1] which included thermodynamics, evolutionary theory, physiology, archaeology, statistics, psychoanalysis and philosophy, all of which came to essay "the representability of time".[2] A more general change was also occurring in understandings of temporality under way in a range of modes of life: "Through its rationalization and abstraction, its externalization and reification in the form of pocket watches, standardized schedules, the organization of the work day, and industrialization in general, time becomes other, alienated."[3] On top of the world standardisation of time (resulting from widespread rail travel and telegraphy) in the last two decades of the nineteenth century came the refinement of the law of entropy in physics which dictated the "irreversible linearity"[4] of time, 'scientific management', which championed the notion of time-oriented labour over task-oriented labour (witness the introduction of the punch card in 1890), the large-scale order and temporal predictability of populations 'discovered' by the discourse of statistics and the operational time units discovered by inquiries into the speed at which nerve impulses are transmitted along various pathways. These were just some of the components of the widespread development of 'cinematic time', Doane's metaphor for "a quite precise historical trauma"[5] rather than a property solely of the cinematic apparatus. This sense of time was only participated in, and not precipitated, by cinema: "Although popular accounts tended to endow the cinema with determinant agency—that is, cinematic technology made possible a new access to time or its 'perfect' representation—in fact the emerging cinema participated in a more general cultural imperative, the structuring of time and contingency in capitalist modernity."[6] She argues that the new palpability of time specific to modernity was only "intimately allied" to the arrival of the time-based media of the cinematograph and the phonograph[7]: "The technological basis of the cinema incarnated the regimentation of time in modernity, its irreversibility."[8] The "new technologies" to which Doane alludes (see above)—the various chronophotographic techniques of the 1870s and 1880s plus the 'animated photography' of the 1890s, including the kinetoscope (which Edison's team, headed by William Kennedy-Laurie Dickson, developed between 1889 and 1893) and the many cameras and projectors developed during 1895 in the race for the projecting kinetoscope that gave us cinema—merely expressed and intensified a pre-existing impulse.

Doane provides thorough accounts of cinema's embeddedness in these shifts in notions of temporality. Cinema, she argues, does not present unique conflicts between the streaming of time in shifts and the rupturing of time by cuts, as it shared this treatment of time with scientific management.[9] Film was not characterised by a unique tension between an ability to represent contingency by rendering indeterminate time (anything can be filmed) and the sense of order which framing and the early editing out of 'dead time' suggested, as this tension between an emphasis on the indeterminate and the full meaningfulness of every event was also the conflict of statistics,[10] an "episteme of contingency" that was itself, she argues, crucial to the emergence of the representational technology of cinema.[11] The same was the case for the other conflicts endemic to 'cinematic time' she identifies: structure vs. event, determinism vs. chance and storage vs. legibility.

THE CONTINUOUS PRESENT

Of course, this new social perception of time can also be seen as one of the developments in the realm of ideas contemporary with the emergence of literary modernism and so as one of its generative forces. But was *nothing* specific to time as it was rendered by cinema? Doane states repeatedly that cinema enforced temporalities that had already arisen from major socio-technical-historical-philosophical changes of the nineteenth century, and makes a range of statements about how film was *used*, but largely keeps away from a theory of the form's singular temporality. This is not ill-considered, as patterns of thought embedded in economic changes tend to prove more realistic causes of changes in aesthetics than the 'ta-da!' of a new technological invention. For Doane this new sense of time was also 'cinematic' because it was the effect of "a historical pressure to rethink time in relation to its representability".[12] Her insight that cinema was in turn "crucial to thinking that [new] representability [of time]"[13] is the strongest statement she makes about cinema itself as a precipitating force for change in the thought underpinning aesthetic activity.[14]

Nonetheless Doane does imply that cinema rendered a very *particular* experience of the wider tangible time that she calls 'cinematic time'. She notes that although music and theatre operate in time, they are not time-based in the sense of temporal invariability, given that duration depends on the personnel involved, which is not the case with film.[15] Cinema is experienced on the basis of "its capacity to record/represent a duration unanchored and potentially without limits".[16] For Doane, "[a] single shot inevitably produces the effect of temporal continuity".[17] Cinema was not the first time-based technology. The phonograph, invented in November 1877 and patented in 1878, has the prior claim to that status. But cinema constituted a major expansion of popular experience of temporal invariability by extending the capacity to record time into the primary sense-domain of vision. While cinematic 'immersiveness' is often mystified, one of its chief aspects is that it depends for its specific quality on the rendering, in vision, of a time index. In May 1900, in the popular *Chambers's Journal*, in a commentary on possible uses for the cinematograph in teaching, a Mrs J.E. Whitby imagined contributions to instruction that could be made by the new technology, "by which moving reflections of the subject under consideration will be distinctly seen by all".[18] The use of the term 'reflection' to describe cinema's image type was quite common at the time. In Marie Corelli's 1900 novel *The Master-Christian*, the Cardinal argues for the existence of God: "The toy called the biograph, which reflects pictures for us in a dazzling and moving continuity, so that we can see scenes of human life in action, is merely a hint to us that every scene of every life is reflected in a ceaseless moving panorama *Somewhere* in the Universe, for the beholding of *Someone*".[19] Given that one of the connotations of 'reflection' is that the viewer is seeing an image of an event occurring at that precise moment, the tendency to use the term about cinema implies that as early as a mere four years after the emergence of cinema in Britain, it was apparent, albeit unconsciously, that cinema possesses the singular characteristic of operating in a continuous present.

This continuous present, occasionally noted by film and narrative historians and theorists,[20] is comprised of two aspects. First, film possesses a characteristic uniformity of text duration and plot duration: the amount of time that it takes for the text to occur is precisely the amount of time that it takes for the plot—that part of the story that is narrated—to occur. If narrative time passes, plot time is also perceived to pass, and so if no blatant evidence of temporal change is presented (for example a change from day to night), the next moment shown will be assumed by the viewer to be the next moment in plot time. This is in stark contrast to written narrative, for which the passing of narrative time does not automatically mean the passing of plot time. Seymour Chatman's analysis of temporality in writing and film, for example, finds that description (where narrative time continues but plot time stops) is "generally impossible in narrative films, . . . story-time keeps going as long as images are projected on the screen".[21]

As early as the late 1930s Jan Mukařovský was distinguishing between three different time registers present in writing, drama and film: plot time, the perceiving subject's time and "the temporal extent of the very work of art as a sign". While writing and drama reflect the plot time in their temporal extent, film, Mukařovský argues, "is the art where all three strata obtain equally, whereas in the narrative [writing] the stratum of plot time comes to the fore, and in the drama it is the stratum of the perceiving subject's time".[22] Film's characteristic uniformity of text duration and plot duration means that it is not characterised by the supremacy of any one of the three temporalities. In film, for Mukařovský, the three temporalities are tightly linked, whereas in writing, he argues, "the perceiving subject's localization is felt as a . . . present without temporal flow reflecting itself against the background of the elapsing past in which the plot takes place."[23] In prose, as plot duration is not tied to a concrete textual duration (given that textual duration is understood to be reader-dependent), writing is framed by the distinct presence of two temporalities, the temporality of the text never interfering with the basic comprehension of the temporality of the plot as a duration located in the past. Film's temporality, in contrast, is singular, and as no distinct narrative duration exists by which the plot's duration is organised as a past, film time has to organise itself. Doing so on the basis of the textual duration elapsing in the viewer's present, film renders a continuous present: any moment seen in a film is experienced as the moment occurring *after* the previously seen moment. In Figure 2.1, although the term 'meanwhile' is used in the subtitle, the "Film Drama" rescue depicted is only funny because each of these moments shown in series is assumed to happen one after the other. The joke does not work if the journey of the heroine is happening in the past of these moments that show the arrow's flight. This cartoon implies that, in film, any given plot moment is experienced as occurring immediately *after* the previously seen moment, because it is only funny that the woman on the horse is covering miles of ground while the arrow is in flight *if* we assume that the time each time we see her is the present and not some time in the past. The humour here therefore derives from the fact that there is actually *no* 'meanwhile', no return to the past of the 'story-NOW' already reached, possible in cinema's depiction of time.

IN THE NICK.

A THRILLING FILM DRAMA OF THE "MEANWHILE-THE-HEROINE" VARIETY.

Figure 2.1 A rescue "of the meanwhile-the-heroine variety", with humour derived from the assumption of an ongoing present, in *Punch* in July 1916.[24]

Because the concrete temporality of textual duration tends to dictate that plot duration relates to the film as a whole only as a continuous present, if any conflict between temporalities exists in film this is therefore likely to be a result of its photographic basis rather than any distinction between textual duration and plot duration. Sigfried Kracauer, André Bazin and Roland Barthes, for example, have all identified a temporality to photography: for Kracauer photography is instant pastness. Antiquated photography "represents what is utterly past, and yet this detritus was once the present."[25] That the photograph is 'of' the present means that it is actually experienced as a lost present, as the instant past: "When the [Kracauer's] grandmother stood in front of the lens, she was present for one second in the spatial continuum that presented itself to the lens. But it was this aspect and not the grandmother that was externalized."[26] For Barthes, the photograph establishes a consciousness of the *"having-been-there"* of the thing, an experience of "temporal anteriority", an experience of the object's existence that intensifies the fact of its existence in the past.[27] However, both Bazin and Barthes commented that while photography conveys a *past* tense, its transformation into film altered this. Bazin's famous summarising of cinema's temporality as *"la momie du changement"* is normally translated as "change mummified"[28]: i.e. the continuous present of a time-record clashing with a photograph's absolute pastness, cinema's ongoing present instantly backdated to the past. The temporality of cinema *may* therefore have been experienced as synthesising the structural past tense of the photograph with the perpetually present tense of cinematic narration/events.[29] But Marco Grosoli suggests a more literal translation: "the mummy of changement", not the mummification of change but the ever-changing mummy, which is implies presentness rather than instant pastness. In 1964 Barthes likewise commented that in cinema photography's instant pastness does not persist: "the distinction between film and photograph is not a simple difference of degree but a radical opposition . . . [f]ilm can no longer be seen as animated photographs". Instead photography's *"having-been-there* gives way before a *being-there* of the thing."[30] An implicit photographic past tense is revised by an implicit cinematographic present tense.

What I have been calling 'textual duration' is more commonly known as 'narrative duration'. To be precise, the three durations conventionally involved in any form of fiction are 1) narrative duration, 2) plot duration and 3) story duration, where 'plot' is the explicitly 'shown' events, and 'story' is the totality of 'shown' events *and* implied events. These distinct three durations of literary fiction become, in cinema, only two, because cinema (when it is presented *as* fiction) lacks any significant separation between narrative duration and plot duration. Of course a separation still exists in film between narrative duration and story duration, insomuch as the total duration of the story will be implied rather than shown in full, but the duration which *is* narrated—the plot duration—will be absolutely simultaneous with the narrative duration. As Richard Maltby remarks, in narrative cinema, "[a]t whatever point in a movie's story an event takes place, the audience always experiences it as being in the here and now of a continuous present."[31] Consequently, in the absence of content cues that force a viewer to understand any given film duration as prior to, or a repeat of, an earlier duration, the viewer's assumptions about temporality are cued by this uniformity of plot duration and narrative duration. Two shots that overlap temporally, for example, are experienced as jarring because, as André Gaudreault points out, "[e]xcept for rare occasions, time characteristically presses forward in cinema; even in flashback, time is felt as a *present*".[32] For example, a four-shot sequence made up of a shot of a fleeing convict, a shot of pursuing guards, another shot of the fleeing convict and another shot of the pursuing guards will appear, to the viewer, to describe a sequential arrangement of events, whereas in written narrative, an equivalent arrangement of serial scenes would not be accompanied by the same intrinsic insistence that time continues to pass in the stream of action not being narrated, meaning that an implicit 'meanwhile' is just as likely to inhere in each change of narrative location.

The second sense in which the time is always the present in film is the dearth of any formal equivalent to tenses. Although the ubiquity of the past tense in written narrative has given film viewers throughout film history a reason to consider filmic plot time as firmly in the past of the present in which the text is being unrolled to them, film itself has no formal equivalent to any of the past tenses, no way of denoting plot time as existing in the past of the act of narration. Cinema's particular indexicality, as many have remarked, is durational. It stores the experience of time. As Friedrich Kittler wrote in 1986, "[w]hat phonographs and cinematographs . . . were able to store was time".[33] When Kracauer, Bazin and Barthes all remarked on photography as a plethora of detail because of its lack of spatial discontinuity, they hinted at film's equivalent.[34] Kracauer, in his 1927 essay, remarked that, in a *photograph*, "[t]he spatial continuum from the camera's perspective dominates the spatial appearance of the perceived object."[35] Consequently, from the perspective of memory, with its ability to select, "photography appears as a jumble that consists partly of garbage."[36] The photograph, he writes, "captures only the residuum that history has discharged."[37] But whereas photography is a plethora of detail because of its lack of *spatial* discontinuity—its representation of a spatial continuum—cinema is plethoric in time, representing a *temporal* continuum in spite of possessing beginnings and endings both formal and incidental.

By providing an abstract experience of duration, film confronts the viewer not in the past tense but in the present tense of the viewing time. As Doane remarks, in film

[t]he image is the imprint of a particular moment whose particularity becomes indeterminable precisely because the image does not speak its own relation to time. Film *is*, therefore, a record of time, but a nonspecific, nonidentifiable time, a disembodied, unanchored time. The

cinema hence becomes the production of a generalized experience of time, a duration.[38]

In effect this means that cinema, in spite of being based on a recorded duration, tends not to render that duration as past in relation to narrative time. As Alain Robbe-Grillet remarked in 1962, in cinema "[t]he essential characteristic of the image is its present-ness. Whereas literature has a whole gamut of grammatical tenses which makes it possible to narrate events in relation to each other, one might say that on the screen verbs are always in the present tense."[39] In Figure 2.2, for example, the joke suggests that in generating a sense of an unbroken forward-moving continuous present, cinema rendered even the stage convention of temporal elision by scene-change a problem.

One aspect of film's absence of a tense system is that it cannot perform any equivalent of the shift from the simple past tense into the past perfect tense: it cannot shift into the story's own past. It cannot, for example, show one event and then show a second event that happened simultaneous with the first event, because the second event occurs in the

[*Life.*]
Mother (explaining moving picture): "Now they're landing in America."

Child: "How can they be, Mother? It's only five minutes since they left England."

Figure 2.2   Cartoon from the American magazine *Life*, 22 January 1914, reprinted in *Pictures and the Picturegoer* 6.6, 28 March 1914.[40]

past of the story-NOW already reached by the account of the first event. Indeed, whereas flashbacks have been seen as one of cinema's lendings to modernism,[41] what is overlooked in such assertions of literary modernist 'cinematicity' is that flashbacks were innovated in cinema (in roughly 1910) *because* cinema is only capable of using a present tense—they signal a shift into a character's memory as it is retrieved in the present, not a shift into a past tense.[42] Pointing out that "[i]t is commonplace to say that the cinema can only occur in the present time",[43] Chatman also notes that while cinema has "ways of indicating temporal changes in the story", "it is not clear whether these amount to anything like a 'grammar'" of verb tenses. Instead, he agrees with Christian Metz that it is more appropriate to consider them as a system of 'punctuation',[44] incapable of implying any temporal change other than the forward movement of 'and then'.

In strict contrast to conventional methods of narrating time in late-Victorian and Edwardian writing, which included the extensive use of formal moves into plot time already in the past of the story-NOW using the conjunction 'while' or the preposition 'before', film emerged as incapable of formal equivalents. Although intertitles could be, and were, used to indicate shifts into the story-PAST (for example, a simple 'MEAN-WHILE'), the intertitle was equivalent to a content cue rather than to a filmic past tense. Intertitles are not a textual aspect of film form; they are the form of one medium (i.e. print) 'remediated', to use Jay David Bolter and Richard Grusin's term, as the content of another (in this case film).[45] Intertitles with time cues were identifiable, for viewers, as content, equivalent to such content cues as the appearance, still living, of a character that died in previous story time, and distinct from filmic narrativity itself.

THE CONTINUOUS PRESENT DISINTEGRATED?

The capacity to render a duration provided a substantial component of cinema's amazement capacity in the first decade after 1895. It was heavily employed by the early practice of starting a film exhibition with a projection of the first frame as if it was a still photograph and then starting the film projector's motive mechanism. Indeed, even well after the end of the cinema of attractions, movement was stated as the essence of cinema. From a letter to a daily paper in 1912 that saw the proof of technological refinements in the cinematic apparatus in the fact that "the whole of the teeming movement of life is shown with absolute faith"[46] to E. Temple Thurston's 1918 case that movement was "the very groundwork of the art of the cinema",[47] movement was persistently figured in the 1910s as the essence of cinema. To valorise cinema as a representation of movement was to specify its indexical capacity as distinctively temporal.

But was this temporality historically specific? Whereas I have argued that cinema was only distinct as a historical entity from 1911, it seems that if there is one characteristic of the new medium that would have impacted upon literary practice before 1911 in a way *not* continuous with other visual technologies and entertainment practices, it is this unprecedented temporality. Nonetheless, the institutional reinvention in process by 1911 was instrumental in shaping the popular experience of cinema's particular temporality. At a basic level, the reinvention of cinema in a fictional mode at cinema's second birth resituated cinema's continuous present as a narrative one. As stated in Chapter 1, it was only when cinema was reinvented, re-discursified in a new set of parameters that broadly defined its "expressive and communicative potential"[48] *as fiction*, that cinema took responsibility for the description of time away from its presentational contexts.

In addition, cinema's temporality entered a new permutation in the period of the cinema of narrative integration. Doane argues that when film began to be used to construct its own temporality on the basis of edited shots (see Chapter 1), there followed a "reduction in the function of film as pure record of a time and a movement outside itself".[49] But this negative assessment follows from an assessment of post-1908 cinema as a bourgeois disappointment of earlier radical possibilities, rather than from the nature of the temporality of the cinema of narrative integration. In the 1895–1908 period, makers of multi-shot narrative films frequently used film as if it was capable of literary fiction's disjunctions between narrative time and plot time, its capacity for movements into the story's own past, drawing on the literary principle that its viewers would not automatically assume the next moment shown to be the next moment in the story-space. Disregarding cinema's implicit injunction against repeating plot duration, they would often reveal events, spaces and objects that could not be seen in shot 1 by showing the same stretch of time from a different position in shot 2. For example, edits in cinema *before* the rise of the race-to-the-rescue film in 1908 were commonly used to repeat story time. Gaudreault, examining shots 8 and 9 of the 1903 version of Edwin S Porter's Edison Company film *The Life of an American Fireman*, explains that the reason the event shown twice (the fireman carrying the woman out of the burning house and returning to get her baby, shown from the inside in shot 8 and from the outside in shot 9) takes much less time when it is seen from the inside of the room (the fireman arrives back in the room too quickly to have carried the woman to the ground, received her pleas to get the baby, and climbed back up the ladder) is because in the cinema of the 1895–1908 period, "the shot's objective is to present not a small *temporal* segment of the action but rather the totality of an action unfolding in an homogenous *space*. Between unity of point of view and unity of temporal continuity, the former takes precedent."[50] In those films of the 1895–1908 era that showed multiple simultaneous events, an operator with a single camera would film from multiple points of view by having the action performed several times and shooting it each time from a different position, but this would then be presented *as such* to an audience, rather than being subject to editing to simulate the temporality of a single event. For example, in Robert Paul's *Is Spiritualism A Fraud?* (1906), towards the end of shot 1, after the staged ghost scene is exposed when one of the participants turns on the light, other angry participants wrestle the man made up as a ghost out of the shot and return to the shot to pick up the sham medium (tied at his own instruction to a chair), stuff him into a chest, nail it shut and carry it out of a door at the back of the shot. Shot 2 begins in the ground floor hallway as the participants emerge into the shot, tumbling the chest down the stairs. They then pick up the chest and carry it out of the front door of the house. Shot 3, an exterior shot, begins with the man made up as a ghost running out of the front door and fleeing down the street, followed shortly afterwards by the participants carrying the chest. That is, the time in shot 3 begins even before the time denoted in shot 1 has elapsed. Hence while cinema may have been experienced by its viewers as a continuous present, film form in the kine-attractography period often contradicted this. While audiences would probably have understood the events of such pre-1908 time-repeating films, this was because content cues forced audiences to mentally rearrange the perceived temporal sequence of events, and so actually lessened their impression of a continuous present. As Doane admits, cinema's identity as a record of duration, for which the duration of its recounting and its occurrence were the *same*, was also undermined by the technique, common in the 1895–1908 period, of playing films in reverse.

Hepworth's *Rescued by Rover* (1905) constituted a watershed moment in the use of editing to emulate, in narrative, the continuous present that was perceived in film itself, signalling the beginning of a disappearance of temporal overlap from film form that intensified in 1907 and was complete by roughly 1908, as the anonymous re-editing of Porter's *The Life of An American Fireman* in c. 1908 to make the time the present—the film now replicating a temporal segment rather than a spatial segment—suggests.[51] While pre-1908 editing methods had openly contradicted the understanding that cinema's time is a continuous present, in continuity editing a system was established that *enforced* this understanding. A fictional time that, before 1908, featured the repetition of duration became, after 1908, a fictional time that mimicked the irreversible duration of real time. In addition, editing in camera, where the camera operator would merely stop winding during the less interesting parts of an event, and which therefore emphasised the lack of continuity in cinema's technological base, was virtually eradicated with the rise of the cinema of narrative integration.

While in 1907 the Vitagraph Company briefly made use of split frames to signal simultaneity, 1908 saw American Biograph spearhead the industry to institutionalise editing as the industry method for signalling *when* events occur in relation to each other. In the new cinema of narrative integration that followed, time was now both *rendered* in each shot through the movement of objects and *articulated* across shots though editing structures. Of course, fetishising editing as the semiotic mandate of cinema sells early cinema short, but there is a clear difference between time marked by the movement of bodies and objects *in* shots and time marked by articulations *between* shots. Both pre-1908 cinema and post-1908 cinema presented as a continuous present, but the nature of their presentnesses differed. Doane herself identifies the move from the dominance of the chase film in 1907 to the dominance of the race-to-the-rescue film in 1908–1909 as an intensification of a temporality: a move from "the insistent linearization of time" to "the dramatization of time".[52] This new system of continuity editing widely *manufactured* a temporality in a medium that had been designed to *record* a temporality. In describing Griffith's frequent and persistent use of cross-cutting (a crucial component of continuity editing) from 1908, Gaudreault points out that Griffith devoted himself to the rule that time always passes in film.[53] According to the principle of cross-cutting, film's point of view is not permitted to leave story strand A for story strand B, stay with strand B for some duration, and then return to the exact moment at which it left strand A: that is, the narrative cannot return to plot time that has already passed.

Doane argues that such narrative editing structures were part of cinema's domestication: "Born of the aspiration to represent or store time, the cinema must content itself with producing time as an effect".[54] But while time as dramatised by editing structures *may* have constituted an alteration of cinema's first temporal effects, the cinema of narrative integration far from recanted the continuous present of the unbroken shot. Whereas Mrs J.E. Whitby and Marie Corelli had *noted* cinema's continuous present in 1900, for contemporaries in the early 1910s, when cinema had emerged as defined by narrativity *and* as a distinct cultural realm in popular thought, the characteristic of the continuous present was both fundamental *and* systemic. Thus while cinema's continuous present confronted its viewers in both the kine-attractography and integrationist eras, in the 1911–1914 period when the newly narrational cinema was becoming familiar to viewers, it doubly enforced a continuous present.

In addition, as film discourse throughout the 1910s eradicated perceptions of the work involved in cinema as transformative (see Chapter 1), even the most ornately edited narratives attained the quality, in popular thought, of *precisely* the "pure record of a time and a movement outside itself" that Doane sees as confined to single-shot, unedited films.[55] Doane even nods to this, stating that although cinema

> moves from the status of a machine that amazes and astonishes through its capacity as a record of time and movement to a machine for the production of temporalities that mimic "real time" . . . the production of temporalities in the classical cinema is ultimately not separable from the idea of the image as a record of time outside itself.[56]

By erasing any distinction between recording and representation, film discourse of the 1910s also helped to motivate viewers to experience film's articulations of time in terms of recorded duration rather than fabrication. The articulations that make up a filmic story-space gave rise to a qualitatively different sense of the 'recorded' material that was nonetheless indistinct from pure recording: through "the inscription of temporality as an internal attribute",[57] editing structures produce, Doane agrees, "the image of a coherent and unified 'real time' that is much more 'real' than 'real time' itself".[58] Cross-cutting between two simultaneous scenes intensified temporal continuity by making time the primary axis on which the film existed. The cinema, Stephen Kern writes, "thickened the present".[59]

In describing the coherence resulting from the potential temporal *discontinuities* of editing in narrative cinema, film discourse of the 1910s suggests that the articulations of editing conveyed a *greater* sense of a continuous present. One October 1912 article in *The Pictures* remarked that

> [o]ne great advantage of the moving picture is its speed. I do not mean merely that there is a delay for scene shifting . . . But there is no delay for talk, and it is only when one is witnessing a film that one realises how unnecessary words generally are. Since the whole thing is action, the action proceeds. The author perhaps tells you that a thrilling incident happened in less time than he takes to tell it—and thereby condemns himself. The picture shows it to you in the same time.[60]

Descriptions of the writing techniques required by film's temporality suggest a popular, although unexpressed, recognition of film's continuous present. The journalist who advised readers, in a May 1913 scenario-writers' column, "not [to] commence the action any earlier in the history of your characters than is necessary to explain subsequent events", was not just emulating short story composition protocols. Maintaining that "photo-plays portray, not the lives of the characters, but one incident or train of connected incidents in those lives",[61] s/ he forbade the denoting of story time preceding plot time that a short story would employ the past perfect tense ("D and E had been child-hood sweethearts") to narrate. The time was to be the present.[62] That the newly narrational cinema's continuous present was at least uncon-sciously perceived by its contemporaries is also suggested by one Sep-tember 1912 article, which argued that the superiority of cinema lay in precisely its ability to create a proper impression of simultaneity by alternating between scenes instead of showing the two scenes whole and in sequence.[63]

This 'second ascendancy' of cinematic temporality—diegetic articu-lation enforcing its continuous present over and against auditorium time—would have intensified the experience of film's singular tempo-rality, placing cinema's continuous present more prominently in the minds of literary practitioners producing their own temporalities. The non-individual structural narrator of cinema described in Chapter 1 is defined by operating in real time, and the common modernist fantasy of growing a new organ—often a visual one[64]—is not just a version of infatuation with the aesthetics of the camera but can also be seen as a fantasy of incorporating a mode of vision *not* based in a person, itself the product of a perception of *temporality* not based in the human percep-tual array. In 1918, when likening Compton Mackenzie's writing to cin-ema, Woolf classified cinema as enforcing a temporality on its viewers. With Mackenzie's characters, "as in a cinema, one picture must follow another without stopping for if it stopped and we had to look at it we should be bored."[65] Woolf tellingly figured the break-down of cinema as the intruding of viewer temporality on the film. Her comment indicates film's dependence on plot duration remaining *indistinct* from the nar-rative duration experienced by its viewers (even when elliptical editing, in which periods of time are skipped, is used). This temporal aspect of cinema also sheds a very different light on one of the most frequently cited of modernism's auto-commentaries,[66] Pound's insistence, in 'Hugh Selwyn Mauberley', in June 1920, that

> The age demanded an image
> Of its accelerated grimace,
>
> . . .
>
> Not, not certainly, the obscure reveries
> Of the inward gaze;
> Better mendacities
> Than the classics in paraphrase!
>
> The 'age demanded' chiefly a mould in plaster
> Made with no loss of time,
> A prose kinema, not, not assuredly, alabaster
> Or the 'sculpture' of rhyme.[67]

Alluding to cinema as incurring 'no loss of time' did *not* suggest that a medium presented to its viewers as *fast*. Pound's 'no loss of time' implicitly cited the parity of plot duration with narrative duration, the continual relation of presentness between the act of narration and story events, with no pause in one while the other continued, demanded not by the age but by cinema. On 10 August 1916 Joseph Conrad also hinted at his sense of cinema when he informed John Quinn that "[a]ll your suggestions will be carried out. . . . But I am not going to run my life like a cinema-film regardless of anything but time to please anybody's temperamental idiosyncrasy".[68] That is, for Conrad, film was characterised by a continuous (indeed, here, rushing) forward movement, a continuous present. In 1921 W.B. Yeats wrote—when arguing that although it was his choice to write in what historical style he wished, it was not necessary to try to recover "the first simplicity" by turning back time—that he "need not reverse the cinematograph".[69] For him the 'cinematographic' encompassed the preservation of a duration, and the cinematograph's present was also the present of its observer: it was experienced as a continuous present. These mentions suggest that even if cinema's time sense was not easily articulated, at least some modernists found it tangible.

MODERNIST TIME

What changes in literary practice were wrought by this time sense? The 'Wandering Rocks' chapter of Joyce's *Ulysses*, first written during January and February 1919 (published in the June and July 1919 issues of the *Little Review*) and revised, along with the rest of *Ulysses*, during the proof stage between 11 June 1921 and 30 January 1922,[70] which has been the subject of more accounts of the impact of cinema on Joyce than any other aspect of the book, can shed significant light on modernist literary form, although *not* via the 'cinematicity' usually ascribed to it. The chapter is comprised of 19 discrete sections, throughout 15 of which Joyce distributed 32 interpolations of short pieces of narration concerning events at some distance from the locales concerned by the narrative into which they interpolated (the interpolations were added at the proof stage). 13 of these interpolations are used to link section 1 (which narrates Father John Conmee's journey from the presbytery of St Francis Xavier's Church in Upper Gardiner St. to the O'Brien Institute for Destitute Children in Artane, interpolated elsewhere three times) with section 19 (which narrates the viceregal cavalcade's journey from the viceregal lodge in Phoenix Park to the Mirus bazaar on the Royal Dublin Society Showground in Ballsbridge, interpolated elsewhere three times) via eight of the intervening 17 shorter sections (sections 2, 4, 5, 7, 8, 9, 11 & 12, between them interpolated elsewhere seven times in total). These moments appear in interpolated form both after and before they appear in their 'original' section

(10 before and three after). The remaining 19 interpolations include six referring to streams of action covered by another section but to events occurring
either before the action narrated in that section commences or after the action
narrated in that section ends, and a further 13 interpolations which refer to
streams of action that are not the subject of a discrete section (comprising nine
additional streams of action in total).

The chapter's use of sections and the 32 interpolated 'shots' have both
been called 'montage'. Keith Cohen claimed in 1979 that even the first readers of *Ulysses* had noted the "montage" effect of the chapter.[71] Arguing that
"'Wandering Rocks' was inspired by the cinema", Kern calls the chapter
"a montage of nineteen sections".[72] Robert Humphrey refers to its use of
interpolations as "a superb example of space-montage",[73] and Ian Gunn &
Mark Wright continue to exemplify the notion that "the interpolations in
the 'Wandering Rocks' episode reflect Sergei Eisenstein's remark on montage *'that two film pieces of any kind, placed together, inevitably combine
into a new concept, a new quality, arising out of that juxtaposition'*".[74] But
to describe either the sequential presentation of 19 sections whose action
occurs roughly simultaneously or the 32 interpolations within them as
'montage' is an error, as film montage is defined as the intentional juxtaposition, in time, of two shots with *no* clear spatial or temporal relation to each
other, a *disruption* of expectations of continuity in both space and time.[75]
Even when the term 'montage' was first being imported into discourse on
film by the Soviet film theorists of the 1920s, it was defined as the join-
ing together of diverse fragments to create an impression out of collision.
Eisenstein defined montage as "[t]he simplest juxtaposition of two or three
details of a material series [that] produces a perfectly finished representation of another order, the psychological", the rendering of "disintegrated
phenomena".[76] He was insistent in this description in his 1929 'Beyond the
Shot': "Collision. Conflict between two neighbouring fragments. Conflict.
Collision. . . . Montage is conflict."[77]

In 'Wandering Rocks', Joyce *did* use a formal literary equivalent of a
particular film editing structure in creating and placing the 32 interpolations, but this was not montage but cross-cutting, a structure of alternation
between multiple simultaneous streams of action, in which time always
passes in stream A while the narrative is showing stream B.[78] Not only does
cross-cutting *not* violate a spatio-temporal continuum, it is operative in
forming one, and it comprised a major component of the cinema of narrative integration. The principle of interpolating into one section a short piece
of action not visible from the viewpoint of any character in the current section, and doing so to show that the two pieces of action are happening at
almost exactly the same time, echoed cinema's narration of time via cross-
cutting. In fact, 'Wandering Rocks' *exclusively* uses a literary equivalent
of cinema's technique for specifying that certain events are happening at
the same time, these instances of literary cross-cutting together generating
a relatively precise time frame in which a total of 28 distinct simultaneous
streams of action occur. Figure 2.3 shows this scheme of interpolations.

Section	Interpolation	Temporal relation
1 Father Conmee	1 Mr Denis J. Maginni . . . Dignam's Court. (282)	*True intercutting (extra stream a)*
2 Corny Kelleher	2 Father Conmee . . . Newcomen Bridge. (288)	'Repeated' intercutting (after 'original'; 1)
	3 a generous white arm . . . forth a coin. (288)	'Repeated' intercutting (before 'original'; 3)
3 One-legged sailor	4 J.J. O'Molloy's . . . with a visitor. (289)	True intercutting (from 8)
4 Katey & Boody Dedalus	5 Father Conmee . . . stubble. (290)	'Repeated' intercutting (after; 1)
	6 The lacquey . . . Barang! (290)	'Repeated' intercutting (before; 11)
	7 A skiff . . . George's quay. (291)	*True intercutting (extra; b)*
5 Boylan	8 A darkbacked figure . . . hawker's cart. (291)	'Repeated' intercutting (before; 9)
6 Stephen Dedalus	None	-
7 Miss Dunne	9 The disk shot down . . . ogled them: six. (294)	'Repeated' intercutting (before; 9)
	10 Five tallwhitehatted . . . they had come. (294)	*True intercutting (extra; c)*
8 Lambert & Love; Lambert & O'Molloy	11 From a long face . . . chessboard. (296)	'Repeated' intercutting (before; 16)
	12 The young woman . . . clinging twig. (296)	'Repeated' intercutting (after; 1)
9 Lenehan & McCoy	13 Lawyers of the past . . . great amplitude. (297)	*True intercutting (extra; d)*
	14 The gates . . . viceregal cavalcade. (299)	'Repeated' intercutting (before; 19)
	15 Master Patrick . . . porksteaks. (300)	*True intercutting (from 18)*
	16 A card . . . Eccles street. (300)	*True intercutting (from 3)*
10 Bloom	17 On O'Connell bridge . . . dancing &c. (302)	*True intercutting (extra; a)*
	18 An elderly female . . . Corporation. (303)	*True intercutting (extra; d)*
11 Simon & Dilly Dedalus	19 Bang of the lastlap . . . College Library. (304)	*True intercutting (extra; e)*
	20 Mr Kernan . . . James's street. (305)	'Repeated' intercutting (before; 12)
	21 The viceregal cavalcade . . . Parkgate. (306)	'Repeated' intercutting (before; 19)

(continued)

Figure 2.3 Scheme of interpolations in 'Wandering Rocks'.[79] Extra streams of action (i.e. those comprised only of interpolations and not narrated as a discrete section): a) Denis Maginni, b) the throwaway, c) H.E.L.Y.'S sandwichmen, d) elderly female, e) Trinity College bicycle race, f) Denis Breen, g) two old women, h) Cashel Boyle O'Connor Fitzmaurice Tisdall Farrell, i) the Revd. Hugh C. Love after he leaves St Mary's Abbey.

Section	Interpolation	Temporal relation
12 Tom Kernan	22 Hello, Simon . . . stopping. (308)	'Repeated' intercutting (before; 14)
	23 North Wall . . . is coming. (308)	*True intercutting (extra; b)*
	24 Denis Breen . . . Collis and Ward. (309)	*True intercutting (extra; f)*
13 Stephen & Dilly	25 Two old women . . . cockles rolled. (310–11)	*True intercutting (extra; g)*
	26 Father Conmee . . . vespers. (311)	*True intercutting (from 1)*
14 Simon Dedalus & Cowley	27 Cashel Boyle . . . Kildare Street Club. (314)	*True intercutting (extra; h)*
	28 The reverend Hugh . . . Ford of Hurdles. (315)	*True intercutting (extra; i)*
15 Cunningham & Power	29 Bronze by gold . . . Ormond hotel. (316)	'Repeated' intercutting (before; 19)
	30 Outside *la Maison Claire* . . . liberties. (317)	*True intercutting (from 5)*
16 Mulligan & Haines	31 The onelegged . . . *England Expects.* . . (320)	*True intercutting (from 2)*
	32 Elijah, skiff . . . with bricks. (321)	*True intercutting (extra; b)*
17 Artifoni/Farrell	None	
18 Patrick Dignam	None	
19 Viceregal Cavalcade	None	

Figure 2.3 (continued)

However, to conclude that Joyce used a literary equivalent of cross-cutting in 'Wandering Rocks' proves nothing about cinema's place in originating literary modernism. 'Wandering Rocks' is just one of 18 chapters in *Ulysses*, the chapter with the least action relevant to the drama of the story—Stephen Dedalus feeling a renewed sense of remorse for not praying for his dying mother on meeting his sister Dilly and Boylan's purchase of expensive treats for Molly constituting the chapter's most significant story events—and also contains the slightest Homeric allusion of all the chapters: after telling Odysseus how to pass the Sirens, Circe tells Odysseus not to take the passage between the wandering rocks as they will smash together and crush his ship,[80] and he does, taking instead the route between Scylla and Charybdis. As Joyce does not use this technique anywhere else in the novel, it might seem that only 'Wandering Rocks', not *Ulysses*, and certainly not modernism as a whole, bears the influence of cinema. If cinema is the basis *only* of 'Wandering Rocks', then 'cinema' is just the more accurate name for the "mechanics" which, according to both the Linati and Gilbert schemas, provided the 'art' for this chapter, and cross-cutting is just the more accurate name for the "labyrinth" technique which both schemas also agree on, again just one of the 18 techniques openly cited by Joyce as the technical bases of the work, and, notably, a technique on which he *consciously* drew in his search for methods of literary experimentation.[81] Cinema is, if cited as the basis of modernism in this guise, just, as David Bradshaw opines, one entry in a lengthy catalogue of secondary and minor influences on the emergence of the form.[82]

That Joyce uses cross-cutting in 'Wandering Rocks' is therefore virtually irrelevant. However, much more relevant to the origins of modernism is *why* he uses it. The answer lies in the reason why film-makers themselves had come to employ the technique of cross-cutting. In his research into the date at which cross-cutting (it is often incorrectly called 'parallel editing', defined as intercutting between two non-simultaneous streams of action) was invented in the US, Gaudreault has discovered that Edison/Porter's 1903 *The Great Train Robbery* was widely misunderstood by contemporary audiences.[83] Using the following possible synopses of the events in the film, and judging from the fact that modern-day audiences will agree that synopsis A is an accurate description of the action in the film, he has concluded that the vast majority of the film's 1903 audiences would have concluded the same also.

A

As the train pulls into the station, four bandits attack the telegraph operator and knock him unconscious. Having tied him up they board the train which has stopped to take on water. When it is once again in motion, two of them hold up the mail car while the other two take control of the locomotive and halt the train. The passengers are forced off the train and robbed at gunpoint. The bandits return to the locomotive, which has been uncoupled from the rest of the train, and use it to reach their horses, which await them in the underbrush. They then continue their getaway on horseback. *At this moment* the telegraph operator *revives* and *is untied*. He runs to warn the posse-to-be, who *are dancing* in a saloon. Hearing of the robbery all dash out in pursuit. *Shortly afterwards* the bandits are overtaken by the posse and shot dead as they divide the loot.

B

As the train pulls into the station, four bandits attack the telegraph operator and knock him unconscious. Having tied him up they board the train which has stopped to take on water. When it is once again in motion, two of them hold up the mail car while the other two take control of the locomotive and halt the train. The passengers are forced off the train and robbed at gunpoint. The bandits return to the locomotive, which has been uncoupled from the rest of the train, and use it to reach their horses, which await them in the underbrush. They then continue their getaway on horseback. *In the meantime* the telegraph operator *has been revived* and *untied*. He *has run* to warn the posse-to-be, *who were* dancing in a saloon. Hearing of the robbery, they *had set out* in pursuit, and, returning to the present, the bandits are overtaken by the posse who have caught up with them by now, and shot dead as they divide the loot.[84]

Explaining that minor pieces of evidence in the film (a clock and the time taken to cover certain distances on horseback) actually indicate that the intended synopsis of the film was B (the two streams of events—first the train robbery and second the revival of the operator and the forming of and pursuit by the posse—happen largely simultaneously), Gaudreault argues that the fundamental misunderstanding—that the two streams of events are understood to happen consecutively—occurs because "cinematic time is always perceived as the present".[85] Because the film's two simultaneous streams of action are shown consecutively, the perception of cinematic time as a continuous present means that they are perceived to *occur* consecutively. In the absence of any mechanism for denoting a return in time to an earlier event to narrate an occurrence simultaneous with an occurrence already narrated, audiences were unable to understand that the second stream of action was meant to occur in the past tense, mainly because of cinema's unique continuous present.

The tendency amongst viewers to misunderstand this and contemporary films was so problematic as to constitute one of the motives for the eventual introduction of the technique of cross-cutting into general film practice. This innovation occurred in spite of the fact that cross-cutting can be construed as a drastic jump from one place to another. Cross-cutting was also introduced only with the aid of stories that used communications via telephones and telegraphs to iterate dramatic links between multiple, geographically distant locations, links that explained the potential disjunctions created by editing. In compliance with the dictates of cinema's continuous present, events occurring simultaneously were shown to be simultaneous through alternating between two unvarying time streams.[86]

The same logic determines the narration of 'Wandering Rocks'. Joyce subscribed to the maxim that the only way to denote that multiple streams of events are occurring simultaneously is to state them, as near as possible, *at the* same time: in the case of 'Wandering Rocks' by stating again a piece of the stream of action already featured. And Joyce did not emulate the technique of cross-cutting because he liked cinema. He used it because he had elected, since moving from writing *A Portrait of the Artist as a Young Man* to writing *Ulysses* in late 1914, to commit to the idea that plot time must always be the present, meaning that all literary ways of stating that two actions occur simultaneously, ways that delve into plot time that has already passed, were off-limits, leaving a literary equivalent of cross-cutting as the *only* way of showing that multiple streams of action are occurring simultaneously. According to this new maxim, if certain story events are happening at the same time as other story events described by the narrative, the only way that this simultaneity can be iterated is the way that cinema iterates it, by stating action so that the reader *experiences* both lines of actions as happening at the same time—in the case of 'Wandering Rocks' this means stating a piece of the 'earlier' stream of action again. In section 9, instead of writing, after "Tom Rochford took the top disk from the pile he clasped against his claret waistcoat", 'just as Miss Dunne was rolling the sheet of gaudy notepaper into her typewriter, Tom Rochford's disc shot down the groove etc., which would mean designating section 9 as starting at a point in the plot duration already narrated and so repeating some of that duration, Joyce states the two durations at the same time, by interpolating a part of Tom Rochford's experiment with the machine from section 9 into the account of Miss Dunne's work in section 7 (interpolation 9).

Indeed, this maxim was not restricted to 'Wandering Rocks'. Plot time across the whole of *Ulysses* is virtually always the present, always compelled to pass as long as narrative time is passing, the narrative never moving the story-NOW into the past of a previous plot moment. Joyce told Jacques Mercanton that in *Ulysses* "there is not past, no future; everything flows in an eternal present."[87] For example, in 'Lestrygonians', when Bloom uses the toilet in Davy Byrne's and then leaves first the toilet and then the pub, the narrative stays with the other men in the pub, hearing their conversations about Bloom, and then rejoins Bloom, but, notably, *not* at the moment in plot time when Bloom left the bar (which is now in the story-PAST) but at a time when he is some distance away down Duke Street, indicating that the passing of narrative time, for Joyce, entailed the passing of plot time.[88] For the first 11 of the 18 chapters of *Ulysses*, and for virtually all of the last seven, the 'story-NOW' is a continuous present. The multiple streams of action in 'Sirens'—the events that occur in the street and the gathering in the bar of the Ormond Hotel—are all narrated in a continuous present, with time always passing in the stream of action not currently being narrated while the narrative attends to the other stream. The same is the case for the narration of the simultaneous events in the Star of the Sea church and on Sandymount strand in 'Nausicaa'.

Indeed, it is remarkable that this work, in which six of the 18 chapters ('Cyclops', 'Nausicaa', 'Oxen of the Sun', 'Circe', 'Eumaeus' and 'Ithaca'—chapters 12–17 of 18) included significant segments of literary parody, features the past perfect tense—e.g. 'he had placed the rock on the bench three days previously'—with its moving back in plot temporality while narrative temporality continues, just a handful of times. Some of the parodies interspersed in 'Cyclops'—such as the description of the Citizen's handkerchief[89]—do include the disparity between narrative time and plot time involved in description (where plot time stops while narrative time continues), but only as the subject of parody—hence they are deliberately rendered in contrast to this chapter's anonymous narrator's unified narrative and plot duration. Remarkably, even *his* narrative only reverts to a 'story-NOW' previous to his own progressing narrative duration in two brief instances.[90] The sentimental fiction satirised in the first half of 'Nausicaa' does include description and plot duration previous to narrative duration using the past perfect tense,[91] but not only are these the subject of parody, every paragraph then fades into either Gerty's interior monologue or third-person narration focalised in her, both in a continuous present. The parodies of 'Oxen of the Sun' and the clichés parodied in 'Eumaeus' include just four and six brief instances respectively of reversions to previous plot time, again as part of the forms being parodied.[92] In spite of the disparities between narrative temporality and plot temporality characterising the literary modes he thoroughly emulated to so thoroughly parody, Joyce maintained an almost exclusive simultaneity of narrative duration and plot duration: he seems to have found it almost impossible to depart, even in these parodies, from the narrative maxim that the time must always be the present. In line with the dictates of cinema's simultaneity of narrative duration and plot duration, the only part of *Ulysses* where description (usually involving a pausing of plot time) is openly provided is the chapter based on a linguistic method in which the language is not narrative and so has *no* duration *as* narrative: the catechism of 'Ithaca'. Although these last seven chapters after 'Sirens' have been described as composing a different work from the first 10 chapters of *Ulysses*,[93] the two extremes of stylistic variation they contain—'Circe' and 'Penelope', the play script and the pure internal monologue—are also nonetheless uniform in that they still render uniform plot duration and narrative duration.

That Joyce used the past perfect tense in his earliest written chapter—'Telemachus', first written before June 1915—but then took pains to stress that this described a memory occurring in the 'story-NOW', suggests the dominance of cinema's continuous present from the point in late 1914 when he began writing the work in earnest. Stephen discusses his refusal to pray for his mother with Mulligan and then Mulligan starts shaving: "Silently, in a dream she had come to him after her death, her wasted body within its loose brown graveclothes giving off an odour of wax and rosewood, her breath, that had bent upon him, mute, reproachful, a faint odour of wetted ashes."[94] Later, as Mulligan leaves him, he remembers again: "In a dream, silently, she had come to him, her wasted body within its loose graveclothes giving off an odour of wax and rosewood, her breath bent over him with mute secret words, a faint odour of wetted ashes."[95] The slight variation of phrasing indicates that these phrasings report Stephen's own thoughts and therefore that the 'had' summarises his experience of pastness in the 'story-NOW' rather than a narrator's movement into the story-PAST.

In Joyce's *A Portrait of the Artist as a Young Man*, written between January 1904 and late 1914, it is not unusual for the narrator to use the past continuous tense: "The plump bald sergeant major was testing with his foot the springboard of the vaulting horse."[96] By the time of writing *Ulysses* between 1914 and 1921, however, instead of *Portrait*'s past continuous ("was testing"), the narrator almost exclusively uses the simple past, as in this from 'Hades' (written c. April 1918): "A team of horses passed from Finglas with toiling plodding tread, dragging through the funereal silence a creaking waggon on which lay a granite block. The waggoner marching at their head saluted."[97] By the time of writing *Ulysses* the explicit pastness and uncertain duration of the past continuous tense had become intolerable, and was largely replaced by the presentness-at-that-time of the simple past tense, even when the former would be appropriate: "Grossbooted draymen rolled barrels dullthudding out of Prince's stores and bumped them up on the brewery float."[98] The past continuous narrates something which at that time in the story had been occurring for some of the story's own past already, and which existed in the past of the story-NOW, whereas the simple past implies that the time in the story-NOW was a continuous present.

Indeed, the only point in *Ulysses* when Joyce significantly suspended the maxim that the time must be the present was 'Wandering Rocks', where in organising the temporally simultaneous sections in series Joyce made a number of small forays into plot time that had already passed. Even here though, Joyce quickly returned to the continuous present: while he made the method of 'Wandering Rocks' apparent to the reader via the use, in 11 of the sections, of 13 'shots' which the reader would recognise from other sections, the act of interpolating a phrase or sentence appearing elsewhere in the chapter, which I have called 'repeated' intercutting (see Figure 2.3), is actually the chapter's *less* used type of intercutting. Of the 32 interpolations in 'Wandering Rocks', 19 are 'true' intercutting, where the interpolated phrase is not duplicated elsewhere in the chapter. These do not carry the implicit specification that the current section exists at the same time as a section narrated previously or subsequently, i.e. that it exists in the story-PAST or story-FUTURE. First figuratively holding up unbroken strips of film and scattering pieces of them through the subsequent sections to show simultaneity, Joyce then quickly shifted to showing action *only* in cross-cutting, the act of repeating a tiny piece of duration in the name of not generally repeating duration gradually transforming into the total parity of plot and narrative duration as he quickly returned to full adherence to the maxim that the time must be the present. I therefore find it impossible to support the common argument, as presented by Ruth Perlmutter, that the impact of cinema on Joyce was to generate in *Ulysses* a text where "[a] complex exchange between listeners and narrators, between direct discourse and the indirect language of inner experience (or sensual thinking) dismantles the spatial and temporal flow".[99]

'Repeated' intercutting in 'Wandering Rocks' does have the purpose of giving time clues that make it possible to work out *when* un-clocked events happen, whereas 'true' intercutting does not provide information about how much time has elapsed between, for example, the lacquey ringing his handbell the first time (interpolation in section 4) and the second time (opening of section 11). On the other hand, there is *some* precision to clock time in 'true' intercutting. When an interpolation in section 9 (number 15) shows Patrick Dignam coming out of Mangan's butcher on the corner of William St and Wicklow St,[100] the fact that by section 18 he has only reached Ruggy O'Donohoe's International Bar, on the opposite corner of the crossroads from Mangan's butcher, shows that section 18 begins only seconds after Lenehan and M'Coy begin their conversation on Wellington Quay in section 9. Likewise, when, in section 7, Miss Dunne writes the date at the head of a letter, the following interpolation of the H.E.L.Y.'S sandwichmen passing Monypeny's corner[101] indicates that, as this corner is just a few metres on from Tangier Lane, where they were seen by Blazes Boylan in section 5, Dunne is writing this less than a minute after Boylan was walking "here and there in new tan shoes about the fruitsmelling shop",[102] as confirmed by her then receiving the phone call he went to place while there. Indeed, these markers of time are part of what Clive Hart calls this chapter's "fully determined" spatio-temporal pattern.[103]

This commitment to a continuous forward-moving literary present even shaped the micro-level of sentence construction. One of the characteristic sentence constructions in *Ulysses* is the immediate adverb. Although not used exclusively, it is ubiquitous, appearing soon after the opening of the first chapter: After Mulligan is joined by Stephen at the parapet of the Martello tower, "[h]e turned abruptly his great searching eyes from the sea to Stephen's face."[104] Another example occurs, when, over breakfast, Stephen and Mulligan discuss washing, and Haines interjects from the corner where "he was knotting easily a scarf about the loose collar of his tennis shirt".[105] Although, in standard construction, adverbs normally follow immediately after verbs when that verb does not have an object, in sentences with objects, adverbs are normally placed after the object: "He turned his great searching eyes abruptly from the sea to Stephen's face", and "he was knotting a scarf easily about the loose collar of his tennis shirt". By departing from this standard construction and placing adverbs immediately after verbs, Joyce refused to split the clarification of the nature of the action from the action itself, as even the separation between the two involved in standard sentence constructions implied the passing of time, making the adverb a narratorial return to a slightly earlier moment in plot time.[106]

The sentence describing Haines's scarf-knotting is also typical of another syntactical peculiarity of *Ulysses*: "Haines from the corner where he was knotting easily a scarf about the loose collar of his tennis shirt spoke: /—I intend to make a collection of your sayings if you will let me." Between the subject "Haines" and the predicator "spoke" a relative clause is inserted ("from the corner where he was knotting easily a scarf about the loose collar of his tennis shirt"), in spite of the vastness of this relative clause (as emphasised by having the relative clause integrated rather than supplementary (i.e. it is not embedded between commas), and in spite of having to place the preposition "from" far from the verb on which it is dependent so that it follows only the sentence's subject "Haines", where the preposition "from" normally either has to succeed a subject *and* a predicate—'Haines spoke from the corner where he was knotting a scarf easily about the loose collar of his tennis shirt:'—or neither in anticipation of both coming later: 'From the corner where he was knotting a scarf easily about the loose collar of his tennis shirt, Haines spoke:'. Joyce sought, albeit unconsciously, to avoid periods of narrative time which did not denote the passing of plot time. By embedding the relative clause between subject and predicate, extra detail (Haines is dressing at the moment) is given within the statement of action (Haines speaks) rather than given after or before, where narrative time would be passing with no connotation of the passing of plot time. Both of these sentence constructions enforced syntactically the presentness that Joyce sought to maintain throughout *Ulysses'* rendering of temporality.

The narratorial agent of the non-parodic chapters of *Ulysses* is almost entirely without subjectivity, yet the placing of interpolations in 'Wandering Rocks' does nonetheless serve to comment. For example, interpolation 28 in section 14, which shows that Reverend Hugh C Love is passing James and Charles Kennedy's rectifiers just before Ben Dollard, on Ormond Quay, asks Love's tenant Father Cowley who his landlord is, implicitly iterates the nature of the relationship between the two. The commentary on social connections that had been embedded in realist narrative was thus not entirely absent from *Ulysses*. Clive Hart has tabulated the purpose of almost all of the interpolations. Interpolation 1, for example, performs "ironic physical contrast". Conmee is walking east along the north side of Mountjoy Square on his journey to see if he can get Patrick Dignam placed in the O'Brien Institute for Destitute Children:

> Father Conmee smiled and nodded and smiled and walked along Mountjoy square east.
> Mr Denis J. Maginni, professor of dancing, &c., in silk hat, slate frockcoat with silk facings, white kerchief tie, tight lavender trousers, canary gloves and pointed patent boots, walking with grave deportment most respectfully took the curbstone as he passed lady Maxwell at the corner of Dignam's court.
> Was that not Mrs M'Guinness?
> Mrs M'Guinness, stately, silverhaired, bowed to Father Conmee from the farther footpath along which she smiled.[107]

As Hart comments, neither Conmee, attending the affairs of the Dignam family, nor the interpolated Maginni, passing the corner of Dignam's court, "is especially involved in 'Dignam'."[108] Likewise, when Lenehan is preparing to tell M'Coy about how he groped Molly Bloom in a carriage on the way back from the Glencree reformatory annual dinner, a 'shot' of Molly restoring the card into the window in 7 Eccles St foreshadows whom his story will concern. Both of these are examples of the use of interpolations to highlight juxtaposition, but even though the uses to which these inter-polations are put might therefore be said to anticipate montage as used in film, the interpolations themselves are not montage since they maintain spatio-temporal continuity, moving the point of view in space but not troubling the sense of a unified story-space by disrupting the continuous present. Indeed, just as Soviet innovators of montage-as-collision sought to establish meaning in film from exclusively non-spatio-temporal links between two shots precisely *because* of the strength of the assumption of spatio-temporal continuity that film encouraged its viewers to bring to shot-to-shot edits, Joyce was impelled to add a secondary layer of non-spatio-temporal commentary to the joins he created in literature only *because* his commitment to the principle of temporal continuity meant that a primary layer of spatio-temporal continuity automatically existed in his 'edits'.

Indeed, the same principle underpins the other major instance of quick-change focalisation: the 'baton-changes' of focalisation in Woolf's *Mrs Dal-loway* (written between October 1922 and October 1924, revised by the end of 1924 and published on the 14 May 1925), which move the point of view in space but not in time, permitting commentary via juxtaposition *because* the primacy of time as the work's main axis means that normal spatial proximity (between two characters, for example) becomes a less determining character-istic of the story-space, the narrative 'viewpoint' only bound to *move* in time. Indeed, a continuous forward-moving literary present also characterises all of *Mrs Dalloway* (see below), as well as H.D.'s *Asphodel* (written between 1921 and 1922, revised in c. 1926 and only posthumously published). For example, the very few uses of the past perfect tense in *Asphodel* (the only suggestions of disparity between narrative temporality and plot temporal-ity in the entire text) are nonetheless used in focalised narration to report thought, H.D. making clear that each 'had' is Hermione's own recollection in the ongoing present: "Someone had met someone. Who? Darrington had met Hermione."[109] In addition, although the principle of a continuous liter-ary present was not in place in the first of Richardson's *Pilgrimage* novels, *Pointed Roofs* (written and revised between October 1912 and early 1913 but not published until September 1915), it gradually began to be enforced as the series progressed (see below). Indeed, a continuous literary present is a major aspect of all of the major literary works produced in the UK that have attracted the label 'stream of consciousness'.

One major ramification of the 'high' modernist commitment to a con-tinuous present is that the narrators of these works have *no memory*: any-thing that happened before the plot duration covered in *Ulysses*, *Asphodel* and *Mrs Dalloway* (and increasingly as the series progresses, Richardson's *Pilgrimage* novels) 'occurs' only as recalled memories on the part of the characters: i.e. in the continuing story-NOW. An amnesiac narrator has no ability to depart the onward-moving continuous present of plot duration for another point in the plot duration. In the later 'stream of consciousness' works, in an intensification of the continuous present narrator-NOW of Ford Madox Ford's *The Good Soldier* (which produced an a-chronological story-NOW), this unvarying continuous present unifies the duration of narration and plot. When, in 'Calypso', Bloom finds that he has left his key in the pocket of his other pair of trousers, instead of a narratorial statement that in the story's own past he had put them there, which would move the story-NOW back to a previous point in plot time while narrative time continued moving forward, this story fact exists only in the continuing present of ongoing plot time: "On the doorstep he felt in his hip pocket for the latchkey. Not there. In the trousers I left off."[110] The amnesiac narrative voice of much of *Ulysses* conveys this synchronisation of plot duration and narrative duration into a continuous present. This is why, as Hart writes of 'Wandering Rocks', "[n]early everything is presented as if seen for the first time. 'A onelegged sailor' in Conmee's section [1] is still 'A onelegged sailor' (not '*The* onelegged sailor') when he reappears in section 3."[111] Father Conmee is almost always "the very reverend John Conmee S.J." This is not a *historical* present; modernism did still set its story-NOW in the past of the narrator-NOW. But it was a temporal present: in this grouping of 'high' modernist texts, narrative time and plot time are always to remain uniform.

By contrast, in realist literature the planes of 1) narrative, 2) plot and 3) story were perceived to have no necessary temporal synchronisation. These were loosely linked, but as temporal plains remained distinct. As with its relations between object language and metalanguage, Arnold Bennett's *The Old Wives' Tale* (1908) displays a concretely realist portrayal of time, in which it was common to separate narrative time and plot time. At the end of chapter 5 and the beginning of chapter 6 of Book One, a set of events occurs as a consequence of Sophia Baines informing the commercial traveller Gerald Scales that she usually visits the Bursley Free Library on a Wednesday:

> At half past one, while Mrs Baines was dozing after dinner, Sophia wrapped herself up, and with the [library] book under her arm went forth into the world, through the shop. She returned in less than twenty minutes.
>
> . . .
> The next day Mrs Baines summoned Sophia into her bedroom.
> 'Sophia,' she said, trembling, 'I shall be glad if you will not walk about the streets with young men until you have my permission.'
> The girl blushed violently. 'I–I–'
> 'You were seen in Wedgwood Street,' said Mrs Baines.[112]

The chapter shortly ends, and chapter 6 begins:

The uneasiness of Mrs Baines flowed and ebbed, during the next three months, influenced by Sophia's moods. There were days when Sophia was the old Sophia—the forbidding, difficult, waspish, and even hedgehog Sophia. But there were other days on which Sophia seemed to be drawing joy and gaiety and good-will from some secret source, from some fount whose nature and origin none could divine. It was on these days that the uneasiness of Mrs Baines waxed. . . .
  . . .
Still, she would have given much to see inside Sophia's lovely head. . . . Sophia was living chiefly on the flaming fire struck in her soul by the shock of seeing Gerald Scales in the porch of the Wedgwood Institution as she came out of the Free Library with *Experience of Life* tucked into her large astrakhan muff. . . .She was walking along Wedgwood Street, by his side slowly, on the scraped pavements, where marble bulbs of snow had defied the spade and remained. She and he were exactly of the same height, and she kept looking into his face and he into hers. . . .
What had happened? Nothing! The most commonplace occurrence! The eternal cause had picked up a commercial traveller (it might have been a clerk or curate, but it in fact was a commercial traveller), and endowed him with all the glorious, unique, incredible attributes of a god . . .
Of course at the corner of the street he had to go. 'Till next time!' he murmured. And fire came out of his eyes and lighted in Sophia's lovely head those lamps which Mrs Baines was mercifully spared from seeing. And he had shaken hands and raised his hat. . . .
And, escorted by the equivocal Angel of Eclipses, she had turned into King Street, and arranged her face, and courageously met her mother.[113]

This instance, in which the narrative returns plot time to the past of the story-NOW already reached in chapter 5, and so separates narrative time from plot time, with narrative time continuing while plot time is repeated, was common throughout the realist novel.

Sections 2 and 3 of this same chapter, in which Gerald Scales's next visit to the shop is narrated, follow a similar structure. Mrs Baines has arranged customers for Sophia that will keep her away from him during his visit, and placed her sister Constance and the apprentice draper Mr Povey in his way, but has not expected Povey, called away to attend to a customer, to become jealous of Scales's attention to Constance:

Their chatter was nothing, and about nothing, but Mr Povey imagined that they were exchanging eternal vows. He endured Mr Scales's odious freedom until it become insufferable, until it deprived him of all his self-control; and then he retired into his cutting-out room. He mediated there in a condition of insanity for perhaps a minute, and excogitated a device. Dashing back into the shop, he spoke up, half across the shop, in a loud, curt tone:

'Miss Baines, your mother wants you at once.'

He was launched on the phrase before he noticed that during his absence, Sophia had descended from the showroom and joined her sister and Mr Scales.[114]

The next section begins with the narration of Sophia leaving the shop later that day to see her friend Mrs Chetwynd and meet secretly with Scales. The third paragraph, in order to explain why she does this (Scales has passed her a note), then returns to the morning in the shop to explain why she was with Constance when Povey emerged from his cutting-out room:

> In the morning she had heard the voice of Mr Scales from the showroom. . . .
> The customer sent up by Constance had occupied the surface of her life for ten minutes, trying on hats; and during this time she was praying wildly that Mr Scales might not go, and asserting that it was impossible he should go without at least asking for her. Had she not counted the days to this day? When the customer left, Sophia followed her downstairs, and saw Mr Scales chatting with Constance. All her self-possession instantly returned to her, and she joined them with a rather mocking smile.[115]

As is common in realist fiction, this narrative features a move of focalisation (seen, for example, in the narrator's subtle endorsement of Sophia's self-consciousness by explaining that it must be her body, and not a gossip, that has revealed the liaison to Mrs Baines) from Mrs Baines to Sophia to Mr Povey and then to Sophia, which at rare points even becomes free indirect discourse. But the temporality of narrative was not yet regarded as having any necessary relationship to the temporality of the plot. The passing of narrative time does not forbid a return to plot time already passed.

The same loose connection between narrative duration and plot duration also threw up instances in realism where the narrative departs from the story-NOW for a story-FUTURE. In the last chapter, after Sophia's death, the narrator describes Constance's revulsion at the idea of the federation of the five towns into one: "The attempted suicide of Mrs Critchlow [because of the evacuation of business from Bursely to nearby Hanbridge] sealed the fate of Federation and damped it for ever, in Constance's mind. Her hatred of the idea of it was intensified into violent animosity; insomuch that in the result she died a martyr to the cause of Bursley's municipal independence."[116] After this brief movement into future plot time, 13 pages of text continue the 'story-NOW' up to Constance's death: for the realist Bennett, narrative can be in the past to the story's present or, as above, vice versa (and these are not rare examples). As above, continuing narrative time bears no particular relationship to plot time, realism permitting the narrative to move into a 'story-PAST' and 'story-FUTURE': the next moment in narrative duration can be other (past or future) than the next moment in the sequence of narrated plot duration. Moreover, the rise of literary impressionism had done nothing to diminish the use of a-chronological narrative, and even incrementally concentrated it: Conrad intensified the discrepancy between narrative time and plot time through increasingly 'shuffling' his narratives, from *Lord Jim* (written mid-1898 to June 1900 and serialised October 1899 to November 1900) through *Nostromo* (written November 1902 to August 1904 and published 1904) and *Under Western Eyes* to *Chance*.[117]

By contrast, in cinema, and consequently in the formal literary mode it triggered, the narrative discourse expressed itself in time identical with plot discourse. Consequently, in 'high' modernist narrative, while reader's and character's experience of time are still different, narrator's and character's experience of time are identical.[118] Joyce, for example, takes care to follow his 'introduction' of Bloom at the beginning of 'Calypso'—"Mr Leopold Bloom ate with relish the inner organs of beasts and fowls"—with the statement that this is part of reverie occurring in Bloom's mind as he thinks what to have for breakfast: "Kidneys were in his mind as he moved about the kitchen softly".[119] In *Ulysses* the rest of 'Calypso' involves no statement other than the use of the simple past and past continuous tenses to indicate the pastness of the narrated events, featuring a total uniformity between the passing of narrative time and the passing of plot time that, like cinema, makes narratorial description impossible; plot duration, elapsing concurrently with narrative duration, cannot stop. A radical departure, therefore, from the focalization in a specific character's consciousness as practised in the realist novel, the focalisation practised by Joyce, Richardson, H.D. and Woolf followed the injunction not to repeat plot duration. This was not a mere stylistic blip. It meant *not* using a previously standard literary device for explaining cause and effect.

By narrating a day rather than arranging temporality according to narrative requirements, *Ulysses*, as with *Mrs Dalloway*, sought to adequate cinema's "pure record of time".[120] Both works regarded time as pre-existing narration, in conflict with the implicit realist tenet that the act of narration pre-exists the story space. Correspondingly, the world's verifiability in *Ulysses* exists independently of any narrator's ability to represent it. Unlike in Joyce's 'A Mother', completed in September 1905, where Madam Glynn "looked as if she had been resurrected from an old stage-wardrobe",[121] in *Ulysses* no such narratorial implication of the existence of a conscious creativity, pausing plot time (however briefly) to issue a comment while narrative time continues, occurs. All such narrators in *Ulysses* are either character-narrators or their narrative is the subject of parody. This suggests a further reason for the absence of a stable metalanguage in modernism. Discussing the occupants of the funeral carriages in the 'Hades' chapter of *Ulysses*, Terence Killeen states that "[o]ne of the most striking aspects of their dialogue is its obliqueness; allusions are made, names are mentioned, with which the reader may or may not be privy, but no allowance is made for such gaps in readerly comprehension".[122] This is true of much of the text, with reader comprehension having to derive from deduction. One of modernism's absolute defining aspects was that the marked disparity between the temporality at which the statements of a realist literary narrator occur and the past temporality of realist events which the narrative posits was now unpalatable. Because the commentary endemic to realist metalanguage would assert a distinction between narrative duration and plot duration that, in film, cannot exist, this explanatory metalanguage (already relativised by Conrad and Ford (see Chapter 1)) was, in the 'high' modernist narrative works, by and large dropped. In addition, the model of a pre-existing reality that is both indisposed to the comprehension of a spectator *and* nonetheless fictionally fabricated is the precise rendering of events in cinema. So Joyce's fictional Dublin and Woolf's fictional London both 'precede' the work, pursuing the possibility of a narratorless recording implied by film's parity of narrative time and plot time.

Impersonal narration did not prevent Joyce from creating equivalents for recollection. 'Circe', for example, is clearly not a dramatisation of any character's single consciousness, yet it repeats a number of details from their experiences earlier in the day. If these are not recollected by the characters, then a kind of recollecting consciousness is present here. However, the meeting of an urge to recollect with the imperative not to revert to previous plot time suggests why the 'Circe' chapter was written as a playscript: feeling the need to refer experiences from earlier in the day, Joyce could not use his prose narrator with his/her access solely to the present. In addition, although these cornerstones of high literary modernism do seem preoccupied with taking characters back into their own past, 1) their remembering always occupies a more or less precise amount of time, keeping to the maxim that plot duration cannot pause if narrative duration is passing, and 2) the extensive delving into the past through recollection was probably a result of the new maxim that the narrator could not access plot or story time already passed (because this would mean moving from a continuous present story-NOW into the story-PAST), in that it would have challenged writers to find ways of getting the past into the present, and to get as much in as possible.

If Woolf deliberately titled the "entirely new kind of book"[123] she began in March 1929 'The Waves' out of frustration at those using the term 'stream of consciousness' to describe her work, suggesting that she favoured the non-linearity of the wave on a shore over the linearity of the stream to describe her sense of time, then it must be remembered that her provisional title for *Mrs Dalloway* was 'The Hours'.[124] The linearity of *Mrs Dalloway* may have impeded her search for an apposite metaphor for crowd consciousness (see Chapter 3), but this was because, as a consequence of the equally strong influence of cinema, the aim of this linearity was rendering a fictional work in a continuous present. Indeed, there are only two cases in all of *Mrs Dalloway* where Woolf breaks the rule that time is always the present, and Woolf breaks this rule deliberately rather than invalidating it. The first is the point when a 'baton-change' transfers focalisation from Clarissa to Septimus via the back-firing of the unidentified car. Clarissa hears "a pistol shot in the street outside!"[125] and the florist goes to the window to look, apologising for the noise, and then returns. Then, after a section break:

> The violent explosion which made Mrs. Dalloway jump and Miss Pym go to the window and apologise came from a motor car which had drawn to the side of the pavement precisely opposite Mulberry's shop window. Passers-by who, of course, stopped and stared, had just time to see a face of the very greatest importance against the dove-grey upholstery, before a male hand drew the blind.[126]

Septimus is then 'introduced'. As a part of using the car as a connection via which the focalisation is transferred from Clarissa's consciousness to Septimus's, the narration runs twice over the short period of time immediately after the back-firing of the car. The second 'violation' occurs at a later baton-change. Peter Walsh is in Regent's Park, thinking of losing Clarissa as a young man:

> It was awful, he cried, awful, awful!
> Still, the sun was hot. Still, one got over things. Still, life had a way of adding day to day. Still, he thought, yawning and beginning to take notice ... still, presumably there were compensations—when little Elsie Mitchell, who had been picking up pebbles to add to the pebble collection which she and her brother were making on the nursery mantelpiece, plumped her handful down on the nurse's knee and *scudded off again full tilt into a lady's legs*. Peter Walsh laughed out.
> But Lucrezia Warren Smith was saying to herself, It's wicked; why should I suffer? she was asking, as she walked down the broad path. No; I can't stand it any longer, she was saying, having left Septimus, who wasn't Septimus any longer, to say hard, cruel, wicked things, to talk to himself, to talk to a dead man, on the seat over there, *when the child ran full tilt into her*, fell flat, and burst out crying.[127]

Likewise, an event experienced by multiple characters is used as a connection via which to transfer focalisation from one consciousness to another, and this transfer involves the repetition of some duration. Nonetheless, both of these moments 'violate' a continuous fictional present in the same way as the repeated intercutting of 'Wandering Rocks' 'violates' it, not by referring to one event as in the past in relation to another already narrated but by narrating an event as occurring in the present and then doing so again, from, in the case of *Mrs Dalloway*, different viewpoints. Woolf does not write that the violent explosion "had come from a motor car", as this, the past perfect tense, would move into the past of the story-NOW already reached, continuing narrative time but repeating plot time. In order for some plot time that has already been narrated to be referred to again, narrative duration *also* has to occur again. For narrative duration to continue while plot duration is repeated would mean that story time would be experienced as past. Although the narrative is written in the simple past tense, the passing of story time cannot exist in a relation of pastness to the passing of narrative time.

In *Mrs Dalloway*, with the exception of these two brief instances, all references to the past of the novel's single plot day occur in the present during which characters recall memories of that past, and references to the narrative's past through the past perfect or past perfect continuous tense appear in the context of a character thinking or uttering, in their present, that they have been doing something up to now: (e.g. "He [Peter] had only reached town last night, he said" (the past perfect tense) or "all in a clip it came over her, If I had married him, this gaiety would have been mine all day!" (the past perfect continuous tense)).[128] The maxim that narrative time and plot time must remain uniform also determines the status of the 'repeated' plot time (8am–12am) at the beginning of *Ulysses*. This plot time is not given as the present and then the past of the point reached at the end of the first rendering, but as the present twice. The second time that this plot duration is covered, the narrator has no memory of having already covered it, and gives no statement that this plot duration has already occurred before at a previous part of the narrative duration, leaving only clues from within the story-space to indicate *when* 'Calypso', 'Lotus-Eaters' and 'Hades' occur. A repeated plot duration demands a repeated narrative duration—the time is always the present. Indeed, in *The Odyssey* the Telemachia and the first part of Odysseus's journey occur simultaneously, giving Joyce a substantial reason for repeating time, so the narration of this three-hour section *without* any statement that the narrative is moving into the past of the story-NOW already reached is notable.[129] The short 'repeated' duration at the beginning of 'Sirens'—Lydia Douce and Mina Kennedy watch the viceregal cavalcade go by, which has 'already' passed them near the end of 'Wandering Rocks'—is given in the same way.

Like Hermione in *Asphodel*—who laments "[o]h if you only knew how it went on and on. As if a whole book on one single page (like ancient papyrus) rolled on and on"[130]—Woolf seems to have been slightly troubled by her commitment to a continuous present, suggesting that it was unconsciously compelling: she wrote on 18 June 1923 that limiting herself to a day and so denying her narrator access to characters' histories made the work "[t]oo thin and unreal somehow".[131] The often-cited solution to this was her 'revelation' of 30 August 1923: "My discovery: how I dig out beautiful caves behind my characters; I think that gives exactly what I want; humanity, humour, depth. The idea is that the caves shall connect, & each comes to daylight at the present moment."[132] Easily viewed as evidence for her commitment to aesthetic investments in collectivism (see Chapter 3), this "discovery" also reveals the strength of her commitment to a continuous present; the past of each character could not exist except as it was recalled, as with *Ulysses*, at the present moment, on the single day of *Mrs Dalloway*.

The imperative that narrative duration match plot duration also means that in *Mrs Dalloway* even thought has a specified duration. In Bond Street Clarissa thinks of herself as a hostess:

> Much rather would she have been one of those people like Richard who did things for themselves, whereas, she thought, waiting to cross, half the time she did things not simply, not for themselves; but to make people think this or that; perfect idiocy she knew (and now the policeman held up his hand) for no one was ever for a second taken in. Oh if she could have had her life over again! she thought, stepping on to the pavement, could have looked even differently![133]

Often this duration does not correspond to the time it takes to *read* the thoughts (as with much of *Ulysses*), but even lengthy streams of thought occurring in mere seconds are specified as having a duration nonetheless. For example, Clarissa passes a glove shop in Bond Street and, as she approaches the flower shop, thinks of her daughter Elizabeth's disdain for gloves and so proceeds on to think of her hatred of Elizabeth's religious partnership with Miss Kilman (and of her hatred of this hatred). This thought process, narrated in 485 words, is then cut off: "Nonsense, nonsense! she cried to herself, pushing through the swing doors of Mulberry's the florists."[134] The 2–3 minutes that it takes to read this is subordinated by the text to the concrete duration of the time it takes to walk between the two shops. Likewise, Peter's 350 words of thoughts, after leaving Clarissa's house, about their past at Bourton, are specified by Woolf as occurring in the time it takes to walk the roughly 500 metres from Parliament Square to half–way up Whitehall.[135] 551 words of Peter's thoughts about Clarissa and Daisy occur in the time it takes to walk about 530 metres from the Madame Tussaud's exit of Regent's Park and east along Marylebone Road to the crossing to Regent's Park Tube Station.[136] Arranging the narrative in relation to wider events such as the work of the sky-writing plane does of course relate to the collectivist commitment to narrating social rhythms rather than events as they occur for individuals (see Chapter 3), but the work of the sky-writing plane in particular also serves to provide an event with limited duration that can be used to specify that the events occurring while people are looking at the writing are occurring *within* this duration.

That time is always the present in film also means that time never stops passing. By contrast, even in theatre a frozen tableau suggests the halting of narrative duration. In literary modernism, absorbing cinema's new definition of narrative, *a sentence passes duration*, whereas, in previous and ongoing realist literary practice, while a sentence *might* narrate the passing of duration it does not automatically involve the passing of plot duration. This means that Joyce and Woolf's decision to set their actions in recognisable urban locations may itself have been a consequence of their commitment to cinema's continuous present. In an intercut sequence in cinema, viewers know how much time has passed for characters in stream A because it is the same as the amount of time that has just elapsed for us as we have been watching the characters in stream B (or at least it is definitely not *less*). As this is not the case in literature, and as a statement of the amount of time elapsed would imply the presence of a narrator with the ability to look back and measure it (and so intensify the pastness of story temporality in relation to narrative temporality), Joyce and Woolf used real-world geography to provide relatively accurate estimates of duration.

In addition, the modernist feature at its most explicit in *Mrs Dalloway*— the baton-change pattern of focalisation that occurs on the basis of incidental relationships or proximity between characters—is also related to cinema's parity of narrative duration and plot duration and its accompanying continuous present. As early as 1954 Robert Humphrey referred to the book's "seemingly arbitrary choosing of subject after subject"[137] as acceptable on the basis of an understanding that the novel contains a "roving camera".[138] But this camera is again metaphorical: the influence *is* that of cinema, but the baton-change narration pattern of *Mrs Dalloway* occurs because the story's axis of occurrence is *time*. Although the baton-change pattern also suggests Woolf's fascination with the mobile non-individual consciousness of the mass mind (see Chapter 3), it was made possible by cinema's rigidity of time, the implication in the continuous present that character's movements are secondary to the forward movement of the present moment. Likewise, in 'Wandering Rocks' the 19-section structure iterates a connectedness between the Dubliners that exceeds their social connections, and this is made possible by the notion that the story's axis of occurrence is time. In *Mrs Dalloway* too the simple past tense—'she walked'—is used overwhelmingly to describe ongoing actions instead of the past continuous tense—'she was walking'—as the latter implies a slice of an ongoing event where the former implies the event as a completed action. The latter also iterates more explicitly the pastness of the action. The present is as much a source of fascination for Woolf-as-Clarissa as "those wild beasts, our fellow men"[139] with whom Woolf experienced temporary thrilling contact: "what she [Clarissa] loved was this, here, now, in front of her; the fat lady in the cab."[140] In addition, Woolf continued her commitment to a continuous present in her next novel, *To the Lighthouse* (written between August 1925 and February 1927 and published on 5 May 1927), even permitting herself one exception in the form of an overlapping 'edit' in the style of Elsie Mitchell's crash into Rezia's legs in *Mrs Dalloway*: the launching of the boat from Lily's viewpoint and from Mr Ramsay, James and Cam's viewpoint, each stated as if it is happening for the first time.[141] This commitment to a continuous present even seems to have strengthened: the present she used in *To the Lighthouse* did not even have any necessary relation to the *scale* of time experiences by a human consciousness: Woolf devoted the first 60% of the text to less than a day, the next 8.7% to ten years, and the last 31.3% to roughly four hours. 'Time Passes', which detaches from any human consciousness by staying with the house while no-one is there, 'intercuts' its square-bracketed 'shots' of events occurring elsewhere only at the moments when these events occur, the 'disjunctions' functioning on the basis of ongoing time. So committed was Woolf to a method in which time moves forward in the story-space automatically that the only way she could indicate a departure from this implicit rule was typographical: simultaneous events are given in square brackets (seven in 'Time Passes' and two in 'The Lighthouse'), and, in 'The Window', one two-paragraph section and one entire chapter, both of which occur in the story-PAST, are given in parentheses.[142]

While Woolf seems to have warmed to the narrative principle of a continuous present well after Joyce, Richardson and H.D., Woolf's earlier *Jacob's Room* (written between April 1920 and 4 November 1921, revised in July 1922, and published on 27 October 1922) bears signs of the beginning of a transition to a continuous present. Woolf employed the amnesiac narrator, foregrounding this in the work's first line: "'So of course,' wrote Betty Flanders, pressing her heels rather deeper in the sand, 'there was nothing for it but to leave'."[143] Instead of a cause-and-effect description of the story-PAST that has led to present circumstances, this narrative admits of no story-PAST, in spite of the narrative events clearly demanding the kind of backstory usually conveyed in the past perfect tense—'Seabrook Flanders had recently died', for example. As a part of this amnesiac description of the present, Seabrook's recent death is, in fact only explained in the present tense: "Scarborough is seven hundred miles from Cornwall: Captain Barfoot is in Scarborough: Seabrook is dead."[144] Disparities between narrative temporality and plot temporality are correspondingly rare in *Jacob's Room*. In chapter 4 only one narration of the story-PAST occurs (with use of the past perfect) when Jacob and Timothy arrive at the Durrant house: "After six days of salt wind, rain and sun, Jacob Flanders had put on a dinner jacket. The discreet black object had made its appearance now and then in the boat among tins, pickles, preserved meats, and as the voyage went on had become more and more irrelevant, hardly to be believed in. And now. . . ."[145] The one disparity between narrative temporality and plot temporality in chapter 6 occurs when some are remarking that real flowers seem to be looking on at the instant doom of the paper flowers that open on contact with water: "Mr. Stuart Ormond made this very observation; and charming it was thought; and Kitty Craster married him on the strength of it six months later."[146]

At one point *Jacob's Room* returns to a previous story-NOW (now in the story-PAST) and then, narrating the consequences of Betty Flanders's refusal of Mr Floyd's proposal of marriage while Jacob is a child, relates the story-NOW to a much later 'narrator-NOW'[147] in which Mr Floyd recognises Jacob Flanders as a grown man in the street, not simply repeating a realist tendency but *emphasising* the sense of disparity between a realist narrator's present and the story-NOW.[148] Cinema's lack of a past tense would seem to have no relation to this aspect of the book. However, since all realist work is based on the assumption of the story's pastness in relation to the narrator's own present,[149] an explicit parody of this in Woolf's work of 'bankrupt realism' indicates that this sense of temporal disparity, and its associated sense of narratorial control over events that would end in the narrator's present, was becoming intolerable.

In contemporary realist fiction, the major technique for moving the viewpoint between distant locations was to shift into the past perfect tense and to narrate how that character or set of circumstances came to be in that place. For modernism, this was unacceptable because it involved moving into the story-PAST. Assigning Woolf's technique of omitting periods of time, at its most elaborate in *Jacob's Room*, the label 'cinematic' overlooks the impact of cinema on modernism. Her 'jumps' are recognisable *as* jumps because they are *specified* as movements on to a point later in time by certain techniques used to inform the reader *when* the new present is, techniques that have to be used because Woolf was already writing under the injunction that the fictional time is always the present. Thus in *Jacob's Room* a germinal form of the 'baton-change' narration characterising *Mrs Dalloway* occurs when Betty Flanders is looking down at Scarborough pier: what seems like narratorial commentary about flower-beds, the aquarium and events on the pier that Betty Flanders could not possibly see or hear are identified as the thoughts of "the young man leaning against the railings" to whom the baton was evidently passed as soon as the narration moved to the pier, and not an omniscient narrator touring the pier.[150] This suggests that in writing *Jacob's Room* Woolf already felt the pull of a story thread which is not the interaction between characters but the movement forward of time.

Arnold Hauser describes film as enjoying complete chronological freedom on the basis of its capacity to narrate the life of a character out of order through flashbacks—"[i]n this way the film often produces the effect of someone playing on a keyboard ad libitum"[151]—and sees this as the force that made modernism "cinematic".[152] But chronological disorganization was not, and is not, the temporal behaviour of film. Robert Humphrey's 1954 argument that stream-of-consciousness fiction was "cinematic"[153] was based on a perceived use of montage defined as having the purpose of "transcending or modifying arbitrary and conventional time and space barriers."[154] But the editing structures which faced Joyce and Woolf during the 1910s (which also faced Winnifred Holtby when she first described

Jacob's Room as cinematic on a very different model from the later montage orthodoxy),[155] and which informed their conceptions of narrative space-time, were *not* transgressions of continuous space-time. Humphrey argues that consciousness demands "the freedom of shifting back and forth, of intermingling past, present and imagined flows",[156] but as Seymour Chatman points out of *Mrs Dalloway*,

> discourse-time [narrative duration] equals story-time: story-time is not the thirty years or so of elapsed life, but rather the time of her [Clarissa Dalloway] thinking about them. Structurally, the summarized material is secondary to the principal narrative event . . ., namely Clarissa's act of reminiscing.[157]

Cinema's chronology is not based on disruption but on temporal continuity. For example, Woolf's praise, in 1926, for the capacity of edits to eliminate "the gulfs which dislocate novels"[158] was for film's capacity to cut across *space*, not time. Indeed, the ability to cut across vast spaces was a function of the introduction into cinema after 1908 of the implicit structural assurance that the next moment shown was *not* a previous moment in story time: audiences could be expected to handle spatial transporation because they were structurally assured of temporal continuity. This reference to cinema suggests that, for Woolf, cinema was defined by the dominance and primacy of temporal continuity. Indeed, the only sense in which a gulf could be seen to dislocate a narrative would be where the narrative was seen as tied to rendering duration. Where this was not the case, a shift in location would not be experienced as a jump.

What, then, of the 'originator' of interior monologue in English, Richardson, whose first *Pilgrimage* novel, *Pointed Roofs*, written between October 1912 and early 1913 (at a time in Richardson's life when it was unlikely that she been exposed to the new cinema of narrative integration),[159] significantly predates *Ulysses*, *Asphodel* and *Mrs Dalloway*? It was, after all, in reference to the first three *Pilgrimage* novels (*Pointed Roofs* (published September 1915), *Backwater* (published July 1916) and *Honeycomb* (published October 1917) that, in April 1918, Sinclair wrote that "[n]othing happens. It is just life going on and on. It is Miriam Henderson's stream of consciousness going on and on."[160] Insomuch as the method Richardson adopted in these novels—to provide direct access to *only* Miriam Henderson's consciousness via either third-person focalisation or first-person interior monologue—remained relatively stable over time, most, if not all, of the allusions to moments in the story-space previous to the moment reached by the present can be understood as recall in an ongoing present, even if not overtly specified as recall, and even if rendered in the third-person, in that they can be regarded as free indirect discourse rather than reversion to previous story time by a narrator. For example, Minna asks if Miriam will live with her when the school term ends and Miriam thinks of this prospect:

Minna's garden, her secure country house, her rich parents, no worries, nothing particular to do, seemed for a moment to Miriam the solution and continuation of all the gay day. There would be the rest of term—increasing spring and summer—Fräulein divested of all mystery and fear, and then freedom—with Minna.

She glanced at Minna—the cheerful pink face and the pink bulb of nose came round to her and in an excited undertone she murmured something about the Apotheker.

'I should love to come—simply love it,' said Miriam enthusiastically, feeling that she would not entirely give up the idea yet. She would not shut off the offered refuge. It would be a plan to have in reserve. She had been daunted, as Minna murmured, by a picture of Minna and herself in that remote garden—she receiving confidences about the Apotheker—no one else there—the Waldstrasse household blotted out—herself and Minna finding pretexts day after day to visit the chemist's little town.[161]

The last sentence, an account of a sensation that Miriam has experienced several seconds before the moment reached by the story-NOW when the sentence begins, can be regarded as a description of the continuing manifestation of that Miriam's sensation of daunting in the ongoing present. Nonetheless in *Pointed Roofs* the narrator frequently moves back to the story-PAST (filling in details from her/his memory) while narrative time continues before returning to precisely the point left off in the story-NOW (indicating that the past is not character recall occurring in the story-NOW), narrative time passes in lengthy narratorial commentary on her/his knowledge of several weeks rather than in narrations of specified segments of time, the time of character recall is often left unspecified, and a number of lengthy descriptions pause plot time while narrative time continues.

However, as Richardson, living in London from early 1913 (having finished *Pointed Roofs*), worked on further *Pilgrimage* novels, she committed further to a unity of a continuing narrative present with a continuing plot present. This took time. For example, even in the second novel, *Backwater* (written between the middle of 1915 and early 1916 and published in July 1916), Richardson seemed to be comfortable reaching a point with the story-NOW and then having her narrator reach back into the story-PAST of this present. One section begins:

The next day, after tea, Eve arrived home from Gloucestershire.

Miriam had spent the day with Harriet. After breakfast, bounding silently up and downstairs, they visited each room in turn, chased each other about the echoing rooms and passages of the basement and all over the garden. Miriam listened speechlessly to the sound of Harriett's heels soft on the stair carpet, ringing on the stone floors of the basement, and the swish of her skirts as she flew over the lawn, following, surrounding, responding to Miriam's wild tour of the garden. Miriam listened and watched, her eyes and ears gladly gathering and hoarding visions. It could not go on. Presently some claim would be made on Harriet and she would be alone. But when they had their fill of silently rushing about, Harriett piloted her into the drawing-room and hastily began opening the piano.[162]

The account of the day Miriam and Harriett spend together continues for a total of roughly 2% of the novel, and is ended by a section break, after which a new section begins with Miriam addressing Eve (so bringing the narrative back to the story-NOW established by "The next day, after tea"). By contrast, by the fourth *Pilgrimage* novel, *The Tunnel* (written between August 1917 and late 1918 and published in February 1919), the reader is informed of time previous to the story-NOW differently. In one instance, a short section describes Miriam boarding a train. The next section begins:

> That extraordinary ending of fear of the great man at the station. Alma and the little fair square man not much taller than herself, looking like a grocer's assistant with a curious, kind, confidential . . . unprejudiced eye . . . they had come, both of them, out of the house to the station to meet her . . . 'this is Hypo' and the quiet shy walk to the house, he asking questions by saying them—statements. You caught the elusive three-fifteen. This is your bag.[163]

The visit with Alma and Mr Wilson which ended with her boarding the train (as narrated in the previous section) is presented to the reader from Miriam's arrival at the beginning of the visit, the total account comprising roughly 7.5% of the novel, but in contrast to the earlier method, here Richardson begins the account in tightly focalised prose by describing it in terms of the effect on Miriam's consciousness, making the account of the visit with Alma and Mr Wilson more clearly indentifiable as recalled memory, even though it occupies a much higher percentage of the novel than the foray into the story-PAST in *Backwater*. Indeed, while, in *Backwater*, the account of the day before Eve arrives occupies no time in the story-space, further suggesting that it is a reversion to the story-PAST on the part of a narrator rather than recollection on the part of Miriam Henderson, in *The Tunnel* the lengthy account of the visit with Alma and Mr Wilson ends with the arrival of Miriam's train back in London: the account has taken time in the story-space, further identifying it as recall.[164]

In addition, while, in *Pointed Roofs*, Richardson had deployed a narrator permitted to spend one of the 12 chapters in general description of Miriam's experience during her early days at the German boarding school, the narrator became far less tangible as the series progressed, diminishing any agency with the capacity to pause the ongoing story-NOW. Chapter 6 of *Pointed Roofs* begins:

During those early days Miriam realized that school-routine, as she knew it—the planned days—the regular unvarying successions of lessons and preparations, had no place in this new world. Even the masters' lessons, coming in from outside and making a kind of framework of appointments over the otherwise fortuitously occupied days, were, she soon found, not always securely calculable. Herr Kappelmeister Bossenberger would be heard booming and intoning in the hall unexpectedly at all hours.[165]

By contrast, by the time of writing *The Tunnel*, although the third-person is still the dominant voice, the narrator is little more than a function of Miriam's consciousness, the following chapter opening exemplifying the new norm:

It was . . . jolly; to have something one was obliged to do every evening [visit Miss Dear]—but it could not go on. Next week-end, the Brooms, that would be an excuse for making a break. She must have other friends she could turn to . . . she must *know* one could not go on. But bustling off every evening regularly to the same place with things to get for somebody was evidently good in some way . . . health-giving and strength-giving.[166]

Indeed, by *The Tunnel*, with the narratorial presence so much less conspicuous, an automatic forward-movement of time is relied upon to carry the narrative on (rather than a narratorial comment that "Two days later . . ." the next narrated events occurred), meaning that it is often unclear how much further on the story-NOW is at the start of each new chapter, as with *Ulysses*.

TIME AND SPACE

Joseph Frank's 1945 essay 'Spatial Form in Modern Literature' and its updates have formed one major basis of the continuing belief that literary modernism constitutes a disruption of linear temporality. Malcolm Bradbury and James McFarlane's major work upheld it in 1976, for example, and in 2007 Michael Whitworth listed 'spatial form' as the fifth of the 12 major characteristics of literary modernism in the eyes of contemporary scholarship.[167] Modernism, Frank argued, made it impossible to comprehend the meaning of a work without first grasping a pattern of synchronic relations subordinating the temporality of the work to "a purely physical limit of apprehension, which conditions but does not determine the work".[168] For him, Eliot, Pound, Marcel Proust, Joyce and Djuna Barnes all "ideally intend the reader to apprehend their work spatially, in a moment of time, rather than as a sequence", in spite of the impossibility of actually achieving this.[169] He renewed this thesis well into the 1970s, arguing in a 1977 answer to his critics that "the structure of modern works took on aspects that required them to be apprehended 'spatially' instead of according to the natural temporal order of language."[170] In his discussion of what he sees as a germinal manifestation of spatial form in Flaubert's *Madame Bovary* (1857), Frank calls Flaubert's handling of a scene which alternates between three 'levels' of simultaneous activity in close proximity "cinematographic":

> For the duration of the scene, at least, the time-flow of the narrative is halted; attention is fixed on the interplay of relationships within the immobilized time-area. These relationships are juxtaposed independently of the progress of the narrative, and the full significance of the scene is given only by the reflexive relations among the units of meaning.[171]

There are two problems with this. First—and this is an analogy he repeated in his 1977 answer to critics, in what amounts to a hint that cinema may have been the influence on the emergence of spatial form[172]—to regard this technique as an abandonment of temporality because it resembles cinema is to misread cinema. Resembling cross-cutting, it resembles cinema's primary technique for the *dramatisation* of time, the opposite of a *dissolution* of time into sheer simultaneity. A cross-cut scene does not show two temporally simultaneous events occurring one after the other (an erroneous belief that forms the basis of Frank's analogy between cinema and the spatialisation of action). It alternates between events whose occurrence in time is not deleted but intensified by the dramatisation of time elapsing in the currently *seen* stream of action as *also* elapsing in the currently *unseen* stream of action. Before such stipulations about *when* streams of action are occurring in relation to each other were generated through cross-cutting, a shot that followed another did not have any necessary relation to the time in that previous shot, as with the sequences in *The Great Train Robbery* (1903) where ensuing shots return to an earlier moment (the telegraph operator left tied up in the station). Cinema does not *show* simultaneity by 'stopping time'. It connotes simultaneity through creating a single time axis. In post-1908 cinema we never actually (with the exception of the split screen) see two events that are happening at the same time *at the same time*; we see that stream A has influenced stream B through the changes that have occurred in B since it was last seen, and this creates an impression of simultaneity through a viewer's inference of influence, an inference *only* made possible by the understanding that the elapsing of time in A also means the elapsing of time in B.[173] Second, Frank's argument is based on the assumption that language's time-dimension leads to a natural progression of story time in prose fiction, which Flaubert is violating by narrating several events occurring simultaneously one after the other. But what he points out in Flaubert as violating the rules of narrative was actually *normal*—ease with narrating simultaneous streams of action one after the other was a feature of realism's elastic link between narrative duration and plot duration.

Frank argues that "like Flaubert, Joyce aimed at attaining the same unified impact, the same sense of simultaneous activity occurring in different places. As a matter of fact, Joyce frequently makes use of the same method of Flaubert (cutting back and forth between different actions occurring at the same time),"[174] counter-acting the problem of his book being read as a sequence by offering fragments of information and allusions hundreds of pages apart which require the reader, "by reflexive reference, . . . [to] link them to their complements . . . independently of the time sequence of the narrative."[175] He identifies in the work of Barnes "a pattern arising from the spatial interweaving of images and phrases independently of any time-sequence of narrative action."[176] The spatiality involved in, for example, cross-referencing the ages of certain characters between chapters in *Ulysses* to discover that Leopold Bloom was Stephen Dedalus's age when he first met Molly (then Marion Tweedy) may have been a *reaction* to cinema rather than (as Frank implies) an *imitation* of it. The unconscious feeling that cinema had got under their skin, or even the conscious awareness of what model they were basing their new temporality on, would have moved modernists to emphasise the spatiality of literature, but this does not mean that modernism is 'spatial form'. This is not evidence that modernists "attempted to overcome the time elements involved in their structures",[177] which is, if anything, a misinterpretation of a literary mode in which time is always the present. Frank, for example, writes that instead of giving the personal history of his characters,

> What Joyce does, instead, is to present the elements of his narrative—the relations between Stephen and his family, between Bloom and his wife, between Stephen and Bloom and the Dedalus family—in fragments, as they are thrown out unexplained in the course of casual conversations or as they lie embedded in the various strata of symbolic reference.[178]

This, for Frank, demands spatial reading. But it precisely describes what Woolf called "digging out beautiful caves behind my characters", the method of description demanded by the requirement that narrative duration and plot duration proceed hand in hand—the plot cannot be paused while narrative duration continues in description or return to earlier plot/story time duration to exist in a relationship of pastness to continuing narrative duration. Information that is relevant can only 'occur'—usually in thought or conversation—in a continuous present. While Robert Green is accurate in using Frank's ideas to describe the scrambling of the order of the story-NOW by the narrator-NOW in *The Good Soldier*,[179] in these 'high' modernist works produced after *The Good Soldier* the opposite had become the case: a strict chronological consecutiveness of the story-NOW.

Hart remarks that timing his re-enactments of the movements of the characters in 'Wandering Rocks' provides "direct confirmation of Joyce's fundamentally realist intentions": the intersecting paths and simultaneous events are all possible.[180] Using 'realist' to mean 'realistic', he indicates that modernism manifested an intensified search for ways of referring to reality, a search for which cinema's continuous present can be seen as a significant provocation. One of these ways of referring to reality was modernism's use of history. The federation of Bennett's five towns into one in *The Old Wives' Tale* (1908) is the fictional transcription of the creation of twentieth-century Stoke-on-Trent, and Sophia Baines/Scales's fortune is made during the 1870 siege of Paris, but Bennett nonetheless continued a realist literary tradition which did not conceive of the duration of the narrative as part of history. While not timeless, realist time is distinct from and only co-exists with historical time—what Frank Kermode referred to in 1965 as the *aevum*. This was the term used by St Thomas Aquinas in the thirteenth century to describe the 'time of the angels', a time that was neither mortal time nor eternity, a *duration* which was nonetheless *outside* of history, and which Kermode pointed out had been incorporated by writers to finally compose "the time-order of novels".[181] "Characters in novels", Kermode wrote, "are independent of time and succession, but may, and usually do, seem to operate in time and succession".[182] In contrast to this realist time co-existing alongside historical time, modernism situated its narratives directly in historical time. This might be taken to suggest that cinema's continuous present did not wholly generate modernism's relationship with time. The historical specificity of *Ulysses* and *Mrs Dalloway*—not just to the year but to the exact day—identifies them as continually historically past, a disparity that would seem to be intolerable from the standpoint of cinema's continuous present. But cinema's dearth of acknowledgment of 'being uttered' leads its viewers directly to history. As Christian Metz states, while "a discourse must necessarily be made by someone", cinema is just views of the world, and "one of the characteristics of the world is that it is uttered by no one."[183] In spite of widespread discursive *avowal* of film's fictionality, the film text nonetheless presented as history rather than discourse. The instant pastness of the photographic aspect of the cinematic image refers not to a fictional duration co-existing with a historical past but to the historical past *itself*, in which writers following cinema's time sense would have felt their fictional events to have been located. Thus modernism left the *aevum* and entered history.

HENRI BERGSON

One 'revolution' in notions of time commonly incorporated into discussions of the temporality of literary modernism is Henri Bergson's philosophy of time, proposed in his *Time and Free Will* (1889) and *Creative*

Evolution (1907), a philosophy not unreasonably perceived behind literary modernism given the wide dissemination of Bergson's ideas in the UK in the 1909–1911 period.[184] Bergson argued that while change is commonly seen as occurring in the transition from one stable state to another ("I am warm or cold, I am merry or sad, I work or I do nothing"[185]), these 'transitions' are just the moment when constant change becomes visible: "just because we close our eyes to the unceasing variation of every physical state, we are obliged, when the change has become so considerable as to force itself on our attention, to speak as if a new state were placed alongside the previous one. Of this new state we assume that it remains unvarying in its turn, and so on endlessly."[186] In reality, even "the most stable of internal states, the visual perception of a motionless external object", is a state of unceasing change.[187] Every 'state' is "only the best illuminated point of a moving zone which comprises all that we feel or think or will—all, in short, that we are at any given moment." States are therefore not distinct elements: "They continue each other in an endless flow."[188] Our attention, however, having distinguished and separated this flow into discrete states,

> is obliged next to reunite them by an artificial bond. It imagines, therefore, a formless ego, indifferent and unchangeable, on which it threads the psychic states which it has set up as independent entities. Instead of a flux of fleeting shades merging into each other, it perceives distinct and, so to speak, *solid* colours, set side by side like the beads of a necklace.[189]

Consequently, "never can these solids strung upon a solid make up that duration which flows. What we actually obtain in this way is an artificial imitation of the internal life, a static equivalent which will lend itself better to the requirements of logic and language"[190] *only* because the element of real time has been eliminated from it. In Deleuze's words, in Bergsonian philosophy "duration is change",[191] reality a "pure ceaseless becoming".[192]

For Bergson, as the self is constantly changing, behaviour manifests the impact of every past event, thought, action, desire, etc.: "it is with our entire past . . . that we desire, will and act."[193] Consequently,

> it follows that consciousness cannot go through the same state twice. The circumstances may still be the same, but they will act no longer on the same person, since they find him at a new moment of his history. Our personality, which is being built up each instant with its accumulated experience, changes without ceasing. By changing, it prevents any state, although superficially identical with another, from ever repeating it in its very depth. That is why our duration is irreversible.[194]

The 'high' modernist commitment to narrating an ongoing present may well therefore have derived from Bergson's concept of the self. As Shiv Kumar noted as early as 1962, the novelist of the stream of consciousness method "does not conceive character as a state but as a process of ceaseless becoming in a medium which may be termed Bergson's durée réele."[195]

Bergson's ideas may account for the micro-narratives of *Ulysses* and *Mrs Dalloway*; as the self is constantly changing, a fictional account of a self can only pertain to the self if it documents second by second, and more precisely without sectioning into separate states, a self "which is being built up each instant with its accumulated experience",[196] a "becoming" rather than a 'being'.[197] Modernist novels render time as the psychological time of Bergsonian 'pure duration',[198] an aim directly advocated by D.H. Lawrence in 1920 when he prefaced the American edition of his 1918 *New Poems* with the assertion that poetry that took as its subject "the incandescence and the coldness of the incarnate moment . . . the immediate present, the Now."[199] Lawrence argued that this so far neglected poetry would be "the unrestful, ungraspable poetry of the sheer present, poetry whose very permanency lies in its wind-like transit".[200] He closely echoed Bergson's notion of *durée* when he argued that "the poetry of the instant present cannot have the same body or the same motion as the poetry of the before or after".[201] Given that, for Bergson, 'becoming' occurs in a temporal plane and human attention and literature both reconstruct it spatially, his supporters may have seen literature's task as documenting this temporal plane in a way that would not spatialise it.

Bergson's argument that "the element of real time"[202] was missing from the common perception of the self certainly suggests that time had become a tangible dimension at the end of the nineteenth century, both as a result of the industrial and technological developments listed by Doane and *before* the emergence of the cinematograph in 1895. Arnold Hauser is therefore too hasty when, noting the Bergsonian influence, he claims that "[t]he agreement between the technical methods of film [which he does not define] and the characteristics of the new [Bergsonian] concept of time is so complete that one has the feeling that the time categories of modern art altogether must have arisen from the spirit of cinematic form".[203] The Bergsonian idea that no moment is ever perceived as external to the living of it until after it has been experienced may have kick-started the dissolution of realist metalanguage—with its implications of a narrator's perception of the moment as external to the living of it, projected into the fictional world—regardless of the impact of cinema on literary precepts discussed in Chapter 1. Bergson's statement that "our duration is irreversible"[204] was made in 1907 and *might* signal the addition, by the emergence of cinema's continuous present, of a notion of time as irreversible to his earlier description of *durée réele* in *Time and Free Will*: "duration properly so called has no moments which are identical or external to one another, being essentially heterogeneous, continuous, and with no analogy to number".[205]

Although it is possible that Bergson did not directly influence some, or indeed any, of the modernist writers (Woolf almost certainly did not read any of his works, for example),[206] the account of time he expressed was nonetheless rooted in the temporal imagination of late nineteenth- and early twentieth-century Europe. Richardson, Wyndham Lewis and Proust all later stated as much. For Richardson, "Bergson influenced many minds if only by putting into words something then dawning within the human consciousness: an increased sense of the inadequacy of the clock as a time-measurer."[207] Bergson's works may have been linked to modernism in that they explained a sense that was emerging in the cultural unconscious anyway. Whatever the route via which modernists experienced the notions of becoming and *durée réele*, it must be noted that fiction's absorption of such ideas was prompted: that Bergson was popular with British intellectuals is not an explanation for *why* literary practice endorsed his notion of consciousness. The emergence of 'high' modernism did, after all, ante-date Bersgon's writing by some time. Lawrence's 1920 lament that the "pure present" was the "[o]ne realm we have never conquered"[208] only arose following cinema's "dramatization of time". The subject of narrative only changed dramatically for the 'high' modernists because they were now holding themselves to the maxim that the time must always be the present; narrator commentary, lengthy description of objects and actions, explanations of psychological reactions and discussions of the underlying logic of interactions between characters were all now taboo areas as they all in some way involved abandoning the continuous present. Woolf's 1919 invitation to writers, in 'Modern Fiction', to abandon 'materialism' and "record the atoms as they fall upon the mind in the order in which they fall, . . . trace the pattern, however disconnected and incoherent in appearance, which each sight or incident scores upon the consciousness",[209] was an invitation to discard realist conventions of ordering material that were now anathema to a continuous present. Instead, the drama of the psychodynamic unconscious/conscious psyche, its thoughts, imaginings and memories, became the subject of literature, for the simple reason that, as Alain Robbe-Grillet noted in 1961,

> an imagining . . . is always in the present. The memories one "sees again", the remote places, the future meeting or even the episodes of the past we each mentally rearrange to suit our convenience are something like an interior film continually projected in our own minds, as soon as we stop paying attention to what is happening around us. But at other moments, on the contrary, all our senses are registering this exterior world that is certainly there.[210]

In contrast to realist shifts into the story-PAST past to explain events in the story-NOW, in the narrative model proposed by cinema's continuous present, imaginary and exterior world were now occurring in exactly the same register.

Hence the prevalent form of 'high' modernist narration, as in this from the 'Lestrygonians' chapter of *Ulysses*, written c. 1918:

A squad of constables debouched from College street, marching in Indian file. Goose step. Foodheated faces, sweating helmets, patting their truncheons. After their feed with a good load of fat soup under their belts. Policeman's lot is oft a happy one. They split up into groups and scattered, saluting towards their beats. Let out to graze. Best moment to attack one in pudding time. A punch in his dinner. A squad of others, marching irregularly. Bound for their troughs. Prepare to receive cavalry. Prepare to receive soup.[211]

Given the maxim that the time must always be the present, the temporality of plot action was now, Joyce would have at least unconsciously realised, the same temporality as the ongoing present of human mental processes. Literary modernism was not some inward turn; instead it was a result of the discovery that narration and the psyche were now occurring in *exactly* the same temporal register. Although modernism's time sense has traditionally been viewed as a consequence of a commitment to new models of the psyche which articulated the persistent nature of psychological change, the singular nature of filmic temporality suggests that the reverse may be the case: those writers we now call modernists moved towards the psyche as their exclusive literary subject because they were committing, with cinema's model of narrativity as a motive, to the principle that time in fiction must always be the present.

Kumar argues that as a consequence of the new concept of time articulated by Bergson, "psychological time thus becomes the distinguishing feature of the stream of consciousness novel. The new novelist accepts with full awareness inner duration against chronological time as the only true mode of apprehending aesthetic experience."[212] The clocks which feature as slicing mechanisms in both *Jacob's Room* and *Mrs Dalloway*—ineffectually trying to segment time—seem to support this, as does Richardson's allusion to Bergson's "sense of the inadequacy of the clock as a time-measurer". But this movement towards psychological time in modernism did not occur because, as Robert Humphrey asserted in 1954, its writers despised clock time.[213] It occurred because, as a result of cinema's continuous present, clock time now *resembled* chronological time: where Richardson and Kumar used 'clock' to connote 'divisible', the record of time provided by the cinema showed that 'clock time' was durational flow. Robert Humphrey was therefore right when he summarised the aim of *Ulysses* as "to represent . . . the inner life simultaneously with the outer life."[214]

Joyce's *A Portrait of the Artist as a Young Man* and Richardson's *Pointed Roofs*, both written before the full formal development of cinema's continuous present, *could* be seen to evidence a commitment to the constantly passing "inner duration" of the conscious/unconscious psyche *before* the possible impact of cinema. Both works contain interior monologue and both frequently employ 'returns' to previous story time which are actually recollections by characters in the forward-moving story-NOW. In 1918

Sinclair cited both works as exemplary of the literary "immersion" in the "stream of consciousness" she admired.[215] If the later 'high' modernist works represent merely a maturation of this already extant tendency, cinema's impact seems immaterial. However, cinema's impact was actually highly instrumental. Those writers we now call modernists were admittedly already drawn to the conscious/unconscious psyche as proposed by psychoanalysis in the 1890s, but in the works written before the full formal development of cinema's continuous present, even the psychodynamic psyche proposed no model of the unity of plot duration with narrative duration. In *Portrait* and *Pointed Roofs*, rendering the 'utterances' of the conscious/unconscious psyche using free indirect discourse did not banish the disparities between plot duration and narrative duration characterising the narrative methods of realist fiction: interior monologue comprises very small proportions of these works. By *Ulysses*, *Asphodel*, *Jacob's Room* and *Mrs Dalloway*, however, the conscious/unconscious psyche had *become* the narrative method. Cinema's time sense had elevated this psyche to the only subject of fiction by emulating its own time sense. Cinema's continuous present was the basis of the "durational aspect"[216] of the 'high' modernist novel, its continuous present serving as a suggestion of a way of referring to narrative events that perceived the events in the same continuous present tense as psychological experience.

Interior monologue in literature did, it must be noted, predate even the 'first birth' of cinema in 1895/6. The writer whom Joyce persistently cited as the most significant influence on his adoption of interior monologue was Édouard Dujardin, whose *Les Lauriers sont coupés* (written April 1886 to April 1887, published in the *Revue Indépendante*, of which he was editor at the time, May–August 1887, and then published as a book in 1888) he had read while in France in 1903.[217] As Richard Ellmann notes, "in later life, no matter how diligently the critics worked to demonstrate that he had borrowed the interior monologue from Freud, Joyce always made it a point of honour that he had it from Dujardin."[218] On 10 November 1917, at which time he was writing the 'Proteus' chapter of *Ulysses*, Joyce wrote to Dujardin from Zurich asking how to obtain a copy of *Lauriers* (having left his own in Austria), suggesting that he may have been using it as a model.[219] Joyce remarked in 1924 that in *Lauriers*, "the reader finds himself established, from the first lines, in the thought of the principal personage, and the uninterrupted rolling of that thought, replacing the usual form of narrative, conveys to us what this personage is doing or what is happening to him",[220] and in 1934 Frank Budgen recalled a conversation with Joyce in which the latter explained that, in *Ulysses*, "I try to give the unspoken, unacted thoughts of people in the way they occur. But I'm not the first one to do it. I took it from Dujardin."[221] In 1929 Joyce told Harriet Shaw Weaver that Dujardin had recently visited him in Paris, and that he had inscribed Dujardin's copy of the French translation of *Ulysses*: "To E.D. *Annonciateur de la parole intérieure, le larron impenitent* [Speaker of the interior word, the unrepentant thief]. J.J."²²² Joyce also encouraged Gilbert to produce an English translation of *Laurier* in 1930. Dujardin's novel has long been acknowledged as the first known instance of sustained interior monologue.²²³

If Joyce's work was just pure interior monologue, and if Richardson and H.D., producing in the same mode as Joyce at the same time, had known of Dujardin, then Dujardin's priority for the emergence of 'high' literary modernism would be clear. However, there is at least one stark distinction between *Lauriers* and *Ulysses*. In *Lauriers*, the continuous present followed virtually incidentally from the exclusive adoption of interior monologue. If the only way the reader can learn of the story space is through the interior monologue of the narrator, then no narratorial indication of a narrative shift into the story-PAST or story-FUTURE is possible, making it a *de facto* aspect of the technique that the next moment in the interior monologue is the next moment in the story space. In *Ulysses*, however, Joyce enforced the continuous present *in spite* of combining interior monologue with a third-person narrative clearly situated in the past, and for which a continuously forward-moving present was not a given aspect of the method of writing. Indeed, Joyce's very clearly historical past in *Ulysses* serves to highlight the contrast between the past tense of the narration and the continuously forward-moving present rendered by the unity of narrative time and plot time. In *Lauriers* the continuous present was incidental to the commitment to rendering an image of constant change, whereas in 'high' modernism it was a principle that occurred in spite of the use of third-person past-tense narrative. Although Dujardin represents a clear source for Joyce's method of denoting speech, providing Joyce with a way of obviating the need for the too obviously narratorial "said Daniel", Joyce used a third-person narrator nonetheless.

In addition, even though Daniel Prince, the protagonist/consciousness of *Lauriers*, is the reader's only way of accessing the novel's story space, Daniel often 'narrates', in that he thinks as if he is addressing a hearer: "That red-haired girl is stopping before a shop window; bold features she has, to match her hair . . . looking our way now, at me; what alluring eyes! Now we're quite close to her. Awfully fetching girl."²²⁴ This is not to claim that Dujardin's method was a stunted version of what only the modernists later achieved, but to point out that Dujardin used his protagonist/consciousness as if it has a narrator's capacity to pause the flow of plot time:

> I lean on the balcony, bending over the emptiness of space; I take deep breaths of the evening air, vaguely conscious of that loveliness out- side, the shadowed, soft, forlorn remoteness of the air, all this night's beauty; a grey-black sky, here and there suffused with blue, and tiny stars, like tremulous drops of water, watery stars; all around, the misty paleness of open sky; over yonder a solid gloom of trees and, beyond, black houses with lighted windows; roofs, dingy roofs; below, blurred

together, the garden; a chaos of tangled walls and all sorts of things; black houses with lighted windows and black windows; and, above me, the sky, vast, bluish, whitened with its early stars; mild air, no wind, air warm with the breath of May. There is a warmth, a soft caress in this velvety night air; the trees down there are a patch of gloom beneath the grey-blue circle of sky, spangled with tremulous gleams; and vague shadows brood in the garden of night.[225]

Although time is passing because this narrational act is a string of thoughts occupying duration in the story space, the act itself observes no imperative to reflect the passing of time, instead enacting in the narrative acts of its protagonist/consciousness the relaxed, pause-friendly, passing of time undertaken by realist narrators. Likewise, for all of chapter 5 (of nine) Dujardin has Daniel chronologically recollect his encounters with Leah while reading through his collection of letters. Although this recollection occurs in the forward-moving plot present, it creates a close equivalent of the realist provision of backstory.[226] By contrast, Joyce's, Richardson's, H.D.'s and Woolf's interior monologues insist on the passing of time in the story space.

Although *Lauriers* pre-dates the emergence of Sigmund Freud's psychodynamics, even before the 'birth' of psychology (usually placed in 1879) neurophysiology had already begun to propose a model of the mind in which conscious activity consisted not of qualitatively different processes from the rest of the body's nerve cells but merely of a higher and more convoluted volume of the nervous traffic comprising the usual operation of afferent and efferent nerve cells in prompting 'automatic' reactions via reflex arcs located in the spinal cord.[227] Both Dujardin and the later practitioners of 'high' modernism were influenced by neurological conceptions of consciousness. Cinema's place was in asserting that narrative temporality possessed the same register as this conception of consciousness.

'CINEMATOGRAPHICAL METHOD'

An account of cinema's aspect as it would have impacted on modernism could also be easily, but erroneously, gleaned from Bergson's explicit mention of the cinematograph in *Creative Evolution*.[228] Bergson wrote that, conventionally, knowledge, perception, intellection and language about the nature of change would all proceed by a "cinematographical method".[229] In this method "[w]e take snapshots, as it were, of the passing reality, and, as these are characteristic of the reality, we have only to string them on a becoming, abstract, uniform and invisible", an "impersonal movement abstract and simple, movement in general". We then put this "impersonal movement" "into the apparatus, and we reconstitute the individuality of each particular movement by combining this nameless movement with the personal attitudes."[230] This "cinematographical method", he argued, was flawed because of its gaps. Our account of change, he explained,

> symbolises . . . a certain transition of which I have taken some snapshots; of the transition itself it teaches me nothing. Let me then . . . between any two snapshots, endeavour to realize what is going on. As I apply the same method, I obtain the same result; a third view merely slips in between the two others. I may begin again as often as I will, I may set views alongside of views for ever, I shall obtain nothing else.[231]

Though, Bergson claimed, this process may be strained "to the point of giddiness" to give "the illusion of mobility, its operation has not advanced a step, since it remains as far as ever from its goal. In order to advance with the moving reality, you must replace yourself within it."[232] This flawed 'cinematographical' method derived, Bergson opined, from "the absurd proposition that movement is made of immobilities."[233]

Consequently, it could be concluded that cinema appeared to modernists as a rendering of time in immobile sections, alluding to time as *discontinuous*, and appearing as a *failure* to properly document becoming. It might even have heightened anxieties about the impossibility of either literally or metaphorically taking snapshots fast enough to document becoming. But while one of the dominant connotations of 'cinematograph' when used as a metaphor or simile before 1910 *was* 'stroboscopic'—an interrupted vision—Bergson's allusion to cinema as rendering time discontinuously is not representative of how temporality in film was experienced by its viewers. Indeed, this appearance of cinema in Bergson's 1907 work is not a description of the technology, practice or phenomenon. Rather, he selected a form whose technological basis he knew involved intermittency. His description of cinema as missing out bits of time is closer to a description of chronophotography, the series photographs produced by Eadweard Muybridge (who called it 'automatic electro-photography') in 1878–1879 and 1884–1887 and the single plates with multiple exposures produced by Étienne-Jules Marey after 1882 (Marey and Bergson would later become colleagues at the Collége de France), both of which were experienced as attempts at records of time which were nonetheless punctuated by lost time—the time elapsed between one exposure and the next.[234] Indeed, even when Muybridge projected animations of silhouettes of his photographs using the 'zoopraxiscope' on his lecture tours (during 1882 and 1887–1892), he touted these as ways of proving to sceptical audience that his photographs were not faked: the moving image verified the intermittency of the still photographs.[235] By contrast, as André Gaudreault and Philippe Marion point out, although it was initially subjugated to other media (and so worked to continue and extend their methods) "[t]he technology of the cinema was . . . the result not of a steady progression but rather of a brusque qualitative leap. The cinematograph's arrival in the world of media constituted an event whose proportions were nothing less than an epistemological break."[236] In using the term 'cinematographic', Bergson was simply arguing 'we're unable to think time' and deriving an explanatory model from his knowledge of chronophotography, one basis of a recent invention. He was not providing an account of a contemporary viewer's experience of cinema.

Indeed, Deleuze later pointed out that, in describing what he saw as the erroneous ideas endemic to our perception of the changing self, "it is strange that Bergson should give the oldest illusion such a modern and recent name ('cinematographic')."[237] Deleuze insisted that cinema itself was not "the reproduction of a constant, universal illusion"[238] but—he implied—the force which had itself given rise to idea of time as continuous flow. For Deleuze, movement is not added to the cinematic 'photogramme'. The basic unit of cinema, the 'cinematic image', is not literally a still frame. Movement belongs to it "as an immediate given". Disputing Bergson, Deleuze argues that the cinematic image is always perceived as duration: "It does give us a section, but a section which is mobile."[239] For Deleuze, cinema is time experienced *without* the method of intellection which Bergson described as 'cinematographical'[240]: "cinema does not give us an image to which movement is added, it immediately gives us a movement-image".[241] This constitutes a further reason why cinema time presented to its viewers as a continuous present. As Deleuze (paraphrasing Bergson) writes, "to recompose movement with *eternal poses* or with *immobile sections* comes to the same thing: in both cases, one misses the movement because one constructs a Whole, one assumes that 'all is given', whilst movement only occurs if the whole is neither given nor giveable".[242] Occurring in duration rather than as a succession of instants, movement is indivisible, so if cinema succeeds in presenting time as an indivisible continuity, it refers to pure duration without beginning or end, in which past and future have little meaning: unlike time mediated through intellection, which holds onto notions of past and future time, time mediated through cinema is time experienced as a continuous present.

Following the dissolution of metalanguage after 1913 amongst the proto-modernist literary impressionists, therefore, cinema militated a further upheaval in literary form: its time-sense motivated a unification of narrative time with plot time, and this unification in turn motivated a turn to the continuous present time of consciousness, which produced modernism's particular mixture of interior monologue and impersonal third-person narration.

3   Mass Consciousness and Mass Cinema

> Three states or manifestations of life: body, mind, over-mind.
>
> —H.D, *Notes on Thought and Vision*
> *and the Wise Sappho*, 1919, 17.

> [T]hough I try sometimes to limit myself to the thing I do well, I am
> always drawn on and on, by human beings, I think, out of the little
> circle of safety, on and on, to the whirlpools; when I go under.
>
> —Virginia Woolf, letter to Gerald Brenan,
> 25 December 1922,
> *The Question of Things Happening*, 600.

In giving rise to one of the formal attributes that comprised literary modernism, cinema's model of narrative temporality, I argued in Chapter 2, also provided one motivation for literary practitioners to pay particular attention to those models of the psyche being proposed in several areas of the new discipline of psychology. This chapter outlines a tighter connection between cinema and the impact on literary practice occasioned by another of modernism's already established generative influences: a conditioning connection. Indeed, if cinema's impact is not sought out in its propensity to condition the generative impact of modernism's *other* causes, a description of its influence on literary practice could well stray towards the conclusion that modernism was 'cinematic'. In this chapter, I examine how cinema's image-regime changed as a result of the First World War—modernism's clearest occasioning historical crisis—and delineate the impact of this image-regime on one of the major philosophical bases of modernism: collectivist notions of mass consciousness. I do so by laying out an unanswered question in modernist historiography, and then continuing my exploration of the developing institution cinema to provide an answer.

MASS

Of all existing accounts of literary modernism's major originating forces, one of the most compelling is outlined by Michael Tratner in his history of the widespread emergence of notions of collective consciousness towards the end of the nineteenth century. 'High' modernism is symptomatic, Tratner argues, of the concept of the 'mass mind' expressed in the works of, foremost amongst many, the French writers Gustave Le Bon and Georges Sorel, a concept that reformulated ideas regarding the source and destination of aesthetic production. Le Bon's *The Crowd* (1895) in turn influenced a range of tracts on the phenomenon of crowd psychology: William McDougall's *Social Psychology* (1908) and *The Group Mind* (1920), Graham Wallas's *Human Nature in Politics* (1908), Wilfred Trotter's *Instincts of the Herd in Peace and War* (1916–1919) and elements of Sigmund Freud's oeuvre, especially *Group Psychology and the Analysis of the Ego* (1921). All described crowds as both single consciousnesses *and* as inflected by the workings of a newly theorised 'unconscious', and all of these works expressed extreme doubts about whether a private realm was still viable, doubts in turn related to the disintegration of the public sphere and consequent lessening of the economic viability of the notion of the private bourgeois individual, as charted by Jürgen Habermas,[1] and to the rise of organised labour across Europe during the second half of the nineteenth century. Sorel's *Reflections on Violence* (1906), translated into English in 1912 by T.E. Hulme, was fundamental to the founding of continental syndicalism, and was championed both by British anarcho-syndicalist trade unionists and labour leaders and the Frith St circle led by T.E. Hulme and A.R. Orage, which included Ezra Pound and Wyndham Lewis. While neither Le Bon nor Sorel simply authored cultural notions of the mass mind, elements of their work nevertheless formulated the mass mind in ways that were central to literary modernism.

Le Bon both alluded to crowds as a consequence of certain situations—the 'psychological crowd' as distinct from the mere group of individuals—and described crowds as manifestations of "the mind of the masses"[2] or "the collective mind".[3] Drawing, in part, on neurological findings "that unconscious phenomena play an altogether prepondering part not only in organic life, but also in the operations of the intelligence",[4] he asserted that the half-conscious entity of the crowd

> thinks in images, and the image itself immediately calls up a series of other images, having no logical connection with the first. We can easily conceive this state by thinking of the fantastic succession of ideas to which we are sometimes led by calling up in our minds any fact. Our reason shows us the incoherence there is in these images, but a crowd is almost blind to this truth, and confuses with the real event what the deforming action of the imagination has superimposed thereon.[5]

The modernist use of 'the image' and interior monologue—and by extension a significant degree of modernist aesthetics—can only be fully explained, Tratner argues, on the basis of this radical new understanding of the mass mind as the entity to which any public utterance was now, at least in part, addressed.[6]

For those fully subscribing to the ethos of collectivism of which Le Bon's work was one concentrated expression, the mass mind was not the opposite of private individuality but an element of the minds of every person, and it was "in no sort a summing-up"[7] of the minds in a group but a new set of characteristics, often utterly unlike its members. For Sorel, it was for the true historian "to *understand what is least individual* in the course of events; the questions which interest the chroniclers and excite novelists are those which he most willingly leaves on one side."[8] Because the force which forms humans into groups was the only important social force, Sorel argued, "all the discussions by moralists about the motives for the actions of prominent men and the psychological analyses of character are therefore of quite secondary and even negligible importance".[9] Both Le Bon and Sorel expressed, and contributed to, the emerging notion of a mass (un)consciousness that was also being demonstrated by sociolinguistics from Saussure in the 1880s[10] and sociology from Emile Durkheim in the 1890s, as both showed the individual to be part of much larger ways of thinking that *could not* be replicated by the individual. As Le Bon noticed, these disciplines would "reverse the perspective which makes society the result of individual behaviour and insist that behaviour is made possible by collective social systems which individuals have assimilated, consciously or subconsciously."[11]

Also prominent in *The Crowd* and *Reflections on Violence* was the notion that the crowd was the only social force capable of total revolutionary change, yet, directed by images placed in the mass mind by antiquated institutions, had not *yet* realised this potential. Le Bon described "the popular imagination" as the basis of the power of conquerors and the strength of states: "There is no power, Divine or human, that can oblige a stream to flow back to its source".[12] He nevertheless aimed to show "how powerless they [crowds] are to hold any opinions other than those which are imposed upon them, and that it is not with rules based on theories of pure equity that they are to be led, but by seeking what produces an impression on them and what seduces them".[13] For Tratner, these thinkers regarded the crowd as holding "little respect for conventions of realism, merging the subjective and the objective, the conscious and the unconscious".[14] Although a crowd's collective observations, based on a 'contagion' of the illusions held by its members, combined with an inability to tell real from unreal, were, as Le Bon put it, "as erroneous as possible",[15] the fact that these illusions directed mass action meant that they had to be regarded as a reality of sorts. As Le Bon wrote, "[a]ll great historical facts, the rise of Buddhism, of Christianity, of Islamism, the Reformation, the French Revolution, and, in our own time, the threatening invasion of Socialism, are the direct or indirect consequences of strong impressions produced on the imagination of the crowd."[16] From the opposite end of the political spectrum Sorel also looked exclusively to proletarian mass consciousness both to realise catastrophic change and to wipe away regressive constitutional representations of the masses that prevented such change.[17] For Tratner, to excavate the effects of this new notion of mass consciousness is to discover the subterranean narrative of modernist aesthetics, an effort to describe and influence the mass mind, and an abandonment of all other areas as beyond the purpose of aesthetics.

Le Bon's work also expressed ambivalence concerning the crowd's ability to cause its own revolution:

> It is difficult to understand history, and popular revolutions in particular, if one does not take sufficiently into account the profoundly conservative instincts of crowds. They may be desirous, it is true, of changing the names of their institutions, and to obtain these changes they accomplish at times even violent revolutions, but the essence of these institutions is too much the expression of the hereditary needs of the race for them not invariably to abide by it.[18]

For Le Bon, because of the innate conservatism of crowds, "[i]t is fortunate for the progress of civilisation that the power of crowds only began to exist when the great discoveries of science and industry had already been effected".[19] Yet Le Bon also believed that "[w]e should not complain too much that crowds are more especially guided by unconscious considerations and are not given to reasoning. Had they, in certain cases, reasoned and consulted their immediate interest, it is possible that no civilisation would have grown up on our planet, and humanity would have had no history."[20] Historical change, including what appears as 'progress', is brought about by the crowd's aimless spontaneity. The mass mind devolved the individual but to a level more amenable to radical action:

> by the mere fact that he forms part of an organised crowd, a man descends several rungs in the ladder of civilisation. . . . He possesses the spontaneity, the violence, the ferocity, and also the enthusiasm and heroism of primitive beings, whom he further tends to resemble by the facility with which he allows himself to be impressed by words and images . . . and to be induced to commit acts contrary to his most obvious interest and his best-known habits.[21]

This emphasis on the crowd's ability to produce enthusiasm and spontaneity that could overcome bourgeois stultification and produce revolutionary change, present in both *The Crowd* and *Reflections on Violence*, meant that the aesthetic thought that warmed to collectivist philosophy sought to figure the mass mind and its utterances not just to represent it but to influence it too.[22]

Both the right-wing Le Bon and the left-wing Sorel insisted that because institutions are a creation of the 'genius' of the masses, "it is not in institutions that the means is to be sought of profoundly influencing the genius of the masses". Rather, "[i]t is illusions and words that have influenced the mind of the crowd."[23] Indeed, Le Bon wrote, "[t]he masses have never thirsted after truth. . . . Whoever can supply them with illusions is easily their master; whoever attempts to destroy their illusions is always their victim."[24] Sorel developed this idea extensively, using the term "myth" to describe the groups of images by which the mass mind is directed into 'movements'.[25] Myths possessed the power to stimulate the mass mind, where socialist leadership or intellectual operations such as criticism, proof, argument and analysis could not, because they could set up and move waves within the mass mind. As he wrote, "we do nothing great without the help of warmly-coloured and clearly-defined images".[26] Opposed to the rational arguments of politics, myths were 'histories of the future', certainties of the success of coming actions which in turn created the movement necessary to realise that action, and which therefore functioned as historical forces in their own right. For Sorel ordinary language would be useless for unifying a disjointed set of workers' movements in France currently abused by "Parliamentary Socialists"[27]:

> use must be made of a body of images which, *by intuition alone*, and before any considered analyses are made, is capable of evoking as an undivided whole the mass of sentiments which corresponds to the different manifestations of the war undertaken by Socialism against modern society. The Syndicalists solve this problem perfectly, by concentrating the whole of Socialism in the drama of the general strike.[28]

Such myths as 'the general strike', Sorel's "proletarian catastrophic" myth (as opposed to 'bourgeois progressive' myth),[29] would, he argued, bring about socialist revolution through complete disruption of state, politics and economics. The 'general strike' would later become a fundamental of militant labour politics in the UK following the dissemination of anarcho-syndicalism towards the end of the 1900s.

As myth was "a spontaneous product" that could not be submitted to the test of intelligence,[30] for the wave in crowd thought, the distinction between "partial reality" and "product of the popular imagination" was irrelevant.[31] Where Le Bon described crowds as intellectually inferior,[32] for Sorel a proletarian revolution would be possible only when the myth of 'the general strike' revealed the attempts [i of the lower middle-class to subordinate proletarian organisations to their own personal advantage.[33] Sorel also frequently identified 'the mass' with the proletariat ('the mass mind' often becoming "the working-class mind"),[34] a numerically viable identification but a central problematic to a non-proletarian modernist's attempt to excavate the mass mind in her/his own mind. Modernism's retreat from the novel of characterisation was also related to Sorel's declaration that with the adoption of Syndicalism "heroic characters . . . disappear!"[35]

'High' modernism drew on the belief, expressed by Le Bon, that the political battles of the twentieth century were not going to be waged by individual contact with the public sphere or by parliamentary debate, but by competing streams of images in the crowd mind:

> Whatever be the ideas suggested to crowds they can only exercise influence on condition that they assume a very absolute, uncompromising, and simple shape. They present themselves then in the guise of images, and are only accessible to the masses under this form. These image-like ideas are not connected by any logical bond of analogy or succession, and may take each other's place like the slides of a magic lantern which the operator withdraws from the groove in which they were placed one above the other. This explains how it is that the most contradictory ideas may be seen to be simultaneously current in crowds.[36]

The potential in aesthetic products to move waves in the mass mind (where aesthetics had for a century occupied at best a peripheral place in conceptions of political activity) was thus a further cause of literary modernism's departure from realism. As, for Sorel, lofty moral convictions "never depend on reasoning or on any education of the individual will, but on a state of war in which men voluntarily participate and which finds expression in well-defined myths",[37] it was therefore crucial that "the movements of the revolted masses must be represented in such a way that the soul of the revolutionaries may receive a deep and lasting impression."[38] Literary modernism therefore appears as an attempt to establish a literature corresponding to the reduced importance of individual personality and literary character in speaking to and serving the mass mind.[39]

While such realists as H.G. Wells and G.K. Chesterton expressed collectivist ideas in world states and spontaneous revolutionary eddies (i.e. in content), literary modernism was the *formal* literary corollary of collectivist philosophy. Modernism, for Tratner, was a formal attempt to write in the idiom of the mass mind, undertaken by those for whom liberalism and even parliamentary socialism seemed to be characterised by an absence of methods of thinking 'as' the masses.[40] The artist was therefore conceived as a cipher for the mob part of her/his own mind (hence Stephen Dedalus conceiving of history as a nightmare and Joyce not letting him wake up from it).[41] Representational capacity was also surrendered to communicating only what is generated by movements in the 'mob' part of the artist's own mind. This progression in modernist thought was also, Tratner argues, accelerated by the First World War: "before the war, many modernists and most politicians in government feared being drowned by the masses; after the war, they feared being left out of the mass movements transforming society".[42] The seductiveness of collectivism by 1922 is signalled by Woolf's letter to Gerald Brenan of that year quoted at the head of this chapter. The degree to which writers subscribed to collectivism determined their distance from existing concepts of narrative, character and dialogue. While the 'mid-range' modernists E.M. Forster, Joseph Conrad and D.H. Lawrence "developed a variety of methods of maintaining the individual in fictional worlds represented as being without a private space",[43] for Tratner the complexity of the works of Eliot, Woolf, W. B. Yeats and Joyce is correlated instead with their commitment to speaking the language of crowd thought.

As Tratner points out, the micro- and macro-narratives of the one-day *Ulysses* and the 400-year *Orlando* (1928) also exemplify the attempt to build novels around collective rhythms rather than individual destinies, in contrast to the *bildungsroman*, in which the individual's formation is dependent on the considerable stability of social forces.[44] Even in Woolf's earlier works, instead of having their personalities brought out by the situations characters find themselves in, characters' thoughts are influenced by these situations. Writing *Night and Day* (July 1916–21 November 1918, revised January–March 1919 and published 20 October 1919), if not yet to the extent of *Mrs Dalloway*, Woolf already regarded the consciousness of her protagonists as continuous with those around them. Walking from work to Queen's Hall, Katharine Hilbery

> fully intended to use her loneliness to think out her position with regard to Ralph; but although she walked back to the Strand with this end in view, she found her mind uncomfortably full of different trains of thought. She started one and then another. They seemed even to take their colour from the street she happened to be in. Thus the vision of humanity appeared to be in some way connected with Bloomsbury, and faded distinctly by the time she crossed the main road[45]

The London streets are consistently experienced in *Night and Day* as arenas of what Woolf, in *A Room of One's Own* (1929), would call "thinking in common",[46] her concept of the central propulsion behind aesthetic creation.

The portable focalisation in *Mrs Dalloway*—the 'baton change' passing of focalisation between characters through physical proximity or some larger linking device such as the sky-writing plane—is also suggestive of a commitment to narrating a greater consciousness that does not inhere in people. Notably, this has been seen as constituting a 'camera eye' in the same sense of the non-subject-centred 'camera-eye' that was constituted in 1920s Soviet film by the deliberate structuring of edits from shot to shot to breach the expected pursuit of drama by each edit (for example, by editing together a shot of a character passing a ticket to an inspector with a shot of the inspector later passing his ticket-book to his employer), so creating a connection between two shots that does not derive from any character. This 'intellectual montage' in *Mrs Dalloway* has been seen as one of the 'cinematic' properties exhibited by modernist literature which it shares with a stream of 1920s film, but *not* because of cinema. Rather, a preceding common cause created these 'camera-eyes' in both media.[47] One component of this common cause, it seems, was the recent emergence of the notion of the mass mind and the felt need to recognise it with a "unifying presence" that was neither a narrator nor based on the interaction between characters.[48]

Mrs Dalloway also includes two short interregna in which the narrative is briefly not localised in *any* consciousness. In the context of the novel's pervasive (albeit highly temporary) localisation of consciousness these represent moments of true 'thinking in common'. When the unidentified car has left Bond Street, the narration pauses free direct discourse focused on Clarissa:

> She stiffened a little; so she would stand at the top of the stairs.
> The car had gone, but it had left a slight ripple which flowed through glove shops and hat shops on both sides of Bond Street. For thirty seconds all heads were inclined the same way—to the window. Choosing a pair of gloves—should they be to the elbow or above it, lemon or pale grey?—ladies stopped; when the sentence was finished something had happened. Something so trifling in single instances that no mathematical instrument, though capable of transmitting shocks in China, could register the vibration; yet in its fulness rather formidable and in its common appeal emotional; for in all the hat shops and tailors' shops strangers looked at each other and thought of the dead; of the flag; of Empire. . . . For the surface agitation of the passing car as it sunk grazed something very profound.[49]

The narration moves with the car, focusing on a group of men in White's club and then on a crowd outside Buckingham Palace before localising again, after just 603 words, in a crowd member called Emily Coates using indirect discourse. Indeed, along with the earlier interregnum of 177 words, just 780 words of the work's 64,027 words cannot be identified with a character's consciousness. The association of these interregna with events occurring in the presence of crowds also mark them as distinct from omniscient narration.

Collectivity is also repeatedly figured in Woolf's content, as early as *Night and Day*, although the character imagining it is often mistaken in assuming it achieved and in error in placing herself at the centre of it. Mary Datchet, surrounded by piles of correspondence at the women's suffrage society, feels herself at "the centre ganglion of a very fine network of nerves which fell over England, and one of these days, when she touched the heart of the system, would begin feeling and rushing together and emitting their splendid blaze of revolutionary fireworks".[50] Mr Clacton advises those at the suffrage office that "[w]e should consider ourselves the centre of an enormous system of wires, connecting us up with every district of the country".[51] To Katharine, the suffrage society appears to be "flinging their frail spiders' webs over the torrent of life which rushed down the streets outside".[52] That is, by 1918–1919 Woolf was challenging certain images of collectivity as mere middle-class illusions about the collective mind *and* working to figure that collective mind in her own work. *Night and Day* saw Woolf begin to use water metaphors to figure urban collectivity. Katharine watches with fascination as traffic and pedestrians flow up and down Kingsway:

> The deep roar filled her ears; the changing tumult had the inexpressible fascination of varied life pouring ceaselessly with a purpose which, as she looked, seemed to her, somehow, the normal purpose for which life was framed; its complete indifference to the individuals, whom it swallowed up and rolled onwards, filled her with at least a temporary exaltation.[53]

Water imagery also populates *Mrs Dalloway*, from Clarissa's "what a plunge!"[54] when faced with the possibility of a day amongst London's crowds, to her feeling of suspense upon entering a room full of people, likened to "an exquisite suspense, such as might stay a diver before plunging while the sea darkens and brightens beneath him."[55] Virtually always linked with crowds, these water images allude to human experience as immersion in an indivisible continuum.

Le Bon argued that while the crowd had often briefly gained power and consciousness before, it had always slipped back into passivity when a new "intellectual aristocracy" arose.[56] Sorel likewise lamented the influence of "the Intellectuals who have embraced *the profession of thinking for the proletariat.*"[57] When Pound advocated a scrappy underclass of uneducated "savage" artists "whose dangers are subtle and sudden" in his February 1914 'The New Sculpture',[58] he showed his eagerness to side with what he saw as the transformative proletariat. As Sorel distinguished between violence and force—"the object of force is to impose a certain social order in which the minority governs, while violence tends to the destruction of that order"[59]—Pound's essay also described his ideal artists as living "by craft and violence",[60] "aroused to the fact that the war between him and the world is a war without truce".[61] In September 1918 Woolf also advocated a similarly chaotic violence for narrating wartime domestic experience: "coarseness—the quality that is the most difficult of all for the educated to come by . . . By coarseness we mean something vehement, full throated, carrying down in its rush sticks and stones and fragments of human nature pell-mell."[62] Advocating generative violence, modernists also had to take into account that the complete disruption of economic activity (either for its own sake or as a myth to galvanise the crowd mind) also included disrupting aesthetic production. Tratner's analysis also hints at the problem posed for modernism by the unanswered question of whether it was even *possible* for a writer whose utterances were versions or aggregates of mass thinking to author works that might initiate waves in the mass mind.[63]

While Tratner points to the evolution in individualist political thought through the nineteenth century (from Alexis de Tocqueville through J.S. Mill and Matthew Arnold) as indicative of the increasing problematisation of liberal individualism as a base to be defended from the demands made by the mass political voice of the rising trade union, he does not note that, in the decades immediately before the First World War, a version of collectivism also entered British Liberal Party politics.[64] Sarah Wilkinson has shown that political debate in Britain between 1880 and 1918 "centred on the economic implications of the relationship between state and individual for society's least privileged members."[65] With the growing loss of confidence amongst state theorists and the government in the market's ability to self-regulate, the 1880s saw recommendations for greater state intervention in the economic sphere to help individuals achieve their economic goals. The 'New Liberalism' of the 1880s and 1890s, the large-scale social investigations of the 1890s and 1900s, and the work of the British Idealist School from the 1870s, peaking in popularity only in 1915, were a substantial departure from the thinking of the mid-century. The philanthropic work of the 1890s and 1900s (not least Charles Booth's vast 17-volume *Life and Labour of the People of London* (1891–1902)) cast doubt on the established notion that unemployment and poverty were controlled by character. Andrew Mearns's *The Bitter Cry of Outcast London* (1883), J.A. Hobson's *Problems of Poverty* (1891), the works of Sydney Webb and Beatrice Potter/ Webb in the 1890s, Seebohm Rowntree's *Poverty: A Study of Town Life* (1901) and the 1909 Minority Report of the Poor Law Commission were all elements of this literature. L.T. Hobhouse, theorising the state in the light of the dire social and economic circumstances experienced by many in the modern industrial metropolis, contributed heavily, between 1893 and 1924, to identifying for the Commons a concept of individual and state as functioning simultaneously rather than as opposites:

> Within voluntary bodies such as Toynbee Hall, the Charities Organization Society, and Charles Booth's social survey movement, figures as diverse as the Webbs and Bernard Bosanquet developed the sense that the scale of the poverty problem, in London at least, could not purely be the product of the individual's enterprise or lack of it, but had its causes in the economic life which was beyond the control of the individual.[66]

In discussing graduated taxation, Hobson argued that "[w]hen it is said that 'we are all socialists to-day', what is meant is that we are all engaged in the active promotion or approval of legislation which can only be explained as a gradual unconscious recognition of the existence of a social property in capital which it is held politic to secure for public use."[67]

This rising perception of a social aspect to capital meant that the idea of the self-sufficient individual (an idea based on the bourgeois investment of capital) was, for many, gradually rivalled by a sense of a collective subject. In a letter of 1903, for example, Beatrice Webb wrote of her perception of a need for "constructive thought and constructive action" to give freedom to "a genuinely state-conscious collective mind and [to create] the machinery to carry this mind into effect".[68] This new conception remained in conflict with traditional liberalism, but nevertheless influenced the 'New Liberalism' espoused by Henry Campbell-Bannerman and Herbert Asquith's 1906–1916 Liberal government. In this new parliamentary credo, 'old liberal' *laissez-faire* principles lapsed in the face of commitments to redistribution, and the Old Age Pensions Act of 1908, the 'People's Budget' of 1909 and the National Insurance Act of 1911 accelerated a gradual increase, already manifest in earlier hygiene and slum clearance legislation, in governmental presence in private life.

Pre-war London also saw syndicalist thought reach a high point, with the first international syndicalist conference held in London in 1913. That collectivist thought possessed an aesthetic permutation is suggested by its presence in the *New Freewoman/Egoist*, where radical-individualist anti-statism co-existed with anarcho-syndicalist anti-statism. Orage's *New Age* contributed to and charted syndicalism's growing strength as an anti-statist ideology among disaffected socialists. Those in the UK familiar with Sorel's ideas witnessed the alarming spectacle of parliamentary socialism moulded into liberalism, in the form of the new Labour Party's increasing co-operation with the Liberals: most demonstrably in the Lib-Lab pact of 1903, Labour MPs siding against strikers in labour disputes throughout the 1900s, and Labour's support for the 1911 National Insurance Plan.[69] David Kadlec has charted the multiple connections between the Hulme/Orage Frith Street Circle and the anonymous militant industry takeover manifestos circulated by personnel linked with the South Wales Miners Federation, and connects the founding of *BLAST* in July 1914 with a tradition of late nineteenth-century socialist and anarchist workers pamphlets, the title even echoing the contemporary underground Welsh syndicalist circular *Rhondda Socialist*, also known as 'the workers' bomb'. For Kadlec, the 'Hulme evenings' "brought together two strains of English rebellion, with the workers' movement drawing from some of the same continental and late-Victorian London anarchic traditions as the libertarian and reactionary politics surrounding the vorticists".[70] *BLAST*'s "art of individuals" was not anti-collectivist. Its assault on the "PLACID, NON-ENERGIZED FUTURE"[71] suggests an intimate connection with Sorel's definition of myth, and its "End of the Christian Era"[72] echoes the impending class war drummed by syndicalist labour leaders at the time. Also, insomuch as the therapeutic models of the unconscious filtering into British literary circles around the time of the formation of the London Psycho-Analytical Society in 1913 offered a way of understanding irrationality as creative and transformative rather than pathological, they substantiated notions of the crowd's irrationality as a radically generative force.[73]

In September 1914 Pound argued that, in Vorticism, in contrast to the "accelerated impressionism" he saw in Futurism,[74] "the image . . . is a radiant node or cluster; . . . a VORTEX, from which, and through which, and into which, ideas are constantly rushing."[75] Vorticism figured its origins as a force present in the nation, the "Great English Vortex", as *BLAST* was subtitled. Clearly Vorticism sought to power itself with a version of Le Bon's mode of crowd thought, with Pound describing artists as both "the plastic substance *receiving* impressions" *and* as "directing a certain fluid force against circumstance"[76]: i.e. both a scribe for movements in the mass mind and, so he hoped, capable of initiating them. As he wrote in the *New Age* in early 1915,

> By bad verse, whether "regular" or "free," I mean verse which pretends to some emotion which did not assist at its parturition. . . . Where the voltage is so high that it fuses the machinery, one has merely the "emotional man" not the artist. The best artist is the man whose machinery can stand the highest voltage. The better the machinery, the more precise, the stronger; the more exact will be the record of the voltage and of the various currents which have passed through it. . . . These are bad expressions if they lead you to think of the artist as wholly passive, as a mere receiver of impressions. The good artist is perhaps a good seismograph, but the difference between man and machine is that man can in some degree "start his machinery going." . . . At least he can move as a force; he can produce "order-giving vibrations"; by which one may mean merely, he can departmentalise such part of the life-force as it flows through him.[77]

The artist, for Pound, channelled a pre-existing force. Creating, over merely imitating (as impressionism was now retrospectively styled), meant manifesting this force in abstract forms: "The organisation of forms is a much more energetic and creative action than the copying or imitating of light on a haystack".[78] The perceived propensity of the mass mind to think in images also made the step towards a language of form and colour all the more attractive.

While, by the 1920s, the war had contaminated any redemptive revolutionary capacity that could have previously been ascribed to violence, its enormity of collective effort, the alternative forms of social organisation it suggested, and the Syndicalist revolutions in Germany in November 1918 also solidified the idea that collective forces were far more capable than institutions of revolutionary change.[79] Indeed, modernism's intensification, from flirtation with notions of collectivity before the war to wholehearted investment in them after the war, can be explained by Vincent Sherry's work on the wartime crisis of Liberalism. Sherry points out that the weight of rhetoric produced by the Liberal press and Liberal intellectuals in support of Britain's entry into the war contradicted the key Liberal tenet of non-involvement in European conflicts, and that it did so through marshalling the supposedly intrinsically Liberal resource of rational argument: "The logic of the Liberal war devolved its burden of proof . . . from the substance of its case to the prosody of its argument."[80] The Liberal imperialists heading up the wartime governments and the party's associated intellectuals made speeches and wrote articles under pressure from a "need to make sensible a policy previously deemed irrational",[81] compromising the ideals of Liberalism in their use of Liberal reasoned argument. Consequently, amongst modernists, what belief in the existence of a public sphere defined by civic rationality still remained "was convulsing under the effort to legitimize this war."[82] There was a daily revelation in the press, during the war, of the vacuousness of the rational argumentation believed to substantiate Liberal ideals, and, from the viewpoint of modernists already warming to collectivist notions of crowd consciousness, this emptying of Liberal rhetoric implied the bankruptcy of individualism.

The First World War also continued to extend the sphere of the 'social' far beyond the scope of New Liberal or even Labour theorisation in the UK (albeit identifying economic collectivity with armed conflict). While the war signalled the failure of any international socialist movement capable of pre-empting such a conflict, it also signalled a massive set of re-articulations of the relationship between individual and state. The corollary of an (as yet un-envisioned) British continental army was a powerful government reorganisation of unanticipated parts of the economy. If munitions and other supplies in required quantities were to be produced, Trevor Wilson points out,

> the peacetime form of large sectors of industry would need to be distorted. They must cease production for established customers, even though they might be under contract to them. They must expand workshop space and machinery and the labour force. They must introduce untrained workers into processes of production formerly reserved for the experienced and qualified. They must aid in the establishment and management of factories set up and owned by the government. And all this must be done in order to provision a market that, it was devoutly hoped, would disappear in short order. Whatever the terms or prices offered, no version of market economics would satisfy such a proceeding.[83]

The Ministry of Munitions and the Coalition Government both emerged in May 1915, James Garvin noted at the time, out of the "vaster question of organising the entire nation for the industrial as well as the military purposes of the war".[84] By the middle of 1916 the Ministry of Munitions controlled almost the entire process of armaments production: research and development, raw materials and machinery, supervision of both private and state factories and provision to the War Office. The new Ministries of December 1916 and early 1917 (Labour, National Service, Food and Shipping) signalled the increasing strength of commitment to the philosophy of state control beyond simply the control of industry. Because of the Somme debacle this involved 'combing out' an extra 45,000 men from industry while simultaneously increasing the labour force to keep the army better supplied than it had been in 1916. While this did not involve the imposition of service on *all* adult males, the National Service Ministry's management of the British workforce was substantial, involving the 'clean cut' method of releasing labour for essential industries and reinvigorating under-farmed land to reduce dependence on imports.[85]

Factories manifested a sense of identity between the working-class and the nation at war (indicated by a preference among even those men *not* of military age for working in government establishments where they would be badged as a worker in an essential industry). Even though the April 1917 reports prepared for the Cabinet on the labour situation stressed that the labour force was by no means moving irresistibly in a class-conscious direction or away from supporting the nation at war, the British working-class did overcome some of its powerful internal divisions on the basis of skill, status and sex. In spite of the banning of all wartime strikes with the agreement of union leaders, strikes amounted to five and a half million working days in 1917, and six million working days in 1918. Although this did not approach the all-time peak of 41 million working days in 1912, it indicated that the wartime worker still experienced her/himself as a part of a labour collective.[86] Alisdair Reid examines the improvement in the bargaining position of British workers as employers competed with each other for scarce labour, as blackleg labour disappeared and as low unemployment and high earnings strengthened the power of trade unions. Consequently, the state took the far more active role in labour politics of encouraging consultation between industry bosses and employees and their representatives—the role of recognising a mass voice.[87] "Never before" wrote G.D.H. Cole in 1919, "has the extent to which the whole community depends upon the working class been so fully realised, either by the other classes or by the workers themselves."[88] Between 1914 and 1918 union membership in the UK rose from four million to 6.5 million, with the highest proportional increases amongst the previously least responsive (the poorly paid and women). That Lloyd George could overthrow Asquith in December 1916 with the support of only half of the 272 Liberals but could *not* form a government without the support of just 42 Labour MPs was just one sign of a much wider, if less explicitly expressed, government reliance on concord with the institutions of organised labour to continue the war[89]: "By the same token, no blow that might be struck in the world of politics could be permitted to damage the Labour party to the degree that it might arouse trade union resistance."[90] The placing of a Labour MP in Lloyd George's five-man war cabinet shows how central the relationship between labour and state had become to the understanding of the meaning of government.

Whereas, for most of the war, class had determined hunger, the adoption of national rationing in early 1918 was an unprecedented socialist move. After food shortages began at the end of 1916, while such foodstuffs as bread were always available, changing foodstuff shortages meant that fixed income families suffered from the consequent price increases as much as actual scarcity. The lengthy queues

> aroused profound working-class resentment, which spread even to soldiers serving at the front. And working-class organizations began drawing conclusions that, however much in tune with wartime notions of equality of sacrifice, severely challenged the existing structure of society. At Nottingham late in September, a report on the labour situation recorded, 'an important joint meeting' of miners and railwaymen passed with enthusiasm a resolution calling on the Food Controller to 'take all the foodstuffs in the country and share them out equally to every household in proportion to the number of the family.'[91]

Whereas the disruption of meetings intended to set up Workers' and Soldiers' Councils in June 1917 aroused little working-class indignation, the combination of a rise in the cost of living, queues at food shops and rumours of profiteering produced a national mood of working-class indignation that began to be expressed in industrial action, which by October 1917 reached proportions sufficient to shake the government. An early February 1918 report on the labour situation stated that "[t]he number of workers involved in the short strikes which are occurring all over the country as protest against the food situation is becoming a matter of serious national importance".[92] Widespread calls in 1917 for rationing were indicative of a widening section of society entertaining the notion that the government was responsible, in spite of established class differences, for provisioning all of its citizens. As Wilson notes, "[i]n a situation where commodities were available but not in sufficient quantities to meet normal demand, the discomforts of a free market were far worse than any inconveniences resulting from state regulations."[93] Outrage against profiteering impugned the profit motive and thus called into question on a national scale some basic tenets of liberal capitalism, tenets which the government largely, if tardily, likewise rejected. The Ministry of Food, albeit slowly, followed suit, bringing 85% of food eaten by civilians under the control of government instrumentalities and 94% under price control between February and July 1918.[94] While queues outside food shops were blatantly at their worst in working-class areas, this expressed an idea of the state as an expression of collective conscious rather than as a management institution.

Of course, left-wing activists were concerned that the war might validate a notion of collective effort as a crutch for governments rather than workers. Beatrice Webb worried at the beginning of 1916 that the War Cabinet's decision in favour of compulsory service was the penultimate step before the establishment of a system of military and industrial conscription, the hallmark of "[t]he 'servile state'".[95] In *Jacob's Room* (1922), following a description of battle, Woolf's narrator remarks that "[t]hese actions, together with the incessant commerce of banks, laboratories, chancellories, and houses of business, are the strokes which oar the world forward, they say",[96] combining certainty of institutional control with scepticism towards this certainty. In the wake of the large-scale economic interventions of the various wartime Ministries and the various Acts of the Coalition Governments, the mass mind could appear to be both in thrall to government 'interference' in the life of the individual *and* the only force capable of destroying these institutions. Woolf's approach to these forces was therefore to criticise not their impersonality, but that they were "dealt by men as smoothly sculptured as the impassive policeman [whose] face is stiff from force of will . . . It is thus that we live, they say . . . driven by an unseizable force."[97] The forces associated with the gestalt of the mass mind were only harmful insofar as the illusion persisted that they were controlled by men with power and were not the operations of the mass mind itself. By the time Woolf was writing *Jacob's Room* in the middle of 1920, the war had significantly enhanced the validity of perceptions that collective entities were uniquely generative and transformative. She had commented in September 1918 that "many whose minds have not been used to turn that way must stop and ponder what thoughts the country people carry with them to their work in the fields, or cogitate as they scrub the cottage floor."[98] That the multiple de-privatisations of the means of production brought by the war fed into and adhered closely to growing notions of the mass mind is evident in the imperative being to know what the working-class are *thinking*, not just what they are doing.

The true realm of activity for Woolf's characters in *Night and Day* (although not the realm in which they can yet move) is "the impersonal life",[99] a far cry of 'the inner life' often attributed to modernism. Notions of the mass mind also moved Woolf to valorise the abilities of 'the common reader' above the literary abilities of "the critic and the scholar"[100] in her introduction to the collection of essays *The Common Reader* (1925). This reader

> is guided by an instinct to create for himself, out of whatever odds and ends he can come by, some kind of whole—a portrait of a man, a sketch of an age . . . He never ceases, as he reads, to run up some rickety and ramshackle fabric which shall give him the temporary satisfaction of looking sufficiently like the real object to allow of affection, laughter, and argument.[101]

The reader-projected image in the crowd mind of Le Bon and Sorel clearly bore on Woolf's understanding of the act of reading undertaken by 'the common', as did the idea that the illusion, though unwittingly fabricated, is also an instrumental force. Tratner indicates that in the work of the right-wing Eliot, the images of alienated labour and urban slavery in *The Waste Land* (written January–December 1921, revised by Eliot and Pound between November 1921 and January 1922, and published October 1922) expressed a different element of belief in the mass mind, figuring a social body that, deprived of leaders intellectually devoted to the study of its currents, would always try, and always fail, to express itself.[102]

MODERNIST PUBLISHING

In looking at how cinema conditioned the impact of notions of mass consciousness on literary practice, I first pose an unanswered question about modernism's most overt public-oriented activity—its marketing institutions. An account of cinema's new dimensions during the war can, I go on to observe, provide one answer to this question.

Joyce, Woolf, Eliot and Yeats, Tratner argues, "did not wish to speak comprehensibly to average men because doing so was irrelevant to the job of creating deep waves" in the mass mind.[103] Modernism wished to avoid duplicating the scant effect on the mass mind achieved by government and education. Central to Tratner's analysis is the idea that because mass consciousness was largely unrealised by existing institutions, including those of mass culture, modernism's ambivalent attitude towards mass culture does not mean that it was a reactionary or aristocratic cultural venture. Rather, given that it saw the ability of institutions to address the mass as inversely proportional to their capacity to speak its language—a disparity increasingly apparent as circulation figures for popular newspapers and magazines grew dramatically between 1890 and 1910—it follows that modernism was, rather than a rejection of mass culture, "an effort to *produce* a mass culture, perhaps for the first time, to produce a culture distinctive to the twentieth century, which Le Bon called 'The Era of the Crowd.'"[104] In an early instance of flirtation with collectivity, as Tratner points out, Yeats wrote in 1901 that "what we call 'popular poetry' never came from the people at all."[105] Instead "the poetry of the coteries"[106] spoke the language of the people. The poetry of the coteries and "the true poetry of the people",[107] Yeats argued, "are alike strange and obscure, and unreal to all who have not understanding, and both, instead of that manifest logic, that clear rhetoric of the 'popular poetry,' glimmer with thoughts and images."[108] Ford Madox Ford exemplified a common assessment of the new generation of newspapers and short fiction magazines that had emerged in the 1890s when he stated, in 1909, that "[a]n immense reading public has come into existence and the desire of those who cater for it is not to promote thought but to keep it entertained."[109] Collectivist thinkers could not dismiss the political power evidenced by the mass-circulating publications of the Newnes, Pearson,

Harmsworth and Odhams publishing empires, even if it could dismiss their ability to speak to 'the masses'. Hence in 1922 Clive Bell saw modernism not as an elite practice but as a thin strip of cultural territory, located "between the uncompromising artists and the barbarous horde—painters and writers who while giving the semicivilized public what it wanted inveigled that public into wanting something better than the worst".[110]

As it was now incumbent on modernists to see realist popular culture as either involved in imposing individualist myths on the mass mind (and thus limiting its spontaneity) or as effectively talking gibberish to it, modernism's self-delineation against mass culture through strategic difficulty was not the same, in the minds of its practitioners, as retreat from the mass mind: "Many modernists believed that they were gaining contact with the mass mind by using their strange forms", Tratner argues, because, in their view, "if they wrote in clear, easily comprehensible, realistic forms, they would be disconnected from the masses."[111] Tratner surmises that in 'Nineteen Hundred and Nineteen' (1919) and 'Ancestral Houses' (1923), Yeats "speculates that great works that outlast the violent social spirit that gave birth to them get in the way of social change"[112] and that it was central to 'high' modernism that, in line with Sorelian thinking on catastrophe, "[c]ultural products lose their value when they are separated from the rich streams that flung them up."[113] In Joyce's *A Portrait of the Artist as a Young Man*, Stephen Dedalus experiences this language necrosis: walking past shops, "he found himself glancing from one casual word to another on his right or left in stolid wonder that they had been so silently emptied of instantaneous sense until every mean shop legend bound his mind like the words of a spell and his soul shrivelled up sighing with age as he walked on in a lane among heaps of dead language."[114] If modernist aesthetics was an engagement with the mass mind, this means that modernism would have embraced the idea of their productions as immediately disposable. In his study of *The English Review*, *The Freewoman/New Freewoman/Egoist*, *Poetry and Drama*, *BLAST* and *The New Age* in the 1908–1915 period, Mark Morrisson concludes that "[r]ather than fostering the rejection of commercial culture, which has long been attributed to modernism, the birth of British . . . modernism sparked an explosion of publication and self-promotion and several serious attempts to address the institutions of the dominant culture."[115] He makes a strong case that, in the immediate pre-war period, none of the modernists "wished to retreat into the private and elite confines of coterie publication."[116] When Ford founded *The English Review* in 1908, for example, he departed from Victorian precedents that dictated that wildly unorthodox material could only be published in small, purely literary and mainly coterie periodicals (like the Pre-Raphaelite *Germ*) or radical political magazines (like the anarchist *Torch*) and created for radical writers a version of the far more widely circulating Victorian review journal.[117] Why, then, did this series of optimistic attempts by modernist little magazines to engage with commercial culture end in 1915? If 'high' modernist thought was focused on the felt necessity of erecting an alternative mass culture, how can we account for the fact that *BLAST*'s 1914–1915 aesthetics of the "jarring appeal of the advertising poster"[118] was the last incarnation of this? *Can* modernism thereafter be claimed to have been attempting to make its replacement mass culture popular?[119]

While arguments about the 'accessibility' of *Ulysses* and *The Waste Land* are fraught, the publication institution constructed to create these objects reveals some clear aspects of modernism's agenda about 'the popular'. The strategies used to sell modernist works may seem separate from modernist aesthetics, but, "[l]ike any cultural work," as Lawrence Rainey argues, any given modernist work "was more than a sum of meanings implanted or intended by its author; it was inseparable . . . from the contradictory network of uses in which it was historically constituted".[120] A concern with 'the public' was a permutation of the beliefs about the processes of textual production held by those who took part in it. The elements of other discourses that came together in these beliefs were instrumental in the manufacture of modernism as a certain type of publishing institution, to a degree not evident in any 'purely textual' modernist work partitioned from its existence as a literary object. Rainey concentrates on the circumstances of the publication of the first edition of *Ulysses* on 2 February 1922 and the publication of *The Waste Land* in the November 1922 issue of *The Dial*, as well as the commercial edition and limited editions published in December 1922 and 12 September 1923 respectively. I will briefly survey Rainey's account and his explanation of the evidence it comprises about the shared cultural attitudes of modernists.

A Portrait of the Artist as a Young Man was published in book form in February 1917 by Harriet Shaw Weaver's Egoist Press in an edition priced at 6s, and until July 1921 Weaver proceeded on the basis of the assumption that she would imminently be doing much the same with *Ulysses*. Joyce himself seems to have initially envisioned a similar publication destination for *Ulysses*, even requesting that the retail price be set even lower than with *Portrait*. Writing from Zurich in July 1919, he told Weaver that "[i]f it should be decided to publish *Ulysses* in the distant future I should like to propose (as I did repeatedly to Mr [Grant] Richards) that it be published in paper covers at a price equivalent to that current in France. I have seen English novels offered here in the shop windows at 11 and 12 francs beside French novels offered here at 3.80 or 4 francs."[121] Shortly afterwards, he told her that he "should prefer to see my book (*Ulysses*) priced at 3/- which is about its value, I think."[122] Just after his arrival in Paris on 9 July 1920, Joyce first encountered the prospect of a special edition during abortive negotiations with John Rodker's small Ovid Press to print *Ulysses*, and he encountered this idea again when he and Sylvia Beach, manager of Shakespeare & Company, agreed at the beginning of April 1921 that she would publish *Ulysses*. The low print runs that Weaver had arranged for T.S. Eliot's *Prufrock and Other Observations* (June 1917, 100 copies) and

Wyndham Lewis's *Tarr* (July 1918, 1000 copies) had corresponded, for her, with their status as ordinary editions published by a financially restricted press, available to a general public of common readers with more print runs to come if economically viable, but the parameters of the first edition of *Ulysses* were very different from those envisioned by Weaver.[123]

Rainey points out that, in late 1920 and early 1921, while awaiting the obscenity trial which he was deliberately trying to postpone, the *Little Review*'s lawyer John Quinn made plans to have *Ulysses* published in America as a private edition by Ben Huebsch. 'Private' publication, as it was understood in America at the time, involved sale directly from publisher to reader through a system of subscription, so that if the publisher and printer were accused of obscenity then the book's non-appearance in any retail outlet would make it possible to claim that the work had not actually been 'published' in the sense of being made publicly available. This planned edition of *Ulysses*, although various circumstances prevented it, had a proposed price tag of £2, a normal multiple of standard prices involved in 'private' publications, which resulted from the absence of a need to accommodate the preferred pricing structures of booksellers and from a genuine impulse to increase profits. Even this edition, however, did not anticipate the parameters of the first edition of *Ulysses* as arranged by Beach.[124]

In April 1921, shortly after securing Joyce's consent to her plan for the first edition of *Ulysses*, Beach sent a prospectus to potential subscribers, inviting subscriptions to the 1,000 copies that would comprise the first edition, and detailing the price stratification for these 1,000 copies: 100 copies (printed on Dutch hand-made paper and signed by Joyce) priced at 350 francs/£7 7s/$30, 150 copies (on vergé d'arches) priced at 250 francs/£5 5s/$22, and 750 copies (on hand-made paper) priced at 150 francs/£3 3s/$14.[125] As Rainey notes, these prices were well beyond the capacity of the average working-class weekly income in the UK. Even skilled workers were earning an average of £3, 10s per week at the time.[126] This subscription was not a way of bypassing booksellers, as booksellers were included in the recipients. Indeed, the first edition of *Ulysses* was marketed so as to place nearly 60% of its gross sales in the hands of dealers, shops and export agents, with only 40% of sales going to individual readers (36% taking into account journalists and reviewers), in spite of the fact that this deluxe edition of *Ulysses* received publicity in the *Observer*, with its current average weekly circulation of around 200,000, at both the time of the trial for obscenity in New York in late 1920 and early 1921, and on 5 March 1922.[127] Appreciating that this was not a 'private' publication, Beach offered the trade the discount that they were entitled to expect for virtually all publications, but set this discount very low at 10%, which for an ordinary edition would have made stocking and selling the book barely worthwhile for booksellers.[128] But *Ulysses* was not purposed for general sale. Neither was it aimed at wealthy collectors. The trade purchasers were expected to retain the book to sell on at a higher price at a later date, a price warranted given the scarcity of the 1,000-copy edition. Informed of Beach and Joyce's plans for the first edition of *Ulysses* in late April 1921, Weaver replied that "I have had no experience of limited expensive editions and it had not occurred to me that booksellers make a practice of buying copies to hold up and sell at double or treble the original price."[129] This book was aimed not at individual readers but at a small body of dealers and speculators in the rare book trade. That is, the first instantiation of *Ulysses* as a book was deliberately engineered so as to make it an investment.

This engineering was borne out in the following months. On 27 March 1922, seven weeks on from the publication date (i.e. when the first copies from the printer reached Beach in Paris), Quinn reported that copies of the 150-france issue were circulating in New York for $20 (200 francs/£4), with one having sold for $50 (500 francs/£10).[130] In late June in Paris, copies of the 150-franc issue were selling for 500 francs (£10/$50).[131] The 1,000 copies sold out on about 1 July, and these prices continued to spiral. In London on 12 August, sales at £20 (1,000 francs/$100) were observed.[132] This was the direct and intended result of the book's particular publication and marketing parameters. By 1921, Rainey makes clear, modernists were both content to forfeit assessments of quality to the exigencies of the marketplace *and* intent on creating a distinct sub-marketplace whose exigencies they could influence, a marketplace susceptible to manipulation by a cartel. As he indicates, "[t]he deluxe edition was inherently monopolistic; it presupposed that one could exploit a market by manipulating the ratio of supply and demand".[133] Pound had been amongst the earliest to endorse a capitalist index of aesthetic quality. In May 1917 he had advised Margaret Anderson to advertise his collaboration on the *Little Review* by stating "that a single copy of my first book [*A Lume Spento*, published in 1908 priced 4s/$1] has just fetched £8 (forty dollars)."[134] But by 1921 modernists had incorporated the aim of transforming the literary object into a commodity with the inbuilt tendency to increase in exchange value over time.

In March 1922 Pound made arrangements for a scheme he called the 'Bel Esprit', in which 30 people would agree to each pay 10 pounds a year to T.S. Eliot. Wealthy patrons were invited to 'invest' in a poet guaranteed to increase in production.[135] Similarly, the first edition of *Ulysses* worked to reincorporate a version of patronage into aesthetic production, but this was no struggle to restore anti-capitalist relations. Instead this desired form of 'patronage' was actually much closer to investment.[136] To buy the first edition of *Ulysses* was to invest in an art object guaranteed to increase in value. For Rainey this shows that, for modernists,

> [t]he answer to the levelling effect precipitated by a consumer economy was to defer consumption into the future, to transform it into investment . . . to encourage or even solicit the ephemeral allure of the consumer economy, acknowledging the status of art as commodity, but to

postpone and sublimate its consumption by turning it into an object of investment whose value will be realised only in the future.[137]

While buying a copy of the first edition of *Ulysses* was not a private affair, particularly given that so many of the subscribers were bookshops, it was nonetheless very different from the everyday purchase of a book. Rainey sees Beach's decision to give Joyce a 66% royalty rate (standard editions would have involved 15–20% royalty rates) as reflecting "a broader effort to restore a more direct, less mediated relationship between author and reader. The book was no longer an industrial product, a mere commodity shaped by the conventions of the publishing industry and produced by the machinery of the large publishing house."[138] Instead, its small audience were required to behave as a group of minor patrons. However, as he points out, "it may give pause that it should be only and precisely the highest-priced issue [i.e. the signed issue] that to the greatest degree 'restored' unmediated relations among author, work, and reader, for it suggests that this restoration was partly fictional, if not factitious".[139] Rather than an attempt to engage directly with the reader (and, by extension, the crowd portion of the reader's mind), this 'unmediated' contact between author and reader seems to have been purposed to endorse the initially high price, and subsequent steep increase in value, of the first edition, a direct attempt to endorse a system in which the literary utterance would be perpetuated for as long as the market could be deliberately manipulated to value it highly as a commodity, in strict contrast to a system (which Joyce seems to have sought some years earlier in seeking to price *Ulysses* cheaper than *Portrait*) in which the literary utterance would deliberately last only as long as the wave in the crowd mind that threw it up.

As with the various claims made to market *Ulysses* to collectors, public versions of Pound's private claim that "Eliot's *Waste Land* is I think the justification of the 'movement,' of our modern experiment, since 1900" were used to market the poem to journals and publishers.[140] Pound played the role in the marketing of *The Waste Land* that Beach had played in producing the first edition of *Ulysses*, mediating various figures proposed to Eliot. The offers to publish the poem that Pound began to broker even before Eliot completed it in the first week of February 1922 (Horace Liveright made such an offer on 3 Jan 1922, before it even had a title), including Scofield Thayer's offer of $150 on 5 March 1922, on behalf of *The Dial*, were not the result of an appraisal of aesthetic quality—neither Liveright nor Thayer had read the poem—but, for Rainey, "of an eagerness to buy a product that promised to meet a series of minimum conditions", including a guaranteed increase in material value over time.[141] Thayer and James Sibley Watson Jr, the *Dial*'s editors, would ultimately refuse to elevate their offer over the $150 that they had first offered in March, for fear of setting an unofficial standard significantly above their normal $110–120 rate, but Pound did succeed in so boosting the poem that in late July 1922 they offered to also give Eliot the second Dial Award of $2,000 to bring the payment up to an unofficial $2,150, making the price of the poem nearly three times the national income per capita at the time, when still neither editor had seen the poem.[142] In the same vein as Beach's sale of *Ulysses* to speculators, with *The Waste Land* Pound and Eliot successfully sought to convince potential buyers that they were offered a product guaranteed to increase in value, and although Thayer and Watson could see that the *Dial* would benefit only tangentially from this investment through the increased subscriptions and sales associated with acquiring a reputation as the focal point for a new literary movement, Pound and Eliot had set out to sell *The Waste Land* as a mechanism for producing interest on a capital outlay rather than an utterance.

In spite of the fact that publication in America in the (relatively) high-circulating, advertising-friendly, low-priced *Dial*, which sold in news-stands, rather than the low-circulation, advertising-hostile and subscription-dependent *Little Review* represented one component in modernism's engagement with the marketplace, discussions for publication in the much higher-circulating *Vanity Fair* were abortive, Eliot refusing the proposition in August 1922.[143] If, according to Rainey, "the publication of *The Waste Land* marked the crucial moment in the transition of modernism from a minority culture to one supported by an important institutional and financial apparatus",[144] then although this transition embraced a wider audience than had been involved in earlier confinement to little magazines, Eliot and Pound deliberately avoided mass circulation. Although Eliot claimed, in his 14 August 1922 letter to Edmund Wilson at *Vanity Fair*, that he had to deny them *The Waste Land* because it was already placed at the *Dial*, at this point no agreement with the *Dial* existed.[145]

Furthermore, in spite of contracting with Boni & Liveright in January 1922 for a commercial edition of the poem that was ultimately published in December 1922, Eliot began to liaise almost immediately with various publishers for a limited book edition of the poem, worrying, Rainey judges, that the move straight from periodical publication to a commercial edition "threatened the status of his work".[146] Eventually produced in a print run of about 460 copies by the Woolfs's Hogarth Press on 12 September 1923, this limited edition is very revealing. While previous limited editions had been either merely small print runs of normal commercial editions (such as those produced by Weaver), or collectable items for the few designed to kick off an ensuing commercial edition, Eliot planned a limited edition in clearly different circumstances. That he sought for a publisher to produce a limited edition in spite of a commercial edition already having been published suggests that, for him, the direct move from publication in the *Dial* and *Criterion* to the commercial edition skipped a beat *and* that the commercial edition by Boni & Liveright was not ultimately the form that he wished his work to have. In contrast to earlier limited editions, which were associated with the felt necessity of removing the work as much as possible from the harsh workings of the marketplace, the deluxe and limited editions which modernism now produced were designed to enter into, manipulate and weather these workings, and to increase in value according to the criterion of the marketplace, to, it was intended, the credit of their author. Eliot arranged a limited edition after the commercial edition because he sought to establish this function for his poem in book form just as he had sought for it in his dealings with the *Dial*.

It was this configuration that Pound still expressed when, in his 1934 *ABC of Reading*, he dignified literature as "news that STAYS news".[147] Bryher's part in funding modernism through stipends to Joyce and Richardson and Contac Editions (publishers of Stein, H.D., Mina Loy and Ernest Hemingway) meant that *Close Up*, even though *entirely* removed, courtesy of Bryher's fortune, from the need to sustain its creators, was *also* marketed in 1927 using the same appeal, i.e. that when bound volumes "are sold their value will be trebled".[148] Where the reason to buy the limited edition as it stood before the war was to read it, the reason to buy the editions which Joyce, Beach, Eliot and Pound plotted after the war was to sell it again at profit,[149] suggesting a major alteration in the concepts dear to modernist cultural production.

If, as a consequence of the clear influence of collectivist philosophy on modernists, the products of modernism were to exist only in relation to the streams that threw them up, then how can this institutionalisation of modernist works as products guaranteed to increase in value be explained? How can we explain modernism's effort to produce artefacts rather than pulses in a circuit? If Yeats's and Joyce's regard for a work's value only in terms of the energy that produced it was indicative of a commonplace of modernist aesthetics, it is vital to note that the institution of modernist publishing by 1922 relied on low sales percentages to the general public *and* a prescribed consumption in which the work would increase in value in spite of its temporal distance from the energy that produced it: *both* belie the image of modernism as an attempt to express the waves of the mass mind.

Modernists were not mere canny businesspeople. Stipends were a regular feature of the lives of the major Anglophone modernists, meaning that in 1922 most were not in desperate need of the income that was created by the various editions discussed above.[150] For Eliot the prospect of financial difficulties was erased by the $2,150 provided by the editors of the *Dial*, but despite this, and the prospect of royalties from Boni & Liveright for the commercial edition, he still sought to produce a limited edition in 1923. Why? Rainey argues that when Eliot contracted with Horace Liveright, "the prospect of immediate publication by a commercial firm raised prospects that were largely unimaginable within the logic of modernism."[151] In the above account, Rainey does not claim that modernism had a reactionary relationship with markets but that it had a very *ambivalent* relationship with markets. This move to turn the aesthetic object into an investment object at its birth was, for Rainey, a response to the purported disintegration of the public sphere as defined by Habermas.[152] Witnessing the disintegration of the idea of the public sphere as a judge in matters of aesthetic quality, modernists turned instead to the market for evidence of their own literary excellence, but in doing so deliberately turned to a certain type of submarket whose workings they could manipulate. "[M]odernism", he writes "is a strategy whereby the work of art invites and solicits its commodification, but does so in such a way that it becomes a commodity of a special sort, one that is temporarily exempted from the exigencies of immediate consumption prevalent within the larger cultural economy".[153] But if Tratner is also right, modernism had no reason to shun a general market. Popular consumption was essential if modernists were to regard themselves as capable of reaching the waves in the mass mind which they regarded as ignored by contemporary popular culture. Assuming that Tratner's account of modernism is not erroneous, what could have caused modernism to rescind the idea of surrendering one's works to the mass mind shortly after the end of the war? Cinema, in particular its wartime reinvention, I will show, constitutes one major potential answer.

A NEW IMAGE-REGIME

When definitions of cinema came under increased direction from an organised film production, distribution and exhibition industry in Britain in about 1910, a widespread movement occurred amongst their various attempts to improve popular perceptions of the medium. Given cinema's widely perceived origins in such disreputable media forms as pornographic seafront amusements, crime-based 'shop of horrors' waxwork displays, the voyeuristic freak show and the raucous unlicensed penny theatre (origins reinforced by its early exhibition parameters and its continuing proletarian public), the new entrepreneurial personnel of the rationalised industry of the late 1900s/early 1910s came to perceive that 'animated photography' required a revised account of its innate properties. The *first* consensus of the post-1910 period was that this would be best achieved by defining the cinematograph as an intrinsically educational medium. This account of cinema had a lengthy history already, given that it was rooted in the strongly didactic lecturing tradition that had colonised a segment of film exhibition practice in the earliest years.[154] Charles Urban had argued in a popular publication in 1907 that cinema's didactic capacities deserved more recognition, explaining that it was "invaluable to students who have no opportunities of witnessing the actual demonstrations or phenomena", which made it "one of the chief and coming means of imparting knowledge".[155] The new consensus of the first four years of the 1910s refashioned this extant account to meld it with cinema's new profile as a predominantly fictional medium, drawing in particular on cinema's established profile as a transmitter of news. This attempt was further bolstered by the establishment of regular cinematograph news in the form of the first 'animated newssheets' in the UK in 1910, and the rise of educational films known as 'scenics', 'interests' or 'nature scenes', with the inauguration of the variety programme format of film exhibition in the new picture theatres (see Figure 0.11).

In his 1910 pamphlet *Focussing the Universe*, 'picture theatre' entrepreneur Montagu Pyke argued that "the Cinematograph has abundant functions"[156]: it was just starting to make the world visible to itself and so to dissolve national ignorance, the main source of war;[157] it was educating as much as a newspaper, because, unlike his forefathers who considered the 'grand tour' "a daring event once in a lifetime", the visitor to the picture theatre "can survey all mankind from China to Peru and obtain observation with extensive view";[158] and it was educating children by "opening up to them . . . vast realms of knowledge in an attractive and easily assimilated form" and undertaking "the extension and spread of scientific knowledge generally".[159] It was also archiving important historical events for future generations.[160] He insisted that the cinema, while enjoyable, "combines in due proportion amusement and interesting information respecting the happenings of humanity everywhere."[161] It was of course in order to justify and recommend the rapid spread of picture theatres, of which he was a beneficiary, that Pyke defined the cinematograph as "a vast, enlightening and instructive force",[162] thus citing a need for 'picture theatres' "in every London suburb and provincial town, . . . to elevate, to enlighten, to instruct, and to amuse humanity."[163] Pyke, like others, saw it as necessary to demote the amusements profile enshrined in the existing proto-institution of 'animated photography' and give these educational tendencies priority. In February 1910, *Rinking World and Picture Theatre News* was likewise asserting that cinema had only just been properly 'born', given that it was only then being discovered that it had a supreme capacity "to prove an educational influence of incalculable value."[164]

The first popular film magazines further boosted this attempt to assert the essential moral and social dignity of the picture theatre with reference to educational film content and usage, *The Pictures* designating cinema, in two articles in February 1912, a "public benefactor in educating the masses",[165] "attracting millions of the masses to an uplifting institution".[166] The nascent film industry was going about "the great business of amusing and instructing the public with pictures", as one writer put it in January 1912.[167] One December 1911 article explained that "the whole physiology of the human body, the processes by which we breathe, eat, drink, build up or break down our strength, can be elucidated by the cinematograph, to the benefit of the human race".[168] In the immediate pre-war period, reported attacks on the morality of picturegoing were often merely pretences for the industry to assert new media attributes for cinema through explaining why its 'detractors' were in error. Children were cited as one object of unwarranted concern; one April 1912 plea for the use of moving pictures in schools predicted that "[s]chool under such conditions would not be a place of detention for seven years, and to be hated for the rest of one's life, but an institution to which no attendance officers would be needed to drive the children. In a word, school life would be as it should be, the happiest time of one's life."[169] "Regarding the potentialities of the educational film," one columnist remarked in April 1912, "I would venture to predict that the time will come when the business done in this direction alone will bear, at least, the same proportion to the entire motion picture industry as the enormous text-book business now bears to the entire publishing output."[170] One March 1913 article distinguished between pictures that "belong to an every-day appearing class, and strike no special note in the progress or signs of the times" and "living pictures", those which have preservative merit: "These living pictures are divided into three classes: entertaining, interesting, and educational. The entertaining are usually classed as 'special feature films' and reproduce chiefly works of great authors successfully. The interesting are scenic, travel, descriptive, and illustrating industrials."[171] Cinema here is virtually entirely telegraphic, a broad-cast 'throw' of knowledge. As one March 1914 article insisted, "[s]cience and humanity are finding new uses for the 'pictures' every day".[172] A February 1912 article argued that "[t]he motion picture is making for the nation volumes of history and action. It is not only the greatest impulse of entertainment, but the mightiest force of instruction".[173]

Cinema's beneficiaries, as cited by *The Pictures*, were plentiful: schoolchildren were being shown educational travelogues, pilots were learning their errors from films of their own flights, motion picture microscopy was being employed in France, British police were displaying motion pictures of wanted suspects, the French Army was using projected films for target practice, industrial salesmen were using the cinematograph to show such large machines as railway derricks in action,[174] the London General Omnibus Company was using it to show drivers and the public how accidents happen and might be prevented and the Australian Government was using it for army recruitment.[175] Stutterers were purported beneficiaries: "A new method of curing stuttering by means of the cinematograph was described to the Academy of Science recently. Dr Marage, who devised it, has found that stutterers can be rapidly cured if their mistaken pronunciation of the word is shown to them on film."[176] This version of uplift was shrewdly invoked. One September 1912 article asserted that cinema was superior to the novel because "[t]he power to think appears to diminish in proportion as the fashion for reading other people's opinions increases."[177] These efforts at constructing an image of uplift were, in part, aimed at tackling the issue of Sunday opening. A section from a West London newspaper article on this issue was reprinted in *The Pictures* in January 1913:

> If the kinematograph be not a holy (wholesome, uplifting, expanding) influence, then we would wish they were not open on any day. If in the main they tend to make life better for those who do not seek other

ways—who perchance could not grasp or appreciate other ways—then why close that door on a day when (as they have often confessed) we don't know what to do with ourselves?[178]

One October 1912 commentator pointed out that "[a]nyone who knows the habits of the average English man will see clearly enough that Sunday is the only day when he can really enjoy the Pictures, leaving out of consideration the profit he derives from them from the educational point of view." Claiming that cinema was certainly not work (and so risking connotations of frivolity), this writer insisted that it was, instead, inherently educational entertainment: the average 'British Islander', with too much time on his hands, "wants to be entertained, he has no objection to being instructed at the same time, and he is not too tired to care about anything."[179] Efforts were even made to describe the enlightening tendency of cinema as more capable of ensuring the morality of its audiences than the indoctrination of the Church. One May 1914 article 'reported' that "[a] police office in a South Wales town says there is not a quarter of the hooliganism that there used to be three years ago before the cinema houses opened. In fact, he added, there is now more hooliganism on a Sunday, when the picture-theatres are closed, than on a Saturday."[180]

Although the education 'debate' competed with the cultivation of narrativity described in Chapter 1, the two were not incompatible. Earlier claims of the telegraphic potentials of the camera were retooled as the new fancy for location shooting in narrative film-making was cited to insist that cinema enabled vicarious travel. One writer, describing the Kalem travelling stock company's film-making tour of Egypt (where the films made were all dramas), commented that "[t]he pen of the explorer and the Kodak of the tourist have given us an all too meagre glimpse of its wonders. It remained for motion pictures to bring to the millions who may not travel something of the Egypt as it is now is and, for countless ages has been."[181] As one October 1913 article remarked: "It is not given to all to travel; to visit foreign countries,—yet the motion-picture has brought to our enchanted vision the crystal peaks of Alpine mountain-tops, and the rushing, foaming torrents of great and famous falls."[182] While this writer's frame of reference included the short travel films that were increasingly coming to be seen as mere stop-gaps in film programmes centred on narrative films,[183] it also included those same narrative films, which were establishing prestige by incorporating the outdoor scenery of the travel film.

The US film industry participated in the same drive to educational uplift, in such instances as Lubin company manager Siegmund Lubin's assertion of the cleanliness of the new pastime:

It is our ambition in the future to produce finer and still finer pictures— pictures that will be good not only from the standpoint of acting and photography, but also ethically. To-day in moving picture fields you see no bank robberies, train robberies, murders and so on, as in the early days. (This is indeed true of Lubin films.) The picture business has come to be educational. The stories told are for the uplift as well as the entertainment of those who see them.[184]

Lubin also claimed to have sent a film of the funeral of the Archbishop of the Catholic Church in Philadelphia to Pope Pius X in Rome. *Unlike* American film culture, however, British film culture did not invest in an uplift effort based on the "attempt to cater to women as decision-makers in the new culture of consumption" that Lee Grieveson has located in US industry uplift as early as 1907,[185] until the end of the First World War, in part because of the resistance to the logic of consumption posed by the stronger Protestant work ethic amongst UK industry spokespeople.

The First World War, however, all but eradicated the industry's education-based discourse of uplift. The industry's view that it was unsuccessful—it had been unable to hush real accusations that picture theatres fostered juvenile delinquency, for example—was one reason for its abandonment by 1915.[186] In addition, in the context of the perception that media forms should assume socially responsible roles during a war that demanded a universal rerouting of resources, the educational capacities of the apparatus now seemed unimportant. Educational uplift was also dropped because the public could not be described as possessing educational or moral levels in need of repair during a war in which virtuous national characteristics were being cited to justify Britain's participation. The successor to the education 'debate' was a general industry move to define cinema as a) fostering familial unity and b) supplying necessary relief to workers via its ability to entertain. The industry strove to justify cinema as a necessary leisure form for a country engaged in a war that was, although, strictly speaking, not total, now associated with nations rather than armed forces. Attempts to define cinema were made in the context of industries coming under governmental control and the state prescription of rest as necessary for high productivity during the working day. In January 1917 *Pictures and the Picturegoer* argued that "munition-workers, toiling six and seven days a week, need some recreation. To blot out every glimpse of pleasure and relief would be suicidal."[187] The magazine reported in March 1917 that "Mr Chamberlain [at the time director of the Ministry of National Service] stated recently that the amusement of the people is an essential part of the national work",[188] a later version of the same quotation finishing the sentence "just as essential as to eat or drink".[189] Rachael Low points out that during the war "[t]he new idea of 'morale' made it the patriotic duty of every citizen to enjoy himself",[190] and cinema was at the forefront of this national duty, one Hepworth advertisement designating the company "entertainers-in-chief to the nation-in-arms" in 1915.[191]

Cinema's lasting status as an escape from the rigours of life was not the result of the simple evolution of a bourgeois form. A pure entertainment profile emerged in response to a specific historical moment. Conceptions of cinema's social function were radically transformed during the war. As Michael Hammond notes, a minority pre-war view that "the function of the cinema space was to be a site of refuge from the house or street expanded to become a vision of the cinema as a relief from the anxieties felt across regions and class due to the war."[192] Fred Dangerfield, editor of *Pictures and the Picturegoer*, was a dedicated producer of this new account, with his promise at the outset of the war that "the cinema will continue to provide the staple form of entertainment for the masses."[193] While American cinema culture was working to reinvent cinemagoing as bourgeois leisure, the 'home front' UK from early 1915 was associating cinema with proletarian entertainment by perceiving it as a vital palliative for widespread anxieties about the conflict, "the recreation necessary to health and sanity" in the words of one October 1916 article.[194] In a September 1914 letter, one picturegoer told readers that "[t]hree of my own people are at the front, and I feel very anxious and unhappy about them; but when I get a real fit of the 'blues,' you can't think how much good an hour or two of 'pictures' does me."[195] In January 1915 one columnist claimed that they were receiving scores of letters praising cinema for its capacity to soothe or even completely cure disordered nerves.[196] Even cinema's heightened wartime reportage function, on the basis of which "the cinema would gain a certain amount of respectability," did not ultimately, Hammond argues, threaten cinema's new "status as a form of entertainment rather than education."[197] While factual government film propaganda was introduced during the First World War (see below), "the Roll of Honour films and the feature-length official war films [*Britain Prepared* (Dec 1915), *The Battle of The Somme* (Aug 1916), *The King Visits His Armies in the Great Advance* (Oct 1916), *The Battle of The Ancre and the Advance of the Tanks* (Jan 1917), and *The Battle of Arras* (June 1917)] offered an apparently popular form of practical patriotism that gave way to a conviction that the role of the cinema was to entertain."[198] By 1917 the National Council of Public Morals report on cinema observed that "the cinema is to be regarded as a means of amusement and recreation",[199] and the report was hailed not as a recognition of the uplifting nature of the institution, but as a vindication of "the value of the picture-house as a cheap amusement for the masses."[200]

In addition to stressing its educational profile, Montagu Pyke's 1910 pamphlet had argued that providing wholesome amusement was cinema's secondary virtue: it "provides innocent amusement, evokes wholesome laughter, tends to take people out of themselves, if only for a moment, and to forget those wearisome worries which frequently appal so many people faced with the continual struggle for existence".[201] By February 1916 the much higher currency credited to this appeal by the war was clearly apparent: "The cinemas have proved themselves to be a great reservoir of national confidence. They have put good heart into the masses and given them incalculable cheer." Crucial to the account of cinema as "The War-Time

Medicine for the Masses" was the class distinction made in imaging what would happen if "the millions who now patronise this cheap and healthy recreation are left to their own devices in the gloomy streets. The rich can pursue their pre-war pleasures with little or no inconvenience. But what of the working-classes? Truly a blow aimed at the cinemas is a blow aimed at the masses." This writer added that, "[a]s at home, so at the Front, the cinema has proved itself to be an unfailing tonic".[202] This effort to swell the existing conceit that cinema was a tonic was related to the threats of closure that culminated in the 1916 Entertainments Tax, and as part of this general anxiety even exhibitors claimed the job of keeping up national morale, with *The Picture House News*, a weekly run by two cinemas in West Hartlepool, promising in June 1917 that "if you are feeling jaded after the day's work, just run around to either the Picturedrome or the West End, and we'll fix you up as well as any M.D. or quack, and for only a fraction of the cost."[203] In September 1917 one columnist was explicit about the new configuration: "we don't profess any uplift tendencies where the cinema is concerned, and merely go to the Pictures by way of relaxation".[204]

One March 1918 article, entitled 'Pictures—The Tonic', described wartime London like so:

> Walk around as I do, and come into contact with all sorts of people— fat people, thin people, cheery people, pessimistic people, food hoarders and "queuers"—converse with them, and see if I am not right in saying that the favourite topic, of the ladies at any rate, is invariably "The Pictures." Even food is forgotten when this all-important subject crops up. Nobody nowadays thinks anything of going to "the movies" at least twice a week. Why? The answer is simple. It is because the picture palace is the one place in which you may forget for an hour or so your work, sorrows and anxieties.
>
> "Line up" for the pictures and listen to the scraps of conversation carried on by these pleasure-seeking queuers. "Better than waiting in a food queue, ain't it?" remarks a lady of considerable avoirdupois. "Yus," assents her neighbour; "summat better'n arf o' marjereen at the end of it. My kids 'ud sooner do wivout their grub than wivout their pictures."[205]

One October 1916 personification of cinema, 'vibrant lady motion picture', declared "I cheer and provoke to merriment as well as to tears. I give the depressed a renewed stimulus to fight life's battles more valiantly. . . . I send the rays of sunshine gleaming through the clouds of despondency and discontent. I send worry and melancholy scurrying into the lanes of oblivion."[206] In October 1917 one columnist defined the apparatus as "the machine which banishes trouble and dispels care, and brings into these sordid times a touch of pleasure, happiness and enjoyment."[207] Five years previously the idea that films served a function for the masses would have been ludicrous. Now it was fundamental. In July 1917 *Pictures and the Picturegoer* printed an anecdote by player James Lindsay about arriving back at the hotel ahead of the rest of his stock company:

> Some minutes later the other players appeared. There was Florence Turner, in the shabby black dress of her persecuted heroine, and with a shawl over her head; young Loraine, who was playing the lame boy, 'Chiz', also in rags; a sham priest (my accomplice in crime); and the producer, Larry Trimble. A more wretched collection of human derelicts I have never seen. My friend the [bus] time-keeper looked at them with pity in his eyes, and then turning to me said: 'It's terrible what misery this war's bringing on. Look at them poor refugees! Makes yer 'art fairly bleed, don't it sir?'[208]

Although this joke risked jibing at the frivolity of film production, the journalists printing it could be confident that the expenditure involved in film production was safely couched in terms of serving the populace.

Wartime ideals of leisure provision re-articulated cinema firmly in terms of national collectives. Langford Reed, in *The Chronicles of Charlie Chaplin* (1917), commented that "Chaplin has become a national and permanent British institution along with the war, Lloyd George, fogs, and roast beef."[209] This was typical of wartime descriptions of the cinematic image as consisting in its ownership by 'the public'. After the Entertainments Tax was introduced in early 1916 it was used to associate cinema with patriotism: "the bulk of picturegoers are far too public-spirited to object to contribute their quota to the national exchequer at a time like present when the ultimate fate of our country depends upon financial strength."[210] Reed also commented that "Charlie is a prime favourite with our gallant soldiers and sailors, who feel that the brightness and joy he has brought into their lives outweighs, a million times, any services he might have been able to render as an asthenic little castigator of Huns".[211]

During the war, cinema's image-regime was also generally remodelled, acquiring many attributes that associated it with collectivity in popular thought. While wartime cinema was not solely a matter of high attendance figures, the scale of cinema's wartime public certainly warrants attention. In his history of the gramophone industry, Peter Martland concludes of the 1914–1918 period that "[u]nder the pressure of war people appear to have reacted introspectively, retreated into their own homes, and sought entertainment and solace from gramophone records rather than pubs and other places of public entertainment."[212] Although the gramophone added a further domestic dimension to wartime popular entertainment, this by no means translated to a general decline in the use of public entertainments. Drops in numbers patronising pubs, music halls and sporting events were matched by, and related to, vast increases in picturegoing. While there the exhibition industry had become unstable due to an overprovision of seats in early 1914—with a fifth of cinema exhibition companies, representing roughly 1,000 of the approximately 4,500 picture theatres in the UK, facing bankruptcy—the war put paid to this.[213] Already by August 1914 the seating capacity of London cinemas (140,000) equalled the music hall and legitimate theatre seating put together (76,000 and 64,000 respectively),[214] and by November 1914 it was reported that "the cinemas everywhere are full to overflowing."[215] Whereas at the start of 1915 the estimated total weekly cinema audience was 10,000,000, by March 1916 it was estimated at 18,000,000, and, by July 1916, 20,000,000 (see Figure 0.7). F.R. Goodwin's figure of 1,075,875,000 cinema tickets sold in the year up to 27 January 1917, disclosed to the National Council of Public Morals Cinema Commission of Inquiry, works out at an average of 20,689,903 tickets per week.[216] Even taking into account that half of these ticket sales represented repeat attendances, as Goodwin told the January 1917 Commission, "[r] oughly speaking, half of the entire population, men, women and children, visit a cinematograph theatre once a week."[217]

Robert Baden-Powell noted this new scale when he wrote in his scouting guide *Young Knights of the Empire* (1916) that the size of an amphitheatre in Timgad in Algeria, compared to its small population, shows that "the Romans were as fond of theatrical plays as the English are of cinematograph shows to-day."[218] Commentators had not written of the cinematograph as competition for the theatre before the war, but at the end of 1916 *The Times* theatre reviewer commented that "[w]ar conditions, Zeppelin raids, daylight savings, the entertainment tax, the growing competition of the cinematograph theatre and the music-hall, all have to be faced."[219] Cinema attendance during the First World War was so substantial that it would only *ever* be equalled or exceeded in the period between 1941 and 1956. By contrast, contemporary cinemagoing is somewhat paltry: in 2002, when UK cinema ticket sales peaked at their highest since 1971, this peak averaged just 3.38 million admissions a week.[220] The August 1916 government film *The Battle of the Somme* was seen by an estimated 20 million people in its first six weeks, and may have eventually been seen by the majority of a British population of around 42 million.[221] Lewis wrote in *Self Condemned* in 1954 that the 1914–1918 years "marked in fact the mass-arrival of the cinema, the aeroplane, the motor-car, the telephone, the radio, etc."[222] Not only did cinema have few competitors for the kind of group activity it offered, the war was causing the alternatives that *did* exist to recede. By July 1916 the UK public was now spending as much on cinema tickets as on all other plays, shows, concerts and organised sporting events put together.[223] 1917 also saw race meetings and the football league go into limbo, and towards the end of the year one journalist noted that "[t]he increased tax, the raids, and the war generally seem to make no difference to picturegoing".[224] The following December 1916 joke relied on a common experience of recent speedy growth for its humour:

"Why, over in the States," drawled the American at the Christmas dinner-table, "we start building a thirty-story hotel one month and finish it the next."

Not to be outdone, a burly guest opposite replied. "That's nowt. I've seen 'em in Yorkshire, when I've been going t'work just laying t'foundation-stone of a new picture-theatre, and when I've been coming home at neet they've been putting on the last episode of a forty-reel film serial."[225]

The popular film magazines conveyed an impression of a deluge of new and growing cinemas. In February 1917, Burnley, one reported, possessed "picture theatres with seating accommodation for 18,000 persons—about one in every six of the population"—enough for the whole population to visit every other day.[226]

In addition, a new generation of cinemas, which had emerged around 1912, and were in the majority by the beginning of the war, were confident with showing multi-reel films that lasted 20 or 25 minutes rather than 10. Because of the consequent reduction in the number of showings possible in a day, these cinemas gradually replacing the small roughly 350-seat halls that were normal before 1909 and the 700–800-seat halls that were normal after 1909 had much larger auditoria in order to be able to maintain takings.[227] The enlarged audience were thus also attending in increased concentrations. "There are two classes of people in this world of ours", one September 1917 columnist remarked: "Those who attend the movies every night and those who go three times weekly."[228] While it may not have been statistically accurate, this indicated a sense of generality to cinemagoing during the war, a generality that also inflated previous images of the democratic nature of the cinema, one interviewer informing interviewee Blanche Sweet: "I come as deputy for the British Public".[229] Another columnist, commenting on the lack of good juvenile films, remarked that "[t]he cinema has not yet become anything like as popular a recreation for the 'upper class' children as it is for the democracy".[230] Clearly, even the language of the Long Acre journalist was affected by the notion that 'national collectivity' and 'working-class' were synonymous. In October 1916 one journalist remarked that "'The people' mean that the pictures have come to stay. I refer to them as people. . . . It is a better term than 'audience,' 'crowd,' or 'patrons.'"[231] Rather than any of these specific and exclusive groups, cinema's addressee was merely 'the public'.

In addition to this increased scale, a number of other major changes occurred during the war which propelled the institution cinema to articulate collectivity. The first of these was related to the Defence of the Realm Acts of 1914, 1915, 1916 and 1918. Early in the war the government empowered licensing authorities to impose early closing on pubs and, particularly in cities, these powers were widely used. 'Treating', the purchase of a drink for another person, was banned generally, and the alcoholic content of various beverages was reduced. Licensing hours then became further constricted, first in munitions manufacturing areas but soon quite generally: in Bristol in August 1915 and in London in November 1915, hours of opening were drastically confined to between noon and 2.30 pm and between 6.30 and 9.30 pm. The government's dependence on increased taxation at home (in addition to its dependence on US bankers) meant that, amongst other commodities, beer duties were consistently increased from the outset of the war. The April 1918 budget doubled duties on beer and spirits that were simultaneously having their alcohol content steadily reduced. This meant that arguments for Sunday opening of cinemas could now draw on the logic behind the reduced opening hours of the pub to reinforce the image of the cinema as the sole working-class pastime. The pre-war threat to the pub posed by the appeal, to working-class men and women, of the low-priced and warm space of the cinema continued to intensify. *Pictures and the Picturegoer* keenly reported the conversion of a church in Kirkcudbright at the beginning of 1917: "The congregation thought it was better that the people should go to a picture-house than to a public-house."[232] *Kinematograph Weekly* acknowledged in May 1918 that "people are more and more forsaking the public-house for the kinema".[233] One June 1917 article expressed a link between emptying pubs and overflowing picture theatres when it explained that,

> It being the opinion of the people of Shirebrook (near Sheffield) that it must either be the cinema or the public-house, a seven days' cinema licence has been granted the Town Hall. It was stated in evidence that since the local Empire had ceased showing pictures on Sunday the public-houses had contained scores of young couples who used regularly to go to the picture show.[234]

The provision of the cinema as a response to the requests of the people is here contrasted with the pub's historically local commonality, suggesting that cinema's wartime profile articulated massification. Although the diminishing role of the pub in British life was a significant part of how cinema was experienced during the war, cinema did not 'replace' the pub. D.H. Lawrence's April 1919 short story about a tram system in the industrial north, "Tickets, Please!", gives cinema as the primary purpose of the miners' travel but also mentions pubs: "From village to village the miners travel, for a change of cinema, of girl, of pub."[235] The cinema did, however, supplement the pub's public space of interpersonal discussion as an expression of working-class consciousness with large areas of unified and simultaneous consumption of the same 'text'.

The second of these developments was the solidification of cinema news. At the start of 1915 (with an estimated total cinema audience of 10,000,000), two-thirds of all cinemas included an 'animated newssheet' in their programmes. Whereas in 1916 only half a million people a week were seeing *Topical Budget*, the least-circulating of these, by February 1918 around 3 million people were seeing the newly official *Topical Budget* at least once a week.[236] An advertisement for the West-End Theatre in Piccadilly Circus boasted Max Linder comedies, "War Office Animated News Films—Grand Orchestra—Dainty Teas—Luxurious Surroundings."[237] Particularly because relatively little wartime 'animated newssheet' footage showed images from France, much (roughly four-fifths) of the 'total war' experience delivered to the British cinemagoing public in the 'animated newssheets' was comprised of items about the UK. This was a major element in generating national awareness of itself during, and at, war. Items in *Topical Budget* like 'Bowls at Blackpool', 'Khaki Bank Holiday' (on a fair at Hampstead Heath), 'Women Hay Makers' and 'Devonshire Hospital Buxton' informed the country in general of its regional components, presenting its ability to gather regional loyalties together as a crucial aspect of its commitment to prosecuting the war. A series of short official films about the home front produced in 1917 and 1918, for example, also "emphasised that the non-military war was being fought as much on the home front as it was overseas"[238] and provided audiences with another source of additional information about 'the war' as the life of their own nation. That "Great Britain [w]as one huge military camp",[239] as one journalist commented in March 1917, also contributed to the idea of the UK public as constituting the collective entity known as the 'home front'.

The third development concerned government propaganda. *Pictures and the Picturegoer* noted at the end of July 1917 that "[w]e are beginning to look for the official films as for a regular feature among things cinematic."[240] As Gary Messinger points out, the British government's new priorities during the First World War were a vital early part of the "twentieth century shift to massive state participation in the manipulation of public opinion."[241] Wartime manipulation of British public opinion, initially by unofficial propaganda organisations and then by the government, confirmed both collectivist theories of the mass mind and of the possibility of influencing its pulsions (albeit from the political right). While the official propaganda campaign was wide-ranging and in place from the outbreak of war, in 1914 and 1915, at the hands of the War Propaganda Bureau at the Foreign Office, it mainly took the shape of literature distributed to individuals in positions to influence policy-making in neutral countries. But by the formation of the Department of Information in February 1917, 'propaganda' was beginning to shift its meaning from "any association or scheme for the propagation of a particular doctrine",[242] to the mass-oriented approach to the governmental manipulation of opinion.[243] Nicholas Reeves's exhaustive research has revealed that early on in the war the activity of the Central Committee for National Patriotic Organisations was regarded as distinct from the official propaganda being practised by the War Propaganda Bureau,[244] the Bureau's director C.F.G. Masterman writing at the end of 1914 that the "intrusion of a Government, or of persons notoriously inspired by Government, into the sphere of opinion, invariably excites suspicion and resentment".[245]

This definition gradually changed. On the tail of the formal decision by the Department of Information in mid-1917 to orchestra a concerted programme of domestic propaganda, by the time of the formation of the Ministry of Information on 4 March 1918 under Max Aitken (created Lord Beaverbrook in January 1917), propaganda on a large scale, and aimed at a domestic audience, was understood as the business of government. A mid-1918 memo from the Ministry of Information explained the new conception of propaganda as

> the formation of public opinion. . . . We were suddenly faced with the fact that men in Tokio [sic] or Buenos Aires might know of the Battle of the Marne, and that what these vast and instructed masses thought they knew of these far off events would powerfully determine their practical attitude towards the belligerent powers. Invention had brought them the news, education the means of reading it, and democracy the power to act on it. By these means was propaganda born.[246]

The concept of government propaganda had gradually but noticeably evolved through the war from propagation amongst opinion-makers to an almost exclusive focus on the "vast and uninstructed masses". As it strove to realise the resources necessary to end the near-static stalemate of trench warfare (a logistical problem that had already provoked the political crisis leading to the formation of the Coalition Government in May 1915) the government came to perceive "the crucial role of propaganda in the maintenance of morale."[247]

This perception spread beyond government. As the war developed, social conventions like handing a white feather to an able-bodied young man in the street were no longer seen to be sufficient to marshal the resources the nation could provide. Rather, it became necessary to address the mass mind to demand the delivery of labour as a mass, thus endorsing beliefs that collective potential outstripped a 'summing up' of the potential of individuals. National endeavour was overtly and repeatedly linked with the collective potential of its workers. Whereas in the first year of the war "the two activities of propaganda and the management of news were kept apart because they were seen as different in kind",[248] the distinction between provision of news and dissemination of propaganda was soon abandoned, with the Foreign Office News Department and War Propaganda Bureau being amalgamated as the Department of Information in December 1916. No distinction between news and propaganda was made when the War Office acquired the Topical Film Company to relaunch *Topical Budget* as *Official War Office Topical Budget* in May 1917. Perceptions of the importance of propaganda for marshalling domestic resources had also influenced the War Office and Admiralty's decisions to abandon the earlier policy of making it as difficult as possible for any hard news to reach the public at large, with the formation of the Directorate of Special Intelligence in February 1915, which in turn gave rise to M07, a branch of the War Office wholly concerned with press publicity, and M07's May 1915 decision to lift the press ban of August 1914. In July 1916 Lloyd George, one of the few Liberals who had been wholeheartedly committed to propaganda from the start, became Secretary of State for War (and thus head of the new Directorate of Military Intelligence with responsibility for propaganda and censorship, MI7). The official approach to fact had also changed by 1918, from a preoccupation at the War Propaganda Bureau with "the presentation of facts and of general arguments based upon those facts"[249] (defined *against* the allegations of German atrocities favoured by the unofficial propaganda organisations), to a Ministry of Information that described its 'method', between March and July 1918, as based on the perception that "[i]t is useless to imagine that the mere existence of fact will penetrate everywhere by its own weight".[250]

This idea of media forms engaging directly in manipulating mass opinion further promoted notions of collective consciousness. The statisation of propaganda articulated the validity of theories of collectivity, and this move to state control of propaganda occurred in tandem with the government's adoption of film. A letter from the Foreign Office in August 1916 explained that film propaganda was useless for the old definitions of propaganda as influencing opinion-makers:

> Generally speaking, it seems to me that the cinema business is very difficult, and it is almost impossible to handle it except through the trade, and to get them keen you have to give them terms in which they can see a good profit. . . . If we have a perfectly first-class article . . . the trade are very keen to push it, but they will not push a film merely for propaganda's sake. As the thing to be good propaganda must also have a real popular appeal, their interest and ours really coincide.[251]

Because financial returns were the price the government paid for the co-operation and technological expertise of the film trade, official films needed to have a large-scale domestic existence. Domestic distribution of official films, beginning with the release of *Britain Prepared* on 29 December 1915, was unabashedly commercial, involving adverts placed in popular film magazines and the commissioning of popular press reviews. Film propaganda thus anticipated the massification of propaganda that did not occur more generally until mid-1917. Even the formation of the Department of Information in February 1917 had no provision for domestic propaganda. The use of cinema for propaganda purposes from the beginning of 1916 also involved a widespread public acknowledgment of government involvement, an acknowledgement that had been conspicuously absent from the earlier activities of the War Propaganda Bureau, whose literary publications in 1914 and 1915 were never distributed in the name of the British government, being either sold through normal commercial channels or distributed free through a variety of local organisations either anonymously or under the name of novelist Gilbert Parker.

Government film policy also endorsed the wider assertion of cinema's indispensability to the war effort. A special statement of support for the *Battle of the Somme* was prepared for its release in August 1916 by Lloyd George in his capacity as Secretary of State for War, while shortly after the film's opening *The Times* reported that, following a private screening at Windsor Palace, the King now urged the public to see it.[252] The government's acquisition of *Topical Budget* in May 1917 also explicitly and publicly stated the appropriateness of propaganda to a domestic audience. In July 1917 one journalist remarked that "[t]he growing use of motion pictures by our own and the United States Governments for patriotic purposes is but a sign of the times. This war has brought about the official recognition in all countries of the importance of the movies."[253] Beaverbrook later drew on this image of a cinema-public symbiosis when commenting of the launch of *Official War Office Topical Budget* that "[t]he Topical Budget shown in every picture palace was the decisive factor in maintaining the morale of the people during the black days of the early summer of 1918."[254] By the beginning of 1917 *Pictures and the Picturegoer* could be confident that Defence of the Realm Acts were no danger to the cinema industry because "[t]he Government needs the cinemas to show the official war films, [and] to get into touch with the masses".[255] The feature-length official films of August 1916 to June 1917 were all praised for their inspiration "to war-worker and general public alike."[256] This configured cinema as a direct address to the British public conceived as a single collective entity.

The fourth development occurred in the envisioned *class* of the cinema auditorium. Before the war, when the audience was almost exclusively working-class, trade and popular discourse on film had painted an image of the picturegoing population as bourgeois. But during the war, when middle-class cinemagoing began to comprise a small but significant proportion of total cinema visits,[257] cinema culture took a major part in valorising the audience as comprised of working-class personae, specifically in the figures of the 'Tommy' and the female war worker, although these were by no means exclusively representative of working-class participation in the war (see Figure 3.1). The female war worker was a national statement of the identity of working-class women. The emergence of discussions of the 'servant problem' towards the end of 1916 indicated that, at least in popular consciousness, female labour had been re-defined away from fidelity to middle-class families and was now much more easily articulated as the labour of working-class women for their own ends. Women were now being described as a 'workforce', and the link between the war and the emergence of this workforce entailed a variety of public validations and valorisations of female labour, of which the figure of the female war worker was an aggregate.

Figure 3.1 Picturegoers as defined by advertisements for *Pathé's Animated Gazette* in October and November 1916.[258]

As the home front became coded female, the female war worker provided Pathé with its primary picturegoer, but Tommies were just as regularly employed as part of the cinema institution's account of its own audiences. As one December 1916 article ran, "one could easily conceive the joy with which these tired men looked forward to the brief rest at the pictures after their turn in the trenches".[259] An executive at a British hiring company was quoted at the end of 1918 commenting how far the cinema had come during the war: "Only

a few years ago the cinema was tucked away in the corner, a sort of side-show
... now ... it's considered a necessary adjunct to the lives of Tommy in the
trenches, and big brother Jack upon the sea."[260] Articles on battlefront cinemas figured the events therein and the opinions of the audiences (like love of
Charlie Chaplin) as representative of Britishness (see Figure 3.2):

> A typical Cockney, he loved he cup of "corfee." It reminded of him of
> the stall at home, just round the corner, in a neighbourhood quite near
> the Old Kent Road. But far, far greater was his affection for the picture
> show. Why? Well, that was where he "proposed" to 'Liza, in the days
> when trenches were never dreamt of. And 'Liza, who spent her time
> toiling in a pickle-factory, off the very same Old Kent Rd., had pressed
> his horny hand under the cover of the darkness.[261]

H.D.'s *Bid Me To Live* (1960), based on material written during and after
the First World War, likewise linked the figure of the Tommy with cinema.
In a cinema, "[t]he pit beneath them was filled with smoke of countless
cigarettes that wafted a cosmic brew, a sort of narcotic dope of forgetful-
ness. . . . Below her, below them, were the thousands; it seemed that all
the soldiers in the world, symbolically, were packed into this theatre."[262]
The 'Tommy' and the female war worker provided revolutionised ways of
thinking about the desirability of collective consciousness figured through
the working-class, and picturegoing, figured as the source of increased

Figure 3.2   Working-class picturegoing as armed forces picturegoing (April 1918).[263]

industrial productivity and military labour, provided a popular image of working-class consciousness.

The fifth development was not directly related to the war but was a part of the image-regime developing for cinema during it. The UK picturegoer was "giving up the illusion that one person writes or tells a story that other people hear"[264] well before this was unambiguously accepted by modernist writers. Wartime cinema, as one October 1917 article paraphrased, was seen as "the voice of the multitudes."[265] This statement drew on a tendency to associate cinema's production with its consumers that continued to present a major distinguishing feature of the new regime. Roland Barthes has also suggested an inherently impersonal element to the photograph and, by extension, a democratic element to the film's conditions of existence: his own like of photographs was not of a photographer such as Alfred Stieglitz or Robert Mapplethorpe, as "I could not accede to that notion which is so convenient when we want to talk history, culture, aesthetics—that notion known as an artist's style."[266] The ostensibly raw presence of the referent denies the in-text existence of an artist. As one January 1921 article implied, even with directors newly awarded the status of creative heads, cinema still lacked something equivalent to an author—"the chair is empty"[267] (see Figure 3.3). In place of authorial control, audience control over film was implicit across the utterances of popular film culture. Scenario editor Irene Miller remarked in February 1917 that:

> "Everybody's doing it"—that is to say, concerning themselves in some way about the cinema. Either one wants to act for the screen, or one hero-worships a screen star, or one is agitated over the censorship, or whether the lights be turned up or down, or if the rising generation is being demoralised by the picture-houses, and last, but scarcely least, whether one writes photo-plays?[268]

Elements of the reality of 'cinema' practice in the continuing list depict 'it' as both consumption and production, interest in cinema being tantamount to involvement in it, indicating just how unclear cinema's production/consumption distinction was. This lack of a distinction between author and consumer, which had become endemic to film fandom, was also, Tratner argues, sought by modernists.

These factors all heavily informed the profile of cinema for the group of literary practitioners informed by collectivism. In spite of the absence in Britain of an equivalent of Hugo Munsterberg's *The Photoplay: A Psychological Study* (1916), which included overt discussion of connections between cinema and the collective psyche, and which was written and published in America, popular film discourse of the period nonetheless evidences the emergence of a profile for cinema that understood it as a conduit for mass thought. It was announced in November 1918, for example, that *Nelson*, recently finished, "does more than a hundred

One day the Director shall obey the will of the Creator whom we shall call the AUTHOR, and who will be as like to the scenario-writer of to-day as Barrow-in-Furness is to Paradise.

¶ There is a restlessness abroad. The old tricks are failing, and there are those who are feeling a wee bit tired.

The art is big; but the man with the brush is not big enough.

It is the art of humanity; but it waits for the artist.

The chair is empty.   As yet.

Jo. White

Figure 3.3   Cinema's missing author, January 1921.[269]

books or a thousand stories to convince the mind of the masses of the immensity of the debt we owe to the British Navy."[270] Tellingly, here the public was conceived as a singular "mind". A very telling description emerged in one April 1920 article, which explained that "the screen itself takes the part of the back part (or retina) of the human eyeball. Think of that, next time you are at a picture show. You are, as it were, sitting in the middle of an artificial eyeball, watching upon its retina the picture record of an artificial, photographically formed world".[271] Whereas cinema had been conceived from its inception as technologically replicating a human sensory process,[272] this writer instead emphasised the idea of a group sitting inside the artificial eyeball, connoting a collective seeing as one.

It is crucial to note that even when cinema was institutionally continuous with the magic lantern, the lantern provided Le Bon with no more than a metaphor for the workings of the mass mind (see above). From c.1908 continuity editing, its suturing of the discontinuity of rapidly succeeding images, along with the 'cinema-real', further limited any comparison between cinema and the workings of the mass mind's "fantastic succession of ideas".[273] Cinema's 'reality', as I demonstrated in Chapter 1, was cited as the result not of illusory power but of the ability to construct a grand pro-filmic event. In spite of this, however, Woolf would show in 1926 that she perceived a strong link between cinema and notions of mass consciousness. Her essay on the cinema, written in late March and April 1926 and published in the UK in *Nation and Athenaeum* in July, took the cinema crowd as evidence of the continued existence of 'the savage'. Her description of "the savages of the twentieth century watching the pictures"[274] referred not to a set of mindless units but precisely the collectivist sociological notion of an energised mass, savage because its thought patterns moved to only seemingly nonsensical rules and because these images manifested a powerful consciousness foreign to contemporary individualism. Cinema offered Woolf a glimpse of the hypothesised 'unseizable force' of *Jacob's Room*, which drives the world forward and "goes hurtling through their [novelists'] nets and leaves them torn to ribbons",[275] what she called, in the 1926 essay, a "secret language which we feel and see, but never speak".[276] The cinema is possessed of an 'art' because its audience, described by Woolf in the first paragraph, behaves so as to *seem* at first sight "simple, even stupid"[277]: this is the 'stupidity' of the crowd, the visions of the cinema crowd qualifying as art because they are linked to mass thought. In a cinema, those who doubt that the savage still exists would realise that "no great distance separates them from those bright-eyed naked men who knocked two bars of iron together and heard in that clangour a foretaste of the music of Mozart",[278] Woolf here figuring the mind of the cinema spectator in terms of the *musical* unity also linked at the time to the aesthetic manifestation of the crowd mind.

Cinema's structural narrativity fed into the (still extant) idea that films require no effort to comprehend, but when Woolf wrote that in a cinema the brain "settles down to watch things happening without bestirring itself to think"[279] she was also figuring a link between cinematic images and mass (un)consciousness, positing cinema as amenable to Le Bon's description of crowds as "to some extent in the position of the sleeper whose reason, suspended for the time being, allows the arousing in his mind of images of extreme intensity which would quickly be dissipated could they be submitted to the action of reflection".[280] Neither was it by any means with recourse to notions of an exclusively *individual* unconscious that Woolf described the cinema thus: "if a shadow at a certain moment can suggest so much more than the actual gestures and words of men and women in a state of fear, it seems plain that the cinema has within its grasp innumerable symbols for emotions that have so far failed to find expression".[281] Woolf's widespread use of water imagery to figure the mass mind in her fiction and letters reappeared at a crucial point in this article's argument: cinema holds up the possibility that "the dream architecture of arches and battlements, of cascades falling and fountains rising, which sometimes visits us in our sleep or shapes itself in half-darkened rooms, could be realized before our waking eyes."[282] Even in a damning paragraph on adaptation, Woolf reserved praise for "thinking with the eye" as opposed to "thinking with the brain", in line with the collectivist idea that a crowd thinks in visual images.[283] After the reappraisal, in the light of Le Bon and Sorel, of what *kind* of thought was to be represented and addressed by the literary practitioner, it was attractive to Woolf that such films as *The Cabinet of Dr. Caligari* (1919) proposed to her for just a moment that "thought could be conveyed more effectively by shape than by words."[284] Mass thought drove her question: "Is there any characteristic which thought possesses that can be rendered visible without the help of words?"[285] It also drove her conclusion that thought has "especially in moments of emotion, the picture-making power, the need to lift its burden to another bearer, to let an image run side by side along with it."[286] Opposing this thought to rationality and thus alluding to the mass mind, Woolf produced a figuration that would have been familiar to Le Bon and Sorel. Described as that which "can say everything before it has anything to say",[287] that is playing musical instruments without knowing how, 'the cinema' could very well be seen as exemplifying the thinking of the mass mind. These correspondences in Woolf's essay also suggest that other modernists would have felt the possibility of this link between cinema and modernism.[288]

H.D.'s *Notes on Thought and Vision*, written in July 1919, also implies that cinema interacted with notions of collectivity. Aesthetic creation, for H.D., was a result of moments when one of the "[t]hree states or manifestations of life", "body, mind, [and] over-mind",[289] shifted a level. For example, H.D. regarded Leonardo da Vinci's *Madonna of the Rocks* (before 1508) as a product of da Vinci's over-mind temporarily becoming his brain.

Hence in it "[w]e look through a window into the world of pure over-mind",[290] the result of "[t]he realisation of this over-conscious world".[291] Aesthetic creations then continue to broadcast messages through the over-mind.[292] Clearly her 'over-mind' was a permutation of collective thought, 'over-conscious' rather than subconscious. "The minds of men differ but the overminds are alike",[293] she wrote, and "[o]ur minds . . . are like dull little houses . . . [e]ach comfortable little home shelters a comfortable little soul—and a wall at the back shuts out completely any communication with the world beyond."[294] Imagining it as a foetus or as inhabiting the 'love-region' of the body at times, H.D. linked the over-mind with artistic creativity. Cinema's close affinity with mass thought (supplementing existing descriptions of collective thoughts as visual) influenced the specific qualities she perceived in the 'over-mind': "it seems to me that a cap is over my head, a cap of consciousness over my head, my forehead, affecting a little my eyes."[295] In line with an image of collectivity figured on the basis of the cinema-real, this "jelly-fish"[296] hanging over her head and extending its feelers downwards over her eyes and reaching outwards to other minds does *not* cause fantastic hallucinations: "Ordinary things never become quite unreal nor disproportionate. It is only an effort to readjust".[297] The over-mind renders "the world of vision . . . open to us."[298] H.D. also described herself as a pearl or glass sphere, "for concentrating and directing pictures from the world of vision."[299] While Le Bon had described the mass mind working through fantastic projection, the influence of cinema is apparent in H.D.'s idea that it worked through seeking out and witnessing.

That "[t]here is no great art period without great lovers"[300]—with art, for H.D., based on an interpersonal experience ("sympathy of thought"[301]) and not on an artistic subject—expressed the sense of inherent communality in the processes regarded, by modernists, as generating aesthetic products. "We must," she wrote, continuing the link between collectivity and vision, "be 'in love' before we can understand the mysteries of vision."[302] Further detailing this metaphor, she asserted that the over-mind can be in the brain and 'love-region' simultaneously, and, as two lenses, only when they are properly adjusted can they "bring the world of vision into consciousness."[303] The capacities of the over-mind even bear a resemblance to the picture theatre auditorium. H.D. recounts her character Lo-fu intensively examining a branch in his garden:

> He really did look at it. He really did see it. Then he went inside and in his cool little room out of the sun he closed his eyes. He saw that branch but more clearly, more vividly than ever. That branch was his mistress now, his love. As he saw it in the orchard, that mistress was, as it were, observed in a crowd, from a distance. He could not touch her, his mistress with all the world about. Here, in his little room, the world has ceased to exist. . . . His love, his apple branch, his beautiful subtle mistress, was his.[304]

While popular film culture had sought to identify the film viewer with the isolated private reader of literary fiction,[305] H.D. nevertheless described the darkened space as a locale by which Lo-fu, through the over-mind, could see more vividly than the outside world where he sees "from a distance". This passage suggests that cinema had been intimately connected with images of collectivity in the years immediately preceding H.D.'s essay, this connection dictating the way that she imagined the over-mind.

TWO FORCES

Why, then, did a "logic of modernism", to quote Rainey, for which "the prospect of immediate publication by a commercial firm raised prospects that were largely unimaginable", emerge shortly after the First World War? This logic, embraced by Pound, Joyce, Beach and Eliot, had resulted from cinema's wartime influence on notions of collectivity. Articulating mass consciousness at precisely the time when modernism itself turned fully to collectivism, cinema had imagined collectivity via its new wartime profile as entertainment. In October 1915, for example, D.W. Griffith was described as "a genius who makes and unmakes at will the emotions of the public."[306] This entertainment profile thrived on the wartime discourse of cinema-as-tonic. Actor Tyrone Power remarked in January 1917 that

> I thought the industry was but a flash in the pan. But with the advancement, the wonderful strides onward and upward, I experienced a change of art. I was informed that people who never before could afford to see my acting would now be given an opportunity because the prices are not so high. I was informed that picturegoers were exacting . . . as those who frequent the legitimate theatres, . . . and I have been studying the audiences. I believe that I am in a humble way contributing to the enjoyment of the masses.[307]

And in May 1915 a picturegoer recounted that

> I was very miserable the other night, and so went to see the pictures. The Comedy, *The Rounders* [Keystone/Chaplin, 1914], was thrown on the screen—at once there was a great silence in the house—a silence of great anticipation. Five minutes later you could not have heard yourself speak. My misery had disappeared, and by the time the comedy was finished my sides ached, and tears were running down my cheeks with laughing.[308]

As Hammond points out, comedy in particular played a vital role "in the industry's move to respectability through the contention that cinema was a palliative for the pressures and anxieties of everyday life".[309] In

April 1918 one journalist remarked that "the nation should rear a statue to "Pimple" [the comedian Fred Evans], who is helping it, in this picture [*Rations*], to chase away its irritating little troubles with a smile."[310]

In a speech delivered in early 1917, the new British Board of Film Censors chairman T.P. O'Connor described the state of the new image-regime, maintaining that "it is not my business, or the business of any Censor, to dictate to the people of the country what should make them laugh and what should not. The knockabout film is not a matter for me to criticise."[311] The institution cinema, by this date, was conceived as primarily and readily responsive to public demand. Grace Cunard, for example, claimed in February 1917 that 'highbrows'

> do not constitute the majority in a picture audience. The motion-pictures are essentially for the masses, who, no matter what any one may say or write, attend the theatres to be amused—for entertainment pure and simple. The masses love comedy, and adore melodrama—they revel in heart interest.[312]

An article by film star Cleo Madison evidences how deeply embedded ideas of pure entertainment were in the perception of cinema even by the end of 1916:

> it is a mistake to be externally "educating the public" in features which are meant to entertain. This excuse of "educating" is more often than not box-office publicity. . . . I am going to act in pictures which will entertain, and which will be above everything else—clean. . . . So many people make the mistake of thinking that a clean or wholesome picture must necessarily be namby-pamby. Nothing of the sort. Melodrama is wholesome, comedy is wholesome, and our nature demands excitement and fun.[313]

In August 1917 one regular contributor could not help concluding (in spite of her beliefs in cinema's capacity for "the expression of lofty thoughts and noble aims") that cinema's public contracted with it solely for entertainment. These "lofty thought and noble aims" would inspire "the unimaginative town dweller, even though he attends the cinema simply and solely for amusement".[314] In replacing preceding accounts that insisted that cinema was an intrinsically educational medium, in which it was possible for collective seeing to at least nudge the flow of group consciousness, this account styled cinema as one-dimensionally responsive to the demands of the masses. Just as cinema was being thoroughly associated with collectivity, this intrinsic insistence on the primacy of its entertainment function worked to define mass consciousness as *merely* receptive, and therefore not the generative aesthetic wellspring which it had appeared in earlier conceptions. As cinema—the culture with the closest contact with the crowd, and the most rapidly dissipated of cultural forms—came to articulate collectivity, it also worked to associate the rapid dissipation of a cultural object—which the modernists had advocated before the war—with crowd passivity, its misdirection by outside forces.

Consequently, modernists were provided with an implicit model of mass consciousness that defined it as solely receptive rather than creative, which in turn motivated them to abandon the short-term, large-scale audience as the ultimate target of their work. In spite of the scale of publicity for *Ulysses*, for example, as a physical object it was deliberately propelled beyond the energy that had created it. "Modernism required not a mass of readers but . . . a corpus of patron-collectors, or patron-investors"[315] because the *idea* of the mass mind as the source and aim of aesthetic energy had been compromised, and for this its involvement with cinema's new image-regime during the war was at least a substantial cause. Pound indicated the continuing currency of notions of the mass mind when he wrote in the *Criterion* in January 1923 that he was indebted to Yeats for his theory "that a poem should attain some degree of intensity", but he had now detached aesthetic production from collectives, asserting that "one should make NO compromise with the public". No longer envisioned as powered by a pre-existing force—the perceived aesthetic function of the Vortex—aesthetic intensity now *only* began with the artist, Pound concluding that "art begins only when one has ceased to react to the imbecilities of the multitude".[316]

Cinema, then, having been deeply connected with notions of collective conscious by the changes that occurred during the war, influenced how modernists treated the mass mind, this force which they were already committed to articulating in their works. In contrast to earlier attempts to reach into crowd consciousness to power aesthetic works, this group of modernists now tended towards the idea that their relationship with the crowd mind was that of influencing an entity perceived as *solely* receptive rather than as the originating point of their own works. Rather than resubmitting their works to the mass waves figured as their cause, this group of modernists sought to propel them both beyond these waves and into their own very different version of 'the popular', their market surrogate for popular conduction. Although the formal properties of modernism remained rooted, at least in part, in attempts at articulating collectivist notions of the crowd mind, even speaking its language, articulating as 'speaking' the creative mass mind now became articulating as 'addressing' the receptive mass mind, and this articulation, they perceived, could and should become as independent of the mass mind as possible, with no debt to this mind for having thrown it up.

Afterword
'a picture feverishly turned'

[M]ost critical paradigms of literary modernism, based as they often are on the modernists' self-understanding and a general anti-techno-logical bias, have precluded sustained reflection upon the historical conditions and enabling constraints of the modernist enterprise.

Sara Danius, *The Senses of Modernism*, 193.

A section of Danius's *The Senses of Modernism* (2002) is exemplary of the historical approach to cinema that literary historians have recently begun to appreciate. "In the wake of cinematography and its accompanying matrices of perception," she writes, "it is the modalities of visibility that change",[1] a modality which Michael North, in his *Camera Works* (2005), defines as the representation of raw sense data in graphical form.[2] Photography, the phonograph and the cinematograph were just three of the technologies produced by a long-term push amongst inventors in the nineteenth century for the means to give streams of sense data the means to 'write *by* itself'. This tradition also incorporated ways of transcribing efferent neural data, such as Alexander Melville Bell's development, in the 1860s, of 'Visible Speech', a notation system, for the benefit of the deaf, composed of symbols that recorded, for every sound, the position and action of all parts of the speech system. For this most recent model of modernism (able to dwarf anti- or pro-recording accounts of technology's place in originating mod-ernism) nineteenth-century 'notation' technologies proposed that the world contained a linguisticity not oriented towards a human subject. Unlike lit-erary impressionism, which had concentrated on characters' experience of sensory data (see Chapter 1), this strand, what we now call 'high' modern-ism, sought to channel the experience of raw sensory data directly through non-character narrators—i.e. the work's own narrative process. Instead of writing "Bloom paid for the kidney", Danius points out, Joyce, in the 'Calypso' chapter of *Ulysses*, had his narrator state: "His hand accepted the moist tender gland and slid it into a sidepocket. Then it fetched up three coins from his trousers' pocket and laid them on the rubber prickles. They lay, were read quickly and quickly slid, disc by disc, into the till."[3] Modern-ism, for Danius, is a rendering of this newly avowed world of raw sensory data, as distinct from that which the senser *knows* to be there. Molly's recognition and annoyance that Bloom has burnt the kidney, for example, is signified by the observation: "Her spoon ceased to stir up the sugar".[4] For

Ruth Perlmutter *Ulysses* shares, with cinema, "[t]he simulation of an "ocular" experience within an acoustic space (of random ambient sound) via framed partial views".[5] In *Jacob's Room*, women in King's College Chapel are "several hat shops and cupboards upon cupboards of coloured dresses . . . displayed upon rush-bottomed chairs."[6] H.D. also rendered such raw visual sense data in *Asphodel*: "A face was leaning toward another face, a thin highly tinted fox-shaped face with puffs of fox-coloured hair . . . A face was leaning over the back of a Chesterfield and was opening tinted lips to someone".[7] As this influence of cinema on literary fiction was, more accurately, the influence of a growing stream of empirical thought during the preceding 100 years which encompassed a variety of technologies, I have nonetheless tried to show that a focus on cinema's distinct mediativity illuminates at least three areas of influence not anticipated by this one aspect identified by Danius and North. Cinema did command an influence on literary practice in tandem with its associated technologies, but an account of literary modernism has only been possible by considering cinema in its historical specificity.[8]

To ask whether modernism was mostly imitative *of* or mostly reactive *to* cinema is to falsely limit inquiry. Cinema presented not as an aesthetic form but as a revision of ways of understanding—as these three studies have demonstrated—the status of language, time and consciousness. Relativising literary metalanguages, impressing on literary narrative an imperative to unify narrative time and plot time that spurred them on towards the psychodynamic unconscious/preconscious/conscious psyche, and modifying models of the spontaneity of mass consciousness, the institution cinema was a major pillar for the emergence of literary modernism. While cinema seems to have impacted on fiction only at the point when it became widely defined *itself* as a form of fiction, this does not denote a type of influence in which one aesthetic form offered formal possibilities to another. The sense of alertness to literature as an institution that emerges from a reading of the keenness of modernist auto-criticism or the multiple metalanguages of *Ulysses* all point to a historical period in which a new element of the cultural furniture pressured both existing understandings of aesthetic production *and* understandings of the world more generally.

I do not wish to suggest that this complex influence on modernism existed solely in the area of literature. The simplistic picture of modernism as a retreat from representational territory as it was annexed by cinema is equally inadequate as an account of modernist painting. Even the painter commonly cited as the most influential pre-war abstractionist—Wassily Kandinksy—was writing, in the same works as his manifestos for abstraction and an embracing of pure form, that the aims pursued by "[t]he great abstraction" were also achieved by "[t]he great realism."[9] The latter "tries to purge the picture of everything artistic. It wants to manifest content by means of the simple ('inartistic') representation of simple, tough objects.

*. . . Reduced to a minimum the 'artistic' becomes comparable in effective-
ness to the most intense abstraction.*"[10] Why did these two extremes, when
"[t]he great abstraction is the great antithesis to this realism", driven by
"determination to eliminate completely the representational (reality) and
to embody content in 'incorporeal forms'",[11] share the same aim? The ideal
common to both was destroying "conventional prettiness", from either
angle: "Just as the cancellation of abstraction intensifies the inner sound
in realistic art so the inner sound is intensified in abstract art by cancel-
ling out realism."[12] For the "liberation" of both the great realism and the
great abstraction, Kandinsky argued, "one must learn to hear the whole
world exactly as it is without any representational interpretation."[13] The
achievability of this ideal was, in Kandinsky's contemporary Europe, being
iterated by cinema, simultaneously apparent as a creative endeavour and as
utterly devoid of representational interpretation.

Kandinksy could even be said to have moved towards the 'spirit of
the object' as a result of cinema endowing the object with subjectivity, its tendency to a tendency to "dissolve the subject-object split into
object relations".[14] This distinguishes Kandinsky from, for example,
Charles Baudelaire, who, in spite of avowing a 'Painter of Modern Life'
who attaches to "the half of art whose other half is the eternal and the
immutable",[15] saw it as possible to distil the eternal from the ephemeral,
the "transitory, fugitive element" constituting only a defence against a
"tumble into the abyss of an abstract and indeterminate beauty".[16] The
photographic abundance of visual specificity—exemplified in Baudelaire
by fashion (the "muslins, the gauzes, the vast, irridescent clouds of stuff in
which she [the female model] envelops herself")[17]—was for him necessary
to avoid meaninglessness, but he was also committed to the limitations of
visual plethora, stating that at the final execution of the artist's work the
"physical presence of the model and its multiplicity of details disconcerts
and as it were paralyses his principal facility."[18] This had to be resisted. In
Baudelaire, cinema had not yet arrived to assert the primacy of the object,
summarised by Roland Barthes as the "*being-there* of the thing",[19] in the
extra dimension of *time*.

An 'influence' work suggests tenuous links and audacious claims, a ped-
alling of a history whose 'lost' status is largely imagined by the writer, and
given that the discipline of early cinema studies is currently committed to
iterating how the tropes, habits of presentation and modes of perception
in cinema were, even after its 'second birth', shaped by the protocols of
amusements and entertainments industries with which the institution cinema continued to associate itself, a case for the isolated impact of cinema
on modernism seems outdated. In this book, however, I have emphasised
two ideas: first, although few of cinema's modes of operation are intrinsic
to the medium, certain traits and tendencies can be pinpointed as specific
to cinema at certain historical points; second, that it is precisely in dialogue with contemporary sociological and philosophical developments—in

this case well beyond the simple context of amusement and entertainment practices—that cinema constituted an impact on literary practice.

Susan McCabe typifies the contemporary idea that as cinema cannot have been earth-shaking enough to have occasioned modernism, the influence of cinema on modernism was to re-state (and offer ways of engaging with) provocations that had *already* occurred—in McCabe's case the dismembered body produced in various disciplines by the First World War—and so rendering 'cinematic' writers who were modernist already.[20] This seems to be impelled by the imperative to avoid audacious claims that cinema should be seen as an originating cause for modernism. But if caution is needed to avoid rubbishing modernism's historical causes, this should mean not that we avoid seeing cinema as a cause altogether but that we situate it as one of several. The intent to find in cinema the chief or sole originator of modernism is therefore not unjustified: without an image of how the new image-regime of cinema's period of distinct mediativity conditioned the attitudes towards literature that were forming in such areas as collectivist philosophy, accounts of modernism's other generative forces are incomplete. This is why I have sought to make it possible to think of cinema as modernism's single unifying generative cause, even though cinema is ultimately one of half a dozen such major generative influences. The preceding description of the image-regime of cinema can not prove that cinema should replace all of modernism's other major causes, but it can provide as much evidence for cinema as currently stands for those other established causes.

Notes

NOTES TO THE INTRODUCTION

1. For example, Paul Tiessen, a frequent scholar of this dynamic, describes cinema-modernism influence as "literary modernism's reception of cinema" ('Eisenstein' par. 2) Further studies are listed in note 11.
2. Marcus, *The Tenth Muse* 130–72, 437.
3. Bell, 'Art and the Cinema' 39–40. Later examples include Bazin, 'Ontology' 11; Dasenbrock, *Literary Vorticism* 5; Denvier, 'Impressionism' 15.
4. Dasenbrock, *Literary Vorticism passim.*
5. See, for example, Gunning, 'Animated Pictures' 320–1. Jonathan Crary relates the optical technologies of the nineteenth century to physiological investigations into the nature of seeing which widely emphasised the idiosyncrasies of human sight, and regards these technologies as purposed to emphasise these idiosyncrasies as much as to reveal images (*Techniques* 97–136). In a discussion of the influence, on painting, of those photographic technologies oriented around producing accounts of time that emerged during the 1880s, Mary Ann Doane exemplifies recent accounts that regard such technologies as occasioning neither emulation nor disassociation but as drawing painters' attention to the oddities of human optical processes (Doane, *Emergence* 85). Tom Gunning provides examples that suggest the same type of influence (Gunning, 'Never Seen' 238.)
6. Trotter, *Cinema and Modernism* 2–3, 160 (for exemplary debunkings), 3. Trotter notes (4–6) that he adapts and refines an approach proposed by Garrett Stewart in *Between Film and Screen* (1999).
7. Trotter, *Cinema and Modernism* 3.
8. These are, respectively, Sarah Wilkinson's 'The Concept of the State, 1880–1939 (2003), Donald Childs's *Modernism and Eugenics* (2001), Thomas Vargish and Delo E. Mook's *Inside Modernism* (1999) and Michael Whitworths *Einstein's Wake* (2001), April McMahon's 'Language: "History is a nightmare from which I am trying to awake"' (2003), Michael Bell's *Literature, Modernism and Myth* (1997), Peter Collier and Judy Davies's collection *Modernism and the European Unconscious* (1990), Vincent Sherry's *The Great War and the Language of Modernism* (2003) and Michael Tratner's *Modernism and Mass Politics* (1995).
9. Smith, *Origins* 11. For a recent survey of modernism's *prospective* identification *as* modernism see Whitworth, Introduction 22 and 39–41.
10. Beach, *The Twentieth Century Novel* 525.
11. See, for example, Levin, *James Joyce* 82–8; Spiegel, 'Cinematographic Form' 229–30; Spoo, Introduction xiv; Hankins, 'Splice' 108; Senn and O'Flaherty 'Episode 8: Lestrygonians'; Childs, *Modernism* 123; McCabe 'The 'Ballet

Mecanique" 36; Vaglio, 'Cinematic Joyce' *passim*; McCabe, *Cinematic* 11; North, 'Words in Motion' 211; Showalter, Introduction xxi. 1932 was also the year when Winifred Holtby called Woolf's method in 'Kew Gardens' (1921) and *Jacob's Room* (1922) "the cinematograph technique", although she avoided emulation of technique for emulation of (purported) ontology: "The story [*Jacob's Room*] deals mainly with the external evidence of emotions, even thoughts and memories assuming pictorial quality." (*Virginia Woolf* 117). For accounts of the history of work on the influence of cinema on modernism see Kellmann, 'The Cinematic Novel' *passim*, and Tiessen, 'Eisenstein' *passim*.

12. Connor, *H.D. and the Image* 6.
13. The 'montage' tradition was in place as early as 1941: see Levin, *James Joyce* 88; Hauser, *Social* 939; Humphrey, *Stream of Consciousness* 50; Perlmutter, 'Joyce and Cinema' 482, 489, 293–4; Burkdall, *Joycean Frames* 8–17, 49–56; Childs, *Modernism* 127; McCabe, *Cinematic* 3, 5, 9, 10, 14, 21, 25, 32–3, 34, 37, 40–1, 49, 54–5 (just a few examples); Humm, *Modernist* 164, Connor, *H.D.* 7. Marcus's chapter on Woolf in *The Tenth Muse* (99–178) is a rare example of the successful avoidance of this tendency.
14. See Hotchkiss, 'Writing the Jump Cut' 134–5, and Smith, *Dickens and the Dream of Cinema, passim*.
15. Bazin, 'In Defense' 63.
16. See, for example, North, *Reading* 10; Potter, 'Modernism' 2; Morrison, *Public* 7.
17. Tiessen, 'Eisenstein' par. 4; Morris, 'Film and Modernism' 110; Hankins, 'Splice' 106–7; Hankins, 'Across' 176–7; Humm, *Modernist* 153; McCabe, *Cinematic* 161; North, *Camera* 83–105; Walter, 'From Image' 301; Connor, *H.D. and the Image* 19–69.
18. These include Fernand Léger and Dudley Murphy's *Ballet Mécanique*, Hans Richter's *Steigen-Fallen [Rise-Fall]* and Vikking Eggeling's *Horizontal-Vertical*, all of which were abstract works based on the rhythmical movement of geometrical shapes.
19. Léger, 'A New Realism' 8.
20. Beaumont, 'Of What are the Young Films Dreaming?' 73.
21. Shaw, 'Cinema and Ballet in Paris' 179.
22. Block, 'When' 68.
23. Qtd. Hankins, 'Virginia'.
24. Advertisement, *transition* 1 (April 1927).
25. Humm, *Modernist* 135.
26. Marcus, *The Tenth Muse* xiii–xv.
27. See, for example, Hankins, 'Across the Screen' 157–64. This is not just the case in studies of modernism. In his study of H.G. Wells' encounters with cinema in the late 1890s, Keith Williams is preoccupied with aesthetic categories imported from later minority film discourse (*H.G. Wells* 40–7).
28. Bradshaw, Introduction 3.
29. MacCabe, 'On Impurity' 20.
30. See, for example, Williams, 'Ulysses in Toontown' *passim*. Williams also identifies the impact of a specific trend in film practice rather than the experience of film in general, and also tends to identify cinema's influence on Joyce's content rather than on any of his formal modernist properties.
31. Block, 'When' 68.
32. This approach is still followed in studying modernist-authored film culture. See, for example, Gevirtz, *Narrative's Journey* 38–47.
33. McCabe, *Cinematic* 18–20, 24, 26, 28, 41, 133, 135. This 'cinema', as McCabe describes it, is also entirely without historically specific characteristics.

34. Singer, *Melodrama* 101–2; Bordwell, *On the History* 142.
35. Kern, *The Culture of Time and Space* 8.
36. Hansen, 'The Mass Production' 62, 69.
37. Singer, *Melodrama* 103–30. More recent examples include Jacobs, *The Eye's Mind* 8; Doane, *Emergence* 5–11; Gunning, 'Modernity and Cinema' 305–12.
38. Hansen, Introduction x–xii.
39. See, for example, Morris, 'Film and Modernism' 110.
40. Deleuze, *Cinema 1* xii.
41. Bolter and Grusin, *Remediation* 61.
42. Hammond, *The Big Show* 4.
43. North, 'Words in Motion' 211.
44. See Hotchkiss, 'Writing the Jump Cut' *passim*, for a range of examples of modernism's use of stylistic techniques drawn from film.
45. Prodger, *Time Stands Still* 109.
46. Anon., 'The Kinetoscopic Lantern. The Work of Mr. Muybridge and his Precursors', *Amateur Photographer* 23.591 (31 Jan 1896), 90.
47. Anon., 'Lantern Projection of Moving Objects', *Amateur Photographer* 23.597 (13 March 1896), 225–6, 225.
48. Gunning, 'The Cinema of Attractions' 65.
49. Gunning, 'The Cinema of Attractions' 68.
50. Gunning, *D.W. Griffith* 229.
51. Gunning, 'The Cinema of Attractions' 64. This is echoed by several other writers, including Wood, 'Modernism and Film' 215 and Morris, 'Film and Modernism' 111.
52. Gaudreault, 'From "Primitive Cinema"' 85.
53. 'Inferior Religions' 315. Much of this had already been laid out in his 1910 essay 'Our Wild Body'.
54. 'Picture Theatre News', *Rinking World and Picture Theatre News* 1.12 (19 Feb 1910), 14–5, 15.
55. 'The Motion Picture and Photo-Play', *Evening Times*, 18 Sept 1911, 6.
56. *Punch* 145 (15 Oct 1913), 323.
57. See Gillies, 'Bergsonism' 108.
58. Lewis, 'Inferior Religions' 316.
59. Lewis, 'The "Pole"' 216.
60. Lewis, 'Les Saltimbanques' 242.
61. Lewis, 'Les Saltimbanques' 239.
62. Lewis, 'Some Innkeepers and Bestre' 232.
63. Gaudreault and Marion, 'A Medium' 4.
64. Gaudreault and Marion, 'A Medium' 4, 5.
65. See Gaudreault and Marion, 'The Neo-Institutionalisation' 89.
66. Gaudreault and Marion, 'A Medium' 4.
67. Gaudreault and Marion, 'The Cinema' 14.
68. Gaudreault and Marion, 'A Medium' 12.
69. Trotter, *Cinema and Modernism* 5.
70. Rossell, 'Double Think' 29–30.
71. Doane, *Emergence* 15.
72. Ward 'The Green Spider' 435; Wells, *Modern Utopia* 8. In March 1897 Cecil Hepworth wrote that the "applications, for their name is legion—of Edison's kinetoscope to the projection lantern, have caused a boom which is unparalleled in the history of the lantern" ('On the Lantern Screen', *Amateur Photographer* 25.651 (26 March 1897), 247).
73. Steer, *Romance*, 14.
74. See Kember, 'The Cinema of Affections' 3–4 and Toulmin, *Electric Edwardians* 57–84.

75. See Barnes, *Beginnings Vol. 1* 87–150.
76. Braithwaite, *Travelling Fairs* 11.
77. See Kember, 'It was not the show' 63. For a list of similar showman's titles see Barnes, *Beginnings Vol. 2* 177.
78. Toulmin, 'Cuckoo' 73.
79. Francoeur, *Les Signes s'envolent* 69–70n.
80. Gaudreault, 'Méliès the Magician' 172.
81. Gaudreault and Marion, 'The Cinema' 14.
82. Gaudreault, *Cinema* n.p.
83. See Shail, ed., *Reading the Cinematograph, passim.*
84. Gaudreault, 'The Diversity' 10, 12; Gaudreault and Marion, 'The Cinema' 17; Gaudreault and Marion, 'A Medium' 5.
85. Qtd. Gaudreault and Marion, 'A Medium' 15.
86. Gaudreault and Marion, 'The Cinema' 15.
87. 'Between Ourselves', *The Pictures* 3.65 (8 Jan 1912), 11.
88. Blumenfeld *R.D.B.'s Diary* 226–7.
89. Anon., 'Wake up, John Bull!', *Kinematograph and Lantern Weekly* 1.16 (29 August 1907), 245. This commentator remarked that "[a] theatre devoted entirely to the display of living pictures is a new thing in this country, dating back to the time when the Balham Empire opened its doors a few weeks since" (245).
90. See Hiley, 'Nothing More" 113.
91. Qtd. National Council of Public Morals, *The Cinema* 2.
92. F.R. Goodwin, quoted in National Council of Public Morals, *The Cinema* 2–3. See also British Film Institute, 'Film and TV Information'.
93. Burrows, 'Penny Pleasures' 86, 63.
94. See my 'Penny Gaffs and Picture Theatres' for a discussion of this continuity.
95. Wells, *The History of Mr Polly* 143.
96. Burrows, 'Penny Pleasures' 79.
97. A.C. Bromhead, 'A Review of the Cinematograph Business', *The World's Fair*, 2 May 1908.
98. Adapted from Hiley, 'At The Picture Palace' 97.
99. Hiley, 'Nothing More' 120, 118.
100. Hiley, 'Nothing More' 120.
101. Kinematograph and Lantern Weekly, *Handbook*; Kinematograph and Lantern Weekly, *How to Run a Picture Theatre*.
102. Rossi Ashton, 'Six Days Shalt Thou Labour', *The Era*, 24 August 1912.
103. McKernan, 'Diverting' 131.
104. McKernan, 'Diverting' 134.
105. *Punch* 140 (26 July 1911), 53.
106. 'Palace Figures', *Evening Times*, 18 Sept 1911, 6.
107. See BFI, 'Film and TV Information'.
108. Hiley 'The British' 167; McKernan, 'Diverting' 134.
109. McKernan, *Topical* 4.
110. 'Palace Figures', *Evening Times*, 18 Sept 1911, 6; Steer, *The Romance* 13; 'The Cinematograph and Education', *The Times*, 4 March 1914, 8; McKernan, *Topical* 25; Anon., *Bioscope*, 9 March 1916, 1008; *Picture Palace News*, 22 July 1916, 212; F.R. Goodwin, qtd. National Council of Public Morals, *The Cinema* 2–3; 'The All British Firm', *Pictures and the Picturegoer* 15.246 (26 Oct–2 Nov 1918), 422; 'Editorial Chat', *Cinema* 1 (August 1918), 39; G.T. Broadbridge, qtd. 'News and Notes', *Pictures and Picturegoer* 17.300 (15 Nov 1919), 575. In correspondence with the author, Nicholas Hiley observes that the industry was happy with an estimate of

eight million attendances per week in 1913 and lowered this estimation to seven million in 1914 (although there is no evidence of a drop in attendance in 1914), probably because of pessimism about an impending end to the picture theatre boom. I have provided both figures to indicate the possible range being researched at the time with some accuracy, as with the figures of 15 million and 20 million for late 1918. (Other contemporary figures ranged as widely as 28,000,000 in 1913 ('The Cinema's Triumph, *The Pictures* 3.70 (date unspecified, c. Feb 1913), 23) and 14,000,000 in January 1912 (L.D., 'Cinematography', *Evening Standard and St James's Gazette*, 13 Jan 1912, 16)).

111. Gifford, *The British Film Catalogue passim.*
112. Low, *The History . . . 1906–1914*, 145.
113. Anon., 'Latest Productions', *Kinematograph and Lantern Weekly* 1.1 (16 May 1907); Anon., 'Latest Productions', *Kinematograph and Lantern Weekly* 3.53 (14 May 1908); Anon., 'Latest Productions', *Kinematograph and Lantern Weekly* 4.78 (5 Nov 1908); Anon., 'Latest Productions', *Kinematograph and Lantern Weekly* 4.99 (1 April 1909), 1362; Anon., 'Latest Productions', *Kinematograph and Lantern Weekly* 8.188 (15 Dec 1910), 372; Anon., 'Latest Productions', *Kinematograph and Lantern Weekly* 9.228 (21 Sept 1911), supplement i.
114. L.D, 'Cinematography', *Evening Standard and St James's Gazette*, 13 Jan 1912, 16.
115. National Council of Public Morals, *The Cinema* 17.
116. Anon., *Historical Review of the Cinematograph*, 1910, 3.
117. L.D., 'Cinematography: A Weekly Review of the Latest Films', *Evening Standard and St James's Gazette*, 10 June 1911, 8.
118. 'Fan' had to be explained to UK picturegoers as an Americanism in issues of *The Pictures* from July 1912, alongside such terms as stand for ("to support"), spruce up ("to adorn"), to quit ("to leave") and janitor ("watchman") and is defined as 'enthusiast'. ('American Words and Phrases', *The Pictures* 2.38 (6 July 1912), 8.) Picturegoers and journalists brought it into Standard British English towards the end of 1912 and its connotations of extremism—it was seen as an abbreviation for 'fanatic'—were being de-emphasised in conjunction with the availability of new models of film-only patronage that year.
119. See McDonald, 'Forming the Craft' 79.
120. See Shail, 'The Motion Picture Story Magazine' 188–9; Burrows, *Legitimate Cinema* 60.
121. F.R. Goodwin, qtd. National Council of Public Morals, *The Cinema*, 3; Hiley, 'The British' 162.
122. Hiley, 'The British' 161.
123. 1914 Select Committee on London County Council (General Powers) Bill, Sessional Papers (21 July 1914), Qs 3465, 3483–3487 (W.F. Jury).
124. Low, *The History . . . 1906–1914* 18.
125. See, for example, 'Photoplay Gossip', *The Pictures* 1.13 (13 Jan 1912), 13; Herbert, 'The Power' 32.
126. 'Photoplay Gossip', *The Pictures* 1.13 (13 Jan 1912), 13; *Kinematograph Year Book 1919*, (London: Kinematograph Publications 1918), 256–332 (ticket prices for 1413 venues).
127. Burrows, *Legitimate* 103.
128. Manders, *Cinemas* 24–180.
129. Programme for the Theatre Royal, 13 Mar 1911, Tyne and Wear Archives, Newcastle upon Tyne, DX540/6/6; Programme for the Palace Theatre of Varieties, Sunderland, 12 April 1907, Tyne and Wear Archives, Newcastle upon Tyne, DX540/10/2.

130. Low, *The History* ... *1906–1914* 24.
131. Kinematograph and Lantern Weekly, *How to Run a Picture Theatre* 24.
132. Bottomore, *I want* 243 (the total number of cartoons Bottomore has discovered to date).
133. L.D., 'Cinematography: A Weekly Review of the Latest Films', *Evening Standard and St James's Gazette*, 10 June 1911, 8.
134. See Shail, 'Reading the Cinematograph' 3.
135. *Punch* 140 (1 February 1911), 77.
136. 'To Leeds Readers', *The Pictures* 2.51 (5 October 1912), 24.
137. In 1921 Odhams guaranteed minimum average net sales for *Kinematograph Weekly* of 4,500. In April 1914 Odhams certified net weekly sales for *Pictures and the Picturegoer* of 101,025 (*Advertiser's Protection Society Monthly Circular*, February 1921, 25 April 1914). Circulations can be estimated at around 2–3 times these numbers.
138. When *Close Up* was first distributed in Europe in 1927, its editors' decision to sell it solely in bookshops contrasted strongly with the established place of the popular film magazine.
139. Anon., 'The Motion Picture and Photo Play', *Evening Times*, 30 October 1911, 6.
140. Anon, 'Photoplay Gossip', *The Pictures* 1.13 (13 Jan 1912), 13.
141. Anon., 'Our Screen', *The Pictures* 5.114 (13 Dec 1913), 24.
142. Anon., 'In reply to yours', *Pictures and the Picturegoer* 6.4 (w/e 14 March 1914), 96.
143. Donald and Donald, 'The Publicness of Cinema' 114.
144. See, for example, my "a distinct advance in society".
145. The turning-point of 1911 also influenced Lewis's 'Wild Body' stories. Whereas the characters of the May 1909 'The 'Pole'', the June 1909 'Some Innkeepers and Bestre', the August 1909 'Les Saltimbanques', the June 1910 'A Spanish Household', the August 1910 'A Breton Innkeeper', and the Sept 1910 'Le Père François' unleash intermittent and intense violence on each other, the Jan 1911 'Brobdingnag' and the Feb 1911 'Unlucky for Pringle' see these episodes of automatic violence begin to fade.
146. Donovan, *Joseph Conrad and Popular Culture* 42–62, 61.
147. Donovan, *Joseph Conrad and Popular Culture* 51.
148. See Barry, *Let's* 38, 43; Lacoste, 'Sur le'Cubisme' 336; Cox, *Artist* 31; Lynton, *Story* 56, and Apollonio (who remarks that Giacomo Balla's *Little Girl Running on a Balcony* (1912) was based on one of Étienne-Jules Marey's chronophotographs (27–8)).
149. See Burrows, *Legitimate* 1–19.
150. Gaudreault, 'The Diversity' 14.
151. Burrows, *Legitimate* 14.
152. Gaudreault and Marion, 'The Cinema' 16.
153. Fred Dangerfield, 'Screen Gossip', *Pictures and the Picturegoer* 6.26 (15 August 1914), 577. See also 'Picture Notes', *The Pictures* 1.15 (27 Jan 1912), 16; 'Screen Gossip', *Pictures and the Picturegoer* 6.4 (14 Mar 1914), 93.
154. Barry 'The Cinema: *Metropolis*' 540.
155. See Armstrong, 'The Lady of Shalott' *passim*, and *Victorian Glassworlds*, *passim*.
156. Woolf, 22 July 1922, *Diaries* 185.
157. Metz, *Psychoanalysis* 9.
158. Bean, 'Technologies' 9.
159. Friedberg, 'Introduction' 4.
160. Friedberg, 'Introduction' 4.

161. See, for example, Hankins, 'Iris Barry' 497; Hankins 'Across the Screen' 157. Maggie Humm repeats the gesture of describing popular film culture as inane; her examination of a handful of popular notions of cinema serves the sole purpose of identifying female and male modernists as democratic and elitist respectively (164).

162. 'Screen Gossip', *Pictures and the Picturegoer* 6.10 (w/e 25 April 1914), 261.

163. See Hankins, 'The Doctor' *passim* for an account of the impact of a specific film—*The Cabinet of Dr. Caligari* (1919), which, Hankins argues, Woolf saw even before its official arrival in the UK in March 1924—on *Mrs Dalloway* (1925).

164. Ford, *Mr. Fleight* 106.

165. Tiessen, 'A New Year One' 158. Wees, *Vorticism* 147.

166. James Joyce to Stanislaus Joyce, c. 1 March 1907, *Letters*, ed. Ellmann, Vol. II, 217–20, 217.

167. Camerani, 'Joyce' 114.

168. McKernan, 'James Joyce' 17.

169. See Hutchins, 'James Joyce and the Cinema' *passim*.

170. Eliot to Elinor Hinkley, 14 October 1914, 27 November 1914, 3 January 1915, *Letters* 60–5, 70–3, 76–9.

171. See Trotter, *Cinema and Modernism* 125, 141–2, 146 for details of Eliot's overt commentaries on cinema in the early 1920.

172. "The manner in which the Surrender of the German Fleet film was given at Queen's Hall (Jan. 22) was a disgrace to cinematography and to whatever Government department is responsible for the film", he wrote in February 1919. "Low visibility during the surrender would account for the poor quality of the negatives, but to use a secondhand lantern, an amateur operator, a worn-out positive, to give the thing out of focus, with a shatter and a shiver reminiscent of the experimental bioscopes of twenty years ago, is inexcusable impertinence, especially as it is a double price show. . . . The quality of the effects would have disgraced a 3d. house." ('Art Notes: Navy' 241.)

173. For examples of Lewis's hostile attitudes towards film, albeit stated after the time frame of this study, see Tiessen, 'A New Year One' 161.

174. Eliot, 'London Letter, July 1921' 184.

175. Willard, 'More about Conrad' 9.

176. Qtd. Tittle, 'The Conrad Who Sat For Me' 161.

177. Anon., 'Latest Productions', *Kinematograph and Lantern Weekly* 4.95 (4 Mar 1909), 1202.

178. Anon., 'Latest Productions', *Kinematograph and Lantern Weekly* 4.99 (1 April 1909), 1362; Anon., 'Latest Productions', *Kinematograph and Lantern Weekly* 8.188 (15 Dec 1910), 372; Anon., 'Latest Productions', *Kinematograph and Lantern Weekly* 9.228 (21 Sept 1911), supplement, i.

179. *The Pictures* 4.95 (2 Aug 1913), *passim*.

180. Anon., 'Where to send scenarios', *The Pictures* 4.85 (17 May 1913), 22.

181. Anon., 'Screen Gossip', *Pictures and the Picturegoer* 6.11 (w/e 2 May 1914), 261.

182. Anon., 'Picture News and Notes', *Pictures and the Picturegoer* 8.64 (8 May 1915), 86.

183. Eliot, '*Ulysses*, Order and Myth' 101.

184. For an account of how those seeking to dignify cinema during the 1920s looked to recently formed modernist aesthetic principles, see Bordwell, *On the History* 44.

NOTES TO CHAPTER 1

1. Gunning, 'The Cinema of Attractions' 65.
2. Doane, *Emergence* 24.
3. This stance is taken, for example, by McCabe (*Cinematic* 7, 9) and Perlmutter ('Joyce and Cinema' 489). Rachel Connor includes post-1910 editing techniques in her account of cinema's relation to H.D.'s poetry (*H.D. and the Image* 31–40), but sees this influence only as a matter of the literary appropriation of film technique. Trotter also tends to seek out cinema's appeal to modernists in the subterranean persistence of the chaotic tendencies that were most apparent before 1908 (*Cinema and Modernism*, e.g. 77, 188), and identifies as a distinguishing feature of the narrative films of D.W. Griffith their subterranean 'anti-system' and 'contingency' (49–85).
4. See, for example, Keil, *Early American Cinema passim* and Hammond, *The Big Show* 11.
5. Bazin, 'In Defence' 61–2; Wood, 'Modernism and Film' 217. See also Shail, 'a distinct advance in society' *passim*.
6. 'Picture Notes', *The Pictures* 1.16 (3 Feb 1912), 16.
7. F.W. Richardson, *Moving Picture World*, 20 Feb 1909, 196.
8. For examples of remarks from the pre-1911 period that viewed editing as erratic 'jumping', see my 'The Motion Picture Story Magazine' 185.
9. Gunning, 'Non-Continuity' 92. The place of telecommunication technologies in initiating the race-to-the-rescue plot in generating cinematic narrative was witnessed in a joke from 1917: "'Wouldn't it be awful if there were no telephones?' . . . 'Oh, I don't know. Then there wouldn't be any film dramas'" ('Smiles', *Pictures and the Picturegoer* 13.183 (11–18 Aug 1918), 210).
10. Musser, 'The Nickelodeon Era Begins' 271.
11. Gunning, 'Weaving a Narrative' 345.
12. See Aumont, 'Griffith: The Frame, The Figure' 349.
13. Gunning, 'Now You See It' 78.
14. Salt, 'Film Form 1900–1906' 35.
15. Gaudreault, 'Film, Narrative, Narration' 71.
16. See Gaudreault, 'Detours in Film Narrative'; deCordova, 'From Lumière to Pathé'; Burch, 'A Primitive Mode of Representation?'; Musser, 'The Nickelodeon Era Begins'; Bottomore, 'Shots in the Dark'.
17. Metz, 'The Cinema' 226.
18. Gaudreault, 'Detours' 133.
19. Gunning, 'From the Opium Den' 30.
20. See Bowser, *Transformation* 71.
21. Bowser, *Transformation* 58.
22. Anon., 'Licensed Release Dates', 'Independent Release Dates', *The Moving Picture World* 8.25 (24 June 1911), 1468, 1470.
23. Anon., 'Latest Productions', *Kinematograph and Lantern Weekly* 9.228 (21 Sept 1911), supplement i.
24. Anon., 'A Sermon for Exhibitors', *The Top-Line Indicator* 1.11 (8 Jan 1913), 3.
25. Bowser, *Transformation* 71.
26. Salt, 'Vitagraph Films' 67–70.
27. Gunning, 'Primitive Cinema' 101, emphasis added.
28. Bowser, *Transformation* 140.
29. 'A Chat about the Famous Players Company', *The Pictures* 3.78 (date unspecified), 19.
30. 'Motion Picture News', *The Pictures* 3.52 (12 Oct 1912), 31.
31. Hansen, 'Early Cinema' 233.

32. Gunning, 'From the Opium Den' 31.
33. 'The Writing of a Photo-Play', *The Pictures* 5.109 (8 Nov 1913), 22.
34. 'Cinema Gossip from the Seaside', *Pictures and the Picturegoer* 6.26 (15 August 1914), 566–7, 567.
35. This extract indicates the need for specificity when investigating the relationship between cinema and modernism. Michael North refers to Eugene Jolas's preoccupation with mechanisation in his poetry collection *Cinema* (1926) as employing a linguistic version of the projector. Language in these poems, he argues, "is an endless associative unrolling of one episode into another" ('Words in Motion' 208). Clearly, as film narrative since 1910 had ceased to depend on associative unrolling, either North has over-simplified Jolas's connection with cinema, or 'cinema' as a fantasy for certain modernists hoping to effect their 'revolution of the word' was not identical with cinema's popular image-regime.
36. James Cotter, 'The Picture-Play and its Makers. No III—The Producer', *Pictures and the Picturegoer* 6.21 (11 July 1914), 436.
37. Bannister Merwin, 'An Expert on Photo-Plays', *The Pictures* 5.118 (10 Jan 1914), 8.
38. Swinton, 'The Sense of Touch' 224; Furniss, *Our Lady Cinema* 28–9, 31–4.
39. 'To Introduce Ourselves', *The Pictures* 1.1 (21 October 1911), 1.
40. On the role of film discourse in reinventing cinema as a bourgeois practice involving isolated spectatorship, see my 'a distinct advance in society'.
41. 'To Introduce Ourselves', *The Pictures* 1.1 (21 Oct 1911), 1.
42. Gorky, 'Review of Lumière programme' 407.
43. Tolstoy, Interview with I Teneromo 410.
44. 'Motion Picture News', *The Pictures* 3.76 (date unspecified, c. March 1913), 22.
45. 'Selfish Playgoers', *The Pictures* 3.53 (19 Oct 1912), 31.
46. 'Photoplay Gossip', *The Pictures* 1.16 (3 Feb 1912), 15.
47. 'Bouquets and Brickbats', *Pictures and the Picturegoer* 13.199 (1–8 Dec 1917), 596.
48. 'Superfluous Correspondence', *The Pictures* 4.93 (19 July 1913), 24.
49. 'Picture Notes', *The Pictures* 1.16 (3 Feb 1912), 16.
50. 'A School for the Screen-Struck', *Pictures and the Picturegoer* 6.8 (11 April 1914), 170–1, 171.
51. Editorial, *The Pictures* 1.10 (23 Dec 1911), 21.
52. 'Mutes Have Best of it at Pictures', *The Pictures* 3.62 (21 Dec 1912), 23.
53. 'Screen Gossip', *Pictures and the Picturegoer* 6.5 (21 March 1914), 117.
54. Gunning, 'Non-Continuity, Continuity, Discontinuity' 93.
55. Bowser, *Transformation* 261.
56. Bordwell, *Narration in the Fiction Film*, 61.
57. Souriau, Preface 7
58. Metz, 'The Cinema' 98–9.
59. 'News and Notes', *Pictures and the Picturegoer* 13.194 (27 Oct–3 Nov 1917), 460.
60. Burgoyne, 'Cinematic' 9.
61. Burgoyne, 'Cinematic' 7.
62. Metz, 'History/discourse' 228.
63. Metz, 'The Cinema' 98.
64. Metz, 'The Cinema' 64.
65. Metz, 'The Cinema' 40, 66.
66. Metz, 'The Cinema' 75.
67. Metz, 'The Cinema' 69.
68. Metz, 'The Cinema' 81.

69. Metz, 'The Cinema' 67.
70. Metz, 'The Cinema' 99.
71. Metz, 'The Cinema' 65.
72. Metz, 'The Cinema' 70.
73. Bordwell, *Narration in the Fiction Film* 25.
74. Bordwell, *Narration in the Fiction Film* 62.
75. Benveniste, *Problèmes de Linguistique passim.*
76. Deleuze, *Cinema 1* 13.
77. Bordwell, *Narration* 62.
78. Booth, *Rhetoric of Fiction* 70–76.
79. Levinson, 'Film Music and Narrative Agency' 252.
80. Gunning, 'Weaving a Narrative' 346, emphasis added.
81. Lothe, *Narration in Fiction* 29.
82. See Levy, 'Re-constituted Newsreels' *passim.*
83. Hepworth, *Came The Dawn* 122.
84. See my 'Penny Gaffs and Picture Theatres' for an account of the techniques employed in popular film discourse for distancing the picture theatre from its predecessors.
85. See Burrows, *Legitimate* 106–9. For example, a writer in *The Cinema* claimed on 13 August 1913 that "a cinematograph version of a West-End production, so far from having a deleterious effect upon the receipts, is calculated to act as a feeder to the theatre, and, of course, vice versa" (qtd Burrows, *Legitimate* 107).
86. Bowser 203–4.
87. 'My Thrilling Experiences at Finchley', *Pictures and the Picturegoer* 6.20 (w/e 4 July 1914), 444–5, 445.
88. 'The Story of Siegmund Lubin', *The Pictures* 3.59 (30 Nov 1912), 5.
89. 'The Cinematographing of the Melancholy Dane', *Dress and Vanity Fair* 1.1 (Sept 1913), 28.
90. 'Aeroplanes in a Romaine Fielding Film', *The Pictures* 5.121 (31 Jan 1914), 8.
91. *Pictures and the Picturegoer* 6.13 (16 May 1914), 290.
92. 'Screen Gossip', *Pictures and the Picturegoer* 6.5 (21 March 1914), 117.
93. 'Motion Picture News', *The Pictures* 3.53 (19 Oct 1912), 31.
94. 'The Price of Realism', *The Pictures* 4.85 (17 May 1913), 22.
95. J.P. McGowan, 'The Price of Realism', *The Pictures* 2.37 (29 June 1912), 19.
96. J.P. McGowan, 'An Account of the Kalem World-Tour: Around the World with a Moving Picture Camera', *The Pictures* 2.48 (14 Sept 1912), 18.
97. *The Pictures* 1.14 (20 Jan 1912), 15.
98. 'At the Queen's Hall', *The Pictures* 3.56 (9 Nov 1912), 7–8, 7.
99. 'Birthplaces of British Films', *Pictures and the Picturegoer* 6.14 (23 May 1914), 320–2, 322.
100. 'Pars for Picturegoers', *Pictures and the Picturegoer* 6.13 (16 May 1914), 302.
101. 'A Little Hero', *The Pictures* 4.83 (3 May 1913), 7–8, 8.
102. Bowser, *Transformation* 166.
103. 'Real Clouds—Not Canvas', *The Pictures* 3.54 (26 Oct 1912), 20. This was of course a partial comparison, as the stage at the end of the nineteenth century had itself attained a degree of intense realism, with the use of such techniques as constructing real buildings on stage.
104. 'Screen Gossip', *Pictures and the Picturegoer* 6.1 (21 Feb 1914), 21.
105. 'Picture Notes', *The Pictures* 2.30 (11 May 1912), 23.
106. 'Screen Gossip', *Pictures and the Picturegoer* 6.26 (15 August 1914), 577.

107. Leonard Donaldson, 'Photoplay Gossip', *The Pictures* 2.34 (8 June 1912), 19, my emphasis.
108. 'Lurid Melodrama and its 'Thrills'', *Pictures and the Picturegoer* 6.24 (1 August 1914), 524.
109. Qtd. Roxbury Sault, 'My 10,000 Lovers. Miss "Lucille Love" tells of her adventures in search of a husband', *Pictures and the Picturegoer* 6.24 (w/e 1 August 1914), 522–4, 523.
110. 'Moving-Picture Mistakes', *Pictures and the Picturegoer* 6.12 (9 May 1914), 273.
111. Margaret Chute, 'Cinemitis', *Graphic* 88.2294 (15 Nov 1913), 894. Cambridge University Library, NPR.C.53.
112. See Gaudreault, 'Méliès the Magician' 168–9.
113. See, for example, 'Photoplay Gossip' *The Pictures* 1.20 (2 Mar 1912), 16.
114. 'People we Admire', *London Opinion* (21 Feb 1914), 340. BOD Nuneham N. 2289 d. 10.
115. 'Smiles', *Pictures and the Picturegoer* 6.14 (23 May 1914), 335.
116. 'Daphne Wayne's Champion', *The Pictures* 3.53 (19 Oct 1912), 31.
117. 'Reel Life in Real Life', *Pictures and the Picturegoer* 6.4 (14 March 1914), 74–5, 74.
118. 'Mr Romaine Fielding', *The Pictures* 4.79 (date unspecified), 21.
119. 'Mr Punch's Holiday Film', *Punch* 147 (8 July 1914), 48–50.
120. Doane, *Emergence* 25.
121. Metz, 'The Cinema' 43.
122. Bean, 'Technologies' 17.
123. Elsaesser, 'Early Film Form' 18.
124. Of course, while early cinema was continuous with earlier practices, later cinema was not independent—it was only continuous with *other* preceding practices—the commuter short story magazine, the legitimate stage, literary fiction, the sketch and the newspaper.
125. Doane, *Emergence* 140–1
126. Reeves, *Official* 49.
127. MacCabe, 'Realism and Cinema' 8.
128. MacCabe, 'Realism and Cinema' 8.
129. MacCabe, 'Realism and Cinema' 8.
130. MacCabe, *James Joyce* 14.
131. Bennett, *The Old Wives' Tale* 288–9.
132. MacCabe, 'Realism and Cinema' 24.
133. Bordwell, *Narration in the Fiction Film* 18–20.
134. Morris, 'Film and Modernism' 111.
135. See my 'a distinct advance in society' and 'The Motion Picture Story Magazine'.
136. Levenson, *Genealogy* 49.
137. Levenson, *Genealogy* 22.
138. See, for example, Peters, *Conrad and Impressionism* 15–6.
139. Peters, *Conrad and Impressionism* 8–11.
140. Levenson, *Genealogy* 14.
141. Ford, 'Joseph Conrad' 83.
142. Ford, 'Joseph Conrad' 84.
143. Ford, 'Joseph Conrad' 90.
144. Ford, 'On Impressionism' 174.
145. Levenson, *Genealogy* 36.
146. Pound, 'The Serious Artist' 46.
147. Ford, 'On Impressionism, Second Article' 323.
148. Ford, 'Joseph Conrad' 84.

149. Ford, 'Modern Poetry' 190.
150. Ford, 'Impressionism—Some Speculations' 222.
151. Ford, 'Impressionism—Some Speculations' 224.
152. Ford, 'Joseph Conrad' 84.
153. Pound, 'A Few Don'ts By An Imagiste' 132.
154. Hulme, 'Searchers after reality II: Haldane' 10.
155. Hulme, 'A Lecture on Modern Poetry' 72.
156. Hulme, 'A Lecture on Modern Poetry' 72.
157. Hulme, 'A Lecture on Modern Poetry' 72.
158. Hulme, 'A Lecture on Modern Poetry' 73, 75.
159. Pound, 'Status rerum' 125.
160. Pound, 'Status rerum' 126.
161. Pound, 'The Serious Artist' 43.
162. Pound, 'The Serious Artist' 56.
163. Conrad, *Under Western Eyes* 181.
164. Conrad, *Under Western Eyes* 18.
165. Conrad, *Under Western Eyes* 150.
166. Conrad, *Under Western Eyes* 289.
167. Conrad, *Chance* 90.
168. Conrad, *Chance* 181.
169. Conrad, *Chance* 310.
170. Conrad, *Chance* 242.
171. Conrad, 'The Partner' 127.
172. Conrad, 'The Inn' 180.
173. Conrad, 'The Planter' 47.
174. Conrad, 'Because of the Dollars' 248–9.
175. Conrad, 'Because of the Dollars' 249.
176. Conrad, *Victory* 36–7, 42.
177. Conrad, *Victory* 25.
178. Conrad, *Victory* 53.
179. Conrad, *Victory* 54.
180. Conrad, *Victory* 73.
181. Conrad, *Victory* 80.
182. Conrad, *Victory* 83–4.
183. Conrad, *Victory* 160.
184. Conrad, *Victory* 224.
185. Conrad, *Victory* 249.
186. Conrad, *Victory* 176.
187. See, for example, Peters' *Conrad and Impressionism* on Conrad's *The Shad-ow-Line* (written c. Feb–c. Dec 1915 and published in March 1917).
188. This historical transition has been noted since the turn to formal analyses of Conrad in the 1980s. Thomas Moser alluded to it when he called *Chance* "the last, most intricate instance of Marlovian impressionism" (*Life in Fiction* 122). Robert Hampson notes *Victory*'s enhanced "technical experimen-tation" compared to its predecessors, although he ascribes one aspect of this, Conrad's relatively objective presentation of dialogue from *Victory* onwards, to Conrad's renewed interest in drama ('The Late Novels' 144–5).
189. Peters, *Conrad and Impressionism* 37; Watt, *Conrad* 175–9.
190. See Moser, *Life in Fiction* 149–59 for an example of an understanding of *The Good Soldier* as expertly impressionist.
191. Meixner, *Ford Madox Ford's Novels*, 145.
192. Ford, *A Call* 303–4.
193. Ford, *The Good Soldier* 12, 15, 21, 21, 51, 57, 89, 104, 139, 141, 159, 169, 181, 220. Moser has also noted some of these differences between *The*

Good Soldier and impressionism (*Life in Fiction* 159–61). As early as 1980 Avrom Fleishman exemplified an altered understandings of *The Good Soldier* as an *"accession ad absurdum"* of the Impressionist method ('The Genre of the *Good Soldier'* 40), pointing to Dowell's statements about impressionism to show that, for Ford, "to adopt the moves of Impressionism to tell a "real" story amounts to an estheticizing act." For Fleishman, Dowell's "narration adds complexity to complication, refinement to rarity, so that it emerges as one of the most artificial tales ever told" (40). For Fleishman, a great deal of the work's comedy comes from literary parody, the result of Ford's perception of "the comic dimension of modern limited narration" (42), and that this is one of the components that make it the first modernist novel.

194. Ford, *The Good Soldier* 15.
195. Ford, *The Good Soldier* 18.
196. Conrad and Ford, *Romance* 17.
197. Ford, *The Good Soldier* 17.
198. Ford, *The Good Soldier* 31.
199. Ford, *The Good Soldier* 51.
200. Ford, *Joseph Conrad* 129–30.
201. Saunders, *The World Before the War* 406.
202. Ford, *The Good Soldier* 147–8.
203. See Chatman, *Story* 81.
204. Ford, *The Good Soldier* 110.
205. Trotter, *Paranoid Modernism* 220.
206. Conrad, *Chance* 21.
207. Qtd. Jean-Aubry, *Joseph Conrad: Life and Letters*, Vol. 2, 283.
208. Qtd. Schwab, 'Conrad's American Speeches' 345.
209. Pound, 'Art Notes: Kinema, Kinesis, Hepworth etc.' 352.
210. Pound, 'The Book of the Month' 122.

NOTES TO CHAPTER 2

1. Doane, *Emergence* 21.
2. Doane, *Emergence* 3.
3. Doane, *Emergence* 221.
4. Doane, *Emergence* 5.
5. Doane, *Emergence* 221.
6. Doane, *Emergence* 3–4, 24.
7. Doane, *Emergence* 4.
8. Doane, *Emergence* 108.
9. Doane, *Emergence* 9.
10. Doane, *Emergence* 19.
11. Doane, *Emergence* 19.
12. Doane, *Emergence* 21.
13. Doane, *Emergence* 3.
14. Doane refers only once to the shape of the cultural consequences of the arrival of the regimes of time she describes: "Representational systems (art, literature) address themselves to the ephemeral, the contingent, the moment. The credibility of any static universal or eternal is diminished" (*Emergence* 176).
15. Doane, *Emergence* 248.
16. Doane, *Emergence* 171.
17. Doane, *Emergence* 184.

18. Mrs. J.E. Whitby, 'The Future of the Cinematograph', *Chambers's Journal* 3.129 (19 May 1900), 391–2, 391.
19. Corelli, *The Master-Christian* 110–1.
20. See, for example, Jurji Lotman, *Semiotics of Cinema* 77.
21. Chatman, *Story* 74.
22. Mukařovský, *Structure* 199.
23. Mukařovský, *Structure* 193.
24. *Punch* 151 (19 July 1916), 59.
25. Kracauer, 'Photography' 56.
26. Kracauer, 'Photography' 56.
27. Barthes, 'Rhetoric of the Image' 44.
28. "Pour la première fois, l'image des choses est aussi celle de leur dureé et comme la momie du changement" (Bazin, 'Ontologie' 14). "Now, for the first time, the image of things is likewise the image of their duration, change mummified as it were" (Bazin, 'Ontology' 15).
29. I am very grateful to Nicola Kielty for this suggestion.
30. Barthes, 'Rhetoric of the Image' 45.
31. Maltby, *Hollywood Cinema* 432.
32. Gaudreault, 'Temporality and Narrativity' 316.
33. Kittler, *Gramophone* 3.
34. Bazin, 'Ontology' 15–6. Barthes uses the term 'punctum' to refer to the photograph's interference with the narrowness of the pre-photographic code of poses and everyday cultural signifiers that the photographer has sought to capture (Barthes, *Camera* 43–9). Stephen Donovan also cites evidence that suggests that Conrad was typical amongst his contemporaries in regarding photography "as defined by undiscriminating inclusiveness and relentless equivalence" (*Joseph Conrad and Popular Culture*, 28).
35. Kracauer, 'Photography' 58.
36. Kracauer, 'Photography' 51.
37. Kracauer, 'Photography' 55.
38. Doane, *Emergence* 162–3.
39. Robbe-Grillet, *Last Year* 11.
40. 'Smiles', *Pictures and the Picturegoer* 6.6 (28 March 1914), 143.
41. See, for example, Humphrey, *Stream* 121.
42. For an example of a common tendency to regard filmic temporality as inherently non-linear, see Hauser, *Social* 941.
43. Chatman, *Story* 83.
44. Chatman, *Story* 80.
45. Bolter and Grusin, *Remediation* 45.
46. *The Pictures* 1.16 (3 Feb 1912), 16.
47. E. Temple Thurston, 'The Future of the Author for the Film', *Pictures and Picturegoer* 14.211 (23 Feb–2 Mar 1918), 198–9, 199.
48. Gaudreault and Marion, 'The Neo-Institutionalisation' 89.
49. Doane, *Emergence* 30.
50. Gaudreault, 'Temporality and Narrativity' 322.
51. Gaudreault argues that it was only the rapid rise to dominance of plots that involved time situations in 1908 (last minute rescues, deadlines and dramatic suspense in general), plots that necessitated the simulation of time, that caused temporal overlap to finally disappear ('Temporality and Narrativity' 326–7).
52. Doane, *Emergence* 187.
53. Gaudreault, 'Temporality and Narrativity' 326–9.
54. Doane, *Emergence* 67.
55. Doane, *Emergence* 30.

56. Doane, *Emergence* 31.
57. Doane, *Emergence* 161.
58. Doane, *Emergence* 163.
59. Kern, *Culture* 88.
60. 'Actions or Words?', *The Pictures* 2.52 (12 Oct 1912), 4.
61. 'Scenario-Writers' Column', *The Pictures* 4.83 (3 May 1913), 21.
62. For other examples of film-specific scenario-writing advice see 'The Writing of a Photoplay', *The Pictures* 5.109–5.113 (8 Nov 1913–6 Dec 1913).
63. 'Real Clouds—Not Canvas', *The Pictures* 3.54 (26 Oct 1912), 20.
64. See, for example, Woolf, 'Pictures' 44 and H.D., *Notes* 18.
65. Woolf, 'The "Movie" Novel' 290.
66. See, for example, Connor, *H.D. and the Image* 32.
67. Pound, 'Hugh Selwyn Mauberley' 157.
68. Conrad, *Collected Letters, Vol. 5* 632.
69. Yeats, *Four Years* 89.
70. Groden, Ulysses *in Progress* 43; Trotter, *Cinema and Modernism* 114–5.
71. Cohen, *Film* 2.
72. Kern 76–7. Indeed, the persistent use of the term 'montage' to describe the technique of *Ulysses* in general (see Introduction) has almost always been a mere metaphor, Valery Larbaud using in October 1922 (before the term 'montage' was popularised in the UK in the 1930s) "the art of mosaic" (Larbaud, 'The "Ulysses" of James Joyce' 102).
73. Humphrey, *Stream* 53. Other 'montage' proponents include Spiegel, *Fiction and the Camera Eye* 171, Barrow, *Montage* 100–16 and Pearce, *The Novel in Motion* 46.
74. Gunn and Wright, 'Visualising Joyce' para 13. Eisenstein, *The Film Sense* 14.
75. See, for example, Bordwell and Thompson, *Film Art* 91.
76. Eisenstein, 'Beyond' 84, 85.
77. Eisenstein, 'Beyond' 87–8.
78. Edward Murray and Lee Jacobus are the only scholars to have correctly identified Joyce's interpolations as literary equivalents of cross-cutting (Murray, *Cinematic Imagination* 130–1; Jacobus, 'Bring the Camera' 531).
79. Killeen (*Ulysses Unbound* 104–10) and Hart ('Wandering Rocks' *passim*) give similar lists of interpolations. As with most Joyce scholars, I do not see an instance when one stream of action intersects with another (for example, when the H.E.L.Y.'S. sandwichmen pass in sight of Boylan outside Thornton's Fruiterer & Florist on Grafton Street in section 5) as an interpolation, as the action occurs within that one stream. Also, to qualify as an interpolation, the 'shot' cannot occur within a line of sight of the current stream (as it could be intended as a part of that stream). Hence, unlike Terence Killeen (but like Clive Hart), I do not see the following short paragraph in section 15 as an interpolation: "On the steps of the City hall Councillor Nanetti, descending, hailed Alderman Cowley and Councillor Abraham Lyon ascending" (*Ulysses* 316). This event occurs both close enough to be seen by the current stream's protagonists and close enough for them to recognise Nanetti, Cowley and Lyon's faces. Even if it is established that characters must be *looking at* a described event for it to count as within that stream (this particular event happens behind Cunningham and Power) John Wyse Nolan has just caught up with them from behind, meaning that they could conceivably have both turned around to look at Nolan and therefore also see Nanetti, Cowley and Lyon. Although interpolation 2 occurs conceivably within Corny Kelleher's line of sight (he has just come to his door, from which the tram stop on Newcomen Bridge is distantly visible), the fact that,

unlike the above sentence from section 15, it closely duplicates text from section 1 qualifies it as an interpolation (here I differ from Hart). In addition, I have also differed from Hart in my categorisation of those interpolations which describe repeated (as opposed to singular) action (interpolations 6, 8, 11 and 29). Hart argues that unlike the majority of the interpolations, which can correspond to only one moment, and so specify the current stream of action as occurring at precisely the same moment as the stream of action from which the interpolation is taken, these four interpolations (the lacquey ringing his bell, the darkbacked figure scanning books on the hawker's cart, Howard Parnell's face and beard hanging over a chessboard and the appearance of Lydia Douce and Mina Kennedy's heads over the crossblind of the bar of the Ormond Hotel) do not necessarily 'clock' the action into which they are interpolated at exactly the same time as the moment when these phrases appear in context, as they could refer to any moment from four quite substantial periods, and so, based on his re-enactments of the many streams of action in 'Wandering Rocks', interpolation 8 cannot refer to the moment in section 9 when a similar phrase reappears (*Ulysses* 216). He makes this judgement, however, on the basis of the assumption that textual similarity is to be subordinated to real-world possibility, and, therefore, that Joyce made no errors in orchestrating the time-scheme of the chapter. Given that most of the interpolations clearly correspond to precise instants, there is every reason to assume that *all* of the interpolations are intended to do so (indeed, Hart's own re-enactments show that three of the four 'continuing action' interpolations *can* be matched temporally to the pieces of text they closely duplicate), and so that if re-enactment shows that, for example, a character would have had to sprint to get from A to B in time, this is because Joyce was slightly inaccurate in his timings. The interpolations in the above table are therefore categorised on the basis of most probable textual intention rather than real-world timings—in spite of the relative overlap between the two—making all four of these interpolations of continuing action instances of 'repeated' intercutting.

80. Homer, *The Odyssey* 158.
81. The schema posted to Carlo Linati in September 1920 is reprinted in Ellmann, *Ulysses on the Liffey* 188–99, and the schema as provided to Jacques Benoît-Méchin and distributed privately by Sylvia Beach is in Gilbert, *James Joyce's* Ulysses, 41.
82. Bradshaw, Introduction 3.
83. Gaudreault, 'Detours' 139–41.
84. Adapted from Gaudreault, 'Detours' 139–40.
85. Gaudreault, 'Detours' 140.
86. Nine years later, Gaudreault would argue that editing in film *does* inscribe a pastness into cinema, the past tense of a narrator's previous perception and arrangement, which identifies cinema as realist narrative (*Du Littéraire au Filmique* 110). Cinema (by the time of the development of narrative editing structures) might therefore be said to combine the past tense of realist narrative with the present tense of the action. Given that only cinema *not* dominated by narrative could be described as producing "temporalities with no referent other than that of the representational system" (Doane, *Emergence* 68), this seems persuasive: a fictional referent for cinema would seem to distract from the medium as a time record. However, given the self-effacing nature of cinema's system of narration (film, according to Metz, "abolishes all traces of the subject of the enunciation" ('History/discourse' 548)), the manifest pastness of cinema's events, as Gaudreault's earlier study found, does not mean that cinema possesses a past tense.

87. Qtd. Jacques Mercanton, 'The Hours' 702.

88. Joyce, *Ulysses* 225–8.

89. Joyce, *Ulysses* 430–1.

90. Joyce, *Ulysses* 402, 406.

91. Joyce, *Ulysses* 453, 460.

92. Joyce, *Ulysses* 504, 510, 521, 545; 704, 709, 716, 722, 735, 747.

93. 'Sirens', for Michael Groden, signals the beginning of "a series of narrative techniques that are themselves as prominent and as important as the characters" (Groden, Ulysses *in Progress* 38). Although Joyce himself drew a line after the ninth chapter of *Ulysses* (between 'Scylla and Charybdis' and 'Wandering Rocks') in a brief account of the Odyssean scheme of the book in a September 1920 letter to John Quinn, he added that "the dotted line represents the first half, but not part or division" (Letter to John Quinn, 3 September 1920, *Letters*, ed. Gilbert, Vol. 1, 145). During the writing of *Ulysses*, the only division that Joyce spoke of was the Telemachia/Odyssey/Nostos division (e.g. Letter to Harriet Shaw Weaver, 18 May 1918, *Letters*, ed. Gilbert, Vol. 1, 113.)

94. Joyce, *Ulysses* 4.

95. Joyce, *Ulysses* 10.

96. Joyce, *Portrait* 74.

97. Joyce, *Ulysses* 126–7.

98. Joyce, *Ulysses* 148.

99. Perlmutter, 'Joyce and Cinema' 486.

100. Joyce, *Ulysses* 300.

101. Joyce, *Ulysses* 294.

102. Joyce, *Ulysses* 291.

103. Hart, 'Wandering Rocks' 215.

104. Joyce, *Ulysses* 4.

105. Joyce, *Ulysses* 18.

106. I am very grateful to David Trotter for pointing this out.

107. Joyce, *Ulysses* 282.

108. Hart, 'Wandering Rocks' 203.

109. H.D., *Asphodel* 102.

110. Joyce, *Ulysses* 67.

111. Hart, 'Wandering Rocks' 189. Joyce, *Ulysses* 288

112. Bennett, *The Old Wives' Tale* 115–6.

113. Bennett, *The Old Wives' Tale* 116–8.

114. Bennett, *The Old Wives' Tale* 121–1.

115. Bennett, *The Old Wives' Tale* 123–4.

116. Bennett, *The Old Wives' Tale* 570.

117. See, for example, Peters, *Conrad and Impressionism* 22–3.

118. The disparity between author's experience of time and reader's experience of time in fiction was *also* being ridiculed as early as May 1895, when the narrator of H.G. Wells's short story 'Pollock and the Porroh Man' commented that the many events of an attack "all happened in less time than it takes to read about it" (Wells, 'Pollock' 178). In 1926 Woolf referred to the same disparity when she wrote that, in film, "[t]he most fantastic contrasts could be flashed before us with a speed which the writer can only toil after in vain" ('The Cinema', 272).

119. Joyce, *Ulysses* 65.

120. Doane, *Emergence* 30.

121. Joyce, 'A Mother' 145.

122. Killeen, *Ulysses Unbound* 3.

123. Virginia Woolf to Quentin Bell, 20 March 1929, *A Reflection* 34–5, 35.

124. 30 August 1923, *Diaries Vol. 2: 1920–1924,* 263.
125. Woolf, *Mrs Dalloway* 14.
126. Woolf, *Mrs Dalloway* 14–5.
127. Woolf, *Mrs Dalloway* 71; emphasis added.
128. Woolf, *Mrs Dalloway* 44, 51.
129. See Shail and Trotter, 'Cinema and the Novel' 383–5, for more on cinema's place in stimulating this kind of repeated duration (specifically in Conrad's *The Secret Agent* (written February–November 1906, serialised 6 October to 15 December 1906, published in revised book form on 12 September 1907).
130. H.D., *Asphodel* 46.
131. Holograph notebook, 9 Nov 1922–2 August 1923, Berg Collection, New York Public Library.
132. 30 August 1923, *Diaries Vol. 2: 1920–1924,* 263.
133. Woolf, *Mrs Dalloway* 10–1.
134. Woolf, *Mrs Dalloway* 12–3.
135. Woolf, *Mrs Dalloway* 54–5.
136. Woolf, *Mrs Dalloway* 86–8.
137. Humphrey, *Stream* 56.
138. Humphrey, *Stream* 56.
139. Woolf, 'Street Haunting' 28.
140. Woolf, *Mrs Dalloway* 9.
141. Woolf, *To the Lighthouse* 184–5.
142. Woolf, *To the Lighthouse* 145, 146–7, 150, 151, 152, 153, 161, 205, 213, 34–5, 85–91.
143. Woolf, *Jacob's Room* 5.
144. Woolf, *Jacob's Room* 5.
145. Woolf, *Jacob's Room* 55.
146. Joyce, *Jacob's Room* 82.
147. Chatman, *Story* 81.
148. Woolf, *Jacob's Room* 18–20.
149. Chatman writes that even present-tense narratives involve this, "for the narrator knows the outcome of the story, and it is evident that his present remains posterior to that of the characters" (Chatman, *Story* 83).
150. Woolf, *Jacob's Room* 15–6.
151. Hauser, *Social* 942.
152. Hauser, *Social* 946.
153. Humphrey, *Stream* 49.
154. Humphrey, *Stream* 50.
155. Holtby, *Virginia* 117.
156. Humphrey, *Stream* 50.
157. Chatman, *Story* 77.
158. Woolf, 'The Cinema' 269.
159. On Richardson's rural locations between 1907 and 1913, see Fromm, *Dorothy Richardson* passim.
160. Sinclair, 'The Novels of Dorothy Richardson' 444. The source usually cited for Sinclair is William James, who wrote (in the 1890 work which elaborated a January 1884 article) that '[c]onsciousness . . . does not appear to itself chopped up in bits. Such words as "chain" or "train" do not describe it fitly as it presents itself in the first instance. It is nothing jointed; it flows. A "river" or a "stream" are the metaphors by which it is most naturally described. *In talking of it hereafter, let us call it the stream of thought, of consciousness, or of subjective life*" (James, *Principles of Psychology*, Vol. 1, 233).

161. Richardson, *Pilgrimage 1* 126.
162. Richardson, *Pilgrimage 1* 296–7.
163. Richardson, *Pilgrimage 2* 110, ellipses in original.
164. Richardson, *Pilgrimage 2* 132.
165. Richardson, *Pilgrimage 1* 77.
166. Richardson, *Pilgrimage 2* 263, emphasis and ellipses in original.
167. Bradbury and McFarlane, 'The Name' 25; Whitworth, Introduction 12. Michael Hollington, one of the few to have disagreed with Frank, does so only to argue that modernism disrupts both the spatial *and* the temporal ('Svevo' 432).
168. Frank, 'Spatial Form' 236.
169. Frank, *Widening* 9.
170. Frank, 'Spatial Form' 234.
171. Frank, *Widening* 14–5. Leon Edel agrees that this "was a striking instance of literary *montage* before it had been thought of as possible on the screen" ('Introduction' xvi).
172. Frank, 'Spatial Form' 237.
173. Frank arrives at his understanding of cinema as "a structure of juxtaposition rather than of sequence" ('Spatial Form' 236) through a focus on montage, commenting that "the juxtaposition of disparate images in a cinematic *montage* automatically creates a synthesis of meaning between them; and this supersedes any sense of temporal discontinuity" ('Spatial Form' 237). The fact that Eisenstein was militating *against* the dominant practice and understanding of cinema before and during his period of film-making and writing seems to be irrelevant to Frank.
174. Frank, *Widening* 17.
175. Frank, *Widening* 18, 16.
176. Frank, *Widening* 49.
177. Frank, *Widening* 57.
178. Frank, *Widening* 18.
179. Green, *Ford Madox Ford* 88–9.
180. Hart, 'Wandering Rocks' 216.
181. Kermode, *The Sense of an Ending* 70–89, 72.
182. Kermode, *The Sense of an Ending* 72.
183. Metz, 'The Cinema' 20.
184. See Gillies, 'Bergsonism' 95–7. In J.D. Beresford's 1911 novel *The Hampdenshire Wonder*, the eight-year-old 'Wonder' hurriedly reads a collection of philosophical works brought to him by the narrator, who notices that "Kant, Hegel, Schelling, Fichte, Leibnitz, Nietzsche, Hume, Bradle, William James had all been rejected and were piled on the floor, but he had hesitated longer over Bergson's *Creative Evolution*. He really seemed to be giving that some attention" (207–8).
185. Bergson, *Creative* 2.
186. Bergson, *Creative* 2–3.
187. Bergson, *Creative* 2.
188. Bergson, *Creative* 3.
189. Bergson, *Creative* 3–4.
190. Bergson, *Creative* 4.
191. Deleuze, *Cinema 1* 8.
192. Deleuze, *Cinema 1* 11.
193. Bergson, *Creative* 6.
194. Bergson, *Creative* 6.
195. Kumar, *Bergson* 2.
196. Bergson, *Creative* 6.

197. Bergson, *Creative* 20.
198. Gillies, 'Bergsonism' 100–1, Parsons, *Theorists* 109–15.
199. Lawrence, Preface 131.
200. Lawrence, Preface 131.
201. Lawrence, Preface 132.
202. Bergson, *Creative* 4.
203. Hauser, *Social* 939.
204. Bergson, *Creative* 6.
205. Bergson, *Time* 120.
206. See Kumar, *Bergson* 69.
207. Letter to Shiv Kumar, qtd. Kumar, *Bergson* vii. See also, for example, Lewis, *Time* 103.
208. Lawrence, Preface 133.
209. Woolf, 'Modern Fiction' 109.
210. Robbe-Grillet, *Last Year at Marienbad* 12.
211. Joyce, *Ulysses* 205.
212. Kumar, *Bergson* 7.
213. Humphrey, *Stream* 50.
214. Humphrey, *Stream* 50.
215. Sinclair, 'The Novels of Dorothy Richardson' 443.
216. Kumar, *Bergson* 10.
217. *Les Lauriers sont coupés* is a quotation from a French folksong: "Nous n'irons plus au bois, les lauriers sont coupés. [We'll go no more to the woods, the laurels are cut down]." This was also the first line of Théodore de Banville's 1847 poem 'Nous n'irons plus au bois'. *Lauriers* was translated into English by Stuart Gilbert in 1938 as *We'll to the Woods No More*.
218. See Ellmann, *James Joyce*, 126.
219. James Joyce to Édouard Dujardin, 10 November 1917, *Letters*, ed. Ellmann, Vol. 2, 409.
220. Qtd. Valery Larbaud, 'Préface' 7.
221. Frank Budgen, *James Joyce and the Making of 'Ulysses'* 94.
222. James Joyce, Letter to Harriet Shaw Weaver, 22 November 1929, *Letters*, ed. Gilbert, Vol. 1, 286–8, 287.
223. See, for example, King, 'Édouard Dujardin' 122–3 (in 1953); Kumar, *Bergson* 6–7 (in 1962); Friedman, 'The Symbolist Novel' 455 (in 1976); McKilligan, *Édouard* 16 (in 1977); Walker, 'Formal Experiment' 129 (in 1997); Stewart, 'Post-Impressionism' 308 (in 2003).
224. Dujardin, *We'll to the Woods No More* 14.
225. Dujardin, *We'll to the Woods No More* 53–4.
226. For an account of other points where Dujardin departs from pure interior monologue, see McKilligan, *Édouard* 52–85.
227. See Salisbury and Shail, 'Introduction' *passim*.
228. See, for example, Kumar, *Bergson* 111.
229. Bergson, *Creative* 324.
230. Bergson, *Creative* 322.
231. Bergson, *Creative* 324.
232. Bergson, *Creative* 324.
233. Bergson, *Creative* 325.
234. See Doane, *Emergence* 59.
235. Muybridge, *Descriptive Zoopraxography*, Appendix A, 13, 14.
236. Gaudreault and Marion, 'The Cinema' 12.
237. Deleuze, *Cinema 1* 2.
238. Deleuze, *Cinema 1* 2.
239. Deleuze, *Cinema 1* 2.

240. Deleuze, *Cinema 1* 6.
241. Deleuze, *Cinema 1* 2.
242. Deleuze, *Cinema 1* 7.

NOTES TO CHAPTER 3

1. Habermas, *Structural* 155–83.
2. Le Bon, *The Crowd* 91.
3. Le Bon, *The Crowd* 32.
4. Le Bon, *The Crowd* 30–1. The concept of the mass mind is to be distinguished from Jung's notion of the collective unconscious, although Jung's expression can be traced to the kinds of mixing of psychoanalytic principles and group psychology of which Le Bon was one permutation.
5. Le Bon, *The Crowd* 45–6.
6. Tratner, *Modernism* 16. Of course, this is not to dismiss the origins of a notion of individual consciousness as functioning in and on flux produced by late nineteenth-century psychology, including William James's *Principles of Psychology* (1890).
7. Le Bon, *The Crowd* 30.
8. Sorel, *Reflections* 122.
9. Sorel, *Reflections* 230.
10. Culler, *Saussure* 72.
11. Le Bon, *The Crowd* 9.
12. Le Bon, *The Crowd* 77, 17.
13. Le Bon, *The Crowd* 21.
14. Tratner, *Modernism* 2.
15. Le Bon, *The Crowd* 52.
16. Le Bon, *The Crowd* 77.
17. That a work regarding socialism as a threat could form the lynchpin of Sorel's anarcho-syndicalist *Reflections on Violence* indicated how amenable the concept of the mass mind was to both right and left. The embrace of collectivism can explain, for example, why certain modernists gravitated towards fascism and others towards pacifism. The modernist political aesthetic could straddle quite dissimilar political positions (the conservative Eliot, the nationalist Yeats, and the radical Joyce and Woolf) because re-conceptualising social issues in terms of 'the masses' was not a left/right political movement but a movement 'down' towards the extremes of the horseshoe-shaped political spectrum. As Michael North points out, "[b]efore throwing in his lot with Mussolini, Pound flirted with the thought of Lenin, and submitted himself to the tutelage of Mike Gold and *The Masses*" (North, *The Political* 6).
18. Le Bon, *The Crowd* 62.
19. Le Bon, *The Crowd* 63.
20. Le Bon, *The Crowd* 66.
21. Le Bon, *The Crowd* 36.
22. In contrast to Tratner's interpretation of modernist anti-individualism as a result of the impact of notions of the mass mind, North describes 'high' modernist anti-individualism as part of a negative reaction to the failure of liberal individualism to deliver a revolution (North, *Political* 2). Tratner's account, however, is more compelling, acknowledging a political axis (individualism-collectivism) that North largely ignores.
23. Le Bon, *The Crowd* 101.
24. Le Bon, *The Crowd* 126.
25. Sorel, *Reflections* 125.

26. Sorel, *Reflections* 148.
27. Sorel, *Reflections* 120.
28. Sorel, *Reflections* 122–3.
29. Sorel, *Reflections* 148.
30. Sorel, *Reflections* 149.
31. Sorel, *Reflections* 127.
32. Le Bon, *The Crowd* 36.
33. Sorel, *Reflections* 17–67.
34. Sorel, *Reflections* 129.
35. Sorel, *Reflections* 214.
36. Le Bon, *The Crowd* 65.
37. Sorel, *Reflections* 209.
38. Sorel, *Reflections* 122.
39. Tratner, *Modernism* 37.
40. Tratner, *Modernism* 2.
41. Joyce, *Ulysses* 42; Tratner 154.
42. Tratner, *Modernism* 15.
43. Tratner, *Modernism* 84.
44. Tratner, *Modernism* 24.
45. Woolf, *Night and Day* 177–8.
46. Woolf, *A Room of One's Own* 63.
47. See, for example, Hotchkiss, 'Writing' 134–5.
48. Hotchkiss, 'Writing' 138.
49. Woolf, *Mrs Dalloway* 19.
50. Woolf, *Night and Day* 78.
51. Woolf, *Night and Day* 269.
52. Woolf, *Night and Day* 92.
53. Woolf, *Night and Day* 465–6.
54. Woolf, *Mrs Dalloway* 3.
55. Woolf, *Mrs Dalloway* 33.
56. Le Bon, *The Crowd* 55.
57. Sorel, *Reflections* 138. While advocating collectivism meant endorsing attacks on intellectuals, modernist writers were not entirely robbed of a role. Sorel's own aesthetic theory had suggested the possibility of a political aesthetic in the era of collective consciousness (143–4).
58. Pound, 'The New Sculpture' 68.
59. Sorel, *Reflections* 171.
60. Pound, 'The New Sculpture' 68.
61. Pound, 'The New Sculpture' 68.
62. Woolf, 'War in the Village' 293.
63. Of course, this does not necessarily show that modernists were seeking to cement collective forms of working-class culture that combated the worker's alienating individualisation by her/his working relationship with a manager and by her/his alienation from the means of production, the function of collectivity for the workers themselves (Chanan, *The Dream* 149).
64. Tratner, *Modernism* 80.
65. Wilkinson, 'The Concept' 183.
66. Wilkinson, 'The Concept' 186.
67. Hobson, *Problems* 195.
68. Beatrice Webb, letter to H.G. Wells, Oct 1903, H.G. Wells Collection, Rare Books and Manuscript Library, University of Illinois at Urbana-Champaign, W-122-3.
69. To this Kadlec ascribes the creation of one of the distinctions central to the founding of what came to be called modernism. When Pound met Orage in

1911, the latter "had already begun to inveigh against the realist literary circle that was associated with Fabian socialistic reform. Orage's attacks on Shaw, Wells, Bennett, and Granville Barker centered on both these writers' political statist ideology and on their utilitarian conception of literature as a didactic corrective for social ills"(Kadlec, 'Pound' 1025).

70. Kadlec, 'Pound' 1020.
71. Pound, 'Vortex: Pound' 159.
72. Aldington et al., 'Long Live the Vortex!' 8.
73. Frosh, 'Psychoanalysis' 120.
74. Pound, 'Vorticism' 461.
75. Pound, 'Vorticism' 469.
76. Pound, 'Vorticism' 467–8.
77. Pound, 'Affirmations: As For Imagisme' 350.
78. Pound, 'Vorticism' 470.
79. Tratner argues that, consequently, the centrality of violence to anarcho-syndicalism, while energising the work of Yeats, troubled the pacifist Joyce and Woolf, haunting their works as a condemned though necessary function (*Modernism* 52). In *Night and Day*, for example, Katharine confides to Mary a desire to be able to communicate with crowds, but it comes out as brutality: "'Don't you see how many different things these people care about? And I want to beat them down—I only mean,' she corrected herself, 'that I want to assert myself . . . Ah, but I want to trample upon their prostrate bodies!' Katharine announced, a moment later, with a laugh, as if at the train of thought which had led her to this conclusion" (*Night and Day* 54). This expresses fear of both the violence of the collective mind, exacerbated by the war, and of the possibility that speaking for the mass was merely harmful to it.
80. Sherry, *Great War* 62.
81. Sherry, *Great War* 11.
82. Sherry, *Great War* 9.
83. Wilson, *Myriad* 219.
84. Garvin 2.
85. Wilson, *Myriad* 389–407.
86. Wilson, *Myriad* 519–40.
87. Alisdair Reid, 'Dilution' *passim*.
88. Cole, 4.
89. Wilson, *Myriad* 663–5, 423.
90. Wilson, *Myriad* 198.
91. Wilson, *Myriad* 529.
92. Qtd Wilson, *Myriad* 530.
93. Wilson, *Myriad* 516.
94. Wilson, *Myriad* 540.
95. Webb, *The Power* 244.
96. Woolf, *Jacob's Room* 156.
97. Woolf, *Jacob's Room* 156.
98. Woolf, 'War in the Village' 291.
99. Woolf, *Night and Day* 286.
100. Woolf, 'The Common Reader' 11.
101. Woolf, 'The Common Reader' 11.
102. Tratner, *Modernism* 173.
103. Tratner, *Modernism* 31.
104. Le Bon, *The Crowd* 2; Tratner, *Modernism* 2, emphasis added.
105. Yeats, 'What is Popular Poetry?' 6.
106. Yeats, 'What is Popular Poetry?' 9.

107. Yeats, 'What is Popular Poetry?' 10.
108. Yeats, 'What is Popular Poetry?' 10.
109. Ford, 'The Passing of the Great Figure' 126.
110. Bell, 'Art and the Cinema' 40.
111. Tratner, *Modernism* 27.
112. Tratner, *Modernism* 154.
113. Tratner, *Modernism* 154.
114. Joyce, *Portrait* 178.
115. Morrison, *The Public* 12–3.
116. Morrison, *The Public* 10.
117. Morrison, *The Public* 47.
118. Kadlec, 'Pound' 1015.
119. Morrisson argues that this was a result of the difficulties of marketing and of keeping together the political and literary radicalism that made up the 'counterpublic sphere' around the *Freewoman/New Freewoman/Egoist* and *The New Age*, instead of any factor intrinsic to modernist thought (*The Public* 115).
120. Rainey, *Institutions* 106.
121. James Joyce to Harriet Shaw Weaver, 2 July 1919, *Letters*, ed. Gilbert, 126–7, 126.
122. James Joyce to Harriet Shaw Weaver, 6 August 1919, *Letters*, ed. Gilbert, 127–8, 127.
123. Rainey, *Institutions* 45–7.
124. Rainey, *Institutions* 46–50.
125. James Joyce, Letter to Harriet Shaw Weaver, 10 April 1921, *Letters*, ed. Gilbert, 161–3, 162. Rainey, *Institutions* 62.
126. Burnett, *A History* 300.
127. Rainey, *Institutions* 61.
128. Rainey, *Institutions* 51.
129. Harriet Shaw Weaver to Sylvia Beach, 27 April 1921, Sylvia Beach papers, Princeton University Firestone Library, box 232, folder 2. Rainey, *Institutions* 55.
130. John Quinn to Sylvia Beach, 27 March 1922, Capen Library, Poetry Collection, Beach Papers, 'Ulysses Subscriptions, 1ˢᵗ Edition' folder. Rainey, *Institutions* 69.
131. Sylvia Beach to Harriet Shaw Weaver, 26 June 1922, Harriet Shaw Weaver Papers, British Library. Rainey, *Institutions* 70.
132. Mitchell Kennerley to John Quinn, qtd. Reid, *The Man from New York* 533. Rainey, *Institutions* 70.
133. Rainey, *Institutions* 56.
134. Ezra Pound to Margaret Anderson, 10 May 1917, *Pound/the Little Review*, 49.
135. For more details see Rainey, *Institutions* 73–4.
136. Rainey, *Institutions* 44–5.
137. Rainey, 'The Cultural' 43.
138. Rainey, *Institutions* 64.
139. Rainey, *Institutions* 64.
140. Ezra Pound to Felix Schelling, 8–9 July 1922, *Ezra Pound, Selected Letters 1907–1941* 180. Rainey, *Institutions* 81.
141. Rainey *Institutions* 83, 81.
142. Rainey, *Institutions* 88.
143. Rainey, *Institutions* 91–105.
144. Rainey, *Institutions* 91.
145. Rainey, *Institutions* 104–5.

146. Rainey, *Institutions* 102.
147. Pound, *ABC* 29.
148. Advertisement, *Close Up* 5.1 (July 1929), back cover.
149. Rainey, *Institutions* 56.
150. For details of the income that Joyce received from his patrons at the time see Rainey, *Institutions* 108–9.
151. Rainey, *Institutions* 104.
152. Rainey, *Institutions* 5.
153. Rainey, *Institutions* 3. Rainey sees the publishing events of 1922 as an attempt to produce a literary equivalent of the financial validation experienced by members of the various schools of modernist painting. As a literary work remains the intellectual property of the author, in contrast with a painting which becomes the property of its purchaser, an alternative system was seen as needed to get literary works to produce a spectacle of spiralling financial value that could confirm its aesthetic significance, and the deluxe edition served this need (85).
154. See Kember, *Marketing Modernity* 60–83.
155. Urban, *Cinematograph* 11.
156. Pyke, *Focussing* 4.
157. Pyke, *Focussing* 5.
158. Pyke, *Focussing* 7.
159. Pyke, *Focussing* 9–10.
160. Pyke, *Focussing* 2–4.
161. Pyke, *Focussing* 8.
162. Pyke, *Focussing* 6.
163. Pyke, *Focussing* 11.
164. 'Picture Theatres as an Educational Force', *Rinking World and Picture Theatre News* 1.10 (5 Feb 1910), 15–6, 15.
165. 'Photoplay Gossip', *The Pictures* 1.16 (3 Feb 1912), 15.
166. 'Photoplay Gossip', *The Pictures* 1.17 (10 Feb 1912), 15–6, 16.
167. 'Picture Notes', *The Pictures* 1.15 (27 Jan 1912), 16.
168. Chas. Heydemann, Letter, *The Pictures* 1.9 (16 Dec 1911), 20.
169. 'Picture Notes', *The Pictures* 1.25 (6 April 1912), 23.
170. 'Photoplay Gossip', *The Pictures* 2.27 (20 April 1912), 19.
171. 'Pictures Which Survive', *The Pictures* 3.76 (date unspecified), 22.
172. 'Screen Gossip', *Pictures and the Picturegoer* 6.4 (w/e 14 March 1914), 93.
173. 'Photoplay Gossip', *The Pictures* 1.17 (10 Feb 1912), 15–6, 16.
174. 'How Pictures Help Salesmen', *The Pictures* 3.58 (23 Nov 1912), 12.
175. 'Some More Uses for the Cinematograph', *The Pictures* 3.70 (date unspecified), 17.
176. 'Screen Gossip', *Pictures and the Picturegoer* 6.6 (28 March 1914), 141.
177. 'Moving Pictures or Books?', *The Pictures* 2.49 (21 Sept 1912), 6.
178. 'Sunday Closing', *The Pictures* 3.65 (8 Jan 1913), 23.
179. Russell de Trafford, 'The Voice of the People: Why the average man—and woman—wants Sunday Picture Shows', *The Pictures* 3.53 (19 Oct 1912), 15.
180. 'Screen Gossip', *Pictures and the Picturegoer* 6.15 (30 May 1914), 353–4, 354.
181. 'Tragedy of the Desert', *The Pictures* 2.41 (27 June 1912), 15.
182. 'Writing for the Screen', *The Pictures* 5.106 (18 October 1913), 21.
183. See, for example, Anon., 'A Sermon for Exhibitors', *The Top-Line Indicator* 1.11 (8 Jan 1913), 3.
184. Siegmund Lubin, 'Photoplay Gossip', *The Pictures* 2.31 (18 May 1912), 22.
185. Grieveson, 'A kind of recreative' 70.
186. See Low, *The History . . . 1906–1914*, 35–6.

187. 'Picture Pars and News', *Pictures and the Picturegoer* 11.152 (13 Jan 1917), 334.
188. 'We Hear-', *Pictures and the Picturegoer* 11.162 (24 Mar 1917), 541.
189. 'News and Notes', *Pictures and the Picturegoer* 13.194 (27 Oct–3 Nov 1917), 460.
190. Low, *The History . . . 1914–1918* 33.
191. Advertisement, *Pictures and the Picturegoer* 9.80 (9 Oct 1915), 45.
192. Hammond, *The Big Show* 246–7.
193. Fred Dangerfield, 'Screen Gossip', *Pictures and the Picturegoer* 7.28 (29 Aug 1914), 37.
194. 'Film "Femininities": "Pictures" Page for the Fair Sex', *Pictures and the Picturegoer* 10.141 (28 Oct 1916), 93.
195. Anon., 'Go to 'The Pictures'!', *Pictures and the Picturegoer* 7.32 (26 Sept 1914), 101.
196. 'Pictures a Boon and a Blessing', *Pictures and the Pictuegoer* 7.46 (2 Jan 1915), 328.
197. Hammond, *The Big Show* 215.
198. Hammond, *The Big Show* 247.
199. National Council of Public Morals, *The Cinema* lix.
200. 'We Hear That-', *Pictures and Picturegoer* 13.193 (20–27 Oct 1917), 440.
201. Pyke, *Focussing* 7.
202. 'Don't Close Our Picture Theatres!: "Movies" The War-Time Medicine for the Masses', *Pictures and the Picturegoer* 9.106 (26 Feb 1916), 494.
203. 'News and Notes', *Pictures and the Picturegoer* 13.176 (23–30 June 1917), 28.
204. Elsie Codd, 'Film Types II: The Vampire', *Pictures and Picturegoer* 13.187 (8–15 Sept 1917), 301–2, 302.
205. Ethel Frankum, 'Pictures—The Tonic', *Pictures and Picturegoer* 14.212 (2–9 March 1918), 233.
206. 'The Light of the World', *Pictures and the Picturegoer* 11.140 (21 Oct 1916), 67.
207. Wedgwood Drawbell, 'Winter', *Pictures and the Picturegoer* 13.193 (20–27 Oct 1917), 468.
208. 'His Awful Past: James Lindsay, the Popular Villain on Screen and Stage, confesses to "Pictures"', *Pictures and the Picturegoer* 13.179 (14–21 July 1917), 103–4, 104.
209. Reed, *Chronicles* v.
210. 'Are We Downhearted?', *Pictures and the Picturegoer* 10.115 (29 April 1916), 100.
211. Reed, *Chronicles* vi.
212. Martland, *Business* 433.
213. Hiley, 'Nothing More' 124.
214. 'Flashes', *Pictures and the Picturegoer* 7.28 (29 Aug 1914), 37.
215. Qtd. Hiley, 'The British' 162.
216. F.R. Goodwin, qtd National Council of Public Morals, *The Cinema* 2–3.
217. F.R. Goodwin, qtd National Council of Public Morals, *The Cinema* 3.
218. Baden-Powell, *Young* 67–8.
219. 'The Theatrical Year', *The Times*, 1 January 1917, 11.
220. See British Film Institute, 'Film and TV Information'; UK Film Council, 'Statistical Yearbook 2009'.
221. See Hiley, '*The Battle of the Somme* and British News Media'. The 1911 census recorded a population in Great Britain (England, Wales and Scotland) of 40,834,714 and in the UK (adding Ireland) of 45,216,665 (1, 116). The 1921 census recorded a population in Great Britain of 42,767,530 and omitted a

figure for the UK (i.e. including Northern Ireland) as it came too soon after the passing of the Government of Ireland Act of 23 December 1920 (1, 62), meaning that a rough estimate of just under 47 million for Great Britain and Ireland in 1921 is not unreasonable. Whereas half of ticket sales usually represented repeat visits from the same person, meaning that, for example, a 10 million tickets weekly attendance actually reflects just 7.5 million different people attending a cinema that week, this estimate was of 20 million *people.*

222. Lewis, *Self Condemned* 89–90.
223. *Picture Palace News*, 22 July 1916, 212.
224. 'Editorial', *Pictures and Picturegoer* 13.193 (20–27 Oct 1917), 453.
225. 'Smiles', *Pictures and the Picturegoer* 11.147 (9 Dec 1916), 240.
226. 'We Hear -', *Pictures and the Picturegoer* 11.158 (24 Feb 1917), 465.
227. As given in *Cinematograph Theatres: A Series of Illustrated Plans etc. of Picture Houses, specially reprinted from the issues of Oct 28th and Nov 11th of* The Builder (London: 1921), 1.
228. 'News and Notes', *Pictures and the Picturegoer* 13.188 (15–22 Sept 1917), 316.
229. M. Owston-Booth, 'A Sweet Half-Hour', *Pictures and the Picturegoer* 9.85 (2 Oct 1915), 8–9, 8.
230. 'Film "Femininities": "Pictures" Page for the Fair Sex', *Pictures and the Picturegoer* 9.141 (28 Oct 1916), 93.
231. 'The Popularity of Pictures', *Pictures and the Picturegoer* 11.138 (7 Oct 1916), 25.
232. 'News and Notes', *Pictures and the Picturegoer* 11.161 (17 Mar 1917), 510.
233. 'Southport Notes', *Kinematograph Weekly*, 2 May 1918, 77.
234. 'News and Notes', *Pictures and the Picturegoer* 13.175 (16–23 June 1917), 4.
235. Lawrence, 'Tickets, Please!' 117.
236. McKernan, *Topical* 25.
237. *Pictures and the Picturegoer* 13.175 (16–23 June 1917), 4.
238. McKernan, *Topical* 247.
239. Ivan Patrick Gore, 'Some Screen "Khaki": The Experiences of a Khaki-clad picturegoer', *Pictures and the Picturegoer* 11.159 (3 Mar 1917), 476.
240. 'News and Notes', *Pictures and the Picturegoer* 13.181 (28 July–4 Aug 1917), 148
241. Messinger, 'An Inheritance' 117.
242. 'Propaganda', *OED* 1446.
243. Messinger, 'An Inheritance' 118–9.
244. Reeves, *Official* 10.
245. PRO/FO371/2207/88913/33913, *First Proof of Wellington House Interim Report*, 2 Dec 1914, para 5. Reeves, *Official* 10.
246. HLRO/BBKE-11/300, *Memorandum on the Ministry of Information 4th March to 10th July 1918*, 1–2. Reeves, *Official* 36.
247. Reeves, *Official* 13.
248. Reeves, *Official* 12.
249. PRO/FO371/2207/88913/33913, *First Proof of Wellington House Interim Report*, 2 Dec 1914, para 5. Reeves, *Official* 10.
250. HLRO/BBKE-11/300, *Memorandum on the Ministry of Information 4th March to 10th July 1918*, 1–2. Reeves, *Official* 35–6.
251. PRO/FO395/37/152076/8403, Foreign Office to Brigadier-General John Charteris, 9 Aug 1916. Reeves, *Official* 59.
252. 'The King and the Somme Film' *The Times*, 6 Sept 1916, 9.
253. 'In and Out of the Studio', *Pictures and Picturegoer* 13.181 (28 July–4 Aug 1917), 155–6, 156.

254. Quoted in Taylor, *Beaverbrook* 144.
255. 'Picture Pars and News', *Pictures and the Picturegoer* 11.152 (13 Jan 1917), 334.
256. Fred Dangerfield, 'Editorial', *Pictures and Picturegoer* 11.175 (16–23 June 1917), 21.
257. See, for example, 'Picture News and Notes', *Pictures and the Picturegoer* 11.149 (23 Dec 1916), 266.
258. *Pictures and the Picturegoer* 10.141 (28 Oct 1916), 95; *Pictures and the Picturegoer* 10.142 (4 Nov 1916), 115.
259. 'Edith F. Mitchell Sowerbutts', '"Tommy" at the Pictures', *Pictures and the Picturegoer* 11.150 (30 Dec 1916), 292.
260. Qtd 'X', 'The All-British Firm', *Pictures and Picturegoer* 15.246 (26 Oct–2 Nov 1918), 422.
261. 'Edith F Mitchell Sowerbutts', '"Tommy" at the Pictures', *Pictures and the Picturegoer* 11.150 (30 Dec 1916), 292.
262. H.D., *Bid Me To Live*, 122–3.
263. 'News and Notes', *Pictures and Picturegoer* 14.219 (20–27 April 1918), 406.
264. Tratner, *Modernism* 214.
265. 'The Light of the World', *Pictures and the Picturegoer* 11.140 (21 Oct 1916), 67.
266. Barthes, *Camera* 18.
267. 'The Empty Chair', *Picturegoer* 1.1 (January 1921), 7.
268. Irene Miller, 'A Chat Concerning Scenarios', *Pictures and the Picturegoer* 11.155 (3 Feb 1917), 398.
269. 'The Empty Chair', *Picturegoer* 1.1 (January 1921), 7.
270. 'Nelson', *Pictures and the Picturegoer* 15.246 (26 Oct–2 Nov 1918), 419.
271. *Pictures and the Picturegoer* 18.323 (24 April 1920), 430.
272. See, for example, Stacy Gillis, 'Only from the senses' *passim.*
273. Le Bon, *The Crowd* 45.
274. Woolf, 'The Cinema' 268.
275. Woolf, *Jacob's Room* 156.
276. Woolf, 'The Cinema' 270–1.
277. Woolf, 'The Cinema' 268.
278. Woolf, 'The Cinema' 268.
279. Woolf, 'The Cinema' 268.
280. Le Bon, *The Crowd* 75.
281. Woolf, 'The Cinema' 270.
282. Woolf, 'The Cinema' 272.
283. Woolf, 'The Cinema' 269–70.
284. Woolf, 'The Cinema' 270.
285. Woolf, 'The Cinema' 271.
286. Woolf, 'The Cinema' 271.
287. Woolf, 'The Cinema' 272.
288. Woolf's fascination with the possibility of what we would now call accelerated montage editing—"[t]he most fantastic contrasts could be flashed before us with a speed which the writer can only toil after in vain"(Woolf, 'The Cinema' 272)—seems therefore to be a consequence not of her supposedly 'cinematic' modernism but of the idea that cinema's proximity to the mass mind meant that it ought to take on its properties, including the mass mind's tendency to think in a fantastic succession of images.
289. H.D., *Notes* 17.
290. H.D., *Notes* 18.
291. H.D., *Notes* 40.

292. H.D., *Notes* 26.
293. H.D., *Notes* 40.
294. H.D., *Notes* 41.
295. H.D., *Notes* 18.
296. H.D., *Notes* 19.
297. H.D., *Notes* 18.
298. H.D., *Notes* 23.
299. H.D., *Notes* 50.
300. H.D., *Notes* 21.
301. H.D., *Notes* 22.
302. H.D., *Notes* 22.
303. H.D., *Notes* 23.
304. H.D., *Notes* 44–5.
305. See Shail, 'a distinct advance in society'.
306. 'Eighteen Thousand Actors', *Pictures and the Picturegoer* 9.85 (2 Oct 1915), 4–6, 6.
307. Tyrone Power, 'Tyrone Power', *Pictures and the Picturegoer* 11.153 (20 Jan 1917), 365.
308. Anon., 'A Tonic for Depression', 'Bits from Our Letter-Bag', *Pictures and the Picturegoer* 8.66 (22 May 1915), 136.
309. Hammond, *The Big Show* 214.
310. 'Editorial', *Pictures and Picturegoer* 14.220 (27 April–4 May 1918), 429.
311. 'Sense from the Censor, T.P. O'Connor, M.P., The New Film Censor, Promises Fair Play and Expects it', *Pictures and the Picturegoer* 11.157 (17 Feb 1917), 436.
312. Grace Cunard, 'The Lure of the Serial', *Pictures and the Picturegoer* 11.157 (17 Feb 1917), 444. In October 1917, A.R. Orage remarked much the same in a comparison between contemporary cinema and cinema 10 years earlier.
313. Cleo Madison, 'The Commercial Value of Clean Pictures', *Pictures and the Picturegoer* 11.153 (20 Jan 1917), 362.
314. Leslie Catchpole, 'Literature and the Movies', *Pictures and Picturegoer* 13.185 (25 Aug–1 Sept 1917), 258.
315. Rainey, *Institutions* 76.
316. Pound, 'On Criticism in General' 144.

NOTES TO THE AFTERWORD

1. Danius, *Senses* 167.
2. North, *Camera* 6.
3. Joyce, *Ulysses* 71–2; Danius, *Senses* 163.
4. Joyce, *Ulysses* 74; Danius, *Senses* 164.
5. Perlmutter, 'Joyce and Cinema' 481.
6. Woolf, *Jacob's Room* 31.
7. H.D., *Asphodel* 45.
8. North and Danius also both slide into 'cinematic' and 'montage' claims that involve the idea that cinema was a tool consciously chosen by modernists (North in reference to John Dos Passos (140, 150, 155) and Danius in reference to Proust and Joyce (164)).
9. Kandinsky, 'The Problem of Form' 272.
10. Kandinsky, 'The Problem of Form' 273.
11. Kandinsky, 'The Problem of Form' 273.
12. Kandinsky, 'The Problem of Form' 273.
13. Kandinsky, 'The Problem of Form' 273.

14. Aronowitz, *Dead Artists* 54.
15. Baudelaire, 'Painter' 12.
16. Baudelaire, 'Painter' 13.
17. Baudelaire, 'Painter' 32.
18. Baudelaire, 'Painter' 16.
19. Barthes, 'Rhetoric of the Image' 45.
20. McCabe, *Cinematic* 25.

Bibliography

Aldington, Richard, et al. 'Long Live the Vortex!' *Blast* 1 (20 June 1914): 7–8.

Apollonio, Umbro, ed. *Futurist Manifestos*. London: Thames and Hudson, 1973.

Armstrong, Isobel. '"The Lady of Shalott": Optical Elegy'. *Multimedia Histories: From the Magic Lantern to the Internet*. Ed. James Lyons and John Plunkett. Exeter: University of Exeter Press, 2007. 179–93.

———. *Victorian Glassworlds: Glass Culture and the Imagination 1830–1880*. Oxford: Oxford UP, 2008.

Aronowitz, Stanley. *Dead Artists, Live Theories*. London: Routledge, 1994.

Aumont, Jacques. 'Griffith: The Frame, The Figure'. 1980. *Early Cinema: Space, Frame, Narrative*. Ed. Thomas Elsaesser. London: BFI, 1990. 348–59.

Baden-Powell, Robert. *Young Knights of the Empire: Their Code and Further Scout Yarns*. London: Pearson, 1916.

Ballet Mécanique. Dir. Fernand Léger and Dudley Murphy. 1924.

Banville, Théodore de. 'Nous n'irons plus au bois'. *The Penguin Book of French Poetry 1820–1950*. London: Penguin, 1992. 126.

Barnes, John. *The Beginnings of the Cinema in England 1894–1901. Vol. 1: 1894–1896*. Exeter: University of Exeter Press, 1998.

———. *The Beginnings of the Cinema in England 1894–1901. Vol. 2: 1897*. Exeter: University of Exeter Press, 1996.

Barrow, Craig Wallace. *Montage in James Joyce's 'Ulysses'*. Madrid: Studia Humanitatis, 1980.

Barry, Iris. 'The Cinema: *Metropolis*'. *The Spectator* (26 March 1927): 540.

———. *Let's Go To The Pictures*. London: Chatto and Windus, 1926.

Barthes, Roland. *Camera Lucida*. 1980. Trans. Richard Howard. London: Vintage, 2000.

———. 'Rhetoric of the Image'. 1964. *Image-Music-Text*. Trans. Stephen Heath. London: Fontana, 1977. 32–51.

Baudelaire, Charles. 'The Painter of Modern Life'. 1863. *The Painter of Modern Life and Other Essays*. Trans. & ed. Jonathan Mayne. 2nd ed. London: Phaidon, 1995. 1–41.

Bazin, André. 'In Defense of Mixed Cinema'. c.1958. *What is Cinema?*, Vol. 1, Trans. Hugh Gray. Los Angeles: California UP, 1967. 53–75.

———. 'Ontologie de l'image photographique'. 1945. *Qu'est-ce que le cinema?* Paris: Éditions du Cerf, 1981.

———. 'The Ontology of the Photographic Image'. 1945. *What is Cinema?*, Vol. 1. Trans. Hugh Gray. Los Angeles: California UP, 1967. 9–16.

Beach, Joseph Warren. *The Twentieth Century Novel: Studies in Technique*. New York: Appleton, 1932.

Bean, Jennifer. 'Technologies of Early Stardom and the Extraordinary Body'. *Camera Obscura* 16.3 (2001): 9–56.

Beaumont, Etienne de. 'Of What are the Young Films Dreaming?'. *Little Review* 11.2 (Winter 1926): 73–4.

Bell, Clive. 'Art and the Cinema'. *Vanity Fair* 19.3 (Nov 1922): 39–40.

Bell, Michael. *Literature, Modernism and Myth: Belief and Responsibility in the Twentieth Century.* Cambridge: Cambridge UP, 1997.

Bennett, Arnold. *The Old Wives' Tale.* 1908. London: Penguin, 1954.

Benveniste, Emile. *Problèmes de Linguistique Gènèrale.* Paris: Gallimard, 1966.

Beresford, J.D. *The Hampdenshire Wonder.* London: Penguin, 1937.

Bergson, Henri. *Creative Evolution.* 1907. Trans. Arthur Mitchell. London: Macmillan, 1914.

———. *Time and Free Will.* 1889. Trans. F.L. Pogson. London: Swan Sonnenschein & Co, 1910.

The Big Swallow. Dir. James Williamson. 1901.

Block, Ralph. 'When the Movies Come of Age.' *Vanity Fair* 19.2 (Oct 1922): 68.

Blumenfeld, Ralph David. *R.D.B.'s Diary.* London: Heinemann, 1930.

Bolter, Jay David and Richard Grusin. *Remediation: Understanding New Media.* London: MIT Press, 1999.

Booth, Charles. *Labour of the People of London.* 17 vols. London: Macmillan, 1891–1902.

Booth, Wayne. *The Rhetoric of Fiction.* London: Chicago UP, 1961.

Bordwell, David. *Narration in the Fiction Film.* Madison: Wisconsin UP, 1985.

———. *On the History of Film Style.* Cambridge, MA: Harvard UP, 1997.

Bordwell, David and Kristin Thompson. *Film Art: An Introduction.* 7th ed. London: McGraw-Hill, 2004.

Bottomore, Stephen. *I Want to See This Annie Mattygraph: A Cartoon History of the Coming of the Movies.* Pordenone: Le Giornate del Cinema Muto, 1995.

———. 'Shots in the Dark: The Real Origins of Film Editing'. *Early Cinema: Space, Frame, Narrative.* Ed. Thomas Elsaesser. London: BFI, 1990. 104–13.

Bowser, Eileen. *The Transformation of Cinema 1907–1915.* New York: Scribners, 1990.

Bradbury, Malcolm, and James McFarlane. 'The Name and Nature of Modernism'. *Modernism.* Ed. Malcolm Bradbury and James McFarlane. London: Penguin, 1976. 19–55.

Bradshaw, David. Introduction. *A Concise Companion to Modernism.* Ed. David Bradshaw. Oxford: Blackwell, 2003. 1–5.

Braithwaite, David. *Travelling Fairs.* Aylesbury: Shire Publications, 1976.

British Film Institute. 'Film and TV Information: UK Cinema Admissions 1933–2003.' 4 Jun 2008. *British Film Institute Homepage.* Accessed May 2009. <http://www.bfi.org.uk/filmtvinfo/stats/boxoffice/admissions.html.>

Budgen, Frank. *James Joyce and the Making of 'Ulysses'.* 1934. Oxford: Oxford UP, 1972.

Burch, Noël. 'A Primitive Mode of Representation?'. *Early Cinema: Space, Frame, Narrative.* Ed. Thomas Elsaesser. London: BFI, 1990. 220–7.

Burgoyne, Robert. 'The Cinematic Narrator: The Logic and Pragmatics of Impersonal Narration'. *Journal of Film and Video* 42.1 (Spring 1990): 3–16.

Burkdall, Thomas. *Joycean Frames: Film and the Fiction of James Joyce.* London: Routledge, 2001.

Burnett, John. *A History of the Cost of Living.* London: Penguin, 1969.

Burrows, Jon. *Legitimate Cinema: Theatre Stars in British Silent Films, 1908–1918.* Exeter: University of Exeter Press, 2003.

———. 'Penny Pleasures: Film exhibition in London during the Nickelodeon era, 1906–1914.' *Film History* 16.1 (2004): 60–91.

Camerani, Marco. 'James Joyce and Early Cinema: Peeping Bloom Through the Keyhole'. *Proceedings of the 2007 James Joyce Graduate Conference.* Ed. Frace Rugierri, et al. Newcastle: Cambridge Scholars, 2009. 114–28.

Chanan, Michael. *The Dream That Kicks*. London: Routledge & Kegan Paul, 1980.

———. 'Economic Conditions of Early Cinema'. *Early Cinema: Space, Frame, Narrative*. Ed. Thomas Elsaesser. London: BFI, 1990. 174–88.

Chatman, Seymour. *Story and Discourse: Narrative Structure in Fiction and Film*. London: Cornell UP, 1978.

Childs, Donald. *Modernism and Eugenics: Woolf, Eliot, Years and the Culture of Degeneration*. Cambridge: Cambridge UP, 2001.

Cohen, Keith. *Film and Fiction: The Dynamic of Exchange*. New Haven: Yale UP, 1979.

Childs, Peter. *Modernism*. London: Routledge, 2000.

Cole, G.D.H. *Daily Herald*. (30 June 1919): 4.

Collier, Peter, and Judy Davies, eds. *Modernism and the European Unconscious*. Cambridge: Polity, 1990.

Connor, Rachel. *H.D. and the Image*. Manchester: Manchester UP, 2004.

Conrad, Joseph. 'Because of the Dollars'. *Within The Tides*. London: J.M. Dent, 1915. 223–80.

———. *Chance*. 1914. Oxford: Oxford UP, 2002.

———. *The Collected Letters of Joseph Conrad, Vol. 5: 1912–1916*. Cambridge: Cambridge UP, 1996.

———. 'The Inn of the Two Witches.'. *Within The Tides*. London: J.M. Dent, 1915. 175–20.

———. 'The Partner'. *Within The Tides*. London: J.M. Dent, 1915. 119–72.

———. 'The Planter of Malata'. *Within The Tides*. London: J.M. Dent, 1915. 1–115.

———. *The Secret Agent*. 1907. London: Penguin, 2007.

———. *Under Western Eyes*. 1911. London: Penguin, 1957.

———. *Victory*. 1915. Oxford: Oxford UP, 2004.

Conrad, Joseph and Ford Madox Ford [Hueffer]. *The Inheritors*. 1901. Alan Sutton, 1991.

———. *Romance*. London: Smith, Elder & Co., 1903.

Corelli, Marie. *The Master-Christian*. London: Methuen, 1900.

Cox, Kenyon. *Artist and Public*. London: Allen & Unwin, 1914.

Crary, Jonathan. *Techniques of the Observer*. London: MIT Press, 1990.

Culler, Jonathan. *Saussure*. 2nd ed. London: Fontana, 1985.

Danius, Sara. *The Senses of Modernism: Technology, Perception and Aesthetics*. London: Cornell UP, 2002.

Dasenbrock, Reed Way. *The Literary Vorticism of Ezra Pound and Wyndham Lewis*. Baltimore: John Hopkins UP, 1985.

deCordova, Richard. 'From Lumière to Pathé: The Break-Up of Perspectival Space'. *Early Cinema: Space, Frame, Narrative*. Ed. Thomas Elsaesser. London: BFI, 1990. 76–85.

Deleuze, Gilles. *Cinema 1: The Movement-Image*. 1983. London: Athlone, 2005.

Demolition of a Wall. Dir. Auguste & Louis Lumière. 1896.

Denvier, Bernard. 'Impressionism'. *Modern Art: Impressionism to Post-Modernism*. London: Thames and Hudson, 1974. 11–57.

Doane, Mary Ann. *The Emergence of Cinematic Time: Modernity, Contingency, the Archive*. London: Harvard UP, 2002.

Donald, James and Stephanie Hemlryk Donald. 'The Publicness of Cinema'. *Reinventing Film Studies*. Ed. Christine Gledhill and Linda Williams. London: Arnold, 2000. 114–29.

Donovan, Stephen. *Joseph Conrad and Popular Culture*. Basingstoke: Palgrave, 2005.

Dujardin, Édouard. *We'll to the Woods No More*. 1938. Trans. Stuart Gilbert. New York: New Directions, 1957.

Edel, Leon. 'Introduction.' *We'll to the Woods No More*. 1938. By Édouard Dujardin. Trans. Stuart Gilbert. New York: New Directions, 1957. vii–xxvii.

Eisenstein, Sergei. 'Beyond the Shot'. 1929. *The Eisenstein Reader*. Ed. Richard Taylor. London: BFI, 1998. 82–93.

———. *The Film Sense*. 1943. Trans. Jay Leyda. London: Faber & Faber, 1968.

Eliot, T.S. *The Letters of T.S. Eliot. Vol 1. 1898–1922*. Ed. Valerie Eliot. London: Faber and Faber, 1988.

———. 'London Letter, July 1921'. *The Annotated Waste Land with Eliot's Contemporary Prose*. Ed. Lawrence Rainey. 2nd ed. London: Yale UP, 2006. 183–7.

———. '*Ulysses*, Order and Myth'. Nov 1923. *A Modernist Reader: Modernism in England 1910–1930*. Ed. Peter Faulkner. London: B.T. Batsford, 1986. 100–4.

———. 'The Waste Land'. *Criterion* 1.1 (October 1922): 50–64.

Ellmann, Richard. *James Joyce*. 2nd ed. Oxford: Oxford UP, 1982.

———. *Ulysses on the Liffey*. London: Faber & Faber, 1972.

Elsaesser, Thomas. 'Early Film Form: Articulations of Space and Time'. *Early Cinema: Space, Frame, Narrative*. Ed. Thomas Elsaesser. London: BFI, 1990. 11–30.

The Fatal Hour. Dir. D.W. Griffith. American Biograph, 1908.

The Female of the Species. Dir. D.W. Griffith. American Biograph, 1912.

Fleishman, Avrom. 'The Genre of *The Good Soldier*: Ford's Comic Mastery'. *Studies in the Literary Imagination* 13.1 (Spring 1980): 31–42.

Ford [Hueffer], Ford Madox. *A Call*. London: Chatto & Windus, 1910.

———. *The Benefactor*. Brown, Laugham & Co., 1905.

———. *The Good Soldier*. 1915. London: Penguin, 1946.

———. 'Impressionism—Some Speculations.' *Poetry* 2 (August & September 1913): 177–87; 215–25.

———. *Joseph Conrad: A Personal Remembrance*. London: Duckworth, 1924.

———. 'Joseph Conrad'. 1911. *Critical Essays*. Ed. Max Saunders and Richard Stang. Manchester: Carcanet, 2002. 76–90.

———. 'Modern Poetry'. 1909. *The Critical Attitude*. London: Duckworth, 1911. 173–90.

———. *Mr. Fleight*. London: Howard Latimer, 1913.

———. 'On Impressionism.'. *Poetry and Drama* 2.6 (June 1914): 167–75.

———. 'On Impressionism, Second Article'. *Poetry and Drama* 2.12 (Dec 1914): 323–34.

———. 'The Passing of the Great Figure.' 1909. *The Critical Attitude*. London: Duckworth, 1911. 113–29.

Francoeur, Louis. *Les Signes s'envolent. Pour une sémiotique des actes de langage culturels*. Quebec City: Presses de l'Université Laval, 1985.

Frank, Joseph. 'Spatial Form: An Answer to Critics'. *Critical Inquiry* 4 (Winter 1977): 231–52.

———. *The Widening Gyre: Crisis and Mastery in Modern Literature*. Piscataway, NJ: Rutgers UP, 1963.

Friedberg, Anne. 'Introduction: Reading *Close Up* 1927–1933'. *Close Up 1927–1933: Cinema and Modernism*. Ed. James Donald, Anne Friedberg and Laura Marcus. London: Cassell, 1998. 1–26.

Friedman, Melvin. 'The Symbolist Novel: Huysmans to Malraux'. *Modernism*. Ed. Malcolm Bradbury and James McFarlane. London: Penguin, 1976. 453–66.

Fromm, Gloria. *Dorothy Richardson: A Biography*. London: Illinois UP, 1977.

Frosh, Stephen. 'Psychoanalysis in Britain: "The rituals of destruction"'. *A Concise Companion to Modernism*. Ed. David Bradshaw. Oxford: Blackwell, 2003. 116–37.

Furniss, Harry. *Our Lady Cinema: How and why I went into the Photo-Play world and what I found there*. London: Simpkin, Marshall, Hamilton, Kent & Co, 1914.

Garvin, James. *The Observer* (23 May 1915): 2.

Gaudreault, André. *Cinema delle origini. O della 'cinematografia-attrazione'*. Milan, Il Castoro, 2004.

———. 'Detours in Film Narrative: The Development of Cross-Cutting'. 1979. *Early Cinema: Space, Frame, Narrative*. Ed. Thomas Elsaesser. London: BFI, 1990. 133–50.

———. 'The Diversity of Cinematographic Connections in the Intermedial Context of the Turn of the 20th Century'. *Visual Delights: Essays on the Popular and Projected Image in the 19th Century*. Ed. Simon Popple and Vanessa Toulmin. Trowbridge: Flicks Books, 1999. 8–15.

———. 'Film, Narrative, Narration: The Cinema of the Lumière Brothers.' *Early Cinema: Space, Frame, Narrative*. Ed. Thomas Elsaesser. London: BFI, 1990. 68–75.

———. 'From "Primitive Cinema" to "Kine-Attractography"'. *The Cinema of Attractions Reloaded*. Ed. Wanda Strauven. Amsterdam: Amsterdam UP, 2006. 85–104.

———. *Du Littéraire au Filmique: Système du rècit*. Paris: Méridiens Klincksieck, 1988.

———. 'Méliès the Magician: The Magical Magic of the Magic Image'. *Early Popular Visual Culture* 5.2 (July 2007): 167–74.

———. 'Temporality and Narrativity in Early Cinema, 1895–1908'. *Film Before Griffith*. Ed. John L Fell. Berkeley: California UP, 1983. 311–329.

Gaudreault, André, and Philippe Marion. 'The Cinema as a Model for the Genealogy of Media'. *Convergence* 8.4 (Winter 2002): 12–8.

———. 'A Medium is Always Born Twice. . .'. *Early Popular Visual Culture* 3.1 (May 2005): 3–15.

———. 'The Neo-Institutionalisation of Cinema as a New Medium'. *Visual Delights Two: Exhibition and Reception*. Ed. Vanessa Toulmin and Simon Popple. Eastleigh: John Libbey, 2005. 87–95.

Gevirtz, Susan. *Narrative's Journey: The Fiction and Film Writing of Dorothy Richardson*. New York: Peter Lang, 1996.

Gifford, Dennis. *The British Film Catalogue 1895–1985: A Reference Guide*. 2nd ed. Newton Abbot: David & Charles, 1986.

Gilbert, Stuart. *James Joyce's* Ulysses: *A Study*. London: Faber & Faber, 1930.

Gillies, Mary Ann. 'Bergsonism: "Time out of mind"'. *A Concise Companion to Modernism*. Ed. David Bradshaw. Oxford: Blackwell, 2003. 95–115.

Gillis, Stacy. '"Only from the Senses": Detection, Early Cinema and a Giant Green Spider'. *Reading the Cinematograph: The Cinema in British Short Fiction 1896–1912*. Ed. Andrew Shail. Exeter: University of Exeter Press, 2010. 144–54.

The Girl and Her Trust. Dir. D.W. Griffith. American Biograph, 1912.

Gorky, Maxim. 'Review of Lumière programme'. 4 July 1896. *Kino: A History of the Russian and Soviet Film*. Ed. Jay Leyda. London: George Allen & Unwin, 1960. 407–9.

Grandma's Reading Glass. G.A. Smith. 1900.

Great Britain. *Census of England and Wales 1911. Preliminary Report with Tables of the Population Enumerated in England and Wales (Administrative, Registration and Parliamentary Areas), and in Scotland, Ireland, the Isle of Man and the Channel Islands on 3rd April 1911*. London: HMSO, 1911.

———. *Census of England and Wales 1921. Preliminary Report including Tables of the Population Enumerated in England and Wales (Administrative, Registration and Parliamentary Areas), and in Scotland, the Isle of Man and the Channel Islands on 19th/20th June 1921, Together with the Population Recently Enumerated of Certain Other Parts of the British Empire*. London: HMSO, 1921.

The Great Train Robbery. Dir. Edwin S. Porter. Edison, 1903.

Green, Robert. *Ford Madox Ford: Prose and Politics.* Cambridge: Cambridge UP, 1981.

Grieveson, Lee. '"A kind of recreative school for the whole family": Making Cinema Respectable, 1907–09'. *Screen* 42.1 (Spring 2001): 64–76.

Groden, Michael. Ulysses *in Progress.* Princeton, NJ: Princeton UP, 1977.

Grosoli, Marco. '"Cinema has not been invented yet": The Second Birth of Cinema According to André Bazin'. *The Second Birth of Cinema.* Newcastle University. 1–2 July 2011.

Gunn, Ian, and Mark Wright. 'Visualising Joyce'. *Hypermedia Joyce Studies* 7.1 (2005–6). n. p.

Gunning, Tom. '"Animated Pictures": Tales of Cinema's Forgotten Future, After 100 Years of Films.' *Reinventing Film Studies.* Ed. Christine Gledhill and Linda Williams. London: Arnold, 2000. 316–31.

———. 'The Cinema of Attractions: Early Film, Its Spectator and the Avant-Garde.' *Wide Angle* 8.3/4 (Fall 1986): 63–70.

———. *D.W. Griffith and the Origins of American Narrative Film: The Early Years at Biograph.* Urbana: University of Illinois Press, 1991.

———. 'From the Opium Den to the Theatre of Morality: Moral Discourse and the Film Process in Early American Cinema'. *Art and Text* (Sept 1988): 30–41.

———. 'Modernity and Cinema: A Culture of Shocks and Flows.' *Cinema and Modernity.* Ed. Murray Pomerance. London: Rutgers UP, 2006. 297–315.

———. 'Never Seen This Picture Before: Muybridge in Multiplicity'. *Time Stands Still: Eadweard Muybridge and the Instantaneous Photography Movement.* By Philip Prodger. Oxford: Oxford UP, 2003. 222–72.

———. '"Now You See It, Now You Don't": The Temporality of the Cinema of Attractions'. *Silent Film.* Ed. Richard Abel. Piscataway, NJ: Rutgers UP, 1996. 71–84.

———. 'Non-Continuity, Continuity, Discontinuity: A Theory of Genres in Early Films'. 1984. *Early Cinema: Space, Frame, Narrative.* Ed. Thomas Elsaesser. London: BFI, 1990. 86–94.

———. 'Primitive Cinema: A Frame-Up? Or the Trick's on Us'. *Early Cinema: Space, Frame, Narrative.* Ed. Thomas Elsaesser. London: BFI, 1990. 95–103.

———. 'Weaving a Narrative: Style and Economic Background in Griffith's Biograph Films'. 1981. *Early Cinema: Space, Frame, Narrative.* Ed. Thomas Elsaesser. London: BFI, 1990. 336–47.

H.D. *Asphodel.* 1921–2. Durham: Duke UP, 1992.

———. *Bid Me To Live.* 1960. London: Virago, 1984.

———. *Notes on Thought and Vision and The Wise Sappho.* San Francisco: City Lights, 1982.

Habermas, Jürgen. *The Structural Transformation of the Public Sphere.* 1962. Trans. Thomas Burger and Frederick Lawrence. Cambridge: Polity, 1989.

Hammond, Michael. *The Big Show: British Cinema Culture in the Great War 1914–1918.* Exeter: University of Exeter Press, 2006.

Hampson, Robert. 'The Late Novels'. *The Cambridge Companion to Joseph Conrad.* Ed. J.H. Stape. Cambridge UP, 1996. 140–59.

Hankins, Leslie. '"Across the Screen of My Brain": Virginia Woolf's "The Cinema" and Film Forums of the Twenties'. *The Multiple Muses of Virginia Woolf.* Ed. Diane Gillespie. Columbia: Missouri UP, 1993. 148–79.

———. 'The Doctor and the Woolf: Reel Challenges—*The Cabinet of Dr. Caligari* and *Mrs. Dalloway*'. *Virginia Woolf: Themes and Variations.* Ed. Vara Neverow-Turk and Mark Hussey. New York: Pace UP, 1993. 40–51.

———. 'Iris Barry, Writer and *Cinéaste,* Forming Film Culture in London 1924–1926: The *Adelphi,* the *Spectator,* the Film Society and the British *Vogue*.' *Modernism/Modernity* 11.3 (2004): 488–515.

———. 'A Splice of Reel Life in Virginia Woolf's "Time Passes": Censorship, Cinema and "the usual battlefield of emotions"'. *Criticism* 35.1 (Winter 1993): 91–114.

———. 'Virginia Woolf and Writers and *Cinéastes* in *The Little Review, The New Criterion*, and the British *Vogue*'. MLA Convention. Philadelphia. 29 December 2004.

Hansen, Miriam Bratu. 'Early Cinema: Whose Public Sphere?'. *Early Cinema: Space, Frame, Narrative*. Ed. Thomas Elsaesser. London: BFI, 1990. 228–46.

———. 'Introduction'. *Theory of Film: The Redemption of Physical Reality*. By Siegfried Kracauer. 1960. Princeton, N.J.: Princeton UP, 1997. vii–xlv.

———. 'The Mass Production of the Senses: Classical Cinema as Vernacular Modernism'. *Modernism/Modernity* 6.2 (1999): 59–77.

Hart, Clive. 'Wandering Rocks'. *James Joyce's* Ulysses: *Critical Essays*. Ed. Clive Hart and David Hayman. London: California UP, 1974. 181–216.

Hauser, Arnold. *The Social History of Art*. 2 vols. London: Routledge & Kegan Paul, 1951.

Henley Regatta. Dir. Cecil Hepworth. 1899.

Hepworth,Cecil. *Came The Dawn*. London: Phoenix, 1951.

Higson, Andrew, ed. *Young and Innocent?: The Cinema in Britain 1896–1930*. Exeter: University of Exeter Preee, 2002.

Hiley, Nicholas. '"At the Picture Palace": The British Cinema Audience, 1895–1920'. *Celebrating 1895: Proceedings of the International Conference on Film Before 1920*. Ed. John Fullerton. Eastleigh: John Libbey, 1998. 96–103.

———. '*The Battle of the Somme* and British News Media'. Centre de Recherche de L'Historial de la Grande Guerre. Péronne. 21 July 1992.

———. 'The British Cinema Auditorium'. *Film and the First World War*. Ed. Karen Dibbets and Bert Hogenkamp. Amsterdam: Amsterdam UP, 1995. 160–70.

———. 'Nothing More than a "Craze"': Cinema Building in Britain from 1909 to 1914.' *Young and Innocent?: The Cinema in Britain 1896–1930*. Ed. Andrew Higson. Exeter: University of Exeter Press, 2002. 111–27.

Hobson, John A. *Problems of Poverty*. 1891. London: Methuen, 1895.

Hollington, Michael. 'Svevo, Joyce and Modernist Time.' *Modernism*. Ed. Malcolm Bradbury and James McFarlane. London: Penguin, 1976. 430–42.

Holtby, Winifred. *Virginia Woolf*. London: Wishart & Co., 1932.

Homer. *The Odyssey*. London: Penguin, 1991.

Horizontal-Vertical. Dir. Vikking Eggeling. 1924.

Hotchkiss, Lia M. 'Writing the Jump Cut: *Mrs Dalloway* in the Context of Cinema'. *Virginia Woolf: Texts and Contexts*. Ed. Beth Rigel Daugherty and Eileen Barrett. New York: Pace UP, 1996. 134–9.

How it Feels to be Run Over. Dir. Cecil Hepworth. 1900.

Hulme, T.E. 'A Lecture on Modern Poetry'. 1911. *Further Speculations*. Ed. Samuel Hynes. Minneapolis: Minnesota UP, 1955. 67–76.

———. 'Searchers after Reality II: Haldane.' 1909. *Further Speculations*. Ed. Samuel Hynes. Minneapolis: Minnesota UP, 1955. 7–14.

Humm, Maggie. *Modernist Women and Visual Cultures: Virginia Woolf, Vanessa Bell, Photography and Cinema*. Edinburgh: Edinburgh UP, 2002.

Humphrey, Robert. *Stream of Consciousness in the Modern Novel*. 1954. Berkeley: California UP, 1958.

The Hundred-to-One Shot. Vitagraph, 1906.

Hutchins, Patricia. 'James Joyce and the Cinema'. *Sight and Sound* 21.1 (Aug–Sept 1951): 9–12.

Jack the Kisser. Dir. Edwin S. Porter. Edison, 1907.

Jacobs, Karen. *The Eye's Mind: Literary Modernism and Visual Culture*. London: Cornell UP, 2001.

Jacobus, Lee. 'Bring the Camera Whenever You Like: "Wandering Rocks", Cinema Ambulante, and the Problems of Diegesis'. *Images of Joyce*. Vol 2. Ed. Clive Hart, et al. 2 Vols. Gerrards Cross: Colin Smythe, 1998. 526–38.

James, Henry. *The Princess Casamassima*. London: Macmillan, 1886.

James, William. *The Principles of Psychology*. 1890. 3 Vols. Cambridge, MA: Harvard UP, 1981.

Jean-Aubry, G. *Joseph Conrad: Life and Letters*. 2 Vols. Garden City, NY: Doubleday, 1927.

Joyce, James. *Letters of James Joyce*. Vol. 2. Ed. Richard Ellmann. London: Faber and Faber, 1966.

———. *Letters of James Joyce*. Ed. Stuart Gilbert. London: Faber and Faber, 1957.

———. 'A Mother'. 1905. *Dubliners*. London: Penguin, 1976. 134–48.

———. *A Portrait of the Artist as a Young Man*. 1916. London: Harmondsworth, 1960.

———. *Ulysses*. 1922. London: Penguin, 1992.

Kadlec, David. 'Pound, *Blast* and Syndicalism'. *ELH* 60.4 (Winter 1993): 1015–31.

Kandinsky, Wassily. 'The Problem of Form'. 1912. *Modernism: An Anthology of Sources and Documents*. Ed. Vassiliki Kolocotroni, Jane Goldman, and Olga Taxidou. Edinburgh: Edinburgh UP, 1998. 270–5.

Keil, Charlie. *Early American Cinema in Transition: Story, Style, and Filmmaking, 1907–1913*. Madison: University of Wisconsin Press, 2001.

Kellman, Stephen G. 'The Cinematic Novel: Tracking a Concept'. *Modern Fiction Studies* 33.3 (1987): 467–77.

Kember, Joe. 'The Cinema of Affections: The Transformation of Authorship in British Cinema before 1907'. *Velvet Light Trap* 57 (Spring 2006): 3–16.

———. '"It was not the show, it was the tale that you told": Film Lecturing and Showmanship on the British Fairground'. *Visual Delights: Essays on the Popular and Projected Image in the 19th Century*. Ed. Simon Popple and Vanessa Toulmin. Trowbridge: Flicks Books, 2000. 61–70.

———. *Marketing Modernity: Victorian Popular Shows and Early Cinema*. Exeter: University of Exeter Press, 2009.

Kenner, Hugh. *Flaubert, Joyce and Beckett: The Stoic Comedians*. London: W.H. Allen, 1964.

Kermode, Frank. *The Sense of an Ending: Studies in the Theory of Fiction*. 1965. Oxford: Oxford UP, 1966.

Kern, Stephen. *The Culture of Time and Space, 1880–1918*. London: Weidenfeld and Nicolson, 1983.

Killeen, Terence. *Ulysses Unbound: A Reader's Companion to James Joyce's Ulysses*. Bray: Wordwell, 2004.

Kinematograph & Lantern Weekly. *Cinematograph Theatres: A Series of Illustrated Plans etc. of Picture Houses, specially reprinted from the issues of Oct 28th and Nov 11th of The Builder*. London: 1921.

———. *The Handbook of Kinematography: The History, Theory and Practice of Motion Photography and Projection*. London: E.T. Heron, 1911.

———. *How to Run a Picture Theatre*. London: E.T. Heron, 1912.

King, C.D. 'Édouard Dujardin, Inner Monologue and the Stream of Consciousness'. *French Studies* 7.2 (April 1953): 116–28.

Kittler, Friedrich. *Gramophone, Film Typewriter*. 1986. Trans. Geoffrey Winthrop-Young and Michael Wutz. Stanford: Stanford UP, 1999.

Kracauer, Siegfried. 'Photography'. 1927. *The Mass Ornament: Weimar Essays*. Trans. and ed. Thomas Y Levin. London: Harvard UP, 1995. 47–63.

Kumar, Shiv. *Bergson and the Stream of Consciousness Novel*. London: Blackie, 1962.

Lacoste, Charles. 'Sur le 'Cubisme' et la peinture'. *Temps Présent* (2 April 1913): 332–40.

Larbaud, Valery. 'Préface'. *Les Lauriers sont coupés*. By Édouard Dujardin. Paris: Albert Messein, 1924.

———. 'The "Ulysses" of James Joyce'. *Criterion* 1.1 (Oct 1922): 94–103.

Lawrence, D.H. 'Preface'. *New Poems*. 1920. *A Modernist Reader: Modernism in England 1910–1930*. Ed. Peter Faulkner. London: BT Batsford, 1986. 129–34.

———. '"Tickets, Please!"'. *Strange Tales from the* Strand *Magazine*. Ed. Jack Adrian. London: Sutton, 1991. 116–27.

Le Bon, Gustave. *The Crowd: A Study of the Popular Mind*. 1895. London: T. Fisher Unwin, 1896.

Lěger, Fernand. 'Film by Fernand Lěger and Dudley Murphy, Musical Synchronism by George Antheil'. *The Little Review* 10.2 (Autumn and Winter 1924–1925): 42–4.

———. 'A New Realism—The Object (Its Plastic and Cinematographic Value)'. *The Little Review* 11.2 (Winter 1926): 7–8.

Levenson, Michael. *A Genealogy of Modernism: A Study of English Literary Doctrine 1908–1922*. Cambridge: Cambridge UP, 1984.

———, ed. *The Cambridge Companion to Modernism*. Cambridge: Cambridge UP, 1999.

Levin, Harry. *The Gates of Horn: A Study of Five French Realists*. Oxford: Oxford University Press, 1963.

———. *James Joyce*. Norfolk, CT: New Directions, 1941.

Levinson, Jerrold. 'Film Music and Narrative Agency'. *Post-Theory: Reconstructing Film Studies*. Ed. David Bordwell and Noël Carroll. Madison: Wisconsin UP, 1996. 248–82.

Levitt, Morton. *James Joyce and Modernism: Beyond Dublin*. New York: Edwin Mellen, 2000.

Levy, David. 'Re-constituted Newsreels, Re-enactments and the American Narrative Film'. *Cinema 1900/1906: An Analytical Study*. Ed. Roger Holman. Brussels: Federation Internationale des Archives du Film, 1982. 243–60.

Lewis, Wyndham. 'A Breton Innkeeper.' September 1910. *The Complete Wild Body*. Ed. Bernard Lafourcade. Santa Barbara: Black Sparrow, 1982. 269–73.

———. 'Brobdingnag.' January 1911. *The Complete Wild Body*. Ed. Bernard Lafourcade. Santa Barbara: Black Sparrow, 1982. 274–81.

———. 'Inferior Religions'. September 1917. *The Complete Wild Body*. Ed. Bernard Lafourcade. Santa Barbara: Black Sparrow, 1982. 315–9.

———. 'The "Pole"'. May 1909. *The Complete Wild Body*. Ed. Bernard Lafourcade. Santa Barbara: Black Sparrow, 1982. 209–18.

———. 'La Père Francois.' September 1910. *The Complete Wild Body*. Ed. Bernard Lafourcade. Santa Barbara: Black Sparrow, 1982. 266–8.

———. 'Les Saltimbanques'. August 1909. *The Complete Wild Body*. Ed. Bernard Lafourcade. Santa Barbara: Black Sparrow, 1982. 237–47.

———. *Self Condemned*. 1954. Chicago: Henry Regnery, 1965.

———. 'Some Innkeepers and Bestre'. June 1909. *The Complete Wild Body*. Ed. Bernard Lafourcade. Santa Barbara: Black Sparrow, 1982. 221–33.

———. 'A Spanish Household.' June 1910. *The Complete Wild Body*. Ed. Bernard Lafourcade. Santa Barbara: Black Sparrow, 1982. 259–65.

———. 'Unlucky for Pringle'. *The Tramp* (Feb 1911).

The Life of an American Fireman. Dir. Edwin S. Porter. Edison, 1903.

Lothe, Jakob. *Narration in Fiction and Film*. Oxford: Oxford UP, 2000.

Lotman, Jurji. *Semiotics of Cinema*. Trans. Mark E. Suino. Ann Arbor: University of Michigan Dept. of Slavic Languages and Literature, 1976.

Low, Rachael. *The History of the British Film 1906–1914*. London: Allen & Unwin, 1949.

———. *The History of the British Film 1914–1918*. London: Allen & Unwin, 1980.

Lynton, Norbert. *The Story of Modern Art*. 2nd ed. Oxford: Phaidon, 1989.

MacCabe, Colin. *James Joyce and the Revolution of the Word*. 2nd ed. Basingstoke: Palgrave, 2003.

———. 'On Impurity'. *Literature and Visual Technologies: Writing After Cinema*. Ed. Julian Murphet and Lydia Rainford. Basingstoke: Palgrave, 2003. 15–28.

———. 'Realism and Cinema: Notes on Some Brechtian Theses'. *Screen* 15.2 (1974): 7–27.

Maltby, Richard. *Hollywood Cinema: An Introduction*. 2nd ed. Oxford: Blackwell, 2003.

Manders, Frank. *Cinemas of Newcastle: A Comprehensive History of the Cinemas of Newcastle upon Tyne*. Newcastle: Newcastle City Library, 1991.

Marcus, Laura. *The Tenth Muse: Writing About Cinema in the Modernist Period*. Oxford: Oxford UP, 2008.

Martland, Peter. *A Business History of the Gramophone Company 1890–1918*. PhD Diss. U of Cambridge, 1992.

Mary Jane's Mishap. Dir. G.A. Smith. 1903.

McCabe, Susan. 'The 'Ballet Mecanique' of Marianne Moore's Cinematic Modernism'. *Mosaic* 33.2 (June 2000): 35–53.

———. *Cinematic Modernism*. Cambridge: Cambridge UP, 2005.

McDonald, Ian W. 'Forming the Craft: Play-writing and Photoplay-Writing in Britain in the 1910s'. *Early Popular Visual Culture* 8.1 (January 2010): 75–89.

McDougall, William. *An Introduction to Social Psychology*. London: Methuen, 1908.

———. *The Group Mind*. Cambridge University Press, 1920.

McKernan, Luke. 'Diverting Time: London's Cinemas and Their Audiences, 1906–1914'. *The London Journal* 32.2 (July 2007): 125–44.

———. 'James Joyce and the Volta Programme'. *Roll Away the Reel World: James Joyce and Cinema*. Ed. John McCourt. Cork University Press, 2010. 15–27.

———. *Topical Budget: The Great British News Film*. London: BFI, 1992.

McKilligan, Kathleen. *Édouard Dujardin: 'Les Lauriers sont coupés' and the interior monologue*. Hull: University of Hull Publications, 1977.

McMahon, April. 'Language: "History is a nightmare from which I am trying to awake"'. *A Concise Companion to Modernism*. Ed. David Bradhsaw. Oxford: Blackwell, 2003. 138–57.

Le Médecin du château. Pathé Frérés, 1908.

Meixner, John. *Ford Madox Ford's Novels: A Critical Study*. Minnesota UP, 1962.

Mercanton, Jacques. 'The Hours of James Joyce, Part I'. *Kenyon Review* 24 (1962): 702.

Messinger, Gary. 'An Inheritance Worth Remembering: The British Approach to Official Propaganda During the First World War'. *Historical Journal of Film, Radio and Television* 13.2 (1993): 117–27.

Metz, Christian. 'The Cinema: Language or Language System?'. Feb 1964. *Essais Sur la Signification au Cinema*. 1968. Trans. Michael Taylor, as *Film Language: A Semiotics of Cinema*. Oxford; Oxford UP, 1974. 31–91.

———. 'History/discourse: a note on two voyeurisms'. 1975. *Theories of Authorship*. Ed. John Caughie. London: Routledge & Kegan Paul, 1981. 225–231.

———. *Psychoanalysis and Cinema: The Imaginary Signifier*. Trans. Celia Britton. London: MacMillan, 1982.

Morris, Nigel. 'Film and Modernism'. *Encyclopaedia of Literary Modernism*. Ed. Paul Poplawski. London: Greenwood, 2003. 110–20.

Morrison, Mark. *The Public Face of Modernism: Little Magazines, Audience, and Reception 1905–1920*. Madison: Wisconsin UP, 2001.

Moser, Thomas. *The Life in the Fiction of Ford Madox Ford*. Princeton, NJ: Princeton UP, 1980.

Mukařovský, Jan. *Structure, Sign and Function: Selected Essays.* Trans. and ed. John Burbank. London: Yale UP, 1978.

Munsterberg, Hugo. *The Photoplay: A Psychological Study.* New York: Appleton, 1916.

Murray, Edward. *The Cinematic Imagination: Writers and the Motion Pictures.* New York: Frederick Ungar, 1972.

Musser, Charles. *The Emergence of Cinema: The American Screen to 1907.* Berkeley: California UP, 1990.

———. 'The Nickelodeon Era Begins: Establishing the Framework for Hollywood's Mode of Representation'. *Early Cinema: Space, Frame, Narrative.* Ed. Thomas Elsaesser. London: BFI, 1990. 256–73.

———Muybridge, Eadweard. *Descriptive Zoopraxography, Or The Science of Animal Locomotion Made Popular.* Pennsylvania UP, 1893.

National Council of Public Morals. *The Cinema: Its Present Position and Future Possibilities.* London: Williams and Norgate, 1917.

North, Michael. *Camera Works: Photography and the Twentieth-Century Word.* Oxford: Oxford UP, 2005.

———. *The Political Aesthetic of: Yeats, Eliot and Pound.* Cambridge: Cambridge UP, 1991.

———. *Reading 1922: A Return to the Scene of the Modern.* Oxford: Oxford UP, 1999.

———. 'Words in Motion: The Movies, the Readies, and "the Revolution of the Word"'. *Modernism/Modernity* 9.2 (April 2002): 205–23.

One is Business, The Other Crime. Dir. D.W. Griffith. American Biograph, 1912.

The Painted Lady. Dir. D.W. Griffith. American Biograph, 1912.

Parsons, Deborah. *Theorists of the Modernist Novel: James Joyce, Dorothy Richardson, Virginia Woolf.* London: Routledge, 2007.

Pater, Walter. *The Renaissance: Studies in Art and Poetry.* London: Macmillan, 1915.

———. 'Style'. 1888. *Appreciations.* London: Macmillan, 1890. 1–36.

Pearce, Richard. *The Novel in Motion: An Approach to Modern Fiction.* Columbus: Ohio State UP, 1983.

Perlmutter, Ruth. 'Joyce and Cinema'. *Boundary 2* 6.2 (Winter 1978): 481–502.

Peters, John G. *Conrad and Impressionism.* Cambridge: Cambridge UP, 2001.

Popple, Simon and Vanessa Toulmin, eds. *Visual Delights: Essays on the Popular and Projected Image in the Nineteenth Century.* Trowbridge: Flicks Books, 2000.

———. *Visual Delights Two: Exhibition and Reception.* Sheffield: National Fairground Archive, 2005.

Potter, Rachel. 'Modernism and Democracy: A Reconsideration'. *Critical Quarterly* 44.2 (Summer 2002): 1–16.

Pound, Ezra. *ABC of Reading.* New Haven: Yale UP, 1934.

———. 'Affirmations: As For Imagisme'. *The New Age* 16.1168 (28 Jan 1915): 349–50.

———. 'Art Notes: Kinema, Kinesis, Hepworth, etc'. *New Age* 23.22 (26 Sept 1918): 352.

———. 'The Book of the Month'. *Poetry Review* (March 1912): 122.

———. 'A Few Don'ts By An Imagiste'. March 1913. *Imagist Poetry.* Ed. Peter Jones. London: Penguin, 1972. 130–4.

———. 'Hugh Selwyn Mauberley'. June 1920. *Selected Poems.* Ed. T.S. Eliot. London: Faber & Faber, 1928. 155–72.

———. 'The New Sculpture'. *The Egoist* 1.4 (16 Feb 1914): 67–8.

———. 'On Criticism in General'. *Criterion* 1.2 (Jan 1923): 143–56.

———. *Pound/the Little Review: The Letters of Ezra Pound to Margaret Anderson.* Ed. Thomas Scott, Melvin Friedman and Jackson Bryer. New York: New Directions, 1988.

———. 'The Serious Artist'. 1913. *Literary Essays of Ezra Pound*. Ed. T.S. Eliot. London: Faber & Faber, 1960. 41–57.

———. *Selected Letters 1907–1941*. Ed. D.D. Paige. New York: New Directions, 1971.

———. 'Status rerum'. *Poetry* 1 (Jan 1913): 123–7.

———. 'Vortex: Pound'. *Blast* 1 (20 June 1914): 159.

———. 'Vorticism'. *The Fortnightly Review* 46.572 (Sept 1914): 461–71.

Prodger, Philip. *Time Stands Still: Eadweard Muybridge and the Instantaneous Photography Movement*. Oxford: Oxford UP, 2003.

'Propaganda'. Def 2. *The Compact Oxford English Dictionary*. 2nd ed. 1991.

Proust, Marcel. *Time Regained*. 1927. Trans. Andreas Mayor. London: Chatto & Windus, 1970.

Pyke, Montagu. *Focussing the Universe*. London: Waterlow Bros. & Layton, Ltd., 1910.

Rainey, Lawrence. 'The Cultural Economy of Modernism'. *The Cambridge Companion to Modernism*. Ed. Michael Levenson. Cambridge: Cambridge UP, 1999. 33–69.

———. *Institutions of Modernism: Literary Elites and Public Culture*. New Haven: Yale UP, 1998.

Reed, Langford. *The Chronicles of Charlie Chaplin*. London: Cassell, 1917.

Reeves, Nicholas. *Official British Film Propaganda during the First World War*. London: Croom Helm, 1986.

Reid, Benjamin. *The Man from New York: John Quinn and His Friends*. Oxford: Oxford UP, 1968.

Reid, Alisdair. 'Dilution, Trade Unionism and the State in Britain During the First World War'. *Shop Floor Bargaining and the State: Historical and Comparative Perspectives*. Ed. S. Tolliday and J. Zeitlin. Cambridge: Cambridge UP, 1985. 46–74.

Rescued by Rover. Dir. Cecil Hepworth. 1905.

Richardson, Dorothy. *Pilgrimage 1: Pointed Roofs, Backwater, Honeycomb*. London: Virago, 1979.

———. *Pilgrimage 2: The Tunnel, Interim*. London: Virago, 1979.

Robbe-Grillet, Alain. *Last Year at Marienbad: A Ciné-Novel*. 1961. Trans Richard Howard. London: John Calder, 1962.

Rossell, Deac. 'Double Think: The Cinema and Magic Lantern Culture'. *Celebrating 1895: The Centenary of Cinema*. Ed. John Fullerton. Eastleigh: John Libbey, 1998. 27–36.

The Runaway Horse. Pathé Frérés, 1907.

Salisbury, Laura, and Andrew Shail. 'Introduction'. *Neurology & Modernity: A Cultural History of Nervous Systems 1850–1950*. Basingstoke: Palgrave, 2009. 1–40.

Salt, Barry. 'Film Form 1900–1906.' *Early Cinema: Space, Frame, Narrative*. Ed Thomas Elsaesser. London: BFI, 1990. 31–44.

———. 'Vitagraph Films: A Touch of Real Class'. *Screen Culture: History & Textuality*. Ed. John Fullerton. Eastleigh: John Libbey, 2004. 55–72.

A Salvation Army Lass. Dir. D.W. Griffith. American Biograph, 1908.

Saunders, Max. *The World Before the War*. Vol. 1 of *Ford Madox Ford: A Dual Life*. 2 Vols. Oxford: Oxford UP, 1996.

Schwab, Arnold. 'Conrad's American Speeches and His Reading From *Victory*'. *Modern Philology* 62.4 (May 1965): 342–7.

Senn, Fritz and Gerry O'Flaherty. 'Episode 8: Lestrygonians'. *Reading Ulysses*. 20 episodes. RTÉ Radio 1. Dublin. Prod. Ann Marie O'Callaghan. 17 May 2004.

Shail, Andrew. '"a distinct advance in society": Cinema's "Proletarian Public Sphere" and Isolated Spectatorship in Britain 1911–1918.' *Journal of British Cinema and Television* 3.2 (2006): 209–28.

————. 'The Motion Picture Story Magazine and the Origins of Popular British Film Culture'. *Film History* 20.2 (2008): 181–97.

————. 'Penny Gaffs and Picture Theatres: Popular Perceptions of Britain's First Cinemas'. *Multimedia Histories: From the Magic Lantern to the Internet.* Ed. James Lyons and John Plunkett. Exeter: University of Exeter Press, 2007. 132–47.

————. 'Reading the Cinematograph'. *Reading the Cinematograph: The Cinema in British Short Fiction, 1896–1912.* Ed. Andrew Shail. Exeter: University of Exeter Press, 2010. 1–17.

————. '"She looks just like one of we-all!": British Cinema Culture and the Origins of Woolf's Orlando.' *Critical Quarterly* 48.2 (Summer 2006): 45–76.

Shail, Andrew, and David Trotter. 'Cinema and the Novel'. *The Oxford History of the Novel: 1880–1940.* Ed. Patrick Parrinder and Andrzej Gasiorek. Oxford University Press, 2010. 370–86.

Shaw, Walter Hanks. 'Cinema and Ballet in Paris'. *New Criterion* 4.1 (Jan 1926): 178–84.

Sherry, Vincent. *The Great War and the Language of Modernism.* Oxford: Oxford UP, 2003.

Showalter, Elaine. 'Introduction'. *Mrs Dalloway.* By Virginia Woolf. London: Penguin, 1992. xi–xlviii.

Sick Kitten. Dir. G.A. Smith. 1903.

Sinclair, May. 'The Novels of Dorothy Richardson'. April 1918. *The Gender of Modernism.* Ed. Bonnie Kime Scott. Bloomington: Indiana UP, 1990. 442–8.

Singer, Ben. *Melodrama and Modernity: Early Sensational Cinema and its Contexts.* New York: Columbia UP, 2001.

Smith, Grahame. *Dickens and the Dream of Cinema.* Manchester: Manchester UP, 2003.

Smith, Stan. *The Origins of Modernism.* London: Harvester Wheatsheaf, 1984.

Sorel, Georges. *Reflections on Violence.* 1906. Trans T.E. Hulme. Toronto: The Free Press, 1950.

Souriau, Étienne. 'Preface'. *L'Univers Filmique.* Ed. Étienne Souriau. Paris: Flammarion, 1953. 1–11.

Spiegel, Alan. 'Cinematographic Form'. *Novel* 6.3 (Spring 1973): 229–43.

Spiegel, Alan. *Fiction and the Camera Eye.* Charlottesville: University Press of Virginia, 1976.

Spoo, Robert. 'Introduction'. *Asphodel.* Durham: Duke UP, 1992. ix–xxi.

Stanford, W.B. *The Ulysses Theme: A Study in the Adaptability of a Traditional Hero.* Oxford: Blackwell, 1954.

Steer, Valentia. *The Romance of the Cinema: A Short Record of the Development of the Most Popular Form of Amusement of the Day.* London: Pearson, 1913.

Steigen-Fallen [Rise-Fall]. Dir. Hans Richter. 1924.

Stewart, Garrett. *Between Film and Screen: Modernism's Photo Synthesis.* Chicago: Chicago UP, 1999.

Stewart, Jack. 'Post-Impressionism'. *Encyclopaedia of Literary Modernism.* Ed. Paul Poplawski. Westport, CT: Greenwood, 2003. 305–9.

Swinton, Ernest Dunlop. 'The Sense of Touch'. *Reading the Cinematograph: The Cinema in British Short Fiction 1896–1912.* Ed. Andrew Shail. Exeter: University of Exeter Press, 2010. 219–39.

Taylor, A.J.P. *Beaverbrook.* London: Hamish Hamilton, 1972.

That Fatal Sneeze. Dir. Cecil Hepworth. 1907.

Tiessen, Paul. 'Eisenstein, Joyce and the Gender Politics of Literary Modernism'. *Kinema:* 1 (Spring 1993). <http://www.kinema.uwaterloo.ca/tiess931.htm>

————. 'A New Year One: Film as Metaphor in the Writings of Wyndham Lewis'. *Words and Moving Images: Essays on Verbal and Visual Expression in Film and Television*. Ed. William Wees and Michael Dorland. Montreal: Mediatexte, 1984. 153–69.

Tittle, Walter. 'The Conrad Who Sat for Me'. *Joseph Conrad: Interviews and Recollections*. Ed. Martin Ray. Basingstoke: Macmillan, 1990. 153–63.

Tolstoy, Leo. Interview with I. Teneromo. 1908. *Kino: a History of the Russian and Soviet Film*. Ed. Jay Leyda. London: George Allen & Unwin, 1960. 410–1.

Toulmin, Vanessa. 'Bioscope Biographies'. *In the Kingdom of Shadows: A Companion to Early Cinema*. Ed. Colin Harding and Simon Popple. London: Cygnus, 1996. 249–61.

———. 'Cuckoo in the Nest: Edwardian Itinerant Exhibition Practices and the Transition to Cinema in the United Kingdom from 1901 to 1906'. *The Moving Image* 10.1 (Spring 2010): 52–79.

———. *Electric Edwardians: The Story of the Mitchell and Kenyon Collection*. London: BFI, 2006.

Tratner, Michael. *Modernism and Mass Politics: Joyce, Woolf, Eliot, Yeats*. Stanford: Stanford UP, 1995.

Trotter, David. *Cinema and Modernism*. Oxford: Blackwell, 2007.

———. *Paranoid Modernism*. Oxford: Oxford UP, 2001.

Trotter, Wilfred. *Instincts of the Herd in Peace and War*. London: Ernest Benn, 1916.

UK Film Council. 'Statistical Yearbook 2009'. October 2009. *UK Film Council Homepage*. 28 October 2009. <http://www.ukfilmcouncil.org.uk/media/pdf/2/p/2009.pdf>

An Unseen Enemy. Dir. D.W. Griffith. American Biograph, 1912.

Urban, Charles. *The Cinematograph in Science, Education and Matters of State*. London: Charles Urban Trading Co., 1907.

Vargish, Thomas and Delo E Mook. *Inside Modernism: Relativity Theory, Cubism, Narrative*. London: Yale UP, 1999.

Vaglio, Carla Marengo. 'Cinematic Joyce'. *XVIII International James Joyce Symposium*. Stazione Marittima. Trieste, Italy. 17 June 2002.

Walker, David. 'Formal Experiment and Innovation'. *The Cambridge Companion to the French Novel From 1800 to the Present*. Ed. Timothy Unwin. Cambridge: Cambridge UP, 1997. 126–44.

Wallas, Graham. *Human Nature in Politics*. London: Constable & Co., 1908.

Walter, Christina. 'From Image to Screen: H.D. and the Visual Origins of Modernist Impersonality'. *Textual Practice* 22.2 (2008): 291–31.

Ward, Arthur Henry Sarsfield. 'The Green Spider'. *Pearson's Magazine* 18.106 (October 1904): 428–35.

Watt, Ian. *Conrad in the Nineteenth Century*. Berkeley: California UP, 1979.

Webb, Beatrice. *The Power to Alter Things. The Diary of Beatrice Webb, Vol 3, 1905–1924*. Ed. Norman MacKenzie and Joanne MacKenzie. London: Virago, 1984.

Wees, William. *Vorticism and the English Avant-Garde*. Toronto: Toronto UP, 1972.

Wells, H.G. *The History of Mr Polly*. 1910. London: Penguin, 1946.

———. *A Modern Utopia*. 1905. London: Penguin, 2005.

———. 'Pollock and the Porroh Man'. 1895. *The Complete Short Stories of H.G. Wells*. Ed. John Hammond. London: Phoenix, 2000. 178–89.

White, Eric Walter. *Parnassus to Let: An Essay About Rhythm in Films*. London: Hogarth, 1928

Whitworth, Michael. *Einstein's Wake: Relativity, Metaphor and Modernist Literature*. Oxford: Oxford UP, 2001.

———. 'Introduction'. *Modernism*. Ed. Michael Whitworth. Oxford: Blackwell, 2007. 3–60.

Wilkinson, Sarah. 'The Concept of the State, 1880–1939: "The discredit of the State is a sign that it has done its work well"'. *A Concise Companion to Modernism*. Ed. David Bradshaw. Oxford: Blackwell, 2003. 179–99.

Willard, Grace. 'More About Conrad'. *New York Evening Post Literary Review*. 30 August 1924. 9.

Williams, Keith. *H.G. Wells, Modernity and the Movies*. Liverpool: Liverpool UP, 2007.

———. 'Ulysses in Toontown: "vision animated to bursting point" in Joyce's "Circe"'. *Literature and Visual Technologies: Writing After Cinema*. Ed. Julian Murphet and Lydia Rainford. Basingstoke: Palgrave, 2003. 96–121.

Wilson, Trevor. *The Myriad Faces of War: Britain and the Great War 1914–1918*. Cambridge: Polity, 1985.

Wood, Michael. 'Modernism and Film'. *The Cambridge Companion to Modernism*. Ed. Michael Levenson. Cambridge: Cambridge UP, 1999. 212–32.

Woolf, Virginia. *Between the Acts*. 1941. London: Penguin, 2000.

———. 'The Cinema'. 1926. *Collected Essays. Vol 2*. London: Chatto & Windus, 1967. 268–72.

———. 'The Common Reader'. *The Common Reader: First Series*. London: Hogarth Press, 1925. 11–2.

———. *The Diaries of Virginia Woolf. Vol 2: 1920–1924*. Ed. Anne Olivier Bell and Andrew McNeillie. London: Hogarth, 1978.

———. *Jacob's Room*. 1922. London: Hogarth, 1945.

———. 'Kew Gardens'. 1921. *Monday or Tuesday*. London: Hesperus, 2003. 32–7.

———. 'Modern Fiction'. 1919. *A Modernist Reader: Modernism in England 1910–1930*. Ed. Peter Faulkner. London: BT Batsford, 1986. 105–12.

———. 'The "Movie" Novel'. 1918. *The Essays of Virginia Woolf. Volume 2: 1912–1918*. Ed. Andrew McNeillie. London: Hogarth, 1987. 288–91.

———. *Mrs Dalloway*. 1925. London: Penguin, 2000.

———. *Night and Day*. London: Hogarth, 1919.

———. 'Pictures'. 1925. *The Moment and Other Essays*. London: Hogarth, 1947. 140–4.

———. *The Question of Things Happening: The Letters of Virginia Woolf. Vol 2: 1912–1922*. Ed. Nigel Nicolson. London: Hogarth, 1976.

———. *A Reflection of the Other Person: The Letters of Virginia Woolf. Vol 4: 1929–1932*. Ed. Nigel Nicolson. London: Hogarth, 1978.

———. *A Room of One's Own*. 1929. London: Grafton, 1977.

———. 'Street Haunting: A London Adventure.' 1930. *The Death of the Moth and Other Essays*. London: Hogarth, 1945. 19–29.

———. *To the Lighthouse*. 1927. London: Penguin, 1964.

———. 'War in the Village'. 12 Sept 1918. *The Essays of Virginia Woolf. Volume 2: 1912–1918*. Ed. Andrew McNeillie. London: Hogarth Press, 1987. 291–93.

Yeats, W.B. *Four Years 1887–1891*. Dundrum: Cuala Press, 1921.

———. 'What is Popular Poetry?'. 1901. *Essays*. London: MacMillan, 1924. 5–11.

Index

Page numbers in *italic* denote illustrations
n = endnote